CAPITALISM
AND CLASSICAL
SOCIAL THEORY

CAPITALISM AND CLASSICAL SOCIAL THEORY

THIRD EDITION

JOHN BRATTON AND DAVID DENHAM

UNIVERSITY OF TORONTO PRESS

LIBRARY AND ARCHIVES CANADA CATALOGUING IN PUBLICATION

Title: Capitalism and classical social theory / John Bratton and David Denham.
Other titles: Capitalism and classical sociological theory
Names: Bratton, John, author. | Denham, David, 1944– author.
Description: Third edition. | Originally published under the title: Capitalism and classical sociological theory. | Includes bibliographical references and index.
Identifiers: Canadiana 20189069368 | ISBN 9781487588199 (cloth) | ISBN 9781487588182 (paper)
Subjects: LCSH: Sociology—Philosophy—Textbooks. | LCSH: Capitalism—Textbooks. | LCGFT: Textbooks.
Classification: LCC HM435 .B73 2019 | DDC 301—dc23

We welcome comments and suggestions regarding any aspect of our publications—please feel free to contact us at news@utorontopress.com or visit our internet site at utorontopress.com.

North America
5201 Dufferin Street
North York, Ontario, Canada, M3H 5T8

2250 Military Road
Tonawanda, New York, USA, 14150

ORDERS PHONE: 1-800-565-9523
ORDERS FAX: 1-800-221-9985
ORDERS E-MAIL: utpbooks@utpress.utoronto.ca

UK, Ireland, and continental Europe
NBN International
Estover Road, Plymouth, PL6 7PY, UK

ORDERS PHONE: 44 (0) 1752 202301
ORDERS FAX: 44 (0) 1752 202333
ORDERS E-MAIL: enquiries@nbninternational.com

Every effort has been made to contact copyright holders; in the event of an error or omission, please notify the publisher.

This book is printed on paper containing 100% post-consumer fibre.

University of Toronto Press acknowledges the financial assistance to its publishing program of the Canada Council for the Arts and the Ontario Arts Council, an agency of the Government of Ontario.

Printed in Canada.

**Canada Council
for the Arts**
**Conseil des Arts
du Canada**

**ONTARIO ARTS COUNCIL
CONSEIL DES ARTS DE L'ONTARIO**
an Ontario government agency
un organisme du gouvernement de l'Ontario

Funded by the
Government
of Canada
Financé par le
gouvernement
du Canada

Canadä

MIX
Paper from
responsible sources
FSC® C016245

To the memory of Bernard Igwe—educator, trade unionist, and close friend. I miss him.

To my wife Carolyn, Amy, Andrew and Elizabeth, Jennie and James, and our grandchildren Owen and Colbie.

—John Bratton

To my wife Ann, Steven and Jennifer, Sarah and Rick, and our wonderful grandchildren Georgia, Imogen, Ella, and Edward.

—David Denham

About the Authors

JOHN BRATTON is a visiting professor at Edinburgh Napier University, Edinburgh, UK, and a visiting professor at the University of Strathclyde, Glasgow, UK. He has taught a wide range of sociology courses, including classical social theory. His research interests traverse the sociology of work, and he is author of *Japanization at Work: Managerial Studies in the 1990s* (1992); co-author of *Workplace Learning: A Critical Introduction* (2004); co-author of *Organizational Leadership* (2005); co-author of *Human Resource Management: Theory and Practice* (2017), now in its sixth edition; and author of *Work and Organizational Behaviour* (2015), now in its third edition.

DAVID DENHAM is an honorary research fellow at the University of Wolverhampton, UK, where he taught a wide variety of sociology courses, including classical social theory, over a career of 35 years. He has published articles on the sociology of law, criminology, and the sociology of sport, and is co-author of *Victimology: Victimization and Victims' Rights* (2008).

Contents

PART IV: CLASSICAL SOCIAL THEORY TODAY

Acknowledgments

This book is a result of teaching classical social theory to undergraduates at Thompson Rivers University, Canada. During that time I benefited from the questions posed by students, and I learned a great deal from my colleagues there: the late Linda Deutschmann and Bernard Igwe, Bruce Baugh, and David MacLennan. I also benefited from comments and suggestions by Sue Hughes, formerly at Leeds Trinity and All Saints College, England, for improving chapters 2 and 3. Dr. Bruce Baugh gave valuable feedback on an earlier version of chapter 4, as did Dr. Jennifer Kelly, University of Alberta, on an early draft of the W.E.B. Du Bois chapter. David Denham would like to thank Paul Grant, University of Wolverhampton, for his comments and Dr. Pauline Anderson, Head of the School of Social, Historical and Political Studies at the University of Wolverhampton, for her continued support over the years and, most recently, for her assistance in setting up his honorary research fellowship. Both of us owe a debt of gratitude to the anonymous reviewers of the 2018 manuscript. They are, of course, absolved of all responsibility for the final outcome. We thank all publishers, where necessary, for permission to republish images, tables, and graphs. We would also like to thank Karen Taylor for finding alternative online sources, helping us to select the images, the editorial work, and improvements made to the text in earlier editions, and Eileen Eckert for her copyediting on this edition. We are also indebted to Anne Brackenbury, our acquisitions editor at the University of Toronto Press.

John A. Bratton
Edinburgh, Scotland

Preface

SINCE THE SECOND EDITION of this book, we have witnessed seismic social-economic and political changes that have reverberated worldwide. For North America, the UK, and Europe, these changes seem to have engendered a sense of crisis—a sense of impending war, terrorist attacks, political turmoil with popular insurrections and riots, racism, xenophobia, and general foreboding as health provisions are commodified or scaled back. That's not all. Technological acceleration has transformed our planet, our societies, and ourselves. The surfeit of well-documented reports link climate change to human activity and provide irrefutable evidence of an ecological crisis. The replacement of human labor power by robotic production and artificial-intelligence systems points to "jobless growth," threatening the last vestiges of job security in manual and core professional occupations. Digital technologies are complicit in the transformational challenges we face today. It is possible for workers to be engaged, surveilled, and managed by text messages. Digital platforms harvest our personal tastes and preferences, which are sold to commercial advertisers and political lobbying groups. Data are the key resource of twenty-first-century capitalism—as crucial as coal, electricity, and oil in the nineteenth and twentieth centuries—creating global giants such as Amazon, Google, Facebook, and Apple (the first trillion-dollar corporation) with immense corporate power.[1]

Have we experienced a period of crisis before? There have indeed been other dramatic years of rupture and uncertainty, such as 1926, when the British Trades Union Congress called a general strike that led the national government to mobilize the army; 1968, when police and the National Guard with fixed bayonets clashed with protestors against the Vietnam war on the streets of Chicago, and students and workers rioted on the streets of Paris; 1989, when the Berlin Wall came down; 1994, when elections in South Africa led to a coalition government, marking the official end of the apartheid system; 2008, when the global financial crisis, triggered by the collapse of Lehman Brothers, shook the world; and 2011, when we witnessed the pro-democracy revolts in North Africa and the Arab world, the short-lived anti-capitalist Occupy movement, and the environmental disaster caused by severe damage to the Fukushima nuclear plant in Japan. Since 2014, we have witnessed the election of an ex-TV celebrity star, Donald Trump, as President of the United States; the United Kingdom voted to sever its 44-year membership in the European Union—the so-called Brexit; and, in an age of unprecedented migration of people, there have been election gains for alt-right politicians across Europe including the UK, France, Germany, Hungary, and Poland.

There are some parallels between the election of Trump and the surprising Brexit result in that in both countries a large swathe of voters, often white working class, were discontent with the status quo. These voters felt increasingly insecure—left behind by economic globalization and socially marginalized by neoliberal welfare policies—and had lost faith in mainstream politicians meant to serve them.[2] Economically depressed "rust belt" manufacturing and coal-mining regions and mid-American states voted for Trump,[3] just as the post-industrial towns in the north of England, Wales, and rural England voted heavily to leave the European Union. Seven of the poorest ten regions in Northern Europe are in England. All seven had substantial Brexit majorities.[4] In 2016, Barack Obama attributed the two electoral earthquakes partly to social dislocations that have resulted from a rapidly changing world: "Globalization combined with technology combined with social media and constant information have disrupted people's lives, sometimes in very concrete ways ... A manufacturing plant closes, and suddenly an entire town no longer has what was the primary source of employment ... making people less certain of their national identities or their place in the world."[5] The election of Trump and the EU referendum result have left the US and Britain acutely divided by age, class, gender, and education. These social fissures are not new but reflect the consequences of post-1990 economic globalization and neoliberal ideology.

Added to this cauldron of uncertainty and social turmoil is the phenomenon of post-factual politics and "fake news" written and disseminated through social media with the intent to mislead in order to damage an entity or politician, and/or gain political advantage. Social media platforms and global-spanning corporations have challenged the traditional sources and centers of authority as never before across the developed world.[6] Even in the age of Amazon, Google, Apple, and Facebook, the argument of this book is that the classical social thinkers speak to the present as much as the past. We shall attempt to illustrate the startlingly contemporary relevance of the classical analysis of capital's crisis-generation *modus operandi* and its ever-expanding destruction of industrial jobs and the planetary environment.

In the second edition, we made reference to the profound changes in global capitalism and in perspectives that have taken place, which affect the way that modernity has been studied over the last three decades. Changes in the condition of modernity include the ascendancy of neo-liberalism, the emergence of new major economic players such as the People's Republic of China, India, and Brazil, and the all-pervasive diffusion of labor-saving digital technology. And, in addition to movements of capital and goods, the mass migration of people to Western Europe and North America has made multiculturalism, the politics of equality, and managing diversity in organizations major areas of research.[7] A key issue for social scientists is the effect of globalization on the workplace, society, and beyond. An important theme in the literature is *convergence* in capitalism, which affects production and employment practices in different regions of the world. The convergence debate has a long antecedence in neoclassical economic theory. Detractors, however, emphasize the existence of "varieties of capitalism" and *divergence* in capitalist behavior as evidence of the importance of the power of local culture, politics, and agency. Over the last 40 years, sociologists have witnessed the ascendancy of rival intellectual approaches to the study of social phenomena. For example, under the rubric of postmodernism, the traditional approach to researching aspects of society, loosely described as positivism, has been challenged by *constructionism* and *intersectionality*. The constructivist's view challenges researchers to re-examine their frames of reference, the research process itself, and the production of knowledge.[8] The concept of intersectionality has been utilized by social scientists as an analytical and organizing tool for investigating social injustices and developing social policy.[9] It has been defined in various ways, but this inspirational description points toward a general consensus:

> Intersectionality is a way of understanding and analyzing the complexity in the world, in people, and in human experiences. The events and conditions of social and political life and the self can seldom be understood as shaped by one factor. They are generally shaped by many factors in diverse and mutually influencing ways. When it comes to social inequality, people's lives and the organization of power in a given society are better understood as being shaped not by a single axis of social division, be it race or gender or class, but by many axes that work together and influence each other. Intersectionality as an analytic tool gives people better access to the complexity of the world and of themselves.[10]

Importantly, the postmodern approach, as Eagleton and Lyotard notably argue, eschews *meta-narratives* such as Marx's conception of history, whose function was to legitimize the illusion of a universal human history, and celebrates the triumph of local fragmented specificities over any kind of totality.[11]

In this intellectual climate, inevitably, there will be disagreement among contemporary sociologists over which classical social theorist should be included in a text on classical theory. The membership of the classical canon is important, for the canon provides a shared language, a focus, some kind of identity for the discipline, and it shapes both the intellectual discourse and the trajectory of social research. In the first edition of *Capitalism and Classical Social Theory*, we chose to be more inclusive and extended the coverage of the familiar sociological canon established around the 1970s—that is, the trio of Marx, Durkheim, and Weber—to include the German sociologist Georg Simmel and four women intellectuals who theorized about gender roles, gendered work, and new patterns of family life that were the consequences of the emergence of industrial capitalism. Our choice was influenced by a common criticism of the classical canon: the marginalization of gender in its authors' theories. We examined the gendering of social theory in the nineteenth and early twentieth centuries through the work of Mary Wollstonecraft, Harriet Martineau, Charlotte Perkins Gilman, and Jane Addams.

In the second edition, we extended the coverage of Max Weber's sociology and examined in more depth his analysis of rationalization processes in modern Western capitalism. The new chapter explored some contemporary applications, such as Ritzer's McDonaldization thesis, as an example of formal rationality. We also added the intellectual contribution of W.E.B. Du Bois. His work strengthened the book by probing the problems bequeathed and advantages created when race is incorporated into the classic analysis of the social world. We critically examine Du Bois's substantive ideas on race and on the interplay of race and class in American society.

For this new edition, we have chosen to extend further the coverage of the classical sociological canon by adding the intellectual enterprise of the American academic George Herbert Mead. The inclusion of Mead strengthens the text by examining the foundations of the distinctively American microinteractionist and interpretive sociology.[12] We critically examine Mead's concept of the social self and society and its contemporary relevance for sociological theory and research. We have also added the intellectual work of the Polish philosopher, economist, and anti-war activist Rosa Luxemburg. The Hungarian Marxist theorist Georg Lukacs called Luxemburg "a genuine dialectician."[13] Luxemburg's analysis of capitalism will put in perspective and help us understand contemporary debates on global capitalism. In order to accommodate these new classical theorists, we had to make the difficult choice of removing from this edition the chapter on Georg Simmel and substituting the contribution of Luxemburg for Jane Addams.

This new edition also presents an entirely revised final chapter on the relevance of classical social theory to contemporary Western society. With this object, it draws upon, for example, Paul Mason's *Postcapitalism* (2015); Joseph Stiglitz's *Great Divide* (2015); Mike Savage's *Social Class in the 21st Century* (2015); James Bridle's *New Dark Age* (2018); Mike Davis's *Old Gods, New Enigmas* (2018); George Monbiot's *How Did We Get into This Mess?* (2017); Kehinde Andrews and Lisa Palmer's (eds.) *Blackness in Britain* (2016); Rebecca Solnit's *Hope in the Dark* (2016); Margaret Llewelyn Davies's *Life As We Have Known It: The Voices of Working Class Women* (2012); and J.D. Vance's *Hillbilly Elegy* (2016). In discussing the contribution of social theory to public discourse, Alex Law observes, "Social theory ... stands aloof from the action, acting as if it is unaffected by the troubles of daily life and its vulgar interests ... social theory can seem remote and arcane."[14] The approach here, like in the previous two editions, aims to avoid being esoteric and disconnected from real-life experiences. Our intention is to provide insight into the relevance and application of the classical theorists with an emphasis on class inequality, gender, race, and ecological inequalities in post-Trump North America and post-Brexit "Global" Britain.

Capitalism and Classical Social Theory represents a departure from the popular texts on classical social theory currently available on the market in several important respects. It does not attempt to cover all aspects of classical social theory but rather to focus selectively on certain significant thinkers and theories while including a range of other contributors to the expanded canon. Our aim is to provide the reader with *depth* of knowledge concerning the most significant contributions rather than with a superficial outline of all sociological works in the classical period from 1789 to 1920. The familiar adage "Jack of all trades, master of none," when applied to a review of classical social theorists, may be rewritten as "knowledge of many, understanding of none." In our experience of teaching one-semester undergraduate courses in classical social theory, time permits only an adequate coverage of a limited number of social theorists in any depth. Consequently, students become exasperated because only a third of the required text is covered in lectures.

Another feature of *Capitalism and Classical Social Theory* is the inclusion of extended passages from the classical texts. The point of this is to counter the prejudice that classical texts are particularly difficult if not almost impossible to read, as well as to encourage the readers of this book to experience the prose and thoughts conveyed by the original texts. Anyone setting out to read the classical texts in English, however, is faced with an overwhelmingly large collection of writings in different editions. With this in mind, we have endeavored, as far as possible, to include extended passages from the readily available English editions of Marx, Durkheim, Weber, Wollstonecraft, Du Bois, and Mead that are referenced at the end of the book. Most importantly, the book is organized to be easily read alongside the selected editions currently available; it is not designed to be a substitute for the classical texts. As an alternative, Roberta Garner's *Social Theory: A Reader* offers substantial selections from the canonical texts, which may be read in conjunction with *Capitalism and Classical Social Theory*.

When quoting from the canonical works, we have deliberately not changed the words used by the authors. The terms "civilization," "nation," "race," and "Negro" are rooted in the Enlightenment language.[15] Using these terms is important to providing an adequate historical account of the intellectual discourse, but they are to be understood, without exception, in their eighteenth- and nineteenth-century meanings. For example, the discourse on "race" remained yoked to that of "nation" well into the twentieth century, and the latter term was associated with and reserved for political entities that had inherited the social beliefs and mores characteristic of "advanced" societies.

We should note here that we have not changed the original texts to be gender-neutral. When the classical writers use the word man, that is precisely whom they are usually referring to: a conspicuous deficiency in their theorizing, as will be explained. One further point needs to be made with regard to the classical theorists themselves. As Garner (2001) points out, although writing is an individual activity, learning and writing are social at the same time: they are nurtured by collective ideas, thoughts, and discourse. Thus the social theorists matured and changed in the course of their life experiences, so we find that the writings of the precocious Karl Marx or W.E.B. Du Bois are sometimes different from those they wrote in their more mature years. Finally, while attentive to the historical context, the classical social theorists speak directly to the crises of global inequality, environmental destruction, and the profound changes taking place in social relations in a post-Trump, post-Brexit world.

Notes

1 On these developments, see James Bridle, *New Dark Age* (London: Verso, 2018); Mike Davis, *Old Gods, New Enigmas* (London: Verso, 2018); Will Hutton and Andrew Adonis, *Saving Britain* (London: Abacus, 2018); George Monbiot, *How Did We Get into This Mess?* (London: Verso, 2017); Will Hutton, "There's Ingenuity Behind Apple's Great Success. But We Must Guard Against Its Might," *The Observer*, August 5, 2018, 38.

2   M. Jacques, "The Death of Neoliberalism," *The Observer,* August 21, 2016, 31–3.

3   R. Foroohar, "Politics Fuels Trump's Retreat from Paris," *The Financial Times,* June 5, 2017, 11.

4   Will Hutton and Andrew Adonis, *Saving Britain* (London: Abacus, 2018).

5   Barack Obama, "Visiting Europe, Obama Warns Against Rise of 'Crude Sort of Nationalism,'" *The New York Times,* November 15, 2016, A3.

6   G. Hassan, *Scotland the Bold* (Glasgow: Freight Books, 2016).

7   R. Bendl, I. Bleijenbergh, E. Henttonen, and A. Mills, *The Oxford Handbook of Diversity in Organizations* (Oxford: Oxford University Press, 2017).

8   Stewart R. Clegg and Cynthia Hardy, *Studying Organization: Theory and Method* (Thousand Oaks, CA: Sage, 1999); Kathy Charmaz, "Grounded Theory: Objectivist and Constructivist Methods," in *Handbook of Qualitative Research,* 2nd ed., ed. N. Denzin and Y. Lincoln (Thousand Oaks, CA: Sage, 2005), 509–35; Chris Grey, *A Very Short, Fairly Interesting and Reasonably Cheap Book about Studying Organizations* (Thousand Oaks, CA: Sage, 2005); Karen Legge, *Human Resource Management: Rhetorics and Realities* (Basingstoke, UK: Palgrave Macmillan, 2005).

9   Patricia Hill Collins and Sirma Bilge, *Intersectionality* (London: Polity, 2016), 2.

10 Collins and Bilge, *Intersectionality,* 2.

11 Terry Eagleton, "Awakening from Modernity," *Times Literary Supplement* (February 20, 1987), quoted in David Harvey, *The Condition of Postmodernity* (Oxford: Blackwell, 1990), 9; Jean François Lyotard, *The Postmodern Condition* (Manchester: Manchester University Press, 1984).

12 Randell Collins, *Four Sociological Traditions* (New York: Oxford University Press, 1994).

13 Helen Scott, *Rosa Luxemburg: Reform or Revolution* (Chicago: Haymarket Books, 2008), 2.

14 Alex Law, *Social Theory for Today* (London: Sage, 2015), 2.

15 Silvia Sebastiani, *The Scottish Enlightenment: Race Gender, and the Limits of Progress* (Basingstoke, UK: Palgrave Macmillan, 2013).

PART I
CONTEXT

1. Introduction: Why Classical Social Theory?

> Ideas, not armies or even banks, run the world. Ideas determine whether human creativity works for society or against it.
>
> —George Monbiot, 2017[1]

> I have yet to find a student who objects to studying the works of dead white men. But, rightly, they object to studying only the works of white men, dead or alive.
>
> —Jonathan Wolff, 2016[2]

IN *VICTORIAN CITIES*, Asa Briggs notes that most Victorian writers were both horrified and fascinated by new industrial cities that seemed to represent "a system of life constructed on a wholly new principle."[3] The discourse about large polyglot cities in nineteenth-century Europe was part of an intellectual debate about modern life that occurred in France, Germany, and the United States. Also, the conditions of the industrial society provided the context for the development of what is now called classical social theory, which has become the principal frame of reference for modern sociology.[4]

Theorizing about society has deep historical roots. Egyptian prophets, Greek philosophers, and medieval scholars in Western Europe all sought to understand and explain the operations of their societies. In Western Europe during the eighteenth and nineteenth centuries—known as the modern period—there was an extraordinarily high level of philosophical engagement by male and female public intellectuals. In the eighteenth century, the writings of Montesquieu, Rousseau, Bonald, Maistre, Saint-Simon, Comte, Martineau, and Wollstonecraft, as well as those of the Scottish moral philosophers David Hume, Adam Smith, Adam Ferguson, and John Millar, provided the intellectual context for theorizing about new forms of social life and society that came to prevail first in Britain and subsequently worldwide.[5]

What ultimately characterizes eighteenth-century historiography and social thought is their universal perspective and progressive structure, which are grounded in human nature.

Eighteenth-century thinkers were broadly optimistic about social change, confident that the certainties of the natural sciences could be applied without problem to the study of civil society.[6] By contrast, the *classical* theorizing that emerged in the nineteenth and early twentieth centuries—conventionally most closely identified with Karl Marx, Émile Durkheim, and Max Weber—was generally pessimistic. The transition from the premodern to the modern era ushered in profound and unprecedented economic, ideological, cultural, political, and social changes.

This book is an introduction to classical social theory and its legacy. The objective of this chapter is to introduce a selection of classical social thinkers and to make the initial case for studying the classical sociological canon.

Classical Sociological Canon

A theory implies a set of concepts and ideas that, taken together, purport to explain a given phenomenon or set of phenomena. Social theory is, above all, concerned with the development of concepts with which to comprehend modern society: it seeks to identify patterns in social relationships, explain individual or collective human action, elucidate what it is that relates individuals within society and how different types of social institutions connect to each other in the social world, and discern whether features of modernity are inevitable or can be transformed into another form of society. Each of the classical thinkers considered here did more than think about the features of contemporary society; they thought in systematic ways about the nature of modern society and about the extent to which capitalism is its key characteristic. What is the effect of technology on workers, society, and the living planet? What happens to self-identity in a money economy? What is the cause of social inequality? What forms of class, gender, and race inequality are present in contemporary society? And what and who can cause modern society to change?

By classical social theory, we mean a collection of published works that embodies a *canon*, a privileged set of texts that defines the discipline.[7] The canonical texts are essential reading for academics and students in the social sciences, and for those in sociology in particular, because they "systematically developed consciousness of society and social relations,"[8] they have relevance to modern sociology, and they are worth reading and rereading. They are classical not only because they provide a historical context for reading sociology, and are therefore a must-read for any serious student of sociology and political science, but also because they are living artifacts with contemporary relevance to both modern social sciences and to understanding our own society. The classical canon remains at the center of modern sociology. It continues to inspire and guide contemporary social theory and empirical research by providing help in posing better research questions.[9] Contemporary sociologists have gone as far as suggesting that the canonical social thinkers have "entered the air that we breathe."[10] It is not surprising, therefore, that the Marx-Durkheim-Weber triumvirate is to sociology what Shakespeare and Dickens are to English literature, or what Adam Smith and John Maynard Keynes are to economics—the iconic "fathers" or founders of the discipline.

The surviving founders of sociology are also a product of our constructions, the result of the translations of selected classical authors largely undertaken by white, male Anglo-Saxon scholars.[11] As such, the community of sociologists constantly revises the membership of the canon. In early twenty-first-century sociology, Marx, Durkheim, and Weber are well entrenched within the classical canon, but this was not always the case. Sociologists in the early 1900s disagreed about which particular "founding thinker" was actually responsible for the founding of sociology. They cited possible contenders from a range of thinkers in a broad intellectual landscape, including Adam Smith, Auguste Comte, Marquis de Condorcet, Vilfredo Pareto, and Charles Darwin.

As late as the 1920s, the Chicago School listed Durkheim and Simmel as notable contributors to the new social science but not Marx or Weber. Émile Durkheim's work on research methodology and his references to social unity and "bonds of interdependence" secured his place early in the sociological canon. Marx's contribution to sociological theory is immense. Even so, his full membership in the sociological canon is relatively recent; it dates from the mid-1960s and the period of radicalization of the university student movement in Western Europe. In the late 1970s, Marx was beginning to be introduced to American undergraduate students as "the first great radical sociologist."[12] In the 1980s, however, in the context of an ascendancy of the doctrine of neoliberalism, Marx, and particularly the key concept of class, became less intellectually fashionable.[13]

As for Max Weber, he was an economist. Though he was a founding member of the German Sociological Society, his contemporaries and some noted Weber scholars (e.g., Wilhelm Hennis) never regarded him as a founding thinker of sociological theory.[14] It was the American sociologist

Talcott Parsons who established Weber as a full-fledged member of the sociological canon. From Parson's reconstruction of Weber's work, it became the parlance that Weber intended his best-known work, *The Protestant Ethic and the Spirit of Capitalism*, as a refutation of Marx's thesis on capitalism. Thus the Anglo-Saxon sociology community canonized some of the prominent "founding fathers" of sociology 50 years ago. The Marx-Durkheim-Weber triumvirate became further entrenched after Anthony Giddens's book *Capitalism and Modern Social Theory* was published in 1971 and after new English translations and books of readings were released.

By now it should be apparent that the canonizing process is not neutral but reflects the values and indirect yet powerful requirements of members of the dominant culture, sociologists included. The canonical exclusion process therefore is not necessarily about the excluded work's true qualities, which can be demonstrated by comparing the works of Wollstonecraft and Du Bois with the canonical inclusions. For example, *A Vindication of the Rights of Woman* by Wollstonecraft and both *The Philadelphia Negro* and *The Souls of Black Folk* by Du Bois are classics in every respect as significant as Marx and Engels's *The Communist Manifesto*, Durkheim's *The Rules of Sociological Method*, and Weber's *The Protestant Ethic*. However, all of these except Weber's contribution were excluded from the sociological canon at some time.[15] A plausible case can be made that the community of sociologists was blind to issues of gender and color, which rendered the intellectual contributions of early female thinkers and Du Bois invisible and excluded them from the Marxian, Durkheimian, and Weberian traditions.[16] Indeed, these reflections raise the question of how the classical sociological canon has become much richer and even more rigorous by including the theoretical tradition of gender and race to analyze the social world.

Toward an Inclusive Canon

The Marx-Durkheim-Weber triumvirate played a prominent role in developing contemporary thinking about capitalism and class. However, given that the development of the classical sociological canon was predominantly the work of white, male, Anglo-Saxon intellectuals and sociologists, the calls for a more inclusive canon are not surprising. This third edition offers a review of a more inclusive canon by including two neglected dimensions of the social world—gender and race respectively. In the English-speaking world, the roots of feminism can be traced to social movements in England and America. In England, the feminist discourse goes back to at least the 1640s and the Levellers' movement. Leveller women campaigned for political and social reforms, proclaiming their unflagging resolve: "Nor will we ever rest until we have prevailed, that We, our husbands, Friends, and Servants, may not be liable to be abused, violated, and butchered at mens Wills and pleasures."[17] Running through the history of the feminist movement was also the idea that equality for women was necessary to free both man and woman for true emancipation. Over a century ago, in 1913, the British suffragette Emmeline Pankhurst was jailed and Emily Davison killed as they campaigned for women's rights.

Across the Atlantic, after the American Revolutionary War (1775–83) the feminist movement developed alongside the campaign to abolish slavery. In *The Feminine Mystique* (1963), Betty Friedan wrote that feminism in nineteenth-century America was not a "dirty joke" and observed that a decade before Mary Wollstonecraft published her masterpiece, an American woman, Judith Sargent Murray, espoused that women needed knowledge to envision new goals. In 1853, the Rev. Theodore Parker preached in Boston that "[t]he domestic function of woman does not exhaust her powers. To make one half of the human race consume its energies in the functions of housekeeper, wife and mother is a monstrous waste of the most precious material God ever made."[18] Just past the 100-year anniversary of the jailing of suffragette Emmeline Pankhurst and Emily Davison's death, and the centenary of the first British women getting the vote, this book explores the theme of gender through the work of Mary Wollstonecraft, Harriet Martineau, Rosa Luxemburg, and Charlotte Perkins Gilman.

More than 56 years after Martin Luther King, Jr., delivered his historic "I Have a Dream" speech at the March on Washington (August 26, 1963), we explore what has been neglected in the classical canon—race. We turn to the best-known writings of America's pre-eminent African American scholar, W.E.B. Du Bois, who examined race from a unique perspective and, indeed, helped define the African American experience. In a new chapter, we examine the concept of the social self and its relation to society through the intellectual endeavors of George Herbert Mead. In the 1930s, the American sociologist Herbert Blumer helped the posthumous canonization of Mead. However, as we will explain, Blumer's appropriation of Mead's social psychology is contested. It is argued that Blumer's reinterpretation that came to be known as symbolic interactionism erased the reformist and societal components of Mead's ideas.[19] The classical sociological canon seeks to achieve an understanding of the distinctive features, tensions, and paradoxes of a new emerging form of social life—capitalist modernity. Because it is generally agreed that the understanding of the emergence of sociology relies on its purported relation to modernity, it is to the meaning of modernity that we shall first attend.

Modernism is very much an urban phenomenon. It has existed, since 1850, in a complex relationship with the experience of capitalism, explosive urban growth, and a confluence of urban-based intellectual ideas and political movements. *Capitalism* is a way of organizing economic activity. Capitalist activities and institutions began to develop throughout Europe during the Renaissance period, dating from the 1400s, and continued throughout the premodern era. The production and exchange of commodities, however, were restrained by traditional religious and political controls.

Capitalist modernity has come to define the vast and largely unregulated expansion of commodity production and related market and monetary networks. The need to maximize profit from commodity production and exchange, rather than to satisfy the material needs of the producers, is the leitmotiv of capitalism.

Well before the publication of Jane Jacobs's *Economy of Cities* or Richard Florida's *Who's Your City?*, cities have been conceived as the epicenters of innovation, technological progress, and personal freedom. As emblematic of profound changes, cities are equated with modernity. They are "simultaneously the machinery and the hero of modernity."[20] The city, in Weber's *General Economic History*, is the crucible of modernity. It is primarily an economic space: the location of commerce and manufacturing. It is also a place of inventions and reinventions, and new kinds of work and occupations. The city alone is the primary place of cultural development. They are also primary places of scientific thinking, and they house specific religious institutions that produce theological thought.[21] Cities, too, have long been acknowledged as primary places of personal freedom and development, that is, spaces where urbanites can give liberty to imagination and play, challenge orthodoxy, and discover their sense of identity.

In reality, modernity has two sides. The first is the spread of a new economic model located primarily in new urban centers. The second but less obvious side to modernity is its unrelenting change, its insecurity, and its totalizing chaos. Berman provides an insightful description of modernity:

> To be modern is to find ourselves in an environment that promises us adventure, power, joy, growth, transformation of ourselves and the world—and, at the same time, that threatens to destroy everything we have, everything we know, everything we are. Modern environments and experiences cut across all boundaries of geography and ethnicity, of class and nationality, of religion and ideology; in this sense, modernity can be said to unite

all mankind. But it is a paradoxical unity, a unity of disunity; it pours us all into a maelstrom of perpetual disintegration and renewal, of struggle and contradiction, of ambiguity and anguish. To be modern is to be part of a universe in which, as Marx said, "all that is solid melts into air."[22]

The collage of capitalist modernity is a quilt stitched together with patches from both the premodern and the new industrial society—patches of agriculture, small manufacturing, villages, kinship, landed interests, monarchy, religion, tradition, and, with increasing dominance, new patches of factories, cities, individualism, business interests, democracy, science, and reason. Modernity signifies creativity, innovation, aestheticism, wealth, and individual freedom and identity. It also exhibits chaotic change, poverty, human degradation, and inequality.

The uneducated, by definition, leave few written accounts of their lived experiences. For the most part, historians have been the ones to document exhaustively the social reverberations of modernity. Working-class women and children suffered the brunt of the chaotic change and adjustment. As the laboring poor migrated to the old and new cities, the bottom layer of the mid-Victorian social pyramid witnessed growing numbers of paupers and prostitutes. Industrialization and urbanization were accompanied by an increase in homelessness and child prostitution and by the growth of a permanent underclass of the extreme poor—"stunted and debilitated"—living in urban slums. On average, children from upper-class private schools were 12 centimeters taller than children from working-class schools.[23] Behind the picture of urban wealth is a story of the destitute, disempowered, dispossessed, and disinherited: those described by the poet Rainer Maria Rilke as "ones to whom neither the past nor the future belongs"[24] constitute the ugly side of modernity.

The collage of modernity appears similar to a well-known drawing in first-year university psychology textbooks, an image that can be seen at the same time as a beautiful young woman and as an old crone.[25]

Charles Dickens's *A Tale of Two Cities*, published in 1859, perhaps best captures the life experience of capitalist modernity: "It was the best of times, it was the worst of times, it was the age of wisdom, it was the age of foolishness, it was the epoch of belief, it was the epoch of incredulity, it was the season of Light, it was the season of Darkness, it was the spring of hope, it was the winter of despair, we had everything before us, we had nothing before us, we were all going direct to Heaven, we were all going direct the other way."[26]

Enlightenment thinkers in the eighteenth century viewed modernity through a conceptual prism of rationalism, positivism, universalism, and a belief in linear progress. They welcomed the maelstrom of change as a necessary prerequisite for modernity and believed that the sciences would not only control and harness natural forces but also promote understanding of society and of the self.[27] In the early twentieth century, the optimism of Enlightenment thought and modernity was challenged in part by the white male canonical writers but also by early feminist thinkers and by socialist movements, which introduced a class dimension into modernism.

The Legacy of the Classical Canon

In this age of globalization, consumer economies, and neoliberalism, skeptical readers may very well ask what the classical thinkers, whose major works have their roots in the Western European industrial cultures between the early 1800s and the early 1900s and were published over a century ago, can tell us today. Globalization is arguably about the unfettered pursuit of profit.[28] Fundamentally, globalization is the closer integration of the economies of the world that has been brought about by the massive reduction of transportation and communication costs and the dismantling of barriers to the flows of capital, finance, and goods and services across borders. In Western societies, globalization has caused the shift from production economies to consumer economies. Moreover, as the global financial crisis of 2008 affirmed, the unsustainable levels of personal debt in "consumer economies" were not only an integral part of economic growth but also a symptom of economic crisis.[29] The phenomenon of globalization is buttressed by the ideology of neoliberalism. The theory of political economy known as neoliberalism proposes that human well-being can best be advanced by liberating individual entrepreneurial freedoms and creativity within an institutional framework characterized by strong private property rights, free markets, free trade, and, concomitantly, the deregulation of labor and of planning and environmental controls, the privatization of public assets, and the withdrawal of the state from most areas of social provision. As an ideology, its effects today are so pervasive that it has become part of the "common-sense" way many people see, interpret, and understand the world.[30]

In light of these massive economic and cultural changes, it is pertinent to enquire why classic social theory is worth studying. We believe that the social theorists we have chosen to examine in this book remain relevant because they created enduring traditions of thinking about the nature of capitalist modernity but also because these theoretical traditions can inform us greatly about the process of neoliberalization and human experience in our present society. The members of the classical sociological canon sought their own ways to confront and make sense of the processes of transformation and to explain the key characteristics of capitalist modernity as contrasted with premodern society. The overwhelming interest of Karl Marx, Émile Durkheim, and Max Weber, writes Anthony Giddens, was in "the delineation of the characteristic structure of modern 'capitalism' as contrasted with prior forms of society."[31]

Income inequality is as extreme in 2018 in the United States as it was in the late nineteenth century,[32] when Durkheim and Weber were writing. It is perhaps therefore unsurprising that Thomas Piketty's *Capital in the Twenty-First Century*[33]—a reflection of the concern about global capitalism, which was also at the center of the canonical theorists' intellectual endeavors—should find its way onto the *New York Times* best sellers' list for four weeks. As Victor Hugo said, "Nothing is more powerful than an idea whose time has come," and after four decades of neoliberalism and recognition of the fact that the doctrine is increasingly deleterious to the natural world and the living standards of the many—or, as British Prime Minister Theresa May dubbed them, the "just about managing" or "JAMs"—Marx's ideas, and those of Weber, have again acquired fashionable relevance.

At the center of Karl Marx's theorizing is the exploitative nature of capitalist production and how this shapes the political and social life of society. For Marx, Victorian capitalism is modernity, and modernity is capitalism.[34] Max Weber tried to understand modernity through the role of ideas in social change and, above all, of rationalization. He emphasized the role played by the sacred "calling" of Calvinism and wholesale rationalization in all spheres of life, the irreversible development of bureaucracy, and increasing secularization, which brought about disenchantment.[35] For Weber, these developments describe modernity.[36] Significantly, both Marx and Weber noticed how modernity was extremely exploitative of the natural world. Émile Durkheim theorized that the crisis of modernity stemmed from an "abnormal" division of labor and its diverse and conflicting interests, which produced "pathological" forms of restless individualism that he termed "anomie." He emphasized the impact of modernity on social and cultural life. Durkheim was concerned with symbolic forms of moral power.

The canonical writers, however, devoted scant theoretical attention to *gender* and *race* as critical dimensions in the development of modernity. In twentieth-century sociology, empirical research on work continued to be concerned with male workers. The work of women was largely, in Sheila Rowbotham's memorable observation, hidden from history.[37] Over several decades, gender has become a concept to be wrestled with, and we acknowledge that the term "gender," historically, has a variant set of

meanings. Gender is here referred to as a group of ideas that grew out
of and developed through the writings of the classical feminist thinkers
concerned with women's liberation. Indeed, the early feminist writers
spawned ideas on social and cultural interpretations that turn sexual
difference into more than a merely biological distinction.[38] The process of
creating and acting on gendered social constructions underscores theories
of gender roles, gender inequality, power, and women's subordination
and oppression. These problems were all addressed in different ways
by early feminist thinkers. As we shall see in the respective writings of
Mary Wollstonecraft, Harriet Martineau, Rosa Luxemburg, and Charlotte
Perkins Gilman, the question of gender inequalities in society is explicitly
addressed. These early feminist thinkers critically examined the plight of
women oppressed through a variety of entrenched social processes, such
as patriarchal strategies and sexism.

The classical thinkers looked for the essence of modernity through
the prism of "European exceptionalism,"[39] traditional class analysis
that neglected race as a fundamental dynamic of social organization in
the US, and racism that imbued the capitalist labor market.[40] Both the
meaning and significance of "race" have been evolving over centuries;
indeed, race is one of the most contestable concepts in sociology, not least
because of its supposedly "scientific" basis and the previous usage of the
term in eugenics. In many ancient civilizations, distinctions were often
drawn between social groups based on visible differences in skin color,
usually between darker and lighter skin tones. In Europe, premodern
"enlightened" scholars developed racial hierarchies based on "objective"
procedures of observation of the physical differences between human
beings, which would contribute decisively to the development of theories
about racial inferiority. In the sixteenth and seventeenth centuries the
words *monogenism* and *polygenism* appeared in anthropological writings, and these terms designated opposing early explanations of race. The
monogenetic hypothesis had biblical origins, whereas the polygenetic
hypothesis developed as a response to the discovery of "savages" in the
New World.

As we explain in chapter 3, the early intellectual discourse on humanism and race denied the unity of humankind and led to the justification
of slavery in premodern Europe and, later, to the practice of using slave
labor to exploit the colonies.[41] In the nineteenth century, a landmark
publication by Joseph Arthur, Comte de Gobineau (1816–82), *Essai sur
l'inégalité des races humaines*, proposed the idea of three races: white
(Caucasian), black (Negroid), and yellow (Mongoloid). Gobineau's
physical classifications were combined with ideas about the superiority of the "Nordic strain" and then with the general notion of inherent

racial inequalities. Theories of innate racial superiority interacted with the political doctrine of imperialism, which saw England and other European nation-states ruling over colonial lands and populations. For some, race and slavery were the twinned catalysts of capitalist modernity. Race was capitalism's ordering principle, its moral authority, its economy and commerce, and its power.[42]

According to historian Eric Hobsbawm (1917–2012), the idea that humanity was divided by "race" penetrated the ideology of the period between 1875 and 1914 almost as deeply as the notion of "progress" itself. Moreover, racism played a central role in nineteenth-century, egalitarian liberal ideology because it passed the blame for visible social inequalities from society to "nature."[43] The ideas of Gobineau influenced the German Nazi party in the 1930s, the government of South Africa until the end of apartheid, and white supremacist groups such as the Ku Klux Klan in the United States. Stefan Kühl's *The Nazi Connection* provides evidence that American eugenicists influenced Nazi Germany's race policies.[44] These included mass sterilization, the murder of handicapped persons, the killing of ethnic minorities, and the extermination of Jews. Also, Anderson argues that white "progressives" who were "prey to eugenic nightmares" funded Du Bois's social study of the black community in Philadelphia.[45]

After 1945, "race science" and eugenics were thoroughly discredited.[46] Nevertheless, even after these early theories of race have been discredited scientifically, race remains a highly contested concept. This is demonstrated by the fact that some contemporary social theorists refer to race and others to "race." Placing the word race in quotation marks is meant to emphasize that race, like gender, can only be understood as a social and ideological construct.[47] The notion of race as a social construct downplays the extent to which sections of the population may form a discrete ethnic group—that is, learn and share certain characteristics on the basis of common historical origins, supportive patterns of social interaction, and a sense of identity. Because early sociology in Europe and the United States developed within a cultural milieu suffused with centuries of Christian teachings and with ideas concerning the innate intellectual superiority and genetic strength of white Western people, the discipline could hardly avoid being shaped by this ideological climate.

The writings of W.E.B. Du Bois bring to prominence the issues of race and cultural identity that are largely invisible in the official canon of social theory classics. For Du Bois, race was a deeply historical, social, and ideological construct and functioned as a key part of his sociological and political writings, from his exposition of the struggles against segregation, structured racism, and class exploitation to his examination of self-identity and pan-African politics. The approaches of the classical sociological canon, which often privilege a specific class, gender, or race, suggest a need not only for nuanced concepts but also for multidimensional analysis that can call attention to connections—to the commonalities as well as to the differences between dimensions of the social world.[48]

In *A Short History of Sociological Thought*, Alan Swingewood makes the valid point that "the history of sociology is never a history of a selective canon but a dialogue between the present and the past, how ideas born in different historical periods and cultures survive as active elements in contemporary sociological thought."[49] By way of summarizing the selected sociological canon, and as a heuristic device, Figure 1.1 depicts the theoretical dimensions of modernity. It shows the interplay of four major concepts probed by the canonical writers—*materiality* (Karl Marx), *morality* (Émile Durkheim), *rationality* (Max Weber), and *culture* (George H. Mead).[50] It also shows two additional dimensions, *gender* and *race*, which we have added for theorizing about society. Although there are limits to what can be reasonably portrayed in a diagram, our diagram also indicates the antecedents of the development of social thought provided by Europe's dual revolution—industrial and political—and by the intellectual thinking arising from the Enlightenment. The lines and arrows between the selected canonical theorists are not intended to suggest causal relationships; they are meant to convey to the reader that classical intellectual thinking is a complex, rich, interrelated set of accumulated knowledge and ideas. Thus, Figure 1.1 refers to an arena of public discourse constituting the different perspectives and theoretical positions on capitalist modernity that define classical sociological theory.

FIGURE 1.1 The Classical Theorizing of Society

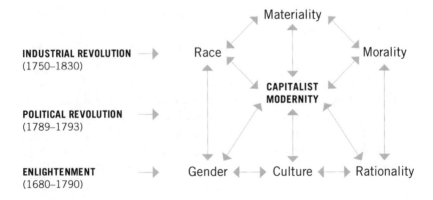

A number of sociologists have questioned the value of the classical canon and of the concepts derived from studies of contemporary modernity. This skepticism has been fueled by two main sets of arguments. First is the claim that advanced Western societies have shifted to a qualitatively new form of society known as late modernity or postmodernity. Adherents to this standpoint argue that, in view of the fact that society has undergone a noticeable shift in sensibility, practices, and also economic, social, and cultural orders,[51] sociological theories should be recast to make them relevant for the new postmodern world. This intellectual climate, in general, and the 1989–90 political collapse of Eastern European communism, in particular, bring into question the intellectual credibility and status of Marx in the canon, as does scholarly interest in postmodernism.[52] However, there is no necessary relationship between Eastern European communism and Karl Marx's social theory.

As evidence of the new social world, critics have argued, for example, that the classical social theorists are irrelevant in the era of postmodernism because neoconservative anti-state ideology has led to a hollowing out of the state and of government services;[53] because global competitive advantage stems from processing information and intellectual capital—the so-called knowledge economy—rather than from commodities and manual dexterity; and because economies and financial systems are closely integrated on a global scale.[54] Although globalization is a contested concept, in essence it is about the unfettered pursuit of profit and the primacy of multinational power over local power.[55] A significant body of literature connects globalization to postmodernity, particularly around themes such as the ever more globalizing of capitalism, space-time compression, the global division of labor and power, and the globalization of mass culture. It also provides theoretical and empirical support for the thesis that postmodernity, in particular its association with globalization, is not simply a quantitative extension of modernity but a qualitatively new phenomenon.

The skepticism surrounding the value of the classical theories has been fueled by a second claim that these theories are, by and large, oblivious to problems concerning gender distinctions within employment (in particular), to male-dominated interests, and to social power. It is contended that Marx, Durkheim, and Weber "gazed upon a masculine world," and their works are said to be blind to gender issues.[56] Another notable related problem with these classical works is that they are ethnocentric and Eurocentric. Sociologists are less divided on the merits of this weakness. The classical theorists saw social transformation as a global phenomenon, but they saw it through a prism that defined modernity in terms of "Euro-American" white culture and religious models.[57] However, colonization and its associated exploitation took place within the violent context of European religious and cultural norms, most notably within the context of Euro-American complicity in colonial genocides in South and North America, in slavery, and in the aggressive proselytizing in Africa and Asia. As a result, analysis to examine the new society independently of the economics and politics of European colonialism and hegemony and of the concomitant national repercussions on social mechanisms becomes increasingly problematic.

The meta-narratives of Karl Marx, Émile Durkheim, and Max Weber can be summarized as referring to commodification, differentiation, and rationalization, respectively. Each of these meta-narratives presumed modernity to be qualitatively different from the past. This dichotomy from traditionalism to modernity was formulated as feudalism to capitalism by Marx, and mechanical to organic forms by Durkheim. For Weber, Western modernity reflected the process of rationalization in all aspects of human life, from business to war. In many late-capitalist, high-carbon societies, there has been increased commodification, and each of these meta-narratives draws critical attention to the malfunctions of free-market societies. Marx's economic analysis emphasizes the process whereby goods and services that were formerly considered essential and collectively supplied—in our recent history, things such as education, health care, drinking water, electricity, and TV airwaves—are privately bought, sold, and operated as for-profit interests. Durkheim's sociology generates an interest in social regulation and the way in which market dynamics lead to rapid and unregulated social change. The deregulated market economies fostered by the new Right can be seen, in Durkheimian analysis, as amoral and damaging to social solidarity. Weber was aware that rational market calculation brings its own social costs. He knew that the rationality of markets could produce irrationalities.

Without the early feminists' efforts, writes Rosemarie Putnam Tong, many women today could not have attained their new-found professional stature.[58] Even after the fiftieth anniversary of Betty Friedan's *The Feminine Mystique*, early feminist writers still inspire[59] and provide sophisticated understanding of the gender-based, persistent, and pervasive injustices that women continue to experience in all areas of life. For example, were Mary Wollstonecraft to reappear today, she would be outraged, but probably not surprised, that, in the twenty-first century, Canadian women can be murdered and then victimized by "the bland racist, sexist and 'classist' prejudices buried in Canadian society."[60] Similarly, if W.E.B. Du Bois were alive today, it's plausible to suggest that he would be incensed, but probably unsurprised, that black drivers on the streets of London can be victims of sustained harassment by police because of the color of their skin[61] or that an independent review could still expose "institutional racism" within a UK police force and city administration.[62]

Sociology as an academic discipline was the product of an emergent industrial capitalism in Western Europe and North America, and overall took for granted society's domination and exploitation of the natural world that enabled the accumulation of capital and new patterns of social life.[63] Social theory attempts to make sense of the complexity of the world, in society and in human experiences. We hope this third edition of *Capitalism and Classical Social Theory* will help readers to better analyze and understand the complexity in the world and contemporary society in the era of Trump and post-Brexit. We aim to demonstrate that the works of Marx, Durkheim, Weber, early feminist writers, Du Bois, and Mead provide powerful conceptual tools for analyzing late modernity and for engaging in debates on globalization, global warming, social inequality, women's subordination and oppression, and issues of race and multiculturalism.[64]

The Structure of the Book

Capitalism and Classical Social Theory is divided into four parts and sixteen chapters. In part I, we explore the context in which the classical theorists were writing. Chapter 2 provides an explanation of how early social theory is shaped by the industrialization and urbanization of nineteenth-century European societies. Chapter 3 examines the intellectual context of early social thought.

In part II, we examine the classical triumvirate. Chapter 4 provides a biographical sketch of Karl Marx and examines the antecedents of his philosophy and methodology. Chapter 5 examines Marx's conception of history, alienation, class-consciousness, and the role of ideology. Chapter 6 examines Marx's economic analysis of capitalism. Chapter 7 examines how Émile Durkheim's theories differed from those of both Marx and Weber. Chapter 8 looks at Durkheim's rules of sociological method and his theory of suicide. Chapter 9 explains his theories on religion and education. Chapter 10 examines Max Weber's pronouncements on methodology and considers his study of the Protestant ethic. Chapter 11 examines Weber's study of the Protestant ethic and its role in the development of modern capitalism and goes on to examine his ideas on the rationalization of modern capitalism. Chapter 12 looks at Weber's treatment of social class, legitimate domination, and his pessimism about the quality of political leadership.

In part III, we expand the traditional sociological canon. Chapter 13 examines the influence of early feminist thinkers and women sociologists and the genesis of feminist social theory. Chapter 14 examines W.E.B. Du Bois's theory of race and his analysis of the interplay between American capitalism, race, and racism. The object is to demonstrate that his work raises the issue of race to a prominence absent in the other classical theorists we have discussed in this volume. Chapter 15 examines the work of George Herbert Mead with a focus on Mead's conception of the social self and society. We explore the argument that the main contemporary interpretations of Mead's social psychology have neglected his ideas on society.

In part IV, chapter 16 attempts to show that serious analytical omissions can arise from classical approaches that privilege class, gender, or race rather than treat their disparate contributions more holistically. We aim to probe connections between class, gender, and race and explore commonalities as well as differences. We ambitiously aim to demonstrate how the analytical perspectives and conceptual tools developed by the classical social theorists presented in this book can be usefully applied to a variety of national contexts in this age of neoliberalism, austerity, Trump, and post-Brexit. We argue that the ideas of the classical social theorists continue to be relevant and exert a profound influence on contemporary social scientists. These ideas have the power to help us analyze and understand contemporary capitalist societies and global capitalism. Indeed, we believe these classics should become part of every citizen's education. We hope that the readers of this book will gain an appreciation of this.

FURTHER THINKING:

Explain the thinking behind the assertion that "the surviving founders of sociology are a product of our constructions." Do white men have a disproportionate influence on public discourse today?

FURTHER READING:

For a reliable historical introduction to sociological theory, see Alex Callinicos, *Social Theory: A Historical Introduction*, 2nd ed. (Cambridge: Polity Press, 2007). For further insight into the development of classical social theory, see R.W. Connell, "Why Is Classical Theory Classical," *American Journal of Sociology* 102, no. 6 (1997): 1511–57. And, for further information on the neglect of early women thinkers, see Jan Thomas and Annis Kukulan, "'Why Don't I Know about These Women?' The Integration of Early Women Sociologists in Classical Theory Courses," *Teaching Sociology* 32 (2004): 252–63.

Notes

1 George Monbiot, *How Did We Get into This Mess?* (London: Verso, 2017), 1.

2 Jonathan Wolff, "Students Don't Mind Studying Dead White Men, But They Want Dead Women Too," *The Guardian*, July 19, 2016, 36.

3 Asa Briggs, *Victorian Cities* (Harmondsworth, UK: Pelican Books, 1968), 12.

4 Anthony Giddens,*Capitalism and Modern Social Theory* (Cambridge: Cambridge University Press, 1971), xi.

5 See Kenneth H. Tucker, *Classical Social Theory* (Malden, MA: Blackwell, 2002); Larry J. Ray, *Theorizing Classical Sociology* (Buckingham, UK: Open University Press, 1999); Alex Callinicos, *Social Theory: A Historical Introduction*, 2nd ed. (Cambridge: Polity Press, 2007).

6 Alan Swingewood, *A Short History of Sociological Thought* (New York: St. Martin's Press, 2000), viii.

7 R.W. Connell, "Why Is Classical Theory Classical," *American Journal of Sociology* 102, no. 6 (May 1997): 1511–57.

8 Dorothy E. Smith, *The Everyday World as Problematic: A Feminist Sociology* (Boston: Northeastern University Press, 1987), cited by Patricia M. Lengermann and Gillian Niebrugge-Brantley, "Early Women Sociologists and Classical Sociological Theory: 1830–1930" in *Classical Sociological Theory*, ed. George Ritzer (New York: McGraw-Hill, 2008), 271–303, see page 300.

9 Ray, *Theorizing Classical Sociology*.

10 Ian Craib, *Classical Social Theory* (Oxford: Oxford University Press, 1997), 2.

11 Sven Eliaeson, *Max Weber's Methodologies* (Cambridge: Polity Press, 2002), 2.

12 Connell, "Why Is Classical Theory Classical," 1542.

13 Alex Law, *Social Theory for Today* (London: Sage, 2015), 29.

14 See Wilhelm Hennis, *Max Weber: Essays in Reconstruction*, trans. Keith Tribe (London: Allen & Unwin, 1988); Wilhelm Hennis, *Max Weber's Central Question*, trans. Keith Tribe (Newbury, UK: Threshold Press, 2000); and Keith Tribe, ed., *Reading Weber* (London: Routledge, 1989).

15 See Silvia Sebastiani, *The Scottish Enlightenment: Race, Gender, and the Limits of Progress* (Basingstoke, UK: Palgrave Macmillan, 2013), 7.

16 See, for example, Charles Lemert, "A Classic from the Other Side of the Veil: Du Bois's *Souls of Black Folk*," *The Sociological Quarterly* 35, no. 3 (1998): 383–96, see page 387.

17 Amy Scott-Douglass, "Women and Parliament in Seventeenth-Century England," *Sites of Cultural Stress from Reformation to Revolution*, accessed January 20, 2013, http://www.folger.edu/html/folger_institute/cultural_stress/parliament_women.html.

18 Quoted in Betty Friedan, *The Feminine Mystique* (New York: W.W. Norton and Company, 1963), 85.

19 Jean-Francois Côté, *George Herbert Mead's Concept of Society: A Critical Reconstruction* (Boulder, CO: Paradigm, 2015).

20 Michel de Certeau, *The Practice of Everyday Life* (Berkeley: University of California Press, 1984), 95, quoted in David Harvey, *The Condition of Postmodernity* (Oxford: Blackwell, 1994), 26.

21 See Max Weber, *General Economic History* (1927; New York: Dover Publications, 2003), chap. 23.

22 Marshall Berman, *All That Is Solid Melts into Air: The Experience of Modernity* (Harmondsworth, UK: Penguin Books, 1982), 15.

23 Eric J. Hobsbawm, *Industry and Empire* (London: Weidenfeld and Nicolson, 1968), 137.

24 The German poet Rainer Maria Rilke is quoted in Naomi Klein, *The Shock Doctrine* (Toronto: Alfred Knopf, 2007), 333. The phrase is from "The Seventh Elegy," in *Duino Elegies and The Sonnets to Orpheus*, trans. A. Poulin, Jr. (New York: Houghton Mifflin, 1975), 51.

25 Derek Sayer, *Capitalism and Modernity: An Excursus on Marx and Weber* (London: Routledge, 1991), 148.

26 Charles Dickens, *A Tale of Two Cities* (1859; London: HarperCollins, 1952), 21.

27 See Harvey, *The Condition of Postmodernity*.

28 Noreena Hertz, *The Silent Takeover: Global Capitalism and the Death of Democracy* (London: Arrow, 2002).

29 Gordon Laird, *The Price of a Bargain* (Basingstoke, UK: Palgrave, 2009).

30 David Harvey, *A Brief History of Neoliberalism* (Oxford: Oxford University Press, 2007).

31 Giddens, *Capitalism and Modern Social Theory*, xvi.

32 Linda Yueh, *The Great Economists* (London: Viking, 2018), 76; see also Joseph Stiglitz, *The Great Divide* (London: Allen Lane, 2015).

33 Thomas Piketty, *Capital in the Twenty-First Century*, trans. Arthur Goldhammer (Cambridge, MA: Harvard University Press, 2014).

34 Sayer, *Capitalism and Modernity*, 12.

35 Sayer, *Capitalism and Modernity*, 12.

36 Bryan S. Turner, *Max Weber: From History to Modernity* (London: Routledge, 1992).

37 Sheila Rowbotham, *Hidden from History* (London: Penguin, 1977). See also Harriet Bradley, "Gender and Work," in *The Sage Handbook of the Sociology of Work and Employment*, ed. Stephen Edgell, H. Gottfried, and E. Granter (London: Sage, 2016), 73–92.

38 Lynn S. Chancer and Beverly Xaviera Watkins, *Gender, Race, and Class* (Malden, MA: Blackwell, 2006), 18.

39 Cedric J. Robinson, *Black Marxism* (Chapel Hill: University of North Carolina Press, 2000), xxix.

40 Evelyn Glenn, "Race, Racialization and Work," in *The Sage Handbook of the Sociology of Work and Employment*, ed. Stephen Edgell, H. Gottfried, and E. Granter (London: Sage, 2016), 93–108.

41 Sebastiani, *The Scottish Enlightenment*, 12. On the history and meaning of race, see also Charles de Miramon, "Noble Dogs, Noble Blood: The Invention of the Concept of Race in the Late Middle Ages," in *The Origins of Racism in the West*, ed. Miriam Eliav-Feldon, Benjamin Isaac, and Joseph Ziegler (New York: Cambridge University Press, 2009), 200–16.

42 Robinson, *Black Marxism*, xxxi.

43 Eric J. Hobsbawm, *The Age of Empire 1875–1914* (London: Abacus, 1994), 252.

44 Stefan Kühl, *The Nazi Connection: Eugenics, American Racism, and German National Socialism* (New York: Oxford University Press, 1994).

45 Elijah Anderson, "Introduction to the 1996 Edition of *The Philadelphia Negro*," in *The Philadelphia Negro*, by W.E.B. Du Bois (1899; Philadelphia: University of Pennsylvania Press, 1996), ix–xxxvi, see page xiv.

46 Anthony Giddens, *Sociology*, 6th ed. (Cambridge: Polity Press, 2009) 632.

47 Lynn S. Chancer and Beverly Xaviera Watkins, *Gender, Race, and Class* (Malden, MA: Blackwell, 2006), 50.

48 Chancer and Watkins, *Gender, Race, and Class*.

49 Alan Swingewood, *A Short History of Sociological Thought* (New York: St. Martin's Press, 2000), x.

50 See Ray, "Figure 1.1: Society as a Multidimensional Concept," in *Theorizing Classical Sociology*, 8.

51 See, for example, Andreas Huyssen, "Mapping the Postmodern," *New German Critique* 33 (Autumn 1984): 5–52; and Harvey, *The Condition of Postmodernity*.

52 Bryan S. Turner, *Classical Sociology* (London: Sage, 1999).

53 B. Jessop, *From the Keynesian Welfare State to the Schumpeterian Workfare State*, Lancaster Regionalism Group Working Paper 45 (Lancaster, UK: University of Lancaster, 1992); Klein, *The Shock Doctrine*.

54 Giddens, *Capitalism and Modern Social Theory*.

55 See Hertz, *The Silent Takeover*; Joel Bakan, *The Corporation* (Toronto: Penguin, 2004); Klein, *The Shock Doctrine*.

56 Ian Macintosh, ed., *Classical Sociological Theory: A Reader* (Edinburgh: Edinburgh University Press, 1997).

57 For a critical interpretation of European historiography, see Sebastiani, *The Scottish Enlightenment*, and Robinson, *Black Marxism*. These authors argue that "enlightened" European scholars spent considerable energy disavowing the interdependence between ancient Western Europe and the cultural and intellectual contributions of North Africa by exorcising the intellectual contributions of Egypt from European history. Further, they contend that the Enlightenment discourse on the universalistic conception of "man" provided the ideological foundation of "racial capitalism" in premodern Europe, which was dependent on slavery, violence, colonialism, and genocide.

58 Rosemarie Putnam Tong, *Feminist Thought* (Boulder, CO: Westview Press, 1998), 53.

59 Ayaan Hirsi Ali, *Infidel* (New York: Free Press, 2007), 295; she states that Wollstonecraft's *A Vindication of the Rights of Woman* inspired her.

60 See Elliott Leyton's review of *The Pickton File*, Stevie Cameron (Toronto: Knopf, 2007); Leyton, "Death on the Pig Farm: Take One," *The Globe and Mail*, June 16, 2007, D3.

61 Shiv Malik and Sandra Laville, "Stephen Lawrence's Brother Lodges Complaint Against Met Police," *The Guardian*, January 9, 2013, 1.

62 Steven Morris, "Bristol Refugee Murder Review Accuses Police of Institutional Racism," *The Guardian*, December 18, 2017, 1, accessed May 12, 2018, https://www.theguardian.com/uk-news/2017/dec/18/bristol-refugee-murder-review-finds-police-institutional-racism-bijan-ebrahimi.

63 See John Urry, *Climate Change and Society* (London: Polity, 2011) for a useful introduction to the sociology of global warming. Space does not permit us to explore this topic thoroughly, but, inspired by the BBC's *Blue Planet* series, the cover of this edition depicts waste plastic in the ocean to draw attention to pollution and the devastation of the living world.

64 See Callinicos, *Social Theory*.

2. Modernity and Social Theory

The self-regulating market ... gave rise to a specific civilization ...
Such an institution could not exist for any length of time without
annihilating the human and natural substance of society; it would
have physically destroyed man and transformed his surroundings
into a wilderness.

—Karl Polanyi, 1957[1]

The city is simultaneously the machinery and the hero of modernity.
—Michel de Certeau, 1984[2]

CLASSICAL SOCIAL THEORY developed as a response to the advent and the
conditions of modernity in Western Europe, which created unprecedented
chaotic change and social upheaval. This great transformation from ancient
times occurred over a period of about 135 years between 1776, when
Adam Smith published his *An Inquiry into the Nature and Causes of the
Wealth of Nations* and Louis XVI still ruled France, and around 1914,
about ten years after Max Weber first published his *The Protestant Ethic
and the Spirit of Capitalism*. Karl Polanyi's book *The Great Transformation* describes how the powerful English bourgeoisie turned land and labor
into "fictitious commodities," in principle very different from the goods
that had previously been exchanged in markets. Polanyi's argument, however, is about much more than the innovation of the self-regulated market;
he makes the case that the great transformation changed not only the social
world but also people—by changing the way they viewed the world and
their place in it. The historical antecedents of classical social theory can be
found in what historian Eric Hobsbawm has called the dual revolution:
the British Industrial Revolution (1780–1830) and the French Revolution
(1789). This dual Anglo-French revolution cannot be understood without

examining conditions many decades before 1780, but such analysis is well beyond the limits of this chapter. As ideas and theories about the great transformation developed, a transformation of vocabulary occurred: new words were formed to explain the historical changes. For example, the word *sociology* was first used by Auguste Comte in 1830 and first appeared in English in 1843.[3] To appreciate the development of vocabulary, consider some of the dominant words that gained their modern meanings during that period: *factory, division of labor, proletariat, working class, capitalism, alienation, anomie,* and *ideology.* These new words reflected an intellectual engagement in the debate about the nature of modernity.

Before reviewing European transformation, we need to highlight some challenges this task presents. Studying social change from a historical perspective and using the word *revolution,* in particular, are problematic for a number of reasons. First, such an exercise involves a compression of time periods and a compression of different modes of social organization. Importantly, we need to avoid presenting the emergence of new social forms as a coherent, orderly, and inevitable process of change. For example, someone looking back from the vantage point of the early twenty-first century might find it reasonable to talk of the emergence of the factory system. However, this development took place sporadically. Many features of paid work in premodernity survived well into the modern era. When compressing the specific into general historical trends, we have to avoid attaching a coherent pattern that is spurious to these changes.[4] The second problem is how to separate the empirical developments from the theoretical perspectives within which these developments are organized and located.[5] History is about interpretation, and much of what follows represents one synthesized account of historical events. How historians assemble and interpret a chosen sample of facts will depend mainly on what methods are chosen, how the data are analyzed, and what kinds of facts are included: "By and large, the historian will get the kind of facts he wants."[6] Each of the classical theorists selected and gave prominence to the empirical developments that they found most significant.

In this chapter we give prominence to the immense social upheaval that occurred primarily in Western Europe or, more precisely, in Britain, France, and Germany. This focus is not because the neglected histories of other countries are less interesting or less important or for reasons of space. Rather, it is because Marx, Durkheim, and Weber witnessed first hand the maelstrom of chaotic social change marked by industrialization and urbanization. In Britain, for example, by 1867, when Marx had completed the first volume of *Capital,* the factory system was well established and the majority of Britons lived in cities. And in Germany and France by 1914, Max Weber and Émile Durkheim could observe for themselves the triumph of industrial capitalism and the social effects of urbanization. This

The factory was a technological and social transformation of paid work, increasing labor productivity but imposing a routine and discipline quite unlike pre-industrial rhythms of work.

chapter aims to provide a general historical synthesis, to make sense of the "great" transformation of Western Europe—insofar as it's reasonable to do so in one chapter—in order to understand how and why European modernity influenced the classical social thinkers that we have chosen to study. Our treatment sketches the processes of industrialization and urbanization in Britain, France, and Germany between 1780 and 1914.

Industrialization

From 1780, the traditional work rhythms and practices of pre-industrial society gave way to those of an industrial society, to a new modus operandi of producing goods. We can define the Industrial Revolution as a fundamental change in the structure of the economy in which the capitalists' pursuit and accumulation of profit guided the mode of organizing work, harnessing technology, and determining the social relations of work. Britain was the classic theater for the transformation of a pre-industrial agrarian economy into an industrialized and urban society. The British Industrial Revolution, which occurred roughly between 1780 and 1830,[7] was, it is posited, partly due to the interplay with European Enlightenment. The quest for knowledge that defined the Industrial Revolution was inspired by the Enlightenment, captured by Kant's injunction *sapere aude*, or "dare to know," that inspired inventors and exposed the world to the forces of reason.[8] In France, the contours of a modern industrial society developed much later, between 1875 and 1914. Germany in 1790 was still essentially a collection of states sharing a common language, and 17 million of her population of 23 million was engaged in agricultural rather than industrial activity. The German "destitution" was evident when compared with economic developments in England, whose industrial sector economy was already well established, and even when compared to those in France, whose economy was transforming from agriculture to manufacture. Between 1800 and 1848, Germany's industrial production was rapidly expanding but still small compared to that of England or France. Typical of this expansion were the tripling of metallurgical output, the 50 percent increase in the output of the coal mines between 1800 and 1830, and the construction of 2,500 kilometers of railway tracks between 1835 and 1847. In 1831, Germany's steam-machine production was still 50 years behind England's. Some German states did industrialize faster than others. In Rhineland-Westphalia, for example, the province where Karl Marx was born, the prefect of the Ruhr could plausibly claim that it was the most industrial region in Europe.[9]

In the late 1840s, the effect of industrialization in Britain, the effect of the French occupation of the Rhineland, and state support acted as catalysts for social transformation in Germany. The unification of the country by force under Prussian leadership and an atmosphere of exacerbated nationalism gave German industrial capitalism its special character. Large-scale expansion of industry occurred in Germany between 1850 and 1900.[10] It would be monotonous to quote data on rates of economic growth; suffice to say that, whereas before 1800 virtually the only quantities measured in millions were populations, by 1890 the quantities of iron, steel, and manufactured goods produced in Britain, France, and Germany were measured in such magnitudes. By 1890, Western Europe was the region of advanced capitalism par excellence.

The common features of industrial capitalism are found principally in the economic forces that produce it. First, industrialization involved a more productive use of the factors of production—land, labor, and machinery—partly obtained by introducing new methods of organization to production: the factory, a combination of power technology, specialized machines, and specialized occupations. Before each Industrial Revolution, most manufacturing operated on a small scale, employed labor-intensive methods, and used little fixed capital. The factory was the most striking outward symbol of the new industrial society. Second, industrialization involved a great increase in the productivity of human labor, in terms of output per head. The factory system provided greater degrees of coordinative and controlling power to the capitalist factory owner. The significance of the concentration of workers lay in the potential for increasing labor productivity by extending the division of labor and installing machines. The factory offered the opportunity to innovate: "The very division of labour ... prepared the ground from which mechanical invention could eventually spring."[11] Third, industrialization required the existence of a reserve army of free labor, the people able and willing to work for wages because they had no other adequate means of support. As we shall explain, the effects of agricultural reforms and population growth created a large pool of cheap labor as people migrated to the new industrial towns.

The role of technology within the factory system has been long debated. In *Capital*, Karl Marx's analysis of the industrial division of labor emphasizes how the process enabled the capitalist to control work processes in ways that were not possible with the traditional domestic, or putting-out, system.[12] Pre-industrial methods made it difficult for entrepreneurs to monitor and control the quantity and quality of the work performed by cottage-based workers because "the domestic weaver or craftsman was master of his time, starting and stopping when he desired."[13] The factory system provided new opportunities for controlling the pace and quality of work by means of the "discipline of mechanization"—the actual speed of the machine—and the hierarchy of direct supervisory control over the work process. Another aspect of the factory system was the need for workers to comply with a new rhythm of work. Factory owners demanded a new mentality toward work, one favorable to the exorable demands of factory rationality. Workers were taught the values of punctuality, obedience, and self-discipline. As noted by social historians, however, the process took several generations: "by fines; bells and clocks; money incentives; preachings and schoolings; the suppression of fairs and sports—new labour habits were formed, and a new time-discipline was imposed."[14] For Marx, as we will explain, the industrial division of labor and its concomitant capitalist relations of production are the prime movers of conflict and social change.

Economic historians have long debated the role of the state in the transition from early modern to modern capitalist society. The role of the state, which Marx famously summarizes as "a committee for managing the common affairs of the whole bourgeoisie,"[15] was central to the process of industrialization. European capitalism depended on a new state apparatus to provide a business-friendly environment: free markets, business laws and regulations, currency control, and, if necessary, defense of commercial interests. In Britain the old Corn Laws, with which the agrarian interests sought to protect farming, were abolished in 1846. To create the most favorable conditions for industrial capital, the British Parliament abolished the fixing of minimum wages. A precondition of the new industrial model was a large supply of labor. Recognizing that a reservoir of free labor is a prerequisite for modern capitalism, Weber writes, "Persons must be present who are not only legally in a position, but are also economically compelled, to sell their labour on the market without restriction.... The development of capitalism is impossible, if such a propertyless stratum is absent, a class compelled to sell its labour services to live; ... Rational capitalistic calculation is possible only ... where ... workers ... under the compulsion of the whip of hunger, offer themselves."[16] In his classic study *The Condition of the Working Class in England*, published in 1845 in German, Friedrich Engels discusses the laws of capitalist competition:

> The worker is, in law and in fact, the slave of the property-holding class, so effectually a slave that he is sold like a piece of goods, rises and falls in value like a commodity. If the demand for workers increases, the price of workers rises; if it falls, their price falls. If it falls so greatly that a number of them become unsaleable, if they are left in stock, they are simply left idle; and as they cannot live upon that, they die of starvation.... The only difference as compared with the old, outspoken slavery is this, that the worker of today seems to be free because he is not sold once and for all, but piecemeal by the day, the week, the year, and because no one owner sells him to another, but he is forced to sell himself in this way instead, being the slave of no particular person, but of the whole property-holding class.[17]

The state is of crucial importance in the workings of capitalism, not only as a major customer of private enterprise (e.g., warships, aircraft, and armaments) but also, in the case of Britain in the nineteenth century and the United States in the twenty-first, because of its readiness to protect business interests with military force. The triumph of British capitalism was achieved, as Eric Hobsbawm notes, "very largely because of the unswerving readiness of British governments to back their businessmen by ruthless and aggressive economic discrimination and open war against all possible rivals."[18] In Western Europe, state intervention supported the birth and growth of capitalism to the extent that it eventually became impossible not to be unaffected by the state's power and interventions in every aspect of modern life.[19]

Some of the classical social thinkers actually witnessed a double transformation in the structure and modus operandi of industrial capitalism.[20] On the one hand, they saw by 1890 the concentration of capital, the emergence of big business and monopolies. On the other hand, they observed the systematic attempt to rationalize production and manage business enterprises by applying scientific methods. The American Frederick W. Taylor (1856–1915) pioneered the so-called scientific management approach to industrial work; hence, the term *Taylorism* represents both a set of management practices and a system of ideological assumptions.[21] The centerpiece of Taylorism includes both the separation of tasks into their simplest constituent elements, the "routinization of work," and the transferring of all decision-making functions to managers. In North America, Henry Ford applied the major principles of Taylorism in his car plant but also added an important innovation, the assembly line. The assembly line intensified work through ever-greater job fragmentation and short task-cycle times. In 1922, Ford described his approach to managing workers: "The idea is that the man ... must have every second necessary but not a single unnecessary second."[22] By measuring tasks, managers gained even more control over the workers' performance. This form of work organization is called *Fordism*. A caustic satire on Fordism is presented in Charlie Chaplin's film *Modern Times*. The inherent problems associated with Taylorism and Fordism—alienation and industrial strikes—became a rich source of sociological inquiry in the twentieth century.

We have already noted that the canonical writers were, by and large, oblivious to the issue of gender (and race). In Western Europe, early industrial capitalism absorbed huge numbers of working-class women and children into the new factories, and this had a rapid effect on public attitudes toward gender roles and patterns of family life. As historians Annette Timm and Joshua Sanborn point out, European industrialization changed not only how people earned money and how they worked but also how they related to others socially and sexually.[23] Gender-based patterns of work and gender inequality were soon omnipresent in European capitalism. The factory owner's need for cheap labor provided new opportunities for working-class women to do paid work. In the later period of industrialization, the 1880s, large-scale food-processing factories and bakeries were female dominated. Emerging stereotypes reinforced the belief that work and family life were two separate spheres: "images ... depicted men as naturally suited to the highly competitive nineteenth-century workplace and women as too delicate for the world of commerce."[24]

Did industrial capitalism segregate home from work and allocate women to the former and men to the latter? Space doesn't allow us to address this question fully, but the evidence suggests that gender-based patterns of work predate modernity: they are socially constructed and not the result of capitalist-induced social change.[25] Work tended to be labeled female or male on the basis of socially changeable expectations of how to view, judge, and treat the two sexes. Enduring patterns of gender inequality at work can be partially explained by the activities of trade unions. According to one union leader, the object of a trade union is "to bring about a condition ... where wives and daughters would be in their proper sphere at home, instead of being dragged into competition for livelihood against the great and strong men of the world."[26] Historian Stephanie Coontz argues that whenever women undertake paid work in large numbers, certain social processes unfold.[27] Women begin to challenge laws and customs that regulate their subordination in the public sphere and within the family. Many working-class women became early supporters and activists in the trade unions and in the women's rights movement. Working women also begin to marry later and have fewer children, especially when they have access to education and attain higher paying careers.

The issue of gender roles and gender inequality at work remains a complex one, but there is no doubt that the case for equality was undermined by the notion of the "breadwinner's wage."[28] James Connolly, the Scottish socialist leader and a proto-feminist executed 103 years ago by the British state for his part in the Easter Rising in Dublin, Ireland, expressed a minority view in the labor movement. He wrote, "The worker is the slave of capitalist society, the female worker is the slave of the slave."[29] The general prevailing opinion meant that, throughout the nineteenth and well into the twentieth century, large numbers of working-class and middle-class women were effectively excluded from many trade and professional occupations, while men used patriarchal strategies to defend skill and profession as male property.[30]

Urbanization

The most obvious symbol of the new industrial society was not only the factory but also its inescapable attendant urbanization. Industrialization required housing for the new urban working class, transportation services, and financial institutions. At the heart of the question about the social effects of industrial capitalism is the disjuncture between pre-industrial and industrial labor. Factory labor imposed a regularity and monotony quite unlike pre-industrial rhythms of work, and labor increasingly took place in cities, which prevented any means of supplementing family income, for example, by growing food. The new manufacturing cities grew exponentially. In Britain in 1750, there were only two cities with more than 50,000 inhabitants: London and Edinburgh. In 1851, there were 29, including 9 cities with over 100,000. In 1831, the industrial city of Manchester had 238,000 inhabitants; Leeds had 123,000; Liverpool, 202,000; and Glasgow, 193,000. The growth of industrial cities was caused by both the general growth of population and the uprooting of people from rural areas. Census returns show the extent of the migration. In 1851, less than 50 percent of inhabitants of Manchester, Liverpool, and Glasgow had been born in these cities. London increased from 2.5 million in 1851 to 3.9 million in 1881; Paris from one million in 1849 to 1.9 million in 1875; and Berlin increased from 378,000 in 1848 to 1.6 million in 1888. With the rapid growth of cities came the most appalling standards of urban squalor known in nineteenth-century Britain. Still, urban conditions have to be related to their context before they can be evaluated. Public services—clean water supply, sanitation, street cleaning, and public spaces—were non-existent or of very poor standard before industrialization began. Comparisons must begin from here, not from twenty-first-century standards. Traditional living practices that were appropriate to the conventions and conditions of a pre-industrial society were carried into the new context, where the sheer numbers of people and the speed of urban development brutalized and degraded the older practices, which then appeared even more brutal and appalling in the new urban environment.

Cities grew rapidly in an unplanned, laissez-faire atmosphere, and they provided only the most basic public services, not to mention affordable housing. Air pollution and water pollution caused mass epidemics of contagious disease, notably cholera and typhoid, which swept through extensive nineteenth-century European working-class enclaves, which created the European division of the "good" west end and a "poor" east end of large cities. The pressure of profit-making shaped the living conditions of the urban working class, as developers and builders constructed railways into the city centers, preferably through the urban slums where real estate costs were low. Most working-class people rented accommodation in high-density tenement houses, typically consisting of one or two rooms only. For the city's powerful social elite, the working-class enclaves were public health hazards. It was only after 1850, when epidemics spread

This 1872 engraving by Gustave Doré shows a typical industrial district of London with back-to-back townhouses built alongside factories. The majority of working people had to live in these squalid conditions. The city caused traditional patterns of human social relationships to change, as did the relationship between the individual and society.

from the slums and began to kill the rich also, and after mass agitation that systematic urban planning and rebuilding were undertaken.

Reflective contemporaries did not deny that the new cities were cauldrons of appalling squalor and misery. In Britain, successive royal commissions, contemporary literature, and individual studies provided empirical evidence of working-class conditions. In 1835, the French liberal Alexis de Tocqueville wrote of Manchester, "From this foul drain the greatest stream of human industry flows out to fertilize the whole world. From this filthy sewer pure gold flows. Here humanity attains its most complete development and its most brutish; here civilization works its miracles, and civilized man is turned almost into a savage."[31] Friedrich Engels's *The Condition of the Working Class in England* is a scathing account of the filth and squalor of working-class housing: "Every great city has one or more slums, where the working class is crowded together ... The houses are occupied from cellar to garret, filthy within and without, and their appearance is such that no human being could possibly wish to live in them."[32] Describing the area of Manchester southwest of the city center and known as "Little Ireland," Engels writes in even more repugnant detail:

> Masses of refuse, offal and sickening filth lie among standing pools in all directions; the atmosphere is poisoned by the effluvia from these, and laden and darkened by the smoke of a dozen

tall factory chimneys. A horde of ragged women and children swarm about here, as filthy as the swine that thrive upon the garbage heaps and in the puddles. In short, the whole rookery furnishes such a hateful and repulsive spectacle as can hardly be equalled in the worst court on the Irk. The race that lives in these ruinous cottages ... must really have reached the lowest stage of humanity.[33]

However, the industrial city, hailed as enterprising by bourgeois contemporaries, was not only more populous than pre-industrial settlements; the increasing atomization of peoples and the migration of large masses unanchored from stable social groups fundamentally changed the social structure. Not only did the new urban working class live in squalid urban enclaves, but also its members' only relationship with their bourgeois employers was constituted by monetary transactions—*a cash nexus*. And the social distance between the urban rich and poor classes widened. Writing about Manchester, which was viewed by some contemporaries as the very symbol of civilization and of the new age,[34] a clergyman in the 1840s exemplified this new sensibility: "There is no town in the world where the distance between the rich and poor is so great, or the barrier between them so difficult to cross ... There is far less personal communication between the master cotton spinner and his workmen ... than there is between the Duke of Wellington and the humblest laborer on his estate."[35]

The city was not merely emblematic of the laboring classes' exclusion from human society; for them, it was a social catastrophe. As a corollary to this, distinctive patterns of social norms and behavior that characterize a modern industrial society became firmly established in industrialized Western Europe, particularly in Britain as early as the 1850s. This fast-paced urban life based on economic rationality, individualism, and a secular worldview gave people a strong sense that they were living in a new age of constant change. As most introductory sociology texts explain, this experience provoked much contemporary discussion on the distinction between traditional and modern societies, a discourse formalized in the celebrated work of the nineteenth-century German sociologist Ferdinand Tönnies (1855–1936), who distinguished the foundations of rural and small-town community life—what he called *Gemeinschaft*—from the foundations of large-city life, which he called *Gesellschaft*.

The clash between, on the one hand, the pervasive influence of religion and the moral economy of the past and, on the other, the principle of self-interest and the rationality of the present was particularly apparent in the realm of social behavior and welfare. The spending habits appropriate to rural life increased social problems when translated into the new high-density urban environment. In the city, the wage is the industrial family's *sole* protection against starvation and destitution, dependent as it is on the vicissitudes of the market. In contrast, although poverty among agricultural laborers was common, money did not usually have such unique importance for agricultural families, which had the opportunity to supplement their income by growing food. In urban centers, when higher wages were fed into traditional spending habits, greater social problems resulted.[36] Laissez-faire industrialization and an urban life based on money exchange exacerbated existing problems of alcoholism, infanticide, crime, prostitution, and suicide.[37]

The urban bourgeoisie, supported by the maxims of liberal economics and utilitarian philosophy, believed that the rational man must make provision for accident, illness, and old age. The social mechanism of the new society was in the profoundest manner inhuman and inequitable, and it left an indelible mark on the emerging discipline of sociology. As the Marxist historian Eric Hobsbawm convincingly explains, the British Poor Law Act of 1834, which made all welfare *less* than the lowest wage offered in the market, forcibly separated husband, wives, and children into institutionalized workhouses in order to punish the poor for being destitute. Yet the gap between the rich and poor classes grew wider and "the poor suffered because the rich benefited."[38] In France and Germany, despotic employers with a strong Catholic and paternalist tradition did, at least, partly offset the inherently insecure factory employment by providing education and welfare. The social relations of Britain's new industrial cities determined the pattern of social movements, as we shall soon discuss. As early as 1819, the year of the "massacre of Peterloo,"[39] *The Times* of London reported on the discontent of the Manchester working classes: "Their wretchedness seems to madden them against the rich, who they dangerously imagine engross the fruits of their labour without having any sympathy for their wants."[40] The development of classical social theory is inextricably tied to this debate about the social effects of urbanization.

Democratization

European industrial capitalism developed predominantly under the influence of the British Industrial Revolution; however, the French Revolution shaped its ideologies and greatly influenced the processes of democratization.[41] In mid-seventeenth-century England, the Leveller movement represented the aspirations of the working poor and campaigned for land reform, democracy, and equality.[42] By the 1790s, democracy was understood as uncontrolled popular power. Edmund Burke expressed the orthodox contemporary view that "a perfect democracy was the most shameful thing in the world."[43] Democracy was still considered a revolutionary term even in the 1850s. Only when it became defined in terms of the liberal tradition of open elections of representatives did it gain wide acceptance. The French Revolution helped spur the process of democratization. On July 14, 1789, the Bastille, a state prison symbolizing the absolute authority of King Louis XVI, was captured, and, by August, the revolution had acquired its manifesto, the Declaration of the Rights of Man and Citizen. The French Revolution inspired radical reform across Europe and ancient civilizations. It was "the first great movement of ideas in Western Christendom that had any real effect on the world of Islam."[44] Revolutions in nineteenth-century Europe were caused largely by the struggle both for and against the principles of 1789.

In his book *The Age of Revolution, 1789–1848*, the late Eric Hobsbawm argues that the French Revolution emerged because of the conflict between the absolute monarchy of Louis XVI and the rising new social forces represented by the middle classes. The bourgeoisie wanted to build a new society according to the maxims of reason and liberal economics. The ideology of the French Revolution, found in the famous Declaration of the Rights of Man and Citizen, is, in essence, a manifesto against the old hierarchical society of aristocratic privilege, as two of its tenets evince: "men are born and live free and equal under the laws" and "all citizens have a right to cooperate in the formation of the law."[45] In Hobsbawm's view, these ideals are rooted in classical liberalism as formulated by such philosophers as Charles-Louis de Sécondat, Baron de Montesquieu, and Jean-Jacques Rousseau, and by liberal economists such as Adam Smith.[46] The leaders of classical liberalism believed in constitutionalism, an enlightened monarchy, and a secular state with civil liberties, guarantees for private enterprise, and a government representing taxpayers and property owners. A second revolution of 1792, the "Jacobin Revolution," inspired the dream of "equality, liberty, and fraternity," and the rise to power of Napoleon Bonaparte (1769–1821).

From 1792 until 1850, Europe experienced almost continual war and three waves of revolution. The first wave occurred in 1820–24, which saw uprisings in Spain and Italy (1820) and Greece (1821). The second wave occurred in 1829–34 and 1837–42 and was confined to Western Europe, with uprisings in Britain, Belgium, Germany, Italy, and Poland. A third wave of revolution broke out in France, Germany, and Italy in 1848, the same year in which Marx and Engels's *Communist Manifesto* was published. In London, a mass demonstration marched to Parliament to demand universal male suffrage. Throughout the second half of the nineteenth century, the state, the power holders of finance, and the big industrialists in Britain, France, and Germany were anxious to prevent revolution on the French Jacobin model. In Germany, the liberalism of England was more of a model than that of France. Radical ideas were confined to groups of German intellectuals, of which the most prominent was the Young Hegelians.[47] It was not until the 1880s that political oligarchs were seriously challenged by the agitations of the labor movement of trade unions and working-class political parties.

The French Revolution and industrial capitalism gave rise to another phenomenon of modernity: nationalism. In the literature of the politics of nationalism, the concept of national identity is often treated as the outcome of capitalist expansion, a development resulting from the pressure of industrial society to produce a large, centrally educated, culturally homogeneous population.[48] Nationalism helped create the notion that people share a collective history and destiny, expressed in the formulation by social elites of shared values and common narratives about the national past and national interests. In the new industrial age, nationalism was a powerful social force in giving the people in advanced capitalist countries a strong sense of culture and social identity. The social experience of those most affected by industrial capitalism was moderated by the "imagined community" of the nation-state. Each nationalist movement tended to justify its principal concern with its own nation. Following the three waves of revolution in Europe, nation building and mass nationalism became important features of European politics.

Mass nationalism was pivotal to capitalist growth.[49] As the British, Belgian, French, and German economies expanded, nationalism helped give rise to a modern global system of "racial capitalism" dependent upon colonialism, slavery, and violence.[50] In simple terms, colonialism refers to the economic, political, social, and cultural domination of an indigenous people by an outside foreign power. The long reign of the British Empire over parts of Africa, India, and North America is an example of colonialism. The same can be said of German rule over parts of East and West Africa and French rule over parts of North Africa. The roots of Western racism took hold in European civilization well before the dawn of the British Industrial Revolution. It was in the West that the "Negro" was first manufactured, and, by extension, another fabrication was created, that of the superiority of white European nations, governed by superior moral and religious beliefs (according to the ideas of "scientific racism," at least) and by European rule of law, and composed of literate citizens and inventors of superior technology. These constructions helped justify colonial expansion and enslavement in those territories deemed to be lawless, illiterate, and inferior. The close relationship among capitalist development, the social construction of race, slavery, and colonialism is complex.[51] But, in Hobsbawm's view, "it is undeniable that the pressure of capital in search of more profitable investment ... contributed to policies of expansion—including colonial conquest."[52]

In Western Europe, the confluence of economic and political forces created the conditions out of which the tensions arose that contributed to the origins of World War I (1914–18). The German industrialists wanted access to international markets for their increasing productive capacity, which only an expansionist foreign policy and colonialism could give. An expansionist foreign policy brought the demand for building a German navy. The economic development of Germany cannot be separated from the politics of colonialism and nationalism.[53] Ideas about colonial backwardness and inferiority when compared with Europe were buttressed by social science. Economists justified colonial expansion through theories of economic growth predicated on the international division of labor, and second-order Darwinism spuriously accounted for the division of races into advanced and backward.

England was not only the birthplace of industrial capitalism but also the cradle of new mass social movements. Disenchantment with the excesses of laissez-faire capitalism gave rise to the Chartist movement, trade unions, and working-class political parties. The fundamental demand of Chartism was political reform, principally universal male suffrage. Universal female suffrage was never asked for, or conceded. In explaining the rise of the working-class Chartist movement in the 1830s, Gammage wrote in 1854, "It is the existence of great social wrongs which principally teaches the masses the value of political rights."[54] For centuries before 1790, popular uprisings of one kind or another had challenged local employers and power holders. But, between the 1780s and the 1830s, mass popular politics gave voice to ordinary people on a wide range of social issues and took several forms: mass national demonstrations, petitions, public statements, and the lobbying of members of Parliament. These political repertoires greatly increased as a means by which members of the middle class and working class made collective claims on the ruling class. Participants and observers alike recognized the maturity of the sporadic surges of political militancy: a transition from relatively parochial to national popular politics. Marx and Engels's *Communist Manifesto* best captures the significance of this new political phenomenon: "All previous historical movements were movements of minorities, or in the interest of minorities. The proletarian movement is the self-conscious, independent movement of the immense majority, in the interest of the immense majority."[55]

In June 2018, to mark the centenary of the Representation of the People Act 1918, which gave some women the right to vote for the first time, UK-wide Processions were held. This image shows two participants at the Edinburgh event.

The British Industrial Revolution and the French Revolution profoundly changed the relative political power of the social classes. As industrial capitalism expanded, the ascendancy of the middle classes became manifest, as did the downward tendency of the aristocracy. War-driven taxation and debt increased Parliament's power and compelled the aristocracy to make concessions: To wage a war against the French Republic, it is argued, the British aristocracy "threw themselves into the arms of the moneied class."[56] The Reform Act of 1832 enfranchised the British middle strata, and was the first example in Europe of an *ancien régime* acquiescing peacefully to the forces of constitutional democracy.[57] After campaigning alongside the bourgeoisie to achieve their own political emancipation, working-class reformers believed that the middle class would campaign in and outside Parliament for the extension of reform to include at least all adult males in the franchise. The fact that the newly enfranchised middle class did not champion working-class rights became known as the great betrayal.

In the 1830s and 1840s, the growing disaffection of the poor was universal in Europe. In Britain, following the 1832 betrayal, the Chartists under the *People's Charter* united the working classes around six points of political reform: universal male suffrage, the secret ballot, payment of members of Parliament, the abolition of property qualifications for MPs, equal electoral districts, and annual parliaments. The Chartist movement was the first national working-class movement in the world, but it was not a revolutionary movement. It demanded inclusion in the political system, not its abolition. Its program of reforms gradually passed into the acts of 1867, 1884, and 1918. As late as 1880, Britain's Queen Victoria opposed political reform. She declared with emphasis that she "*cannot* and will not be Queen of a *democratic monarchy*."[58] The British Labour Party, backed by trade unions and inspired by socialist ideology, was firmly established in 1914. In Britain, after decades of mass demonstrations, physical abuse by police, and the imprisonment and force-feeding of some leaders of the Women's Social and Political Union, women secured the vote in 1918—for those over 30 who owned property and then, in 1928, for all women over 21, well behind the Nordic countries and ex-colonies Australia, Canada, and New Zealand.[59] In France and Germany, the survival and prosperity of substantial sections of the peasantry retarded the development of working-class political movements in a way that was dissimilar to the British experience. In the first half of the nineteenth century, French and German intellectual reformers were not interested in organizing mass political agitation.[60]

From the eighteenth to the early twentieth century, conflict and collective action were further transformed as working-class activity progressed from machine breaking—commonly referred to as Luddism—to unionism. Trade unions have a history that goes back beyond the Industrial Revolution, but most early unions were local and specialized. Until 1824, workers had no legal rights to organize unions to improve their working conditions. In the aftermath of the "great betrayal," British trade unionism developed among skilled male workers—the "aristocracy of labor." In 1851, for example, the Amalgamated Society of Engineers (ASE) had a membership of almost 12,000, large enough to compel employers to negotiate improvements to their working conditions. Leaders campaigned for the legal recognition of unions, which was granted by the Trade Unions Act of 1871.[61] The years following the 1880s saw a significant growth of trade unionism, both in numbers and character. General unions were formed to organize all workers, not just skilled ones, and developed the strike as a weapon of the working class. This new unionism represented an ideological and political "sharp turn to the left."[62] Elsewhere, the situation was rather different. In France, unionism was extremely localized. In Germany, unionism was limited to workers with highly specialized skills. In France and Germany, a wave of labor unrest and strikes did occur during 1868–71, which certainly frightened employers and governments. The raison d'être of trade unionism was, as it remains today, to secure through collective negotiation better terms for the sale of labor power. Exclusionary practices against working-class women persisted, however, and unionism largely remained the preserve of male workers throughout the nineteenth century. The limits of English working-class radicalism were further evident in Anglo-Saxon chauvinism, a racial ideology shared across class lines that allowed the English middle classes to rationalize the low wages given to Irish workers, and even to condone the great exploitation and brutality of the non-European population.[63]

Conclusion

The dynamic social changes occurring between 1780 and 1914 provided the context of the classical assemblage we have chosen to study. The works of Marx, Durkheim, and Weber are inextricably bound up with the conditions of modernity. As we have attempted to capture, Europe in 1914 was qualitatively different than it had been in the eighteenth century. It had experienced colossal technological and social transformation in at least three respects.

First, economies were no longer predominantly based on agriculture. The large-scale industrial production symbolized by the factory and pioneered by Britain had migrated to the mainland of Europe and elsewhere, most notably to North America. In 1848, Britain was the superpower and the "workshop of the world," but the superpowers of 1914 included France, Germany, and the United States. Large-scale industrial production was a technological and social transformation of paid work, which increased labor productivity but imposed a routine and discipline quite unlike pre-industrial rhythms of work. Paradoxically, the period between 1780 and 1914, whose claim to have benefited humanity rests on the enormous triumphs of an industrial capitalism based on natural science and technology, ended with the new technology of mass-produced machine guns, artillery, armored warships, and munitions slaughtering millions in the trench warfare of 1914–18. The second transformation was the unprecedented development of cities where wage labor increasingly took place. With urbanization, traditional social norms and patterns of human engagement were abandoned, and this changed the relationship between the individual and society: society comprised atomized individuals in the anarchy of competition pursuing only their own self-interest. Marx and Engels's description of the transformation of social structure is familiar: "The bourgeoisie ... has pitilessly torn asunder the motley feudal ties that bound man to his 'natural superiors' and has left remaining no other nexus between man and man than naked self-interest."[64] The third transformation was the process of democratization and the creation of mass national social movements that challenged despotism, the logic of capitalism, and inequality. Working-class emancipation and the institutions of working-class self-defense—the trade unions—had become firmly rooted in Western Europe by 1914.

These are some of the dynamic developments of humanity that the classical social thinkers confronted. It was, simultaneously, a new world of perpetual collapse and renewal, extreme wealth and poverty, individual growth and alienation, liberal democracy and political exclusion, and contradiction and struggle. The classical theorists were preoccupied with trying to make sense of the totalizing chaos and with explaining the key characteristics of modernity as contrasted with premodern society. We will explore their works in future chapters, but, before that, we need to examine the intellectual forces that also shaped the theoretical thinking of the founders of sociology.

FURTHER THINKING:

Why were large numbers of working-class and middle-class women excluded from many trade and professional occupations in the nineteenth and well into the twentieth century? Recently, Beatrix Campbell in *The End of Equality* (London: Seagull Books, 2014) has posited that we are seeing a return of patriarchal attitudes encouraged by the advocates of neoliberal capitalism. Do you believe this to be true?

FURTHER READING:

For an interesting and readable introduction to the history of the nineteenth century, see Eric Hobsbawm, *The Age of Revolution, 1789–1848* (London: Abacus, 1962). To help understand how the factory system changed people's lived experience, read the classic piece by Edward P. Thompson, "Time, Work-Discipline, and Industrial Capitalism," *Past and Present* 38 (December 1967), 56–97. For a contemporary article on gender and work, see J. Acker, "Hierarchies, Jobs, Bodies: A Theory of Gendered Organizations," *Sociology* 23 (1990): 235–40.

Notes

1 Karl Polanyi, *The Great Transformation* (Boston: Beacon Press, 1957), 3.

2 Michel de Certeau,*The Practice of Everyday Life*, trans. Steven Rendall (Berkeley: University of California Press, 1984), quoted in David Harvey, *The Condition of Postmodernity* (Oxford: Blackwell, 1994), 26.

3 Raymond Williams, *Keywords: A Vocabulary of Culture and Society* (New York: Oxford University Press, 1976), 291–96.

4 See Craig R. Littler, *The Development of the Labour Process in Capitalist Societies* (London: Heinemann, 1982); Graeme Salaman, *Class and the Corporation* (London: Routledge & Kegan Paul, 1981).

5 Eric J. Hobsbawm, *On History* (London: Weidenfeld & Nicholson, 1997).

6 Edward H. Carr, *What Is History* (London: Harmondsworth, UK, 1961), 22–23; see also Arthur Marwick, *The Nature of History* (London: Macmillan Press, 1970).

7 Dividing social and economic history into periods can only be very approximate, and the date for the beginning of the Industrial Revolution is still a matter of dispute among historians.

8 See Will Hutton and Andrew Adonis, *Saving Britain* (London: Abacus, 2018); Joel Mokyr, *The Enlightened Economy: An Economic History of Britain 1700–1850* (London: Yale University Press, 2009).

9 For a short account of German economic, social, and political background of the period, see David McLellan, *Marx Before Marxism* (London: Harper and Row, 1971).

10   Tom Kemp, *Industrialization in Nineteenth Century Europe* (London: Longman, 1969).

11   Maurice Dobb, *Studies in the Development of Capitalism* (London: Routledge & Kegan Paul, 1963), 145.

12   Karl Marx, *Capital*, vol. 1 (1867; London: Lawrence & Wishart, 1959).

13   David Landes, *The Unbound Prometheus* (Cambridge: Cambridge University Press, 1969), 59.

14   Edward P. Thompson, "Time, Work-Discipline, and Industrial Capitalism," *Past and Present* 38 (December 1967), 56–97, see page 90.

15   Robert Tucker, ed., *The Marx-Engels Reader* (New York: Norton, 1972), 475.

16   Max Weber, *General Economic History*, trans. F. Knight (1927; New York: Dover Publications, 2003), 277.

17   Friedrich Engels, *The Condition of the Working Class in England* (1845; Moscow: Progress Publishers, 1973), 118–19.

18   Eric J. Hobsbawm, *Industry and Empire* (London: Weidenfeld and Nicolson, 1968), 196.

19   Ralph Miliband, *The State in Capitalist Society* (London: Weidenfeld and Nicolson, 1969).

20   Eric J. Hobsbawm, *The Age of Empire, 1875–1914* (London: Abacus, 1994).

21   Craig R. Littler, "Internal Contract and the Transition to Modern Work Systems," in *The International Yearbook of Organizational Studies 1979*, ed. David Dunkerley and Graeme Salaman (London: Routledge & Kegan Paul, 1980), 157–85.

22   Quoted in Huw Beynon, *Working for Ford* (Harmondsworth, UK: Penguin, 1984), 33.

23   Annette F. Timm and Joshua A. Sanborn, *Gender, Sex and the Shaping of Modern Europe* (Oxford: Berg Publishers, 2007), 55.

24   Barbara F. Reskin and Irene Padavic, *Women and Men at Work* (Thousand Oaks, CA: Sage, 1994), 21, and quoted by Mats Alvesson and Yvonne Due Billing, *Understanding Gender and Organizations* (Thousand Oaks, CA: Sage, 1997), 58.

25   See Alvesson and Billing, *Understanding Gender and Organizations*; Maxine Berg, "Women's Work, Mechanization and Early Industrialization," in *On Work*, ed. Raymond E. Pahl (Oxford: Blackwell, 1988); Jane Rendall, *Women in an Industrializing Society: England 1750–1880* (Oxford: Blackwell, 1990).

26   Herbert A. Turner, *Trade Union Growth, Structure and Policy: A Comparative Study of the Cotton Unions* (London: Allen & Unwin, 1962), 185, and quoted in Keith Grint, *The Sociology of Work*, 2nd ed. (Cambridge: Polity Press, 1998), 72.

27   Stephanie Coontz, "Feminism Didn't Fail the Family," *The Globe and Mail*, August 25, 2008, A13.

28   Jane Rendall, *Women in an Industrializing Society*, 62.

29   James Connolly, "The Re-Conquest of Ireland" (1915), in *The James Connolly Reader*, ed. Shaun Harkin (Chicago: Haymarket Books, 2018), 428.

30   David Knights and Hugh Willmott, eds., *Gender and the Labour Process* (Aldershot, UK: Gower, 1986).

31   Alex de Tocqueville, *Journeys to England and Ireland*, ed. J. P. Mayer (New Haven, CT: Yale University Press, 1958), 107–08.

32   Engels, *The Condition of the Working Class*, 66–67.

33   Engels, *The Condition of the Working Class*, 100.

34   See Asa Briggs, "Manchester, Symbol of a New Age," in *Victorian Cities* (London: Pelican, 1968), 88–138.

35 Canon Parkinson, quoted in Briggs, *Victorian Cities*, 114.

36 Peter Mathias, *The First Industrial Nation* (London: Methuen, 1969), 208.

37 Hobsbawm, *The Age of Revolution*, 241–42.

38 Hobsbawm, *The Age of Revolution*, 247.

39 The "massacre of Peterloo" is featured in Mike Leigh's epic film *Peterloo* (2018). To read a review of this film, go to https://www.theguardian.com/film/2018/nov/03/peterloo-review-mike-leigh-epic-history-lesson?CMP=Share_iOSApp_Other.

40 Briggs, *Victorian Cities*, 90.

41 Hobsbawm, *The Age of Revolution*.

42 Christopher Hill, *The Century of Revolution, 1603–1714* (London: Sphere Books, 1961).

43 Quoted in Williams, *Keywords*, 96.

44 Bernard Lewis, "The Impact of the French Revolution on Turkey," *Journal of World History* 1 (1953): 105, quoted in Hobsbawm, *The Age of Revolution*, 76.

45 Hobsbawm, *The Age of Revolution*, 81.

46 See also Hill, *The Century of Revolution*.

47 See David McLellan, *Marx Before Marxism* (London: Harper and Row, 1971), 10–14.

48 Ernest Gellner, *Nations and Nationalism* (Oxford: Blackwell, 1983).

49 Eric J. Hobsbawm, *The Age of Capital, 1845–1875* (London: Abacus, 1977), 110–21.

50 Cedric J. Robinson, *Black Marxism* (Chapel Hill: University of North Carolina Press, 2000), xii–xii.

51 See, for example, Silvia Sebastiani, *The Scottish Enlightenment: Race, Gender, and the Limits of Progress* (Basingstoke, UK: Palgrave Macmillan, 2013).

52 Hobsbawm, *The Age of Empire*, 45.

53 Tom Kemp, *Industrialization in Nineteenth Century Europe* (London: Longman, 1969), 117.

54 Robert George Gammage, *History of the Chartist Movement, 1837–1854* (London: Merlin Press, 1969).

55 Marx and Engels, *Communist Manifesto*, quoted in Tilly, *Social Movements*, 6.

56 Gammage, *History of the Chartist Movement*, 2.

57 Dorothy Thompson, "Chartism, Success or Failure?" in *People for the People*, ed. David Rubinstein (London: Ithaca Press, 1973), 90–97.

58 Henry Pelling, *The Origins of the Labour Party, 1880–1900* (Oxford: Clarendon Press, 1965), 1.

59 For a short history of women's suffrage in Canada, go to http://www.thecanadian encyclopedia.ca/en/article/suffrage/.

60 Hobsbawm, *The Age of Revolution*, 152.

61 For an extended account of early trade union history, see Peter Mathias, *The First Industrial Nation* (London: Methuen, 1969); and Henry Pelling, *A History of British Trade Unions* (London: Pelican, 1963).

62 John Lovell, *British Trade Unions, 1875–1933* (London: Macmillan Press, 1977), 20.

63 Robinson, *Black Marxism*, xiii.

64 Eric Hobsbawm, *The Age of Extremes, 1914–1991* (London: Abacus, 1995), 128.

3. European Enlightenment and Early Social Thought

The time will come when the sun will shine only on free men who have no master but their reason.

—Nicolas de Condorcet (1743–94)

Faith in the power of reason—the belief that free citizens can govern themselves wisely and fairly by resorting to logical debate on the basis of the best evidence available, instead of raw power—was and remains the central premise of American democracy. This premise is now under attack.

—Al Gore, 2007[1]

SOCIAL THEORY DID NOT DEVELOP IN A VACUUM. It emerged from a complex set of interlocking philosophical problems and debates that date back to the middle decades of the seventeenth century. In medieval Europe before the Enlightenment, scholastic theories about humankind were dictated by the church and religious ideology. The Church of Rome denounced as a heretic anyone who sought for truth independently of the church. Views began to change in the seventeenth century when the educated elite adopted secular ideas to debate the nature of society and the direction it was going or ought to go. It is this unprecedented shift in social discourses, the sets of ideas that together form a powerful body of intellectual thought, which we associate with "Enlightenment." But the Enlightenment was a pan-European movement with contributions from French, German, and Scottish thinkers, for example. The multifaceted nature of what has come to be known as the Enlightenment, then, refutes the possibility of encapsulating the various streams of thought within a single history.[2] In reality, the intellectual movements cannot be separated from the social movements, and the former were intimately related to modernity. The Enlightenment, also known as the Age of Reason, not only emphasized reason and science over superstition and blind faith but also negated all legitimation of monarchy, slavery, and woman's subordination to man. Thus, the Enlightenment was a cultural tsunami that swept across western Europe and presaged "a breakthrough in critical consciousness."[3] It is therefore of immense importance for understanding the rise of modernity and social theory.[4]

In this chapter, we provide a brief and selective survey of the core ideas of the European Enlightenment to gain some insight into the philosophies that engaged the classical social theorists examined in this book. The start date of this synthesis, 1648, marked the beginning of a restructuring of Europe's political powers and a secularization of knowledge. The end date, 1789, witnessed the French Revolution and the beginning of a sustained conservative reaction against the ideals of the Enlightenment. After defining *Enlightenment*, the chapter examines the ideas of key Enlightenment thinkers under three thematic headings that interlock and, in many cases, overlap: epistemology, human nature and civil society, and emancipation. The rest of the chapter considers the conservative reaction to Enlightenment ideals and the effects of these social discourses on early sociology.

The Enlightenment

Any coverage of the European Enlightenment that fails to acknowledge its antecedents within the centuries of other intellectual thinkers would be misleading. Enlightenment thinkers were conscious of their debt to the past and, at the same time, aware of the uniqueness of their own historical moment as an age of critique, reassessment, and transformation.[5] The ancient Greeks speculated on the nature of society. *Republic* by Plato (c. 427–347 BCE)[6] describes an organic social division of labor. And *Politics* by Aristotle (384–22 BCE) contains one of the first attempts to analyze systematically different forms of government—tyranny, oligarchy, and democracy. In the two centuries dating from 1400 to 1600, European intellectuals and artists developed an interest in the ancient civilizations of Greece and Rome. This interest sparked what has come to be known as the Renaissance, a movement originating in Italy and extending progressively to the rest of Europe that cultivated "a spirit of enthusiastic inquiry" in the fields of the arts, architecture, literature, philosophy, and politics.[7] However, neither ancient Greek philosophers nor Renaissance intellectuals conceptualized society as something distinct from government or the state. The crucial notion of society as a general and abstract concept had to await the Enlightenment.[8]

What is the Enlightenment? In *The Enlightenment* (2013), Dorinda Outram observes that the answer to this question is nearly as important as the question "What is truth?" Since the seventeenth century, there have been many attempts to define the *European Enlightenment*.

The Prussian Immanuel Kant (1724–1804) famously wrote, "Enlightenment is man's release from his self-incurred tutelage,"[9] and his injunction *sapere aude*, or "dare to know" and have the courage to use your own reason, inspired inventors and philosophers alike. In the twentieth century, Ernst Cassirer's *The Philosophy of the Enlightenment*[10] implies that Enlightenment refers to a desire for human action to be guided by rationality rather than by faith, superstition, or revelation. Written in the immediate aftermath of World War II (1939–45), Horkheimer

FRONTISPICE DE L'ENCYCLOPEDIE.

Designed by Charles-Nicolas Cochin, the frontispiece of Diderot and d'Alembert's *Encyclopédie*, subtitled in English *A Reasoned Dictionary of the Sciences, Arts and Trades*, embodies one of the most common interpretations of the term *Enlightenment*. It depicts Reason and Philosophy pulling away the veil from Truth, while clouds withdraw to open the sky to light. Imagination (left) offers Truth a garland on behalf of all the Arts and Sciences.

and Adorno's 1947 *Dialectic of Enlightenment*[11] is far less positive. The authors argue that at the heart of the Enlightenment lurks political terror in the form of "rational" technological systems utilized to assure mass death in the Holocaust.

In the twenty-first century, there is still no scholarly consensus about which intellectual projects should be given preference. For some, such as Peter Gay, the European Enlightenment represents a unified body of thought developed around the core principle of reason, and it is the basis for human progress.[12] Similarly, for Irving Zeitlin, the Enlightenment is about the advancement of humanity and ever-greater degrees of freedom through "reason and science." For Outram, the Enlightenment is best seen as "a series of interlocking, and sometimes warring problems and debates," where intellectual projects changed society and government on a world-wide basis.[13] In relation to social discourses on Christianity and Islam, some contemporary scholars posit that the Enlightenment is an embodiment of Western cultural imperialism. The Enlightenment was a pan-European phenomenon and was pre-eminently a movement of ideas. The movement's leading thinkers were religious skeptics and cultural critics who shaped intellectual opinion across Europe. In the eighteenth century, the French *philosophes* (a term used to refer generally to all kinds of Enlightenment thinkers) most fervently criticized religious orthodoxy. Some of Enlightenment thought as it relates to the development of social theory we consider next.

Epistemology: Rationalism and Empiricism

The significance of the European Enlightenment for the evolution of social theory lies in large part in the Enlightenment's philosophical trait of rationality and in the secular conceptualization of society and human progress as objective, collective forces. Philosophers ask questions about knowledge: How is knowledge acquired, and how reliable is knowledge? Such questions are known as epistemology or the theory of knowledge. Rationality refers to a philosophical doctrine that gives primacy to the a priori (deductive) method of reasoning in the process of developing knowledge. Rationalism assumes that the human mind is the sole source of truth and hence must reject faith as a source of truth. As such, it is opposed to empiricism, which is an epistemological doctrine that gives primacy to the a posteriori (inductive) method of reasoning to arrive at general truths, which are derived from experience, observation, or experiments.

Historically, rationalism is embodied in the works of two prominent seventeenth-century philosophers, Descartes and Spinoza. The French philosopher René Descartes (1596–1650) is often regarded as the originator of the rationalist method, and he had an important influence on early Enlightenment thinking. Descartes argues that strict deductive reasoning must be the only source of knowledge. In his 1641 *Discourse on Method and Meditations on First Philosophy*, Descartes sets out the conditions necessary for something to be knowledge. He posits that, like the structure of a building, knowledge must rest upon secure foundations, and this foremost principle is based on self-consciousness: "I exist, simply because I am able to doubt my existence." All things that we can conceive of clearly and distinctly exist. In establishing self-consciousness as the basis of absolute certainty, Descartes rejects faith as a possible source of truth and celebrates the universal power of human reason.[14] Cartesian philosophy is part materialist and part idealist: the human is a machine but has a soul. Benedictus (Baruch) de Spinoza (1632–77) attracted notoriety in early Enlightenment Europe because he was the chief progenitor of the medieval Christian doctrine of revelation.[15] In his 1674 *Ethics*, Spinoza conceives the reality of the universe both as the sum of all facts and as the ordering principle that determines the relationship of all those facts in the whole.[16] In other words, all things that exist, exist necessarily and are modes of thought and extension. For Spinoza, reason in humans is akin to reason in nature; one order permeates everything. Reason enables rational human beings to understand themselves and the totality of the universe: it is the key to all of life.[17] The underlying assumption of Spinoza's philosophy is that reality and concept coincide, so relations between ideas correspond exactly to relations in reality. Spinoza's materialist philosophy had the potential of producing a revolutionary ideology, which may be seen as a precursor of Marx's historical materialism.

Empiricism, which is an epistemological doctrine that gives primacy to the a posteriori method of reasoning, is most famously associated with the writings of Sir Isaac Newton, John Locke, David Hume, and Immanuel Kant. In contrast to the emphasis placed solely on deductive reasoning, the English mathematician Sir Isaac Newton (1642–1727) believed in the importance of data based on experience and observation. In *Opticks* (1704), he persuasively puts his case for "experimental philosophy":

> As in mathematics, so in natural philosophy, the investigation of difficult things by the method of analysis ought ever to precede the method of compositions. This analysis consists of making experiments and observations, and in drawing general conclusions from them by induction.[18]

Like Newton, John Locke (1632–1704) and the Scottish philosopher David Hume (1711–76) emphasize the pivotal role of experience in all human understanding and knowledge. Locke's 1690 *Essay Concerning Human Understanding* provides the epistemological foundations of modern empiricism. An *idea*, according to Locke, is "whatsoever is the Object of the Understanding when a Man thinks."[19] Locke acknowledges that, sometimes, humans conceive of things outside their life experience. He asserts that when ideas do not appear to connect directly to experience, they are in fact fabricated by some kind of extrapolation from the ideas that are based upon sensory experience.[20] In *A Treatise of Human Nature* (1739–40), David Hume avers empiricism, and his radical approach involved him in deconstructing the identity of the self: "The true idea of the human mind is to consider it as a system of different perceptions or different existences which are linked together by a relation of cause and effect, and mutually produce, destroy, influence, and modify each other."[21]

The celebrated German thinker Immanuel Kant, arguably one of the most influential philosophers of the European Enlightenment, established his international reputation through his trilogy of critiques.[22] His seminal treatise on epistemology is found in the first of these, his *Critique of Pure Reason*, in which he asks what can be known by a priori reasoning. Although concurring with empiricists such as Locke and Hume that there are no innate ideas, he did not accept that all knowledge could be derived solely from sense experience, which imprints impressions on the human mind. To understand the phenomenal world, humans have to rely upon their own inherent logic and concepts, such as causation, that enable us to make sense of the natural world. The human mind is equipped with several categories of understanding, including cause and effect, which are not learned from sense experience. To Kant, the order of the natural world and the laws of nature are not then inherent in nature but are human *constructs* imposed upon it by human minds. The works of Descartes, Spinoza, Locke, Hume, and Kant offer an overview of the debate on the epistemological question of what is (or should be) regarded as acceptable scientific knowledge. The precise meaning and status of the words *positivism* and *empiricism* later affected the emerging discipline of sociology.

Human Nature and Civil Society

The phrase *civil society* was central to the European Enlightenment as a description of the conditions of organized social life. The French and Scottish *philosophes* were preoccupied with the concept of civil society, its moral values, and its development. John Locke (1632–1704) and Thomas Hobbes (1588–1679) were two early contributors to the debate on human nature. In *Two Treatises of Civil Government* (1690), Locke argues that individuals will readily abdicate their agency and live under the rules of civil society for protection: "To avoid this state of war ... is one great reason of men's putting themselves into society."[23] In *Leviathan* (1651), Hobbes portrays humans as innately and wholly self-seeking and engaged in perpetual war. Hobbes' work is pre-Enlightenment, but it did influence later *philosophes*, such as Rousseau.

The prominent Swiss philosopher Jean-Jacques Rousseau (1712–78) was probably one of the first to use *société* as a key concept and explicitly to reason in terms of social relations.[24] In *A Discourse upon the Origin and Foundation of Inequality Among Mankind*, published in 1755, he declares, "The first man who, having enclosed a piece of ground, took it into his head to say 'This is mine,' and found people simple enough to believe him, was the real founder of civil society."[25] For Rousseau, the natural state was not the cause of human misery; it was the origin of society, principally private property, that placed new chains on the poor and gave new powers to the rich. Rousseau concludes, "The original man having vanished by degrees, society only offers to us an assembly of artificial men and factitious passions, which are the work of all these *new relations*, and without any real foundation in nature" (emphasis added).[26]

This passage from what is now known as Rousseau's "Second Discourse" exemplifies social theory in the making.[27] In his deliberations on the notion of a covenant between individuals and the state, Rousseau presupposes a theory of social life involving new social relations,

William Hogarth, *Gin Lane* (engraving, 1751). The observation and celebration of the ordinary, imperfect world of "common nature" was typical of Enlightenment thinking.

social institutions, and social processes. Whereas Hobbes in *Leviathan* represents human life as "solitary, brutish, and short," Rousseau represents the savage in the state of nature as an innocent who becomes corrupted by the encroachment of civil society.[28] He contends that there must be two kinds of social inequality, one that is natural or physical, and hence beyond human control, and one that is moral or political because it depends upon human choice. Claims to rule put forward by a few who govern the many can have no force unless they are acknowledged to be legitimate by others.[29] Rousseau's secular views, not astonishingly perhaps, influenced the French revolutionaries.[30]

In *The Social Contract* (1762), Rousseau argues that the inequalities established by humans themselves require each individual to enter into relations with other individuals. This situation creates a complex reciprocal arrangement—expressed in the commercial terminology of a *social contract*—that converts the mass into a coherent body and constitutes a society. A social contract emerges as one of the fundamental concepts of Enlightenment thought. It was Rousseau's view that a social contract must have been a hoax perpetrated by the rich upon the poor. As he put it, "All ran headlong to their chains believing they had secured their liberty."[31] It is suggested that Rousseau's Second Discourse expounds a theory of the development of social inequality that is analogous to Marx's own concept of history.[32]

Other scholars conceptualize society as a complex structure of institutions and social processes shaped by specific historical development.[33] In
On the Spirit of the Laws, Charles-Louis de Sécondat, baron de Montesquieu (1689–1755), attempts to theorize society as an organic whole
and to relate its different cultures to specific stages of historical development. Montesquieu's *Spirit* contains the genesis of social theory. In it, he
outlines a comparative analysis of different types of government, each
of which is, effectively, a type of society.[34] He identifies three basic kinds
of government: republican, monarchic, and despotic. His analysis examines the nature of government—that which makes it what it is—and its
principles—that which makes it act. He argues that virtue, the thirst for
glory and self-sacrifice drive republics (e.g., Ancient Greece). Monarchies
are driven by honor or status, meaning the ambition to receive titles (e.g.,
England). And despotism is founded on fear and the will of the despot
(e.g., Asian societies). Human passions make up part of a wider totality
of interrelated conditions, institutions, and cultures that underlie and
sustain that form. This totality he called "the spirit of the laws." Though
society presents itself as a chaotic phenomenon, Montesquieu contends
that beneath the surface exists a definite structure or laws comprising
patterns of human behavior. It was this observation that led Durkheim
and others to argue that Montesquieu founded sociology.[35] Others are
less positive about Montesquieu's scholastic accomplishments,[36] and
argue that the roots of social change are better found in the Scottish
Enlightenment.

In the decades after 1750, a group of Scottish philosophers—Adam
Ferguson, John Millar, David Hume, and Adam Smith—produced works
of genius in social theory.[37] In *An Essay on the History of Civil Society*
published in 1767, Adam Ferguson (1723–1816) traces the development
of society from primitive to capitalist forms: each stage of evolution being
due to a dynamic interaction of social, technological, and psychological
factors. He was the first to point out the socially negative consequences
of the division of labor.[38] Also to be found in *An Essay* is the seed of
C. Wright Mills's idea of the sociological imagination. Ferguson writes,
"The history of the individual is but a detail of the sentiments and
thoughts he has entertained in the view of his species: and every experiment relative to this subject should be made with entire societies, not
with single men."[39] Ferguson was particularly interested in how economic
pressures might affect the psychology of commercial society. He writes,
"Man is sometimes found a detached and a solitary being: he has found
an object which sets him in competition with his fellow-creatures."[40]
These observations by Ferguson are remarkably akin to Marx's concept
of alienation.

Adam Smith (1723–90) is probably the most influential figure in Scottish Enlightenment historiography. In his economic treatise *An Inquiry into the Nature and Causes of the Wealth of Nations* (1776), Smith identifies and explains the fundamental "natural" principles upon which economic wealth and societal development are, and should be, based. Motivated to promote their own economic welfare, all individuals are free to pursue their self-interests. According to Rousseau's *The Social Contract*, the state had absorbed within itself all social and economic spheres. In Smith's view the state became a particular segment of civil society, namely, the institution that legalizes and protects property relations. Smith's fundamental proposition is that markets allocate resources efficiently and are self-correcting. This innovation, what he famously called the "invisible hand," was predicated on the assumption that the unfettered pursuit of private economic gain contributes most to the common good: "It is not from the benevolence of the butcher, the brewer, or the baker that we expect our dinner, but from their regard to their own interest."[41]

Smith's *The Wealth of Nations* exhibits a rudimentary theory of social class. According to Smith, the new society produced three main classes: landowners, capitalists, and wage laborers. Property forms the basis of social differentiation, the natural source of influence and authority. It is easy to caricature Smith's treatise as a heartless justification for market fundamentalism and inequality. But Smith, foremost a moral philosopher, did not mistake self-interest for greed, and he never suggested that the serving of self-interest was the only view of the human endeavor.[42] Neither did he believe that industrial capitalism never required state intervention. In *The Theory of Moral Sentiments* (1759), Smith declares,

> The love of our country seems ... to involve ... an earnest desire to render the condition of our fellow citizens as safe, respectable, and happy as we can ... He is certainly not a good citizen who does not wish to promote, by every means in his power, the welfare of the *whole society* of his fellow-citizens ... Concern for our own happiness recommends to us the virtue of prudence: concern for that of other people, the virtues of justice and beneficence. [emphasis added][43]

The *sine qua non* of Smith's argument is that economic outcomes and the evolution of human life draw on the theory of political economy and moral personality. For this reason, we need to be wary of interpreting his argument solely in terms of the "hidden hand" of modern economics and neoconservative ideology.[44]

Human Emancipation: Slavery and Women

The ideological justification for human slavery predates the European Enlightenment. Aristotle, for example, saw slavery as necessary for the self-sufficiency of the *polis*, and in only rare instances were slaves expected to achieve a virtuous life.[45] In the new age, when philosophers and other public academics believed in a *universal* human being—one possessed of reason—and when they gave primacy to equality and freedom, slavery and women's subordination is a paradox.[46] Though his work predates the main period of the Enlightenment, Hobbes, in his *Leviathan* (1651), declares that reason was found in equal measure in all men: "From this equality of ability [among men], ariseth equality of hope in the attaining of our ends."[47] Yet plantation owners legally treated slaves as private property. By treating humans as a commodity, colonial slavery raised questions about who was a person, who was inside, and who, such as a slave, was outside the boundary of the community. Slavery could exist without the guilt or abhorrence of its beneficiaries if those totally subordinated can be seen as enslavable outsiders. As missionary activity in the colonies increased, more slaves were baptized and became Christians. The problem arose, therefore, of reconciling the ideological language of spiritual equality with the actual legal inequality and servitude of enslaved Christians. How could the quality of being a brother or sister in Christ and of being a subhuman slave coexist in one person? The fact that the abolition of colonial slavery involved the dismantling of a highly profitable economic structure heightened the intensity of the public discourse on slavery.

In Enlightenment thought, property holding and liberty were closely related. The right to possess property gave men a "stake in the country," which stabilized society. By this logic, property rights would be undermined if slaves were freed. Few of the middle class endorsed Rousseau's radical position that private property was the cause of harmful inequality among humans who were naturally equal. In Europe and the Americas, it became easier for the bourgeoisie to justify colonial slavery by linking it to race. On the basis of "scientific" evidence, it was argued that, for the African, slavery was natural to their being because they were inferior. Contradiction therefore informs Enlightenment thinking on slavery. The discourse on universal "man" affirms and simultaneously denies the unity of humankind in order, on the one hand, to sustain the European perspective of human emancipation that flowed into the French and American revolutions and, on the other, to enable the practice of slavery and the exploitation of non-European people.[48] The German philosopher Johann Gottfried Herder (1744–1803) questioned the presumption of *white* racial superiority, as did the progressive Enlightenment thinker Montesquieu. In *De l'esprit des lois*, published in 1748, Montesquieu posited the Enlightenment case against slavery:

> Slavery in its proper sense is the establishment of a right which makes one man so much the owner of another man that he is the absolute master of his life and of his goods. It is not good by its nature; it is useful neither to the master nor the slave: not to the slave, because he can do nothing from virtue; not to the master, because he contracts all sorts of bad habits from his slaves, because he imperceptibly grows accustomed to failing in all the moral virtues, because he grows proud, curt, harsh, angry, voluptuous, and cruel.[49]

The Scottish philosopher Adam Smith also campaigned to eradicate slavery, as this passage from his *The Theory of Moral Sentiments* shows:

> There is not a Negro from the coast of Africa who does not ... possess a degree of magnanimity which the soul of his sordid master is too often scarce capable of conceiving. Fortune never exerted more cruelly her empire over mankind, than when she subjected those nations of heroes to the refuse of the jails of Europe, to wretches who possess the virtues neither of the countries which they come from, nor of those which they go to, and whose levity, brutality, and baseness, so justly expose them to the contempt of the vanquished.[50]

In *The Wealth of Nations*, Smith persuasively presented the economic and utilitarian critique of slave labor. For Smith, slavery was not only morally repugnant but also economically unsound because it was an artificial constraint on individuals acting in their own self-interest and, as such, was an obstacle to improving labor's economic efficiency. He argued that

> The experience of all ages and nations, I believe, demonstrates that the work done by slaves, though it appears to cost only their maintenance, is in the end the dearest of any. A person who can acquire no property, can have no other interest but to eat as much, and to labour as little as possible. Whatever work he does beyond what is sufficient to purchase his own maintenance can be squeezed out of him by violence only, and not by any interest of his own.[51]

Scottish philosopher Adam Ferguson, mentioned previously, had impeccable anti-slavery credentials and added to the intellectual case against the practice. He argued in 1769 that "No one is born a slave; because every one is born with all his original rights ... no one can become a slave; because no one, from being a person, can ... become a thing or subject of property."[52] In the late eighteenth century, as the intellectual and moral climate of the times moved against slavery, Christians began a sustained opposition to it, especially as it was practiced in the colonies.[53] In England, evangelical Christianity helped to drive abolitionism. In France, the case for abolitionism was made by Rousseau in 1762 in *The Social Contract*, which argued that men were born with the right to be free and that "The words 'slavery' and 'right' are contradictory, they cancel each other out."[54] The anti-slavery campaign was also driven by the secular imperatives of the Declaration of the Rights of Man and Citizen, which Condorcet helped to draft. Condorcet's *Réflexions sur l'esclavage des nègres* (Reflections on Black Slavery) of 1781 is the most radical treatise on the justification of abolition. He openly addresses the slaves as his brothers and recognizes in them an unreserved entitlement to full human rights.[55] The abolition of slavery took place in the French colonies over the course of the French Revolution (1789–99), in British Caribbean colonies in the 1830s, and in the United States in 1865.

The shift of societal consensus or, to use the German word, *Zeitgeist*—"spirit of the times"—toward the abolition of slavery was due to the combined influence, directly or indirectly, of the French Revolution, Methodism, and Quakerism, as well as to the writings of Montesquieu, Condorcet, and Wollstonecraft.

The standard history of the European Enlightenment, as Margaret Atherton's *Women Philosophers of the Early Modern Period*[56] points out, is that it obscures the fact that women as well as men wrote and published philosophy during the period. One such woman was Mary Wollstonecraft (1759–97), a product of the Enlightenment and one of the first feminist thinkers. Her contribution is also considered in chapter 14, so we can afford to be brief here on her critique of the Enlightenment. The problem of reconciling the ideological language of spiritual equality and of legal inequality applied to European women in the same measure as it did to slaves. In seventeenth- and eighteenth-century Europe, white women were baptized, but spiritual equality did not result in their legal equality with men. In her seminal work, *A Vindication of the Rights of Woman* (1792), Wollstonecraft persistently draws parallels between the status of slaves in the colonies and the status of white middle-class women in the metropolis.[57] She takes many of the ideals of the Enlightenment and applies them to middle-class women, arguing that it was hypocritical not to do so. In essence, she argues that, if rationality is essentially human, it is irrational not to allot that characteristic to women too: knowledge is learnable by all—men and women. In *A Vindication of the Rights of Woman* she provides a scathing critique of Rousseau's pedagogical treatise *Emile*, in which he proposes that woman's nature disqualifies her from an academic

The Kneeling Slave: "Am I not a man and a brother?" This image is a typical Enlightenment representation of a slave asserting his common humanity.

education. The assumption that woman is essentially inferior to man, she posits, cannot be demonstrated as long as she is subjugated: "He [Man] denies woman reason, shuts her out from knowledge."[58] Wollstonecraft persuasively argues that, excluded from reason and education, women are confined within the arbitrary power of beauty and sensual experience. In Western culture, men constitute women as "the fair sex" by means of rituals of gallantry and courtesy, thereby separating women from the male world of reason. Once trapped within the sensual world of beauty, women's subordination is further strengthened as they are forced into both financial and emotional dependence on men—into a life of "petty" activity.[59] One effect of *A Vindication of the Rights of Woman* is the questioning of any analysis of a capitalist society that segregates studies of paid work from those of family and gender divisions.

The Romantic-Conservative Reaction

The Enlightenment, as even this short selective survey should indicate, did not constitute a simple unitary body of doctrine; it assumed many forms. The term *liberal individualism* is used as a brief description of Enlightenment thought. By this we mean that the individual is seen as the location and source of all the important ingredients in the "liberated" society.[60] A number of core intellectual concepts, or what Richard Hadden calls "intellectual weapons," developed from the Enlightenment and helped to change the way philosophers viewed the relationship between the individual and society. The Rousseauist notion of the social contract entailed *freedom* to engage in contract formation; *equality* between parties to the contract; *universality*, in that the personal character of either party was considered irrelevant; *private property*, the right to acquire and dispose of it as the parties wished; and *religious tolerance*. The individual's religious convictions were considered irrelevant; put in crude commercial terms, religious intolerance was bad for business. The radical ideology of the philosophers was a change catalyst and therefore, not astonishingly, found support among the rising commercial and professional classes. The Enlightenment's confidence in the powers of reason and its agnostic ideology were too partisan to remain unchallenged.

In the 1740s, dissenting voices against the Enlightenment were increasingly heard. Johann Gottfried Herder and Edmund Burke began the critique, which became known as the "Romantic-Conservative reaction."[61] The influential Catholic critic Edmund Burke (1729–97) linked morality and civil government closely to the divine order and to the providential authority of God. In *A Vindication of a Natural Society*, published in 1756, he argues that Rousseau's rejection of inequality meant nothing less than the rejection of the civil order and God-given natural law. In later publications, Burke defended inequality and the consequent strata of the aristocratic hierarchy as natural and progressive phenomena that guarantee the civil order. After 1815, French intellectuals engaged in wide-ranging debates on the nature of modernity. Though initially a reactionary movement that defended the traditional view of the world, the Catholic counter-revolutionary movement developed propositions about modernity that greatly influenced Saint-Simon, Comte, and Durkheim.

The French Catholic intellectuals Joseph de Maistre and Louis de Bonald both rejected the rational core principles enshrined in the social contract; emphasized *natural* social hierarchy, duty, and collective good; and conceptualized society as an organic whole in which *rational* and also traditional elements played an active, constitutive role. Like Burke, Joseph de Maistre (1753–1821), a resolute opponent of the Revolution, repudiated Rousseau's conception of the origin of society because it implied that it had been created without the intervention of divine providence. Maistre's writings may be read as a sustained polemic against secular-rational Enlightenment thinking. But his work is a reformulation of the medieval doctrine of an infallible church.[62] Louis de Bonald (1740–1840) was an influential figure in the Catholic counter-revolutionary movement. In his best-known work, *Théorie du pouvoir politique et religieux* (Theory of Political and Religious Power), Bonald presents a rebuttal of Montesquieu's *On the Spirit of the Laws* and Rousseau's *The Social Contract*. Bonald contends that knowledge is not simply derived from individual reason but is situated in a cultural community and is a product of the social. Art and literature, for example, are expressions of the society that produces the artifacts. For Bonald, the natural man is a meaningless abstraction: Natural man does not exist, only social man.[63] Like Maistre, Bonald argued that humans, by their very nature, are social, moral, and cultural beings, and he repudiated Enlightenment rationalist, humanist, individualist ideology. As Bonald expressed it, "The schools of modern philosophy ... have produced the philosophy of modern man, the philosophy of I ... I want to produce the philosophy of social man, the philosophy of we."[64] Society, moreover, did not consist of simply an aggregate of individuals; rather, it was the expression of a whole culture. Bonald argues that the individual cannot exist outside society, and, consequently, it is the individual, not society, that is an abstraction. Bonald believed that urban industrial capitalism undermined the most natural and sacred of social units, the family, and he extolled the importance of the community and the binding influence of the church.

Although we can detect in the Enlightenment dissidents a strong anti-modernist sentiment, over decades the reaction to the Enlightenment movements mutated into a new, more comprehensive humanism.[65] This essentially *dialectical* view of intellectual history, which was first grasped by Hegel, posits that neither Enlightenment thinking nor reactions against it developed into simple rationalism or simple anti-rationalism. Louis Dupré provides an insightful passage describing the dialectical relation between social change and the roles of ideas: "Whenever human thought has been dominated by some special interest, the most fruitful philosophy of the age has reflected that domination; not passively, ... but actively, by making a special attempt to understand it and placing it in the focus of philosophical inquiry."[66]

What is most significant for our purposes is this: the ongoing engagement between Enlightenment thinkers and detractors contributed substantially to the foundation of classical sociological thought. On the one side, we have Enlightenment individualism with its emphasis on reason and a reverence for science as a way to investigate society. On the other side, we have a conservative collectivism with its emphasis on extra individual concepts and its conception of society as an organic whole. As Irving Zeitlin argues, once expunged of its theological assumptions, Bonald's polemic against Enlightenment ideology becomes the source of core sociological concepts and ideas.[67]

The Beginnings of Sociology: Saint-Simon and Auguste Comte

Sociology, it is argued, has always had an ambivalent relationship to the Enlightenment and to post-Revolutionary conservative thinking. On the one hand, sociology emerged out of and extended Enlightenment thinking on reason and epistemology; on the other hand, it draws upon counter-Enlightenment thinking for its subject matter, particularly the secular, collective concepts of community and culture, rather than focusing on the power of pervasive individualism. Thus, sociology is an amalgam of secular liberal ideology and conservative intellectual thought.[68] Elements of both the Enlightenment and the conservative reaction can be found in the works of French socialists Claude-Henri de Saint-Simon and Auguste Comte, the two academics most closely identified with establishing sociology as a distinct discipline.

Saint-Simon (1760–1825) is credited for conceiving both the name and the essentials of positive sociology.[69] He was fiercely critical of the French Revolution. Like Bonald, Saint-Simon believed that knowledge is a product of a community of ideas. Further, he believed that knowledge is both the binding force of society and a moving power of progress. Like Marx after him, Saint-Simon viewed the historical transformation of society as a result of forces that had been maturing in the old regime. In his view, the *philosophes* had contributed to the disintegration of the *ancien régime*. According to Saint-Simon, the new order needed to be built on a foundation of new intellectual principles. Science would replace religious dogma and would be the defining force of society. His view of French modernity would remain essentially hierarchical, with society divided into *industriels*—(wealth creators)—and *oisifs* (idlers). Saint-Simon, then, envisioned what historian Eric Hobsbawm calls "a Rousseauist 'cult of the supreme being.'"[70]

Auguste Comte (1798–1857) invented the name "sociology."[71] His parents were devout Catholics and ardent royalists. His most famous work, *Cours de philosophie positive*, published in 1830, attempts to understand modernity following the French Revolution of 1789, its excesses, the implosion of the *ancien régime*, and the creation of a new economic regime—industrial capitalism. Comte claimed to be the champion of intellectual positivism, broadly understood as an epistemological position that advocates the application of the methods of the natural sciences to the study of society and social life. For Comte, positivism and the new science of sociology would provide the intellectual and moral basis of the new social order. He argued for giving up the metaphysical search for causes; instead, he advocated the search for invariable relations between things—the regular patterns in social phenomena.

Comte's "Law of Three Stages" is one of his most well-known propositions. In the context of the social turmoil in nineteenth-century France, Comte endeavored to discover the causes of this social phenomena. He claimed to have unearthed a great fundamental law—the human mind evolves through a series of stages, each of which marks a different way of thinking or philosophizing. These three theoretical states are the theological or fictitious state, the metaphysical or abstract state, and the scientific or positive state. Comte believed that, in the positive state, "the human mind, recognizing the impossibility of obtaining absolute truth, gives up the search after the origin and hidden causes of the universe and a knowledge of the final causes of phenomena. It endeavors now only to discover, by a well-combined use of reasoning and observation, the actual laws of phenomena— that is to say, their invariable relations of succession and likeness."[72] Comte believed that metaphysical thought was a rational attempt to explain all worldly phenomena that are beyond the physical, that is, not observable. Catholic theology represented *metaphysical* thought, and, in Comte's opinion, the human mind during the period of European industrialization that was leaving the metaphysical and entering the positive or scientific stage. The crisis in modernity, then, occurred because too many features of the metaphysical remained to sustain the new regime, which should embrace positive philosophy. Comte wrote, "We are theologians in childhood, metaphysical in youth, and natural philosophers in virility."[73]

In *Philosophie positive* Comte's positive doctrine attempts to reconcile two mutually antagonistic principles: *order* and *progress*. Derived from Catholic theology, the principle of order or *static* describes the functioning of a society and its culture that binds society together. The principle of progress or *dynamics* describes the "functional prerequisites" for historical development. This principle was derived from the Enlightenment. As Larry Ray points out, Comte laid the foundations of sociological positivism, which was the dominant paradigm throughout the nineteenth century.[74] Comte's insights on modernity remain influential. Most important is the "centrality of the social"—his insistence that people are significant only as social beings, that society is an organic necessity, which "commands all times and places." He emphasized also the importance of language to transmit cultural mores and values across generations. However, Zeitlin has contested the originality of Comte's social theory. Zeitlin writes, "Auguste Comte ... appropriated virtually all of Saint-Simon's ideas."[75] Other sociologists have given more favorable evaluations. Comte should be given credit for synthesizing the conceptual terrain of sociology and for rejecting metaphysics in favor of positivist empirical methods.[76]

Criticism

The interlocking intellectual projects that was the Enlightenment was internally fractured and riddled by contradictions. The debates on slavery and women's rights are examples of its intellectual anomalies. Enlightenment discourse presents a Eurocentric and "white" interpretation of human nature and history. Silvia Sebastiani's *The Scottish Enlightenment* (2013) offers a critical interpretation of Enlightenment thinking on slavery and women in society. Under Enlightenment humanism, theories of racial hierarchies led to the justification of slavery. Thus, at the very heart of the Enlightenment's universalistic conception of man "sprang the nucleus of Western racist ideology."[77] In *Black Marxism* (2000), Cedric Robinson argues that European scholars "worked hard" to exorcise from European historiography the cultural and intellectual contributions of North Africa, particularly Islam's social and intellectual influence, in order to "whiten the West [and] ... maintain the purity of the European race."[78] For Robinson, the European Enlightenment was responsible for "the invention of the Negro—and by extension the fabrication of whiteness and all the policing of racial boundaries that came with it."[79]

The intellectual legacy of Enlightenment ideology is also, unsurprisingly, a masculine vision of the human nature and of social life. Sylvana Tomaselli's essay offers a feminist view of women in history, which "linked women, not, as is all too swiftly done, to nature, but to culture and the process of historical development."[80] Similarly, Rosalind Sydie's *Natural Women, Cultured Men* has luminously explored the *sex-blind* nature of classical social thought. Canonical writers, she argues convincingly, overwhelmingly viewed the "natural" differences between the sexes based on the reproductive capacity of women to justify the hierarchical relations of female subordination and exclusion from the public sphere. Additionally, this masculine interpretation of nature predates the Enlightenment era. Aristotle, for example, believed that the female was an incomplete version of the male. And one Renaissance writer opined that "men are by nature of a more elevated mind than women."[81]

The European Enlightenment, then, was grounded in the assumption that universal man, in thought and practice, becomes *rational* man, active and able to conquer the forces of the natural world, and that this man is in stark contrast to *subjective* woman, passive and a repository of the natural. Influential Enlightenment writers promulgated the widespread conviction that women were, by nature, less rational, less objective, more prone to hysteria, weaker than men in mind and body, best suited to the domestic sphere, and often inherently inclined to vanity, frivolity, and wantonness. Tension and ambivalences inform Enlightenment thought on women in society. As Sebastiani convincingly argues, "Woman is represented simultaneously as the 'embodiment of the natural' and the 'repository of civilization,' in a complex relationship between the private sphere—increasingly associated with virtue and therefore positioned within the family—and the public sphere, linked instead to the public discourse of rights."[82] The early feminists' critiques of the masculinity of Enlightenment thinking exposed the limits of Enlightenment radicalism, arguing that, if rationality is essentially human, it was irrational to believe that only men had this characteristic. Although expunged of theological ideology and further theorizing by Saint-Simon and Comte, Enlightenment thinking about society, including the idea of a dichotomized social order as natural, became the foundation of sociological positivism, which remained the dominant paradigm until the early twentieth century.

Between 1900 and 1915, Enlightenment thought was increasingly challenged by late-modern thinkers and was ultimately dethroned by an emphasis upon divergent frameworks of thinking. In Germany, writers such as Max Weber and Friedrich Nietzsche no longer accorded Enlightenment reason and rationality a privileged status in the definition of the essence of human nature. Weber argued that universal freedom is suffocated by the growth of rationality. Nietzsche (1844–1900) placed aesthetics above science and rationality and attacked the accepted Enlightenment logic on linear progress, civilization, and morality. In the twentieth century, the logic of Enlightenment rationality led to domination and oppression and the unparalleled institutionalization of state violence,[83] but for the classical social thinkers, these observations were made with the facility of hindsight.

Conclusion

This chapter has covered a lot of material. The Enlightenment is best described as an intellectual and cultural movement that challenged religion's pre-eminent authority to both know and speak the truth, and affected virtually every area of Western knowledge. Its legacy and the post-Revolutionary, conservative philosophical reaction are a number of propositions about society: society has an organic nature, with internal laws of unity and development; it creates the individual, and individuals have no existence outside of a social context; it is composed of relationships and institutions; and it has institutions and customs that are positively functional in that they fulfill human needs either directly or indirectly by serving other essential institutions. We have seen throughout this chapter that the European Enlightenment, like most intellectual movements, was not a unified body of thinking but was internally fractured and riddled by contradictions. The Enlightenment heritage could be restorative. There remains today an ongoing need to instill skepticism about the motives of political elites. For example, Scott McClellan's scathing memoir *What Happened*[84] describes his years at the White House and speaks of a culture of deception, the manipulation of public opinion, and lies to justify the Iraq War. In this context, it is argued, convincingly, that given the abuses of power of world leaders such as George W. Bush and Tony Blair, the critical spirit of Kant and other Enlightenment thinkers is vitally important to us now.[85]

In summary, the chaotic transformation of European societies between 1700 and 1850 was due to what we have called three waves of modernity: the British Industrial Revolution, the French Revolution, and the contemporaneous intellectual revolution consisting of Enlightenment and post-Revolutionary thought. These three revolutions profoundly influenced and shaped the work of the classical canon to which we now turn.

FURTHER THINKING:

Why has the Enlightenment become known as a social movement, rather than an intellectual project? What ideas in this chapter would you advise Donald Trump to read, and why?

FURTHER READING:

For a readable introduction to the Enlightenment, see Dorinda Outram, *The Enlightenment* (Cambridge: Cambridge University Press, 2013). Alexander Broadie, *The Scottish Enlightenment* (Edinburgh: Birlinn, 2001) provides an excellent account of the principal contributors to the Scottish Enlightenment. Silvia Sebastiani, *The Scottish Enlightenment: Race, Gender, and the Limits of Progress* (Basingstoke, UK: Palgrave Macmillan, 2013), looks at the Enlightenment through a feminist perspective. The American ex-politician Al Gore, *The Assault on Reason* (New York: Penguin Books, 2007), gives a very readable account of why Enlightenment principles are important for the present day.

Notes

1 Al Gore, *The Assault on Reason* (New York: Penguin Books, 2007), 2.

2 Silvia Sebastiani, *The Scottish Enlightenment: Race, Gender, and the Limits of Progress* (Basingstoke, UK: Palgrave Macmillan, 2013), 3.

3 Louis Dupré, *The Enlightenment and the Intellectual Foundations of Modern Culture* (New Haven, CT: Yale University Press, 2004), xiii.

4 Jonathan I. Israel, *Radical Enlightenment: Philosophy and the Making of Modernity, 1650–1750* (Oxford: Oxford University Press, 2001), vi.

5 David Williams, ed., *The Enlightenment* (Cambridge: Cambridge University Press, 1999), 1.

6 BCE means "before the common era" and refers to the time that was once known as BC, or "before Christ."

7 Robin Kirkpatrick, *The European Renaissance* (London: Pearson Education, 2002), 1.

8 Alan Swingewood, *A Short History of Sociological Thought*, 3rd ed. (New York: St. Martin's Press, 2000), 4.

9 Immanuel Kant, "What Is Enlightenment?" (1784), and quoted in *The Enlightenment: A Sourcebook and Reader*, ed. Paul Hyland with O. Gomaz and F. Greensides (London: Routledge, 2003), 54.

10 Ernst Cassirer, *The Philosophy of the Enlightenment* (Princeton, NJ: Princeton University Press, 1951).

11 Max Horkheimer and Theodore W. Adorno, *Dialectic of Enlightenment: Philosophical Fragments*, trans. E. Jephcott (1947; Palo Alto, CA: Stanford University Press, 2002).

12 Peter Gay, *The Enlightenment: An Interpretation* (New York: Norton & Company, 1996).

13 Dorinda Outram, *The Enlightenment* (Cambridge: Cambridge University Press, 2013), 3.

14 Dupré, *The Enlightenment and the Intellectual Foundations of Modern Culture*, 3; Hyland, *The Enlightenment: A Sourcebook*, 33.

15 Israel, *Radical Enlightenment*, 159.

16 Michael Morgan, ed., *The Essential Spinoza* (Indianapolis, IN: Hackett Publishing, 2006).

17 Don Garrett, ed., *The Cambridge Companion to Spinoza* (Cambridge: Cambridge University Press, 1996).

18 Quoted in Hyland, *The Enlightenment: A Sourcebook*, 35.

19 John Locke, *Essay Concerning Human Understanding*, section 8 of the introduction, quoted in Peter Sedgwick, *Descartes to Derrida: An Introduction to European Philosophy* (Oxford: Blackwell, 2001), 12.

20 Hyland, *The Enlightenment: A Sourcebook*, 40.

21 David Hume, *A Treatise of Human Nature*, Bks.1, 4, 6, quoted in Dupré, *The Enlightenment and the Intellectual Foundations of Modern Culture*, 49.

22 Immanuel Kant's trilogy is *Kritik der reinen Vernunft* (*Critique of Pure Reason*, 1781), *Kritik der praktischen Vernunft* (*Critique of Practical Reason*, 1788), and *Kritik der Urteilskraft* (*Critique of Judgement*, 1790).

23 John Locke, *Two Treatises of Civil Government*, vol. 2, chap. 3, paras. 16 and 21, quoted in Hyland, *The Enlightenment: A Sourcebook*, 155.

24 Johan Heilbron, *The Rise of Social Theory* (Cambridge: Cambridge University Press, 1995), 88, quoted in Alex Callinicos, *Social Theory: A Historical Introduction*, 2nd ed. (Cambridge: Polity Press, 2007), 10.

25   Jean-Jacques Rousseau, *A Discourse Upon the Origin and Foundation of Inequality Among Mankind* (1755), quoted in Hyland, *The Enlightenment: A Sourcebook*, 178.

26   Quoted in Hyland, *The Enlightenment: A Sourcebook*, 179.

27   Swingewood, *A Short History of Sociological Thought*; Larry Ray, *Theorizing Classical Sociology* (Buckingham, UK: Open University Press, 1999).

28   Alexander Broadie, *The Scottish Enlightenment* (Edinburgh: Birlinn, 2001), 80.

29   Robert Wokler, *Rousseau: A Very Short Introduction* (Oxford: Oxford University Press, 2001), 47.

30   James Miller, *Rousseau: Dreamer of Democracy* (New Haven, CT: Yale University Press, 1984), 1.

31   Rousseau, *A Discourse Upon the Origin and Foundation of Inequality Among Mankind*, quoted in Hyland, *The Enlightenment: A Sourcebook*, 52.

32   Wokler, *Rousseau*, 68.

33   Swingewood, *A Short History of Sociological Thought*, 4.

34   Swingewood, *A Short History of Sociological Thought*, 6.

35   For example, Raymond Aron, *Main Currents in Sociological Thought* (New York: Doubleday, 1970), quoted in Ray, *Theorizing Classical Sociology*, 26.

36   See Swingewood, *A Short History of Sociological Thought*, 26; Callinicos, *Social Theory*, 22.

37   See Swingewood, *A Short History of Sociological Thought*, 6–10; Broadie, *The Scottish Enlightenment*, 78–112; Stephen Copley and Kathryn Sutherland, eds., *Adam Smith's* The Wealth of Nations: *New Interdisciplinary Essays* (Manchester: Manchester University Press, 1995).

38   Sebastiani, *The Scottish Enlightenment*, 2.

39   Adam Ferguson, *An Essay on the History of Civil Society* (1767), in Hyland, *The Enlightenment: A Sourcebook*, 189.

40   Broadie, *Scottish Enlightenment*, 84–85.

41   Adam Smith, *The Wealth of Nations*, edited and introduced by Andrew Skinner (1776; London: Penguin Books, 1999), 119.

42   Knud Haakonssen, "Introduction," in *The Theory of Moral Sentiments* by Adam Smith, ed. Knud Haakonssen (1759; Cambridge: Cambridge University Press, 2002), x.

43   Adam Smith, *The Theory of Moral Sentiments*, ed. Knud Haakonssen (Cambridge: Cambridge University Press, 2002), 272, 309.

44   Noel Parker "Look, No Hidden Hands: How Smith Understands Historical Progress and Societal Values," in *Adam Smith's* The Wealth of Nations, ed. Copley and Sutherland, 122–43.

45   Cedric J. Robinson, *Black Marxism* (Chapel Hill: University of North Carolina Press, 2000), xxix.

46   On slavery and enlightenment, see Dorinda Outram, *The Enlightenment*, chap. 5, 60–76, from which this section is largely based.

47   Thomas Hobbes, *Leviathan*, chap. 13, and quoted in Hyland, *The Enlightenment: A Sourcebook*, 9.

48   Sebastiani, *The Scottish Enlightenment*, 12.

49   Quoted in William Hague, *William Wilberforce: The Life of the Great Anti-Slave Trade Campaigner* (London: Harper Perennial, 2008), 129.

50   Adam Smith, *The Theory of Moral Sentiments*, ed. D. D. Raphael and A. L. Macfie (1759; Oxford: Oxford University Press, 1976), 206–7.

51 Adam Smith, *The Wealth of Nations*, ed. Andrew Skinner, 488–89.

52 Adam Ferguson, *Institutes of Moral Philosophy*, 2nd ed. (Edinburgh: A. Kincaid & W. Creech, and J. Bell, 1773), 201–2, and quoted in Hague, *William Wilberforce*, 129.

53 Hague, *William Wilberforce*, 131.

54 Jean-Jacques Rousseau, *The Social Contract* (1762; London: Penguin Classics, 1968), 58.

55 Williams, *The Enlightenment*, 35.

56 Margaret Atherton, *Women Philosophers of the Early Modern Period* (Cambridge, MA: Hackett Publishing, 1994).

57 Moira Ferguson, *Colonialism and Gender Relations: From Mary Wollstonecraft to Jamaica Kincaid* (New York: Columbia University Press, 1993).

58 Mary Wollstonecraft, *A Vindication of the Rights of Woman* (1792; London: Oxford University Press, 2004), 129.

59 Wollstonecraft, *A Vindication of the Rights of Woman*, 116.

60 See Richard W. Hadden, *Sociological Theory: An Introduction to the Classical Tradition* (Peterborough, ON: Broadview Press, 1997); Ray, *Theorizing Classical Sociology*.

61 Irving M. Zeitlin, *Ideology and the Development of Sociological Theory*, 7th ed. (Upper Saddle River, NJ: Prentice Hall, 2001), 45.

62 Callinicos, *Social Theory*, 74.

63 See Zeitlin, *Ideology and the Development of Sociological Theory*, 54.

64 Quoted in Swingewood, *A Short History of Sociological Thought*, 11.

65 Swingewood, *A Short History of Sociological Thought*, 4.

66 Dupré, *The Enlightenment and the Intellectual Foundations of Modern Culture*, 5–6.

67 Zeitlin, *Ideology and the Development of Sociological Theory*, 58.

68 See Ian Craib, *Classical Social Theory* (Oxford: Oxford University Press, 1997), 3; Robert A. Nisbet, *The Sociological Tradition* (London: Heinemann, 1967); and Zeitlin, *Ideology and the Development of Sociological Theory*.

69 See Zeitlin, *Ideology and the Development of Sociological Theory*, 65–77.

70 Eric J. Hobsbawm, *The Age of Revolution: Europe 1789–1848* (London: Shenval Press, 1962), 219.

71 Peter Berger and Brigitte Berger, *Sociology: A Biographical Approach* (London: Penguin, 1976), 32.

72 Auguste Comte, *Introduction to Positive Philosophy* (Indianapolis, IN: Bobbs-Merrill,1970), 1–2, and quoted in Callinicos, *Social Theory*, 65.

73 Auguste Comte, *The Foundations of Sociology*, ed. K. Thompson (London: Nelson, 1976), and quoted in Ray, *Theorizing Classical Sociology*, 45.

74 Ray, *Theorizing Classical Sociology*, 51.

75 Zeitlin, *Ideology and the Development of Sociological Theory*, 77.

76 See Ray, *Theorizing Classical Sociology*, 55; and Swingewood, *A Short History of Sociological Thought*, 15.

77 Sebastiani, *The Scottish Establishment*, 12.

78 Robinson, *Black Marxism*, xiii.

79 Robinson, *Black Marxism*, xiii.

80 Quoted in Hyland, *The Enlightenment: A Sourcebook*, 400.

81   Leon Battista Alberti, *The Family in Renaissance Florence* (Columbia: University of South Carolina Press, 1969), 207, quoted in R.A. Sydie, *Natural Women, Cultured Men* (Vancouver: University of British Columbia Press, 1994), 5.

82   Sebastiani, *The Scottish Establishment*, 17.

83   See, for example, Mike Berners-Lee, and Duncan Clark, *The Burning Question: We Can't Burn Half the World's Oil, Coal, and Gas, So How Do We Quit?* (London: Profile, 2013).

84   Scott McClellan, *What Happened: Inside the Bush White House and Washington's Culture of Deception* (New York: Public Affairs, 2008).

85   See, for example, Susan Neiman, *Moral Clarity* (Toronto: Harcourt, 2008).

PART II
THE CLASSICAL TRIUMVIRATE

4. Karl Marx:
Philosophy and Methodology

> Marx was not just the product of the culture into which he was born.
> From the beginning, he was determined to impress himself upon the
> world.
>
> —Gareth Stedman Jones, 2017[1]

> As the careful student of Marx eventually discovers, capitalism's
> "laws of motion" come with a lot of fine print. There are few pure
> determinations or simple secular trends in his historical analyses
> and economic manuscripts.
>
> —Mike Davis, 2018[2]

TODAY, TWO HUNDRED YEARS AFTER HIS BIRTH, Marx's ideas still influence
modern sociology. At the center of Marx's social theory is the precept
that the anatomy of civil society is to be found in the social and economic modes of production: society is produced rather than prearranged;
cultural mores are learned, not given; and social conditions determine
human consciousness and patterns of human history and development.
This perspective has important ramifications for sociological theory.[3]
Epistemologically, sociological theory must embody concepts that analyze
the making, not the completion, of social structure, and it must include
the nexus of social relations, cultural conditioning, and the entrenched
interests of powerful social elites. Marx prophetically states, "At the same
pace that mankind masters nature, man seems to become enslaved to
other men or to his own infamy. Even the pure light of science seems
unable to shine but on the dark background of ignorance."[4] Thus, he
addresses a challenge that haunts all thinkers today: the balance between
sustainable development and ecological catastrophe.

The analysis of capitalist society by Karl Marx and his lifelong confidant, generous benefactor, and intellectual companion Friedrich Engels is firmly rooted in the social and political changes stemming from the dual revolution in Britain and France and is organically bound up with the labor and political movements in Western Europe. In the 1880s, Marx and Engels provided the ideological and political vocabulary for much of the socialist and revolutionary movements in Europe. Marx's acknowledgment of the progressive systems of capitalist production and the inevitability of class struggle laid the foundation for European Marxism in the early twentieth century. His work inspired the Russian Revolution of November 1917, a cataclysmic event that profoundly shaped global politics for 70 years. Since his death in 1883, various political and intellectual leaders have reshaped the legacy of Marx, and by the late nineteenth and early twentieth centuries, there were important differences between Marx himself—what he believed, what he thought about—and the ways in which he had come to be represented in political and intellectual discourse.[5] Probably for these reasons, Marx's name, whether revered or reviled, is known to all, and he is likely the only classic social theorist that members of the general public have a strong opinion about, without their actually reading his voluminous works.

The purpose of the next three chapters is to survey Karl Marx's central themes with particular reference to his philosophy, history, and economics and to present a critical account of how these contribute to social theory. The profound intellectual content of Marx's works and their chronological position mean that the other classical social theorists are conventionally seen in relation to him.[6] Naturally, in three short chapters, we cannot elaborate all of Marx's theory, which would require a separate book. This chapter first reviews his life, published works, and intellectual influences before explaining Marx's philosophy and his contribution to the methodology of the social sciences.

Life and Works

Karl Marx was born in 1818 into a middle-class Jewish family in the predominantly Catholic city of Trier, Germany. The city had very little industry, and liberal ideology had much support among large sections of the city's population, as it did in other regions of Germany. Karl Marx's father, Heinrich Marx, was a rabbi in Trier. Little is known of the ancestry of Henriette Marx, Marx's mother, but like her husband she came from the rabbinic tradition. Born in the Netherlands, she was the daughter of Isaac Pressburg, a rabbi in Nijmegen. There were nine children in the Marx family, of whom Karl was the eldest. Anti-Semitism in the Rhineland, where Jews were often blamed for the peasants' increasing poverty, increased Jewish self-consciousness. It is a matter of conjecture how Marx's Jewish ancestry and the social context affected him, but it would be facile to disregard Jewish self-consciousness as a factor that influenced Marx's development. Marx's Jewishness made him an *outsider* in European society, and, it is argued, the experience of prejudice and discrimination is a powerful argument for changing society.[7]

A lawyer, Heinrich Marx had adopted the ideas of the Enlightenment and had considerable influence on Karl Marx's intellectual development as did a family friend, Baron von Westphalen, who introduced the young Marx to the

Karl Marx was born in 1818 in Trier, Germany. In 1836, he married Jenny von Westphalen. The Marx family experienced financial hardship because of Marx's inability to manage his finances. In 1849, Marx was expelled from Paris, and he and his family moved to London, where he died in his study in 1883.

Utopian socialism put forward by Saint-Simon, as well as to Shakespeare, who remained Marx's favorite author all his life. Between 1830 and 1835, Marx attended the Frederick William High School in Trier, which included Enlightenment ideology in the school's curriculum. In 1835, Karl Marx became a student of law at the University of Bonn. Although a diligent student in the first semester, he increasingly became distracted from his studies and was even imprisoned for a day for "disturbing the peace with drunken noise."[8] In 1836, young Marx transferred to the University of Berlin. He also became engaged and married Jenny von Westphalen, a friend from early childhood. At the University of Berlin, Marx made the intellectual transition from romantic idealism to Hegelianism, the philosophy of Georg Hegel, which was probably the most profound intellectual step of his whole life. In 1838 Marx began working on his doctoral thesis, which contained post-Hegelian philosophical themes that he was later to develop in his published works.[9] In particular was the notion of *praxis* that was to become so central to his later philosophy. Whereas Hegel's philosophy had only dealt with the present and the past, *praxis,* on the other hand, focused on the "deed and social activity."[10] In 1841, at the age of 23, Marx was awarded his doctorate in philosophy.

After completing his doctorate Marx was unable to obtain employment as a university professor because of his incendiary ideas. Instead, he accepted the position of editor of *Rheinische Zeitung* (Rhine News), an opposition weekly financed by liberal industrialists. The German government suppressed the paper in March 1843, and Marx emigrated to Paris where he began his lifelong friendship and collaboration with Friedrich Engels, the son of a German cotton spinner whose company had a factory in Manchester. Engels was able to educate Marx with the practical workings of industrial capitalism. During this period, Marx wrote a series of searing essays critiquing Hegelian philosophy and capitalism. In 1845 he was expelled from Paris for subversive journalism, but with Engels was able to write *The German Ideology*. After a visit to London, Marx and Engels were commissioned to write the theory underpinning the political activities of the Communist League. The result was the polemic *Communist Manifesto*, published in 1848. As noted, this was a period of social and revolutionary upheaval in France and Germany, and notoriety followed Marx everywhere. In July 1849, he returned to Paris but was expelled yet again, and the Marx family moved to London where he began what Marx called his "sleepless night of exile."[11]

For the next decade, Marx experienced financial hardship and personal tragedies. His letters to Engels describe his misery and impoverishment: "I am unable to go out for want of the coats I have in pawn, and I can no longer eat meat for want of credit ... My wife is ill. Little Jenny is ill ... I could not and cannot call the doctor because I have no money to buy medicine. For the past eight to ten days I have been feeding the family solely on bread and potatoes ... If possible, therefore, send me a few pounds."[12] We should note that the Marx family was never poor by ordinary standards. In 1851, one of Marx's most poverty-stricken years, his income was three times that earned by an average skilled British worker. Marx's difficulties arose from his unwillingness to seek full-time employment and his inability to manage his financial resources. During the 34 years he lived in London, he sought gainful employment only twice. At heart, Marx was a traditional Victorian middle-class patriarch, with "inverted priorities," who lived beyond his means.[13] Despite his "sub-proletarian" way of life, as he put it, he thought it "unseemly" *not* to have a private secretary.[14] What working-class families considered luxuries—regular holidays, dance, piano, and foreign language lessons for the children, and attendance at a ladies' seminary—Marx considered "absolute necessities." He was often to muse in letters to Engels that while he spent so much time writing about money, he had little skill for managing it. A regular source of income came from his articles for the *New York Tribune*. Marx apparently resented doing what he called "journalism muck" because it kept him away from his research. It was not until 1864, however, that a legacy brought financial relief.

In the early 1850s, Marx began working on his treatise on political economy, *Capital*, a manuscript for which he acknowledged he had "sacrificed ... health, ... happiness and ... family,"[15] but also that procrastination, multiple revisions, frequent bouts of ill health, and political activism delayed its completion. His publisher must have had monumental patience. In the summer of 1846, Marx wrote to his German publisher saying the revised version of the first volume would be complete at the end of November. Two decades later, the manuscript was still unfinished.[16] Volume one of *Capital* was finally completed 21 years later in April 1867. It was Engels who edited and published volumes two and three of *Capital* in July 1885 and November 1894 after Marx's death. The *Grundrisse* (Ground Notes of a Critique of Political Economy) was written during the winter of 1857–8, but the manuscript became lost and was not published until 1953. The *Grundrisse* provide invaluable insight on the "inner logic of *Capital*."[17]

In the 1870s, a generous annuity from Engels enabled Marx to adopt a comfortable upper-middle-class lifestyle, but his writing productivity diminished. Although suffering a mild stroke, Marx did manage to write the second edition of the first volume of *Capital* in 1873 and a critique of the first program of the German socialists under the title *Critique of the Gotha Programme*, published by Engels in 1891. In December 1881, Marx's wife died of cancer, and, two years later, his daughter Jenny also died. Two months after his daughter's death, racked by bronchitis and suffering an abscess in the lung, Karl Marx died stateless in his armchair on March 14, 1883. His lifetime intellectual companion Friedrich Engels died of cancer on August 5, 1895. The rest of this chapter examines Karl Marx's philosophy.

Intellectual Influences

The philosophical context of Marx's early education was the rationalism of the European Enlightenment and the school of German philosophy called idealism. It is not possible to understand Marx's ideas without understanding the work of Georg Hegel, and to understand Hegel we need to be familiar with the work of the German philosophers Immanuel Kant and Ludwig Feuerbach. The sequence was that Hegel improved Kantian idealism, Feuerbach transformed Hegel's dialectical mode of thinking, and Marx extended Feuerbachian dialectics.

Immanuel Kant saw the Enlightenment as a liberating process. Liberty is self-determination, meaning the subjection of one's self and its necessary functions to one's own conscious, rational choice. For Kant, what is real and what is not was a matter of great political importance and was key in the furtherance of self-determination. The Enlightenment insisted on the audacity of relinquishing traditional feudal law for abstract ideals of universal justice. Importantly, the Enlightenment also contested the reality of superstitions. As long as people believed that poverty and disease, for example, were God's punishment for human sin, they were unlikely to explore ways of tackling these social problems. In the political milieu of eighteenth-century Western Europe, Kant's philosophy was widely considered as reflecting the incendiary ideals of the French Revolution. Kant himself averred that his trilogy of major works, *Critique of Pure Reason* (1781), *Critique of Practical Reason* (1788), and *Critique of Judgement* (1790), explained the workings of the human mind: its ability to reason, to form morally correct decisions, and to shape a satisfying aesthetics.

It was largely the writings of the Scottish philosopher David Hume that inspired Kant to refute Scottish empiricism and reaffirm the paramount importance of reason. Although concurring with Hume that there were no innate ideas, Kant rejected the underlying premise that *all* scientific knowledge derives solely from experience, as some knowledge did not spring from experience. Thus, in his seminal work on epistemology, the *Critique of Pure Reason*, he writes,

> There can be no doubt that all our knowledge begins with experience.... In the order of time, therefore, we have no knowledge antecedent to experience, and with experience all our knowledge begins. But ... it does not follow that it [knowledge] all arises out of experience. For it may well be that even our empirical knowledge is made up of what we receive through impressions and of what our own faculty of knowledge ... supplies from itself.... Any knowledge that is thus independent of experience and even of all impressions of the senses ... is entitled *a priori*, and distinguished from the *empirical*, which has its sources *a posteriori*, that is, in experience.[18]

For Kant, the human mind is not simply a *tabula rasa*, a pristine blank slate passively recording the sense impressions it receives from the external world; it is also, and more important, an active agent in understanding those impressions in terms of certain categories and principles that it brings to bear on its experience and on the multiple data coming to it. The human mind's immanent principles include, for instance, cause and effect. These innate principles or categories exist independently of and prior to sense experience. Kant's most creative intellectual idea is that the human mind does not view the external world in a random way; it imposes structure and order on sense experience: "The order and regularity in objects, which we entitle nature, we ourselves introduce."[19] For example, when we make a judgment such as "the sun caused the earth to become warm," we are not simply describing what we perceive because all we perceive is that the sun appears and then the earth becomes warm. We make sense of what we perceive, however, by engaging the principle of causality that we apply to experience. Thus, for Kant, humans do not simply accept what is given to them by perception; rather, they are active, rational beings who understand what they perceive in terms of the mind's categories and principles. The individual human mind, therefore, does not derive the laws of nature *from* the natural world; on the contrary, it imposes its own laws on nature. At least in part, individuals construct the natural world that they perceive. Thus, Kant gave primacy to the subject—the human mind—rather than to the objects of knowledge.

Kant's philosophy contains paradoxes. On the one hand, he is a materialist when he says we can only know the world as it appears to us and is experienced by us, that is, not as it is "in-itself." On the other hand, Kant is an idealist when he insists that ideals are not to be measured by whether they reflect reality: we adjudicate on what is real and what is not by whether it lives up to experience.[20] Kant posits that, if our ideas of what is possible are restricted by our ideas of what is reality, no new ideas can flourish. While providing a foundation for knowledge through reaffirming the validity of knowing by a priori reasoning, Kant also simultaneously defines limits to laws of reason by insisting that, for rational human beings, knowledge is restricted within the boundary of the phenomenon. The effect is to make cognitive space for faith in the existence of divine or mystic forces, beyond the boundary of what humans can know. According to Kant's analysis, human alienation results from the inability of a rational, but finite, being to accept human boundaries. Escaping from the phenomenal world and entering the world of *noumenon* was achievable by an individual's own moral imperatives.

Hegel's philosophy and dialectics

The German philosopher Georg Wilhelm Friedrich Hegel (1770–1831) endeavored to resolve the paradoxes introduced by Kant—dichotomies between faith and reason, between the infinite and the finite.[21] Hegel's philosophy demands our attention for two important reasons. First, his thought is the most ambitious single attempt to demonstrate that modernity contains within itself the intellectual resources to justify, rationally, its rupture with the premodern era.[22] And second, he took seriously the idea that the world contains contradiction. In his most celebrated work, *The Phenomenology of Spirit* (1807), Hegel emphasizes that we cannot ever simply perceive the world, or what is, without preconditions or presuppositions—and here Hegel follows Immanuel Kant—because all human consciousness is informed by innate principles or categories of thought that mediate everything we experience.[23]

In terms of human history, Hegel believed that the French Revolution had been an important and fundamentally positive event in the advancement of the human spirit. Indeed, he expressed this for many years in a quasi-religious way by always lighting a candle on July 14th, Bastille Day.[24] Although Hegel endorses Kant's view on the importance of the human mind and mental instruments in the quest for truth about the world, two of Hegel's criticisms of Kant are particularly important for sociological theory. First, for Kant, the conceptual mental instruments through which humans see the world are static and universal for all finite rational beings. The problem, for Hegel, is the ahistorical character of Kant's conceptual framework. Kant's position is that the basic structure of the human mind is the same in all times and places, whether in Aristotle's ancient Greece or Kant's early modern Germany.

From Hegel's perspective, things are more complex. First, some categories may well be universal, but others, for instance cause and effect, are understood by different cultures in different ways. Hegel posits the existence of a universal human mind or spirit (*Geist*, in Hegel's German) that knows itself as spirit—which develops over time and may differentiate itself in different cultures that exist at the same time. Second, and more important, Hegel's notion of mind develops by interacting with the world—a social process involving self-expression, self-actualization, and self-knowledge.[25] For Hegel, the principles of thought that mediate everything we experience constitute the changing *historical* preconditions of knowledge. The following dense and difficult-to-understand passage from *The Phenomenology of Spirit* contains the essence of Hegel's philosophy:

> The living Substance is being which is in truth *Subject*, or, what is the same, is in truth actual only in so far as it is the movement of positing itself, or is the mediation of its self-othering with itself. This Substance is, as Subject, pure, *simple negativity*, and is for this very reason the bifurcation of the simple; it is the *doubling which sets up opposition*, and then again the negation of this indifferent diversity and of its antithesis [the immediate simplicity]. Only this *self-restoring* sameness, or this reflection in otherness within itself—not an *original* or *immediate* unity as such—is the Truth. It is the process of its own becoming, the circle that presupposes its end as its goal, having its end also as its beginning; and only by being worked out to its end, is it actual.[26]

The subject or consciousness—spirit—is conceived as a *relation*, not a discrete thing; over time "it is the process of its own becoming." Whereas Kant conceptualizes the mind's categories of understanding as being subjective forms that are imposed on the world and provided by sense experience, Hegel's conception of the self is *socially situated*, as each person is a member of a historically specific community of self-conscious human agents. Hegel's idealism, therefore, provides the power to elevate the subject beyond immediate circumstances by placing the individual outside the boundaries provided by empirical limitations. Moreover, his conception of "Absolute Spirit," that is, truth in its totality, evolves and develops and has a circular structure: "a circle which returns upon itself, for mediation bends back its end into the beginning."[27] In Hegel's eyes, human history is the story of the gradual realization of reason in the world; it is a rational process that enables truth to unfold and make itself known to the human mind. This realization of reason involves the full articulation of its internal contradictions.

Georg Wilhelm Friedrich Hegel (1770–1831), a major European philosopher who provided a significant critique of Kantian idealism. His philosophy, particularly his application of the dialectic method to explain human history, profoundly influenced Karl Marx. Marx famously "stood on its head" Hegelian dialectic thought.

This brings us to Hegel's second and equally important view that the human mind develops by grasping the interplay between potential opposites, which results in a third alternative or "unity of opposites."[28] This is a "dialectical" process. As the human mind confronts and tries to make sense of the world, it develops ever-richer and higher-level concepts. As the mind produces such alternative concepts, it changes itself. The dialectic is a concept that predates the European Enlightenment. The etymology of *dialectic* comes from the Latin *dialectica* and Greek *dialecktikē*, and, for Plato, the word described "the art of defining ideas." For Hegel, the essence of dialectical thinking about the world lay in its intrinsic contradictions as well as in a method of interrelated thinking that uses concepts of change, motion, and process. Dialectical thinking is the principle whereby apparently stable thoughts reveal their inherent instability; such thoughts turn into their opposites and then into new, more complex thoughts—as the thought of being is discarded by the thought of nothing and then is discarded by the higher thought of becoming. Through the negation of the antithesis and "the process of its own becoming," consciousness becomes aware of itself as spirit, that is, becomes "conscious of itself as its own world, and of the world as itself."[29] The pinnacle of "absolute knowing" is the point at which spirit reflects on the preceding process and understands it as nothing other than its own self-development.

The dialectical principle, for Hegel, is "the soul of all genuinely scientific cognition," and it is what gives Hegel's thinking its distinctive character by making his thought dynamic. The dialectical principle depicts three moments or concepts of each logical reality: (1) "Thought," (2) the dialectical moment, and (3) the speculative moment or positive "Reason."[30] In his *Science of Logic* (1812), Hegel seeks to demonstrate that, upon conceptual analysis, category A proves to contain a contrary concept, B, and conversely that concept B proves to contain concept A, thus showing both concepts to be self-contradictory. Hegel then seeks to demonstrate that this negative result has a positive outcome, a new concept, C, which is referred to as the "negation of the negation." Concept C *unites* the preceding concepts A and B. When analyzed, the new concept C contains both A and B, but they are united in such a way that they are not only preserved but also discarded. Hegel's term for this paradoxical process is *Aufhebung*; that is, the concepts A and B are preserved in the new C but only with their original meaning modified. This modification of their meaning renders them no longer self-contradictory, so the contradiction between them is overcome. At a new higher level, concept C plays the role that was formerly played by concept A, and the reciprocal containment is repeated.[31] The English poet William Blake, a contemporary of Hegel, captured this view in a phrase: "Without Contraries is no Progression."[32] Sometimes this three-stage process of thinking is conveniently depicted as *thesis* (affirmation of thought which is contradictory), *antithesis* (affirmation of its negation), and *synthesis* (a higher unity which itself becomes a thesis), but we must emphasize that Hegel never used these terms in his formulation. The dialectical method provides the necessary five scientific standards for Hegel's philosophical system. A philosophy must (1) have a method, (2) constitute an entire system, (3) examine the totality, (4) demonstrate the necessity of everything, and (5) give to the subject an a priori character.

The dialectical principle is somewhat abstract, but Hegel gave sociological form to his dialectical reasoning in his famous master-slave analysis. Our treatment here is by no means exhaustive; our aim is simply to flesh out Hegel's dialectical thinking and, in so doing, to introduce the reader to its application in Marx's analysis of industrial capitalism. In *The Phenomenology of Spirit*, Hegel uses the master-slave relation to explain the mutation of two primitive consciousnesses into self-consciousness and its *logical* development into a higher unity of absolute knowledge. Through experience, simple sensuous certainty changes logically into perception and then mutates itself into *understanding*. Hegel then argues that consciousness turns logically into self-consciousness. Fully developed self-consciousness occurs only when two (or more) self-consciousnesses mutually recognize one another. We do not exist as a person unless another person acknowledges our existence. In Hegel's words, "Self-consciousness exists in and for itself when, and by the fact that, it so exists for another; that is, it exists only in being acknowledged."[33]

At the initial encounter, the two primitive self-consciousnesses are perfectly symmetrical; neither would see the other as participating in Reason and committed to mutual recognition. Each demands to be recognized by the other as "being-for-itself," or having freedom, and each wants to end the symmetry by dominating the other. "Absolute negativity" is what Hegel calls the freedom that is determined by the other. The symmetry of mutual recognition between the two self-consciousnesses is unstable; only one self is to be recognized, the other recognizes. One will be master; the other will be slave. Because each primitive self demands to be recognized by the other, a "life and death" struggle for recognition by the other ensues. Each combatant tries to prove to the other how free he or she is by killing the other and by risking his or her life in the struggle. The struggle contains a contradiction: if either combatant should actually be killed, the victorious self would be denied the desired recognition by the dead self-consciousness. The logical "experience" of self-consciousness shows that both combatants must emerge from the struggle alive. Indeed, one must surrender to the other self, if there is to be any conferral of the desired recognition. The self that surrenders out of fear of death, abandoning its effort to be recognized, will become the slave. The dominant self-consciousness, who is recognized by the slave, becomes the master. The slave labors for the master.

In the master-slave relation, each self learns through experience that it is actually the opposite of what he or she initially takes himself or herself to be. The master takes himself to manifest freedom and unfettered power. However, he does not learn the productive potential within himself; he does not produce but consumes, and, paradoxically, despite his freedom, he is in fact *dependent* on the labor of the slave. Further, the master wants recognition from an *equal* other but obtains recognition only from a subordinate human being reduced to an object and a means, a slave. The slave, by contrast, takes herself to be wholly unfree but learns that she does, in fact, experience an *independent* consciousness or spirit of her own. Through labor, the slave learns self-respect and realizes that he, too, has a certain power to transform things: "the bondsman [slave] realizes that it is precisely in his work ... he acquires a mind of his own."[34] Albeit "a freedom which is still enmeshed in servitude ... it is a skill which is a master over some things, but not over the universal power and the whole of objective being."[35] Hegel's master-slave relation logically mutates to a new form of self-consciousness that renders fully explicit the master's state of dependence and the slave's independent consciousness. This truth was always there, implicitly, unconsciously, or, in the Hegelian language effected by Marx, "in-itself"; the *experience* renders it explicit, consciously, or "for itself."

Thus, as each self learns of its reversed relation to being, it brings in its wake a new higher unity, one that is enriched and made self-conscious by the experience of contradiction and antagonism: each self-benefits more from mutual economic cooperation than from domination. For Hegel, the dialectic process is self-transformative and, because it embodies a theory of social change—the slave is the driving force—provides the epistemo-logical paradigm for understanding human history.[36] The philosophy of Hegel has been referred to as "the algebra of revolution."[37] Although this statement is an exaggeration, his ideas, particularly the emphasis on social change, had a profound influence on Marx.

The Critique of Hegel: Feuerbach and Marx's Philosophy

Marx's early conversion from the romantic idealism of Kant to the dialec-tic idealism of Hegel is captured in a letter to his father written in 1837. Marx wrote, "A curtain had fallen, my holy of holies had been shattered, and new gods had to be found. Setting out from idealism ... I hit upon seeking the Idea in the real itself. If formerly the gods had dwelt above the world, they now become its centre."[38] Converted to Hegelianism, Marx changed from a romantic idealist to a materialist who viewed human history as propelled by material forces. On his conversion to Hegelian philosophy, Marx joined in 1836 a group of radical intellectuals that came to be known as the Young Hegelians. Isaiah Berlin summed up the politics of the Young Hegelians by describing the aspiration of each member like this: "To promote revolution by the technical skills which he alone commands, that is by intellectual warfare."[39] Whereas Hegel held that philosophy and religion had different forms but the same content, Marx and the Young Hegelians argued that religion was irrational and, moreover, acted as an impediment to social progress. Thus, the Young

Hegelians' intellectual climate was secular idealism, which is echoed in Marx's proclamation in the preface of his doctoral thesis: "Philosophy makes no secret of it. Prometheus' confession—'in a word, I detest all Gods,' is its own confession."[40]

Marx's critique of Hegel's philosophy was strongly influenced by another well-known German philosopher, Ludwig Feuerbach (1804–72). In his *The Essence of Christianity* (1841), Feuerbach criticizes Hegel's philosophy for preserving a religious world view. He argues that philosophy should not start from God or "the Absolute" but with the human being and the material world, the finite, the real—in other words. Feuerbach argues that religion is an expression of mythical thinking that involves people unwittingly projecting their human essence onto a fictitious entity, whose image represents perfection. For Feuerbach, the human being, fearful and self-doubting, "sets God before him as the antithesis of himself ... God and man are extremes."[41] Thus, God represents the externalization of an idealized human being. This thinking process, then, amounts to an inversion in which the *subject*—a creative human being—is reduced to the status of a *predicate*—a dependent attribute—by a *mystic being*, namely, by God, which is the product of the human imagination. Further, Feuerbach conceives the dialectic as a process of self-alienation because people divest themselves of their best qualities and make these qualities the property of a God or gods.

Hegel's philosophy, according to Feuerbach, remained a repository of religion and, as such, had to be exorcized to end the deception. He asserts that there must be an "inversion of this inversion" so that human beings recognize themselves as the real subject of the process, thereby regaining control over the human attributes, desires, and potentialities that they had ascribed to a God-ideal. Then, they would be in a position to restore to themselves their alienated "species-being" (*Gattungswesen*) or human nature. People will realize that *they* have created religion when intellectuals understand the "true" relationship of thought to being: "Being is the subject, thought is the predicate. Thought arises from being—being does not arise from thought."[42] Though critical of Hegel, Feuerbach still believed that human emancipation from religion is an intellectual process, and that the course of history is determined by the conceptual dialectic of the universal spirit. As such, Feuerbach's thesis remained firmly within a Hegelian framework.[43]

In the winter of 1843–44, Marx developed his critique of religion and idealist philosophy. Marx argues that religion gives expression to a mode of life that is empty, dehumanized, and alienated; it serves the dual social function of compensating for material human suffering, which makes this suffering *seem* tolerable, and of giving expression to a false or illusionary actualization of human's deepest desires. In the early article "A Contribution to the Critique of Hegel's *Philosophy of Right*: Introduction," published in 1844, Marx argues that religion served the purpose of reparation for self-alienation and economic alienation. Though agreeing with Feuerbach that "man makes religion; religion does not make man," Marx thought this observation was too abstract and ahistorical. Marx writes,

> *Man* is not an abstract being, squatting outside the world. Man is the *human world*, the state, society. This state, this society produce religion which is an *inverted world consciousness*, because they are an *inverted world*. Religion is the general theory of this world.... The struggle against religion is, therefore, indirectly a struggle against *that world* whose spiritual *aroma* is religion. *Religious* suffering is at the same time an expression of real suffering and a *protest* against real suffering. Religion is the sigh of the oppressed creature, the sentiment of a heartless world, and the soul of soulless conditions. It is the *opium* of the people.[44]

In other words, people live in such a world, such a system of social organization, that invokes feelings of reverence or religious consciousness, which become the dominant way of thinking about themselves and their world. It is easy to interpret the famous epigram in the sentence about religion being the "opium of the people" as meaning that religious consciousness produces human misery or that *opium* is the problem. Both interpretations are incorrect. To understand Marx's metaphor, we have to know that opium was in common use in Europe as a relief from pain and other forms of distress and that it produces some form of ecstasy in those who use it. If we view the use of opium as a *response*—albeit not a wise one especially if made regularly—to human suffering, we have something approaching Marx's thesis. Religious illusions and the "God hypothesis" give expression to a sense of the emptiness and worthlessness of human life—to alienation.

Religion's social function is to anesthetize people to the misery of their social condition. The belief in the supernatural also offers solace for this alienation, by the false promise of a meaningful and unalienated life in the beyond. Religion, therefore, is an illogical reaction to the finitude of the human condition. Marx's conclusion is that it is necessary to change the material conditions that make false consciousness or illusion necessary: "The abolition of religion as the *illusory* happiness of men is a demand for the *real* happiness. The call to abandon their illusions about their condition is a *call to abandon a condition, which requires illusions*. The criticism of religion is, therefore, *the embryonic criticism of this vale of tears* of which religion is the *halo*."[45] The religious veil may conceal earthly misery, but the task of removing the veil is just a beginning. This is because the phenomenon of religion, the disease, is primarily alienated labor—a state of existence increasingly exacerbated by the division of labor and ever-sophisticated factory machinery in the hands of capitalists—as opposed to abstract ideas in the form of religion. Once alienated labor is abolished and the cause removed, the symptom—religion—will wither on its own. Philosophers must be critical of material conditions not only of their religious reflection. Thus, in his *Theses on Feuerbach* (1845), Marx declares that the chief defect of all hitherto philosophers is that they "have only *interpreted* the world, in various ways; the point, however, is to *change* it."[46] We can now begin to understand why religion is so important to Marx's critique of German idealist philosophy, for "the criticism of religion is the premise of all criticism."[47] His critique of religion ends with the categorical imperative to abolish all conditions that abase, enslave, and alienate human beings.

The concept of alienation figures prominently throughout Marx's critique of idealist philosophy. Originating with Hegel, alienation has become a key concept in modern sociology. Central to Marx's notion of alienation is the idea that human beings progressively forfeit to something (e.g., God) or someone (e.g., the capitalist) something that is the essence of their nature: principally, the control over their own attributes and activities. Marx addresses political alienation in another early article entitled "On the Jewish Question" (1844). In this work, he discusses how the state deprives people of the opportunity for attaining the essence of their nature, and that this deprivation is a form of political alienation. Marx's old mentor Bruno Bauer had argued that Jewish emancipation could not be achieved without the state ceasing to be Christian. Marx, however, countered that the simple secularization of the state was insufficient because it did not entail the emancipation of men and women as human beings. He argued that specific social elements had to be defeated in order to achieve genuine emancipation: "The question of the relation between political emancipation and religion becomes for us a question of the relation between political emancipation and human emancipation."[48] For Marx, human emancipation necessitated democratic control over all human activity.

Marx's *Theses on Feuerbach* contains a critique of Feuerbach's account of materialism. Although Marx accepted much of Feuerbach's critique of Hegel, he argued that the real relation of thought to human life was not Feuerbach's human nature but the social and economic system of production. In Marx's inversion, thought is a product of these concrete

conditions. The opening page of the first thesis contains the essence of
Marx's criticism of Feuerbach's materialism: "The chief defect of all
hitherto existing materialism—that of Feuerbach included—is that the
thing, reality, sensuousness, is conceived only in the form of the object
or of *contemplation*, but not as *human sensuous activity, practice*, not
subjectivity."[49] Marx concludes that Feuerbach's critique of Hegel merely
substituted one mystic for another. In the second thesis, Marx explains
his principle of the unity of theory and practice: "The question whether
objective truth can be attributed to human thinking is not a question of
theory but is a *practical* question."[50] Theory without practice is a form
of pure cognitive gymnastics—graceful perhaps, but ultimately sterile
and of no consequence. And, in the third thesis, Marx identifies the
agent of social change: "The materialist doctrine that men are products
of circumstances and upbringing ... forgets that it is men who change
circumstances and that it is essential to educate the educator himself."[51]
This thesis leads us to Marx's treatment of Hegelian dialectics and his
methodology of social analysis.

Marx's Methodology

Marx employed unobtrusive methods—historical and comparative
research, extensive published data, content analysis—and a particular
form of dialectical reasoning to study social phenomena. In the early
twentieth century, Marx was venerated as the founder of the "science"
of history and, with Engels, as the architect of the scientific philosophy
to accompany it: "dialectical materialism." Posthumous elaborations of
Marx's dialectics were constructed beginning with Engels's *Anti-Dühring*
in 1878, but not without controversy. Marx's contribution to the methodology of social science was his use of contradiction and the idea of
unintended consequences of human action. The genealogy of Marx's
methodology is, without doubt, derived from his critique of Hegelian
and Feuerbachian dialectics. For Marx, Hegel's master-slave dialectic was
mystifying and written from an idealistic standpoint. In the *Economic and
Philosophical Manuscripts*, Marx did recognize the positive elements of
Hegel's dialectic: "The outstanding thing in Hegel's *Phenomenology* and
its final outcome ... is first that Hegel conceives the self-genesis of man as
a process, conceives objectification as loss of the object, as alienation ...
thus grasps the essence of labour and comprehends objective man ... as
the outcome of man's *own labour*."[52] However, Marx criticized Hegel's
dialectic because it still harbors uncritical idealism: "The appropriation
of man's essential powers [is] ... in the first place only an appropriation
occurring in *consciousness*, in *pure thought*—i.e., in *abstraction*."[53]

Although Hegel, according to Marx, only recognizes "abstractly mental labour," Marx defined his position as consistently humanist and as avoiding idealism, which recognizes "real, corporeal man, man with his feet firmly on the solid ground, man exhaling and inhaling all the forces of nature."[54] Marx rejected Hegel's notion of mind or spirit (*Geist*) as an independent reality and replaced its supposed antithesis to the external world by the antithesis between human beings and their *social* being.[55] For Marx, Hegel's philosophy reduces human beings and history to an abstract mental process, which constitutes a form of alienation.

Dialectical processes—dialectics as a feature of the world itself—had "a very powerful grip on Marx's mind."[56] Marx extends the idea of psychological contradiction found in the master-slave analysis to the theory of social contradiction. Marx employs "contradiction" to analyze social phenomena and societal change. The term's most central use is in his theory of social change; over time, the two reciprocally dependent productive forces and the relations of production come into conflict or "contradiction" and turn into "fetters" on human progress.[57] He explains his methodology this way:

> My dialectic method is not only different from the Hegelian, but is its direct opposite. To Hegel, the life-process of the human brain, i.e., the process of thinking, which, under the name of "the Idea," he even transforms into an independent subject, is the demiurgos [the creator] of the real world, and the real world is only the external, phenomenal form of "the Idea." With me, on the contrary, the ideal is nothing less than the material world reflected by the human mind, and translated into forms of thought.[58]

Marx believes that Hegel is close to the truth. The human mind and the world do change together. And history is indeed, as Hegel averred, an arena of human alienation. But Marx argues that the human mind is not the creator of the universe. Marx acknowledges, however, that he is extracting from Hegelian dialectic "the rational kernel within the mystical shell"[59] to develop a "materialist dialectic."

To demystify Hegel's logic, Marx believed it must be "inverted" or "turned upside down" before it could assume a rational shape. For Marx, the "rational kernel" is Hegel's vision of society, organically structured and characterized by inherent social contradictions and unintended consequences—activities undertaken by social actors that do not always turn out as they expect. Marx emphasized the unintended consequences of purposive social action, arguing that they are to be understood in the causal modeling that has become the standard language of the social sciences.[60] The classic sociological example of unintended consequences is found in Max Weber's thesis about the links between the Protestant ethic and the spirit of modern capitalism. The American sociologist Robert Merton outlined several explanations for how the outcomes of any action—policy, program, or other—can deviate from the intended purpose.[61] A well-known case of the law of unintended consequences is provided by a US management study, where the presence of the researchers inadvertently changed the behavior of the workers they were studying, a research phenomenon designated the "Hawthorne effect." A contemporary case of unintended consequences is illustrated by US President Donald Trump's policies; any benefits Americans gain by his tax cuts are soon to be lost by the higher fuel prices caused by Trump's "get-tough" approach toward Iran.[62]

Hegel's psychological contradiction characterized the three stages as, respectively, thesis, antithesis, and synthesis. The most important example of Marx's social dialectical process follows a similar three-stage sequence: in stage one, society begins as a primitive, undifferentiated community. The community dominates the individual and self-realization is stymied. Stage two, the negation of the first stage, occurs with the emergence of class societies. Society is characterized by extreme individuality, exploitation of labor and nature, and the disintegration of community. Stage three, the negation of the negation, reinstates a higher-level community, but without stifling individuality. It is the synthesis of stages one and two. The idea of social contradictions and that of unintended consequences is the essence of Marx's theory of social change, which we examine in chapter 5.

In sum, Marx accepts Hegel's vision of reality but rejects the metaphysics that motivates his vision.[63] For Marx, any dialectical perception of nature is subordinate to the dialectic between human activities and nature, which arises from human beings satisfying their everyday economic needs through their labor. Marx's mode of causal analysis as a particular form of dialectical reasoning is his central contribution to the methodology of human inquiry.[64]

Criticisms

To write about the intellectual assault on Marx's philosophical concepts would be almost tantamount to writing a history of modern philosophy, and would go well beyond the aims of this chapter. This is not to say that we cannot identify a number of criticisms of Marx's early works.[65] Marx, if we recall, draws on a constellation of European philosophers, and one obvious criticism is that the origins of his philosophical concepts are "indisputably Western."[66] Marx never studied religion in any detail, but his discussions underscore that religion is a product of social alienation. People create an imaginary figure known as God in order to find solace from their suffering in the real world; the cause of their suffering is alienation caused by a particular type of social organization; and religious beliefs and values provide justification of social inequality—the theory of ideology. One possible criticism to Marx's hypothesis on religion is that traditional theology is right and Marx is wrong. There is a God who created all things and demands our worship. For those who believe in God or in a higher force, as well as for those who believe in the possibility of the salvation of one's soul through the acceptance of Christ as personal savior, Marx is wrong. Critics also point out that, although there is evidence to support the *secularization thesis* within postmodernity, new religious movements and Christian and Islamic fundamentalism challenge the notion that religious commitment in all its manifestations is about solace or a bourgeois conspiracy to keep down the "lower orders."

An orthodox critique of Marx's dialectic method is that it lacks credibility because it denies the basic law of non-contradiction. This law holds that the presence of a contradiction in a statement or proposition invalidates its claim to truth. For example, we cannot simultaneously say "It is snowing" and "It is not snowing." Formal logic denies that contradictions exist in reality, and, if they do exist in thought, they signify an error and have to be expunged in order to reveal truth. Marx's insistence that contradictions exist in capitalist reality is, critics claim, a repudiation of formal logic. Marx's use of the dialectic logic, critics argue, also exhibits a doctrinaire or "mechanical" use of the concept and a unidirectional notion of human history. This allegedly doctrinaire dialectic is counterposed against the *genuine dialectic* defined in terms of interaction, reciprocity, and multiple causation. In reply, it may be said that dialectic contradictions are different from the contradictions referred to in formal thinking. From this perspective, the principle of non-contradiction has limited value when one is studying a complex system in motion, and, thus, dialectic contradictions do not repudiate the laws of thought but augment and qualify them.

Conclusion

Marx's philosophical concepts are not original but were fashioned from the ideas of an extraordinary constellation of Western philosophers. Specifically, there was continuity in the thinking of Hegel, Feuerbach, and

Marx that certainly looked back at least to the ideas of Immanuel Kant. Hegel provided a major critique of Kantian idealism, and his account of the master-slave dialectic gave sociological form to his philosophy. The paradigmatic account of the master and slave relation, with its contradictory elements of antagonism as well as economic cooperation, resonates in Marx's analyses of both social class and the dynamics of social change.[67] Unsurprisingly, the sociological implications of Hegel's concept of recognition have provided inspiration for the feminist conception of gender relations and inequality and for philosophies encouraging black liberation and black consciousness. Through his critique of German idealism, Marx constitutes society in materialist terms. Thus, he argues that human consciousness does not determine the social being; rather, material conditions and a purposive *praxis* determine human consciousness. His conception of political, religious, philosophical, and economic alienation—a condition in which human beings progressively lose control and become estranged within the society that their labor creates—remains central to his writings.

Is Marx's philosophical legacy relevant today? Confronted with global inequalities, fragmented responses to global warming, and the public discourse on Christianity and Islam, today's society will find his philosophical concepts insightful, suggestive, and a fertile source for social theorizing.[68] Turning to his commentary on religion, for example, we find that Marx's concepts contain much insight for a world of diasporas and multiculturalism. Marx may well have said to followers of different faiths, "Your mind would be much more free if you critically examine your faith and think about the degree to which that faith is itself responsible for your own oppression." Without doubt, we are witnessing a revival of religion in local and global political conflicts.[69] Perhaps once people stop kneeling before an imaginary deity, humanity will be able to address cataclysmic issues such as war, epidemics, and global warming.

As to the relevance of Marx's dialectic, it can be argued that, despite all the knowledge and sophisticated information technologies we possess, we still don't know how to conceptualize the intensified conflict over the earth's shrinking reserves of natural resources, how to think usefully about societal and political solutions to global warming, or, in general, how to make connections between apparently disparate processes and events. Marx's dialectic is the logic of postmodernity that provides us a way to think philosophically about the changes and innumerable instances of contradiction that lie at the heart of the processes of globalization and global warming; for these reasons, we suggest Marx's dialectic is of lasting significance.

FURTHER THINKING:

What does Marx mean when he argues that human consciousness does not determine the social being, but rather that material conditions and purposive *praxis* determine human consciousness? Is Marx's dialectical reasoning relevant in postmodern social research?

FURTHER READING:

For an engaging and witty read about the life and times of Karl Marx, see Francis Wheen, *Karl Marx* (London: Fourth Estate, 2000). Also see Gareth Stedman Jones, *Karl Marx: Greatness and Illusion* (London: Penguin, 2017). For an interesting "rewrite" of Marx by two believers of free-market capitalism, see Rupert Younger and Frank Partnoy, "What Would Marx Write Today?" *The Financial Times, Life & Arts*, March 11, 2018, p. 1. For a short introduction to weighty premodern and modern philosophers, including Marx, see Terry Eagleton's *Radical Sacrifice* (London: Yale University Press, 2018). Raoul Peck's film *The Young Karl Marx* (2017) traces how Marx (August Diehl) and Friedrich Engels (Stefan Konarske) met in the 1840s, bonded over their shared contempt for the Young Hegelians and came to write *The Communist Manifesto*. A review of the film is available at https://www.youtube.com/watch?v=1_z-jx_6beM.

Notes

1 Gareth Stedman Jones, *Karl Marx: Greatness and Illusion* (London: Penguin, 2017), 5.

2 Mike Davis, *Old Gods, New Enigmas* (London: Verso, 2018), 22.

3 Alan Swingewood, *Marx and Modern Social Theory* (London: Macmillan, 1975).

4 David McLellan, *Marx* (London: Fontana Press, 1975), 9.

5 Stedman Jones, *Karl Marx: Greatness and Illusion*, 4.

6 Ian Craib, *Classical Social Theory* (Oxford: Oxford University Press, 1997), 11.

7 David McLellan, *Karl Marx: The Legacy* (London: BBC, 1983), 12.

8 McLellan, *Karl Marx: The Legacy*, 41.

9 Francis Wheen, *Karl Marx* (London: Fourth Estate, 2000), 32.

10 August von Ciezkowski, quoted in David McLellan, *Marx Before Marxism* (New York: Harper Torchbooks, 1970), 65.

11 Quoted in McLellan, *Karl Marx: The Legacy*, 33.

12 Quoted in Wheen, *Karl Marx*, 179–80.

13 Wheen, *Karl Marx*, 180–95.

14   Wheen, *Karl Marx*, 184.

15   Quoted in Robert Tucker, ed., *The Marx-Engels Reader*, 2nd ed. (New York: Norton, 1978), x; hereafter cited as Tucker, *Marx-Engels Reader*.

16   Wheen, *Karl Marx*, 234.

17   Karl Marx, *Grundrisse*, trans. with a Foreword by Martin Nicolaus (1857–58; London: Penguin, 1953), 7; hereafter cited as Marx, *Grundrisse*.

18   Immanuel Kant, *Critique of Pure Reason*, trans. Norman Kemp Smith (1781; New York: St. Martin's Press, 1965), 41–43.

19   Immanuel Kant, quoted in Paul Hyland, ed., *The Enlightenment: A Sourcebook and Reader* (London: Routledge, 2003), 53.

20   Susan Neiman, "Can and Kant," *The Globe and Mail*, May 10, 2008, D13.

21   Other German idealists such as Johann Gottlieb Fichte (1762–1814) and Friedrich Wilhelm Joseph von Schelling (1775–1854) also addressed the paradoxes that Kant had enshrined in his works.

22   This section draws heavily from the chapter on Hegel in Alex Callinicos, *Social Theory: A Historical Introduction*, 2nd ed. (Cambridge: Polity Press, 2007), 39–56.

23   See Stephen Houlgate, *An Introduction to Hegel* (Oxford: Blackwell, 2005), 4–12.

24   Peter Berger and Brigitte Berger, *Sociology: A Bibliographical Approach* (London: Penguin, 1976), 39.

25   Allen W. Wood, *Karl Marx* (London: Routledge, 2004), 199.

26   G.F. Hegel, *The Phenomenology of Spirit*, trans. Arnold V. Miller (1807; Oxford: Clarendon Press, 1977), 10, quoted in Callinicos, *Social Theory*, 50.

27   G.F. Hegel, *Science of Logic*, quoted in Callinicos, *Social Theory*, 52.

28   G.F. Hegel, *Science of Logic*, quoted in Wood, *Karl Marx*, 208.

29   Hegel, *The Phenomenology of Spirit*, quoted in Callinicos, *Social Theory*, 51.

30   G.F. Hegel, *Science of Logic*, quoted in Michael Forster, "Hegel's Dialectical Method," in *The Cambridge Companion to Hegel*, ed. F.C. Beiser (Cambridge: Cambridge University Press, 1993), 130–70, see page 131.

31   Forster, "Hegel's Dialectical," 132.

32   Cited by Jon Elster, *An Introduction to Karl Marx* (Cambridge: Cambridge University Press, 1986), 34.

33   Hegel, *Phenomenology of Spirit*, 111.

34   Hegel, *Phenomenology of Spirit*, 119.

35   Hegel, *Phenomenology of Spirit*.

36   Angelica Nuzzo, "Dialectic as Logic of Transformative Processes," in *Hegel: New Directions*, ed. Katerina Deligiorgi (Chesham, UK: Acumen Publishing, 2006), 94–99.

37   Alexander Herzen, *My Past and Thoughts*, abr. ed., ed. D. Macdonald (Berkeley: University of California Press, 1982), and quoted in Callinicos, *Social Theory*, 79.

38   Quoted in David McLellan, *Marx Before Marxism* (New York: Harper Torchbooks, 1970), 48.

39   Isaiah Berlin, *Karl Marx: His Life and Environment*, 4th ed. (Oxford: Oxford University Press, 1978), 49–50.

40   Quoted in McLellan, *Marx*, 26.

41   Feuerbach, *Essence of Christianity*, 33.

42   Quoted in McLellan, *Marx Before Marxism*, 107.

43 Callinicos, *Social Theory*, 79–80.

44 Karl Marx, "Contribution to the Critique of Hegel's *Philosophy of Right*: Introduction," in Tucker, *Marx-Engels Reader*, 53–65, see pages 53–54.

45 Tucker, *Marx-Engels Reader*, 54.

46 Tucker, *Marx-Engels Reader*, 145.

47 Tucker, *Marx-Engels Reader*, 53.

48 Tucker, *Marx-Engels Reader*, 31.

49 Tucker, *Marx-Engels Reader*, 143.

50 Tucker, *Marx-Engels Reader*, 144.

51 Tucker, *Marx-Engels Reader*, 144.

52 Tucker, *Marx-Engels Reader*, 112.

53 Tucker, *Marx-Engels Reader*, 111.

54 Tucker, *Marx-Engels Reader*, 115.

55 David McLellan, *The Thought of Karl Marx*, 2nd ed. (London: Macmillan, 1980), 118.

56 Elster, *An Introduction to Karl Marx*, 35.

57 See Tucker, *Marx-Engels Reader*, 4–5.

58 Karl Marx, "Afterword to the Second German Edition," in *Capital*, vol. 1, ed. Friedrich Engels, trans. Samuel Moore and Edward Aveling (1873; London: S. Sonnenschein, Lowery & Co., 1887), in *Marx-Engels Reader*, 301.

59 Marx, "Afterword," quoted in *Marx-Engels Reader*, 302.

60 Jon Elster, *Making Sense of Karl Marx* (Cambridge: Cambridge University Press, 1985), 3.

61 Robert K. Merton, "The Unanticipated Consequences of Purposive Social Action," *American Sociological Review* 1 (1936): 894–904.

62 Business editorial, "The Reason the Oil Price Is High Is Also the Reason It's Sure to Fall Again: Economics," *The Observer*, May 20, 2018, 62.

63 Allen W. Wood, *Karl Marx*, 2nd ed. (New York: Routledge, 2004).

64 For a more detailed account see Elster, *Making Sense of Karl Marx*, 3–48.

65 See Jonathan Wolff, *Why Read Marx Today?* (Oxford: Oxford University Press, 2002), 100–08; Lawrence Wilde, "Logic: Dialectic and Contradiction," in *The Cambridge Companion to Marx*, ed. Terrell Carver (New York: Cambridge University Press, 1991), 275–95; Wood, *Karl Marx*; Swingewood, *Marx and Modern Social Theory*, 11–12.

66 This criticism is made by the African American academic Cedric J. Robinson in *Black Marxism* (Chapel Hill: University of North Carolina Press, 2000). In terms of Marx's dialectic, Robinson argues that racism ran deep in the bowels of Western culture, and, as a consequence, it negated its social relations of production and distorted their inherent contradictions.

67 Chris Arthur has argued that the alleged connection between the master-slave relation and Marx's conception of class-consciousness and class struggle, first popularized by Jean-Paul Sartre, is false. See "Hegel's Master-Slave Dialectic and a Myth of Marxology," *New Left Review* (Nov–Dec 1983): 67–75, http://marxmyths.org/chris-arthur/article.htm.

68 See Wolff, *Why Read Marx Today?*, and Nuzzo, "Dialectic as Logic of Transformative Processes," 100.

69 John Gray, *Black Mass* (Toronto: Doubleday, 2007), 3.

5. Karl Marx: Theory of History

There's class warfare, all right, but it's my class, the rich class, that's making war, and we're winning.
—Warren Buffett, 2006[1]

The fundamental fact remains that life outcomes are largely determined by the wealth and social class of one's parents at birth.
—Naomi Eisenstadt, 2017[2]

Racial and sexual oppression have been added to the dynamic of class exploitation. Social justice movements like Black Lives Matter and #MeToo owe something of an unspoken debt to Marx.
—Jason Barker, 2018[3]

CENTRAL TO MARX'S PHILOSOPHICAL WORK is that the labor necessary to satisfy individual and collective material needs leads to ever more complex forms of productive activity and social engagement. It is this view of human interaction with nature and with each other that forms the rudiments of Marx's theory of history. At Marx's funeral, Friedrich Engels paid tribute to him for discovering the primary motive force in human history: "Just as Darwin discovered the law of development of organic nature, so Marx discovered the law of the development of human history."[4] Marx never used the term *historical materialism*, which was coined by Engels; instead he preferred to call his approach "the materialist conception of history."[5] Like Hegel, Marx believed that the French Revolution had been a positive event, but, unlike Hegel, he made the Revolution a central concern for the science of humanity. For Marx, the French Revolution inaugurated a new age of humanity.[6] The French Revolution helped Marx develop many of his basic concepts, which provide an explanatory theory about society's different forms of social life, such as class structure, ideology, and development and transformation over time. For Marx, social classes play a pivotal role in societal change and transformation.

As we pass the bicentennial of Karl Marx's birth, are his ideas on social class and ideology really applicable to our postmodern world, or do we now live in a "classless" post-ideological age? In the 1950s, the United States was described as a "classless society."[7] And, 40 years later, after winning the 1997 general election society, British Labour Prime Minister Tony Blair declared that "the class war is over." A decade after the global financial crisis, extreme inequality has put social class under the public microscope. And the ideology of neoliberalism, it is argued, runs deeply through UK government policies and US and UK corporate strategies.[8] Unsurprisingly, therefore, Marx's empirical theory of history, which has become known as historical materialism, constitutes one of the central elements in his social theory. A thorough treatment of Marx's materialist concept of human history is found in the first part of *The German Ideology* (1845–46), and the most succinct statement of it is in the preface to *A Contribution to the Critique of Political Economy* (1859). This chapter examines the core elements of the general theory. To begin to understand the materialist conception of history, however, we need to recognize the importance Marx gave to human nature and to labor in formulating his theory of history.

Human Nature

Marx's understanding of human history is based on the fundamental premise that people must obtain their basic necessities of life—food, clothing, shelter, and so on—by cooperating with others and by entering into a conscious relation with nature. The most important historical act is the act of productive labor; by this means, men and women develop and exercise their human faculties to transform nature to satisfy their material needs. The human species, according to Marx, is different from all other animal species because it alone produces its own means of subsistence and creates something in reality that previously existed only in an individual's imagination:

> We presuppose labour in a form that stamps it as exclusively human. A spider conducts operations that resemble those of a weaver, and a bee puts to shame many an architect in the construction of her cells. But what distinguishes the worst architect from the best bees is this, that the architect raises his structure in imagination before he erects reality. At the end of every labour process we get a result that existed in the imagination of the labourer at its commencement. He not only effects a change of

form in the material on which he works, but he also realizes a purpose of his own that gives a law to his *modus operandi*, and to which he must subordinate his will.[9]

Marx calls this process whereby humans create external objects from their internal thoughts *objectification*. We can begin to understand Marx's concept of objectification by thinking of the work of an artist. An artwork is a representation of the artist's imagination—a representation of an idea that exists in the artist's head before the commencement of the project.

Marx believed that capitalism destroyed the pleasure associated with socially productive labor. Consequently, humans are alienated from their product, productive activity, species being, and other people. Under capitalism, people are unable to exercise and experience a distinctively human capacity that is critical for human freedom—to make and remake nature. All forms of alienation are thus, according to Marx, located in the real world, and it is necessary to change the conditions that cause alienated labor.

Thus, the artwork is an objectification of the artist. During the creative process, the artist's ideas about the object may change and prompt a new art form that needs objectification. Work, for Marx, provides the means through which humans can realize the fullness of their humanity. It is through the specific conditions of material life that men and women develop the power and capacity for generating consciousness and for collective action to transform society. This is agency in the classical revolutionary sense and the basis of Marx's materialism.

Alienation

Exploitation of labor and alienation are two fundamental flaws in capitalism, according to Marx. These concepts play two distinct roles in his economic theory and his theory of history. Both exploitation and alienation enter into his normative assessment of what is dysfunctional about capitalism and, conversely, what is attractive about communism.[10] Further, both are part of Marx's explanation of the collapse of capitalism and the transition to communism. Marx's theory of history is based on philosophical concepts such as self-estrangement, drawn directly from Feuerbach; on ideas about communism, taken from French socialists François Noel Babeuf (Gracchus) and Charles Fourier; and on his understanding of capitalism, derived from Adam Smith's political economy. For Marx, capitalism perverts the relation between human nature and productive power—thereby stultifying human creativity—and therefore is the locus of *alienated labor*. Alienation occurs because men and women (and children) forfeit the right to control their own labor when they enter the employment of the capitalist (i.e., when they sell their labor power). This means that workers lose autonomy over when and how work should be undertaken. Thus, there is a subordination of workers to their employers (or managers who act as "agents of capital"), which means work becomes a degrading and dehumanizing activity:

> [Under] the capitalist system ... all means for the development of production transform themselves into the means of domination over, and exploitation of, the producers; they mutilate the labourer into a fragment of a man, degrade him to the level of an appendage of a machine, destroy every remnant of charm in his work and turn it into a hated toil.[11]

As a result of the capitalist system, according to Marx, workers experience different types of alienation. The following tour de force contains Marx's classic statement on alienated labor under capitalism:

> The object which labour produces—labour's product—confronts it as *something alien*, as a *power independent* of the producer.... The worker is related to the *product of his labour* as to an *alien* object. For on this premise it is clear that the more the worker spends himself, the more powerful the alien objective world becomes ... the poorer he himself—his inner world—becomes, the less belongs to him as his own.... The alienation of the worker in his product means not only that his labour becomes an object, an *external* existence, but that it exists *outside him*, independently, as something alien to him, and that it becomes a power of its own confronting him; it means that life which he has conferred on the object confronts him as something hostile and alien.... But the estrangement is manifested not only in the result but in the *act of production*—within the *producing activity* itself.... Estranged labour turns ... man's *species being* ... into a being *alien* to him, into a *means* to his *individual* existence. It estranges man's own body from him, as it does external nature and his spiritual essence, his *human being*. An immediate consequence ... is the estrangement of *man from man*.[12]

This dense passage can be read in more than one way. What follows is the traditional interpretation in which Marx contends that humans experience four discrete but related types of alienation: alienation from their product, from their own productive activity, from their own nature or species being, and from other human beings.

The first type of labor alienation is from the *product*. Extensive use of division of labor and machinery means that workers have no creative input into how products are designed or made. In this sense, the product confronts the individual worker "as something alien, as a power independent of the producer." The more sophisticated the productive process becomes, as narrower divisions of labor and increasingly advanced machinery are applied to it, the less significant is the individual worker. In a less obvious way, humans collectively become alienated from the products they create because of two related concepts: mystification and domination. Everything individuals use or encounter in their daily lives is the result of accumulative learning. This process creates a mystery around products because few people have any real understanding of how everyday products actually work or are made. Take, for example, the Internet and the related electronic products that also dominate people's lives. The cumulative effect is that "we are strangers in our own world."[13]

The second type of labor alienation is "within the producing activity itself." Marx emphasizes that the long-term tendency to extend the division of labor and to implement new machinery makes paid work repetitive and monotonous, giving no intrinsic satisfaction: the worker becomes an "appendage of the machine."[14] Marx's notion of alienated labor is an extension of Feuerbach's analysis of religious alienation. In the *Manuscripts*, he makes the parallel with Feuerbach explicit: "Just as in religion the spontaneous activity of the human imagination, of the human brain and the human heart, operates independently of the individual—that is, operates on him as an alien, divine or diabolical activity—in the same way the worker's activity is not his spontaneous activity. It belongs to another; it is the loss of his self."[15]

The third type of alienation is from the human species. Marx uses the term *species being*, taken from Feuerbach, to refer to the free ability of humans to create a world in which to manifest their full creative nature. The human essence is not an abstraction, however; it is concrete and defined by the human capacity to create objects:

> It is just in the working-up of the objective world, therefore, that man first really proves himself to be a *species being*. This production is his active species life. Through and because of this production, nature appears as *his* work and his reality. The object of labour is, therefore, the *objectification of man's species life*: for he duplicates himself not only, as in consciousness, intellectually, but also actively, in reality, and therefore he contemplates himself in a world that he has created."[16]

But, under capitalism, work embodies the opposite qualities: labor is repetitive, boring, and mentally incapacitating. Work is, as a woman factory worker put it, "the blank patch between one brief evening and the next."[17] Workers produce as animals do, and feel human only when they are not engaged in paid work.

The fourth type of alienation is "the estrangement of man from man." Again, Marx draws on Feuerbach's analysis of religion to capture the experience. In the intellectual world, "religious self-estrangement necessarily appears in the relationship of the layman to the priest.... In the real, practical world self-estrangement can only become manifest through the real practical relationship to other men."[18] The essential point is that capitalist production alienates workers from fellow human beings as well as from the communal aspects of their lives. This alienation occurs because people are fixated on going to work to earn money and then going to shopping malls to spend it—a consumer culture develops in which humans are integrated into society, above all, as consumers.[19] By being continuously engaged in the individual aspect of a consumer culture, people have little time for or interest in communal *species essence*. Alienation is an objective condition, and, although it has subjective implications, a "happy" worker is no less alienated than a bored one. Marx's economic analysis of alienated labor is central to his conception of the development of capitalism.

The General Thesis

The materialist conception of history has two sides to it. On the one hand, it is a general theory explaining the primacy of the economic in social life, how productive systems work, and the underlying motive force for change in human history. On the other hand, it is a theory of the historical stages of modes of production, which is the basis for social revolution. The preface to *A Contribution to the Critique of Political Economy*, first published in 1859, is the canonical text that serves as a "guiding thread" for Marx's work:

> In the social production of their life, men enter into definite relations that are indispensable and independent of their will, relations of production, which correspond to a definite stage of development of their material productive forces. The sum total of these relations of production constitutes the economic structure of society, the real foundation, on which raises a legal and political superstructure and to which correspond definite forms of social consciousness. The mode of production of material life conditions the social, political and intellectual life process in general. It is not the consciousness of men that determines their being, but, on the contrary, their social being that determines their consciousness.[20]

Three fundamental, central concepts of Marx's general thesis can be derived from this passage: productive forces, relations of production, and superstructure. The *productive forces* refer to two factors: the "means of production" and "labor power." Although there are some problems of definition, what qualifies as a productive force is an instrument or facility that must be ownable, progressively developed by humans, and capable of being utilized by labor power.[21] In every stage of history, men and women utilize non-human resources such as tools, machinery, and raw materials—the means of production—and harness human resources in the form of physical strength, skill, or knowledge—labor power—to satisfy their needs. The means of production vary with the different ways that human beings attain their subsistence. For example, a fisher needs a net, and a software designer uses more complex instruments of production. Concomitantly, the type of labor power used by the fisher or the software designer differs according to the specific ways these individuals attain their economic needs.

The *relations of production* may be defined in terms of the ownership and non-ownership of the means of production,[22] but the term also refers to the social relations and classes that are formed. Under capitalism, the relations of production that workers enter into, "indispensable and independent of their will,"[23] differ from those of feudalism. Workers are compelled to sell their labor power to an owner of the means of production in order to satisfy their own economic needs. In so doing, they also enter into relations that place them under the control of the owner. The forces and the relations of production constitute the economic base of a society. According to Marx, people's economic activity, their "mode of production in material life," is what primarily characterizes their social life, and a society's economic base determines both the institutions and prevalent ideas in that society. This is Marx's first premise: the level of development of a society's productive forces will determine the nature of its social form. Why should this be the case? As we have discussed, factory production introduced specialized machines and occupations, which changed patterns of ownership and instilled new patterns of social behavior. An equivalent transformation in present society is the new globally oriented communication technology of the so-called knowledge economy. The apparent primacy of economic affairs over social processes illustrates the materialist nature of Marx's theory of history.

The *superstructure* in Marx's socio-economic model includes the legal, political, religious, philosophical, and cultural processes and institutions of society. The legal and political architecture, for instance, embraces criminal and civil law, the law courts, and provincial and federal parliamentary systems. In Marx's view, these non-economic features are important for the continued existence of the economic base. The economic "base" and the social "superstructure," therefore, constitute a totality, the different parts explicable in terms of the whole. The nature of the relationship between the superstructure and the economic base introduces Marx's second premise: the economic base will "determine" (*bestimmen*) the social superstructure of a society, and, moreover, the superstructure and consciousness will change as the economic base undergoes change. Here lies the genesis of Marx's theory of ideology. The causal relationship embodied in Marx's theory and the process of change have been central topics for debate and scholarship.

Critics of Marx regard the idea that the economic base ultimately determines the nature of civilization, the social "superstructure," as a form of determinism. Marx and Engels, however, never meant to suggest that the economic structure of society determines a specific culture, set of ideas, or politics. To borrow a phrase from the eighteenth-century Scottish philosopher David Hume, there is no suggestion of a "necessary connexion" or causal glue between the economic base and the social superstructure.[24] The capitalist economic structure was not the *cause* of Charles Dickens's *Great Expectations* (1860–61). Neither does the economic structure of society generate only those ideas that serve capitalists' interests. If this were the case, Tom Paine's *Rights of Man* (1791–92) or Marx's *Capital* would not exist, and neither would institutions such as the Canadian Co-operative Commonwealth Federation or the Socialist Party of America.

Base and superstructure is an "architectural metaphor," which Marx uses in order to provide a certain perspective on society.[25] The direction of travel between the base and superstructure is not just one way. His premise is simply that the base affects the superstructure and "sets limits" rather than "determines" life experiences and that it is no coincidence that both the state and social consciousness correspond to the economic structure of society—not least because the dominant social class has the capacity to control the material means by which ideas are produced and disseminated.[26] For heuristic purposes, Figure 5.1 shows Marx's socio-economic model, which can be used to explain, in a concrete way, a society.

The notion of *mode of production* is not fully defined by Marx, but it conceptualizes the totality and richness of a society comprising both productive forces and relations of production and also its superstructure at each historical epoch. Thus, the pre-capitalist feudal mode of production subordinates ancient forms of production, such as the use of slaves, and the capitalist mode of production subordinates feudal forms of production, such as domestic handcraft workers, to the logic of factory production.

FIGURE 5.1 Conceptual Schema of Marx's Triadic Model of Industrial Capitalism

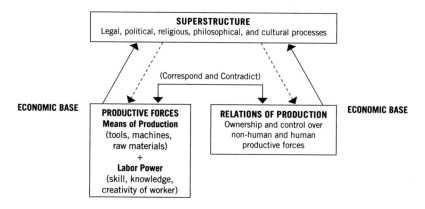

Stages of Historical Development

Like Saint-Simon and Comte in the early nineteenth century, Marx viewed human history as passing through stages of development. These various stages of social forms serve to test Marx's general theory. As Marx explains it, a particular system of forces and relations of production and a class system that develops on the basis of these relationships define different types of society. In *The German Ideology*, five social forms are described: tribal (*Stammeigentum*) or primitive communism, ancient communal, feudalism, capitalism, and communism. The pre-capitalist modes of production were conservative and underdeveloped because of low labor productivity. The first pre-capitalist mode of production is *tribal*, which describes a rudimentary system of social organization in which people live together principally by "hunting and fishing, by the rearing of beasts or, in the highest stage, agriculture.... The division of labour is at this stage still very elementary,"[27] and the social structure is limited to the family or kinship groups of "patriarchal family chieftains, below them the members of the tribe, finally slaves."[28] Property is communal, and, therefore, there is no developed system of class relations. Tribalism did embody a degree of gender equality among non-slaves.[29]

The *ancient* mode of production, such as existed in ancient Rome and Greece, describes a form of society in which tribes create cities and develop complex civil structures. This form "proceeds especially from the union of several tribes into a city by agreement or by conquest, and ... is still accompanied by slavery. Beside communal ownership we already find ... private property developing."[30] Productive forces are based on agriculture and rudimentary industry, with more division of labor. The social structure begins to change too. In particular, a system of class relations develops, and the "antagonism of town and country" intensifies.[31] Marx devotes relatively little time to analyzing pre-capitalist tribal and ancient societies, but he suggests that the construction of irrigation networks and the emergence of a central bureaucracy are examples of the primacy of the productive forces.

The *feudal* mode of production is still predominantly agricultural and community based, but "the directly producing class standing against it is not the slaves, but the enserfed small peasantry."[32] Whereas slaves were at the disposal of their owner, serfs had the right to life and access to common land. The feudal or "petty" mode of production was based on subsistence agriculture, with simple commodity production undertaken by a multiplicity of small capitalists and traditional, skilled guild masters and artisans. Extensive rules governed the making and selling of commodities under the early craft guilds. In terms of relations of production, there was little differentiation between master and journeyman. One historian,

For Marx, different social forms throughout the centuries are to be explained by a changing complex interplay of productive and other material factors and the social and ideological spheres of society.

describing the position of the journeyman to his master, goes so far as to state that it was "rather that of a companion-worker than a hired servant."[33] A distinctive social structure developed with "the differentiation of princes, nobility, clergy and peasants in the country, and masters, journeymen, apprentices and soon also the rabble of casual labourers in the towns."[34] The feudal legal system defined the ownership and privileges of the landowning aristocratic class. The accumulated wealth of the town-based bourgeois class intensified the conflicts between rural and town interests. Marx notes, "As soon as feudalism is fully developed, there also arises antagonism to the towns."[35]

The *capitalist* mode of production, with its antecedents in the development of a market-oriented economy, population growth, and improved domestic agricultural techniques, became historically significant after the rise of the urban bourgeoisie and the decline of feudalism. In volume one of *Capital*, Marx explains the emergence of industrial capitalism by identifying the fettering of the productive forces by feudal relations of production:

> This [feudal] mode of production presupposes parcelling of the soil, and scattering of the other means of production. As it excludes the concentration of these means of production, so also it excludes cooperation, division of labour within each separate process of production, the control over, and the productive application of the forces of Nature by society, and the free development of the social productive powers. It is compatible only with a system of production, and a society, moving within narrow and more or less primitive bounds.... At a certain stage of development it brings forth the material agencies for its own dissolution. From that moment new forces and new passions spring up in the bosom of society; but the old social organization fetters them and keeps them down. It must be annihilated; it is annihilated.[36]

This passage illustrates the complexity of Marx's dialectic process. Although Marx insists on the central role played by the economic in history, the passage suggests that the claim that social change for Marx is determined by the economic alone is a gross oversimplification. A highly complex and technical division of labor and the relation between formally free wage labor and private capital defines *industrial capitalism*. The transition to a large-scale mode of production also saw the development of new relations of production and modes of life. Seen in relation to the alienation process, Gareth Stedman Jones observes "the worker as its victim stands from the outset in a relation of rebellion towards it and perceives it as a process of enslavement."[37] The new workforce consisted of landless workers for whom selling their labor power was their sole source of subsistence, and the capitalists extracted a surplus of production through dominance of the wage nexus.

For members of the new urban bourgeoisie, with their own economic interests, the feudal system was archaic and socially rigid. The politically decisive urban bourgeoisie abolished the privileges of the rural aristocracy, enacted parliamentary legislation, and created a legal system that reflected bourgeois power and suited the needs of a complex industrial society consisting of private ownership and geared toward the needs of the market. Wage legislation and welfare reforms—e.g., the Poor Law Act of 1834—forced long working hours and discipline on the working poor. There were also ideological changes. The triumph of Enlightenment thinking encouraged a moral individualism that stressed individual choice, responsibility, and a strong work ethic. Thus, under capitalism, the forces and relations of production changed, as did the forms of consciousness, which were part of the superstructure. The three main elements of the totality, as depicted in Figure 5.1, are in harmony again.

For Marx, capitalism is the last antagonistic society. The system's inherent contradictions become the driving force for its replacement by the communist mode of production. In Marx's words, "Communism is the position as the negation of the negation, and is hence the *actual* phase necessary for the next stage of historical development in the process of human emancipation and recovery."[38] Under communism, there is no alienation because, writes Marx, "society regulates the production and thus human labour is fulfilling, free from coercion, and will correspond to humans' nature."[39] Thus "socialized production" makes it possible for humans to work and produce as artists would, allowing their creative powers to be expressed.

Marx's Theory of Social Change

Marx's conception of history seeks to explain the underlying motive force in social change. He devotes little time to explaining the process of change in pre-capitalist societies, focusing instead on the transition from feudalism to capitalism in Western Europe. Marx identifies two fundamental drivers of social change. Social change is driven, first, by contradictions between the forces and relations of production and, second, by class antagonisms. Marx offers a highly complex account of his first position. A standard reading of the 1859 preface, mentioned earlier, and of the historical chapters of the first volume of *Capital* is that, at the initial stage of each mode of production, productive forces develop rapidly in society. The relations of production help this process of development as they complement, or *correspond* to, the productive force. Over time, the two reciprocally dependent forces and relations of production come into conflict, or *contradiction*, and turn into "fetters" on human progress. Marx explains his theory of social change like this:

> At a certain stage of their development, the material productive forces of society come in conflict with the existing relations of production, or—what is but a legal expression for the same

thing—with the property relations within which they have been at work hitherto. From forms of development of the productive forces these relations turn into their fetters. Then begins an epoch of social revolution. With the change of the economic foundation the entire immense superstructure is more or less rapidly transformed. In considering such transformations a distinction should always be made between the material transformation of the economic conditions of production, which can be determined with the precision of natural science, and the legal, political, religious, aesthetic or philosophic—in short, ideological forms in which men become conscious of this conflict and fight it out.[40]

The first two sentences of this canonical passage introduce the notion of *fettering*, which has been interpreted two ways. The passage can be read as stating that, by fettering relations of production, all further improvement in productive forces is prevented; this is the *absolute* conception of fettering. Alternatively, fettering can be conceived of as occurring when existing relations of production are suboptimal for the further development of productive forces; this is referred to as the *relative* conception of fettering. At the core of historical materialism is the notion that the system of production of a given society will eventually exhaust its creative and productive potential.[41] Marx also suggests—in the third sentence in the passage—that social revolution installs productively superior relations of production. However, an epoch of social revolution cannot be successful unless it follows from a real change in the economic base, as Marx argues in his preface to *A Contribution to the Critique of Political Economy*: "No social order ever perishes before all the productive forces for which there is room in it have developed; and the new, higher relations of production never appear before the material conditions of their existence have matured in the womb of the old society itself."[42] This text, when taken literally, supports the absolute conception of fettering whereby a social revolution occurs when, and only when, obsolete relations of production fetter all further improvements in the productive forces of society.[43]

There are several problems with this theory. One obvious problem is its determinism. The trajectory of human history unfolds by an inevitable internal inanimate logic. There is a single "driver" of history—productive forces—and these falter, convulse, and throw up different social structures as they march on. Thus, it is not people who make their own history; it is the productive forces, which have a life of their own.[44]

Marx himself offered an alternative doctrine to his own productive-force determinism. In this alternative approach, Marx gives primacy to social relations of production and argues that each form of social production has its own laws of development.[45] The primacy of social relations of production is repeatedly emphasized in Marx's work when he refers to class relations as the "foundation" or the "basis" of a society. Thus, Marx claims, "direct forced labour is the *foundation* of the Ancient world." Similarly, referring to feudal society, he writes that land-tied peasant labor was "the *basis* of the world of the middle ages" and, referring to capitalism, that the separation of the worker from the means of production and wage labor was "the *basis* for capitalist production."

In this alternative interpretation of Marx's historical theory, human agency—the possession of power and a capacity for collective action[46] in the shape of social relations and class struggle—is the primary driver of historical change. In each stage of development, a particular antagonistic class is responsible for the transformation from one mode of production to another. Feudalism was superseded by capitalism not because the latter could promote productive forces more efficiently but because feudalism created the conditions in which feudal social relations were gradually ousted by capitalist ones. The textual evidence shows Marx to have believed that, in the feudal mode of production, the urban bourgeoisie was responsible for ousting feudal social relations. Citing the late Eric Hobsbawm, Mike Davis points out that it was the French bourgeois revolution against feudalism from which Marx "derived the idea of the class struggle in history."[47] In capitalist society, by contrast, it was the proletariat that would overthrow capitalist social relations. The process of these developments, as Marx states in the 1859 preface, is that "men become conscious of this conflict and fight it out."[48] And the *Communist Manifesto*, which shows Marx and Engels as joint authors but was penned by Marx alone, also supports the idea that human agency drives change:

> The history of all hitherto existing society is the history of class struggles. Freeman and slave, patrician and plebeian, lord and serf, guild-master and journeyman, in a word, oppressor and oppressed, stood in constant opposition to one another, carried on an uninterrupted, now hidden, now open fight, a fight that each time ended, either in a revolutionary reconstitution of society at large, or in the common ruin of the contending classes.[49]

In the previous quotation, Marx posits that, in all societies, the most distinctive form of social stratification involves class divisions. This universal feature is viewed in the economic terms of both those who own property and live off the labor of others and those who do productive labor. Hegel's master and slave dialectic, with its inherent contradictions and antagonisms, finds resonance here in Marx's analyses of classes. Just as for Hegel, who described master and slave defining and implicating each other, for Marx, the capitalist and proletariat define each other by the *relation* of each to the means of production. Under capitalism, historical change arises from the antagonistic relations between two opposing class interests, those of the bourgeoisie and those of the proletariat: "The bourgeois relations of production are the last antagonistic form of the social process of production—antagonistic not in the sense of individual antagonism, but of one arising from the social conditions of life of the individuals; at the same time the productive forces developing in the womb of the bourgeois society create the material conditions for the solution of that antagonism. This social formation brings, therefore, the prehistory of human society to a close."[50]

For Marx, classes are change agents, but the precise dynamics of how society is transformed through *class struggles* is ambiguous, and there is a tension in Marx's thought on the primacy of the productive forces to which he was committed by his general theory. For example, pre-capitalist societies did experience class struggle; there were slave rebellions in the ancient world and serf riots in the medieval, feudal period. But action by *oppressed* slaves did not cause the collapse of ancient society. Similarly, in feudal England, the antagonistic classes were not "lord and serf" but the rural aristocracy and the urban bourgeoisie. The serfs, the oppressed class, were rather marginal historical actors in the transformation process. Historical change occurred because feudalism imposed fetters on the further development of the economic system, and the merchant capitalists, not the serfs, were the revolutionary class who dismantled the fetters of the obsolete guilds and caused the demise of feudalism.

Did Marx believe that acute class struggles inevitably generate historical change? There is certainly textual evidence in his writings that support such an interpretation. Thus, describing the social revolution that transformed feudalism into capitalism, Marx declares, "The weapons with which the bourgeoisie felled feudalism to the ground are now turned against the bourgeoisie itself."[51] Yet there is also textual evidence that Marx did not ascribe to a deterministic conception of historical change. His celebrated statement—"Men make their own history, but they do not make it just as they please; they do not make it under circumstances chosen by themselves, but under circumstances directly found, given and transmitted from the past"[52]—recognizes that human agency is constrained by the structural limits constituted by a given society and that historic change is not the inevitable consequence of these limits. Neither is the human factor the isolated individual of Rousseau's philosophy. The individual is embedded in a particular social context and class.[53] Marx's dual theory identifies structure and human agency as the prime drivers of social change. On the one hand, the tendency for the forces and relations of production to enter into a structural contradiction creates fetters on the productive forces. On the other hand, the class struggle is contingent on an unpredictable composite of economic, political, and social factors.

Social Class

As we have already seen, the guiding thread of Marx's general theory had convinced him that, to understand human history and capitalist modernity, one had to analyze the development of productive forces and the relations of production of different societies. Marx's general theory holds that the internal dynamics of each mode of production predicts that class relations, class conflict, and ideology principally flow from the economic structure. For Marx, class performs an essential role in the dialectic process; men and women, not productive forces, engage in revolution and develop societies when historical circumstances provide them with the motives and opportunities for doing so. His account of class is intended to explain the prevalence and forms of collective action in terms of the *class position* and *common interests* of the people engaged in economic and political conflict.[54] As Mike Davis perceptively observes, Marx and Engels believed mass socialist consciousness would be "a dialectical alloy of the economic and the political; of epic battles over rights as well as over wages and working hours; of bitter local fights and great international causes."[55]

We have two questions: What are classes? How many classes are there? Unfortunately, Marx nowhere offers a systematic analysis of class devoted to the first question, but we know that Marx rejected the theory that class is stratified purely according to income and wealth. He wrote, "The size of one's purse is a purely quantitative distinction, whereby any two individuals of the same class may be incited against one another at will."[56]

As to the second question, in the polemical *Communist Manifesto*, society is characterized as divided into "two great classes," with wholly irreconcilable common interests, and class struggles are expressed purely in bipolar terms as a conflict between the bourgeoisie and the proletariat.[57] A salient point here, one frequently missed, is that the *Manifesto* was crafted primarily as a political document to inspire and energize European labor movements in a specific historical context; it was never intended as a treatise on social class. The beginning of a more complete answer to our second question can be found in *The Eighteenth Brumaire of Louis Bonaparte* (1852), where Marx identifies seven classes: bourgeoisie, petty bourgeoisie, financiers, landlords, free farmers, proletariat, and the lumpenproletariat. In his more academic and historical studies, such as the third volume of *Capital*, Marx states that wage laborers, capitalists, and landowners constitute the "three big classes" of modern capitalist society, but he also mentions "middle and intermediate" classes.[58]

As Marx conceives of classes, they have a dynamic or subjective element: classes *potentially* develop or arise out of the material conditions of a given system of production relations. In the capitalist mode of production, each category of people constituting the capitalists and the proletariat is a *class-in-itself* because each class is defined by its common relationship to the means of production. As in Hegel's master-slave dialectic, however, only when a group of people share the same relationship to the means of production, share a common interest, and act together to discover a consciousness that promotes their common interests do they actually constitute a *class-for-itself*. Thus, class formation might be gauged by the development of social movements and ideologies that promote class interests. Based on these criteria, unsurprisingly, Marx was sometimes hesitant as to whether the proletariat had developed sufficiently to constitute itself as a class, and he observed, "The combination of capital has created for this mass a common situation, common interests. This mass is thus already a class as against capital, but not yet for itself."[59] He also noted impediments: "This organization of the proletarians into a class, and consequently into a political party, is continually being upset again by the competition between the workers themselves."[60]

It is common to read in many introductory sociology texts that Marx advanced a "simple two-class model" of social class. When the textual evidence demonstrates that Marx never articulated such a crude model, how can we explain this common misreading of Marx's ideas on class? In part, it can be explained by the fact that Marx predicts the demise of capitalism through the triumph of class struggle, although he does not offer an unambiguous theory of class itself. Marx's methodology also explains the misreading of his

Marx's account of class is intended to explain the prevalence and forms of collective social conflict in terms of the class position and common interests of the people engaging in it. For Marx, classes perform an essential role in the dialectic process. It is people, not productive forces, that engage in social revolution and develop societies when historical circumstances provide them with the motives and opportunities for doing so.

social theory.[61] Marx isolates the "essential" labor-capital relation to analyze capitalism's specific historical character, much as bourgeois economists use the concept of *ceteris paribus* to freeze all other determinate
factors when isolating the price-quantity relation. Thus, the first volume
of *Capital* operates at a high level of abstraction with its assumption of
a two-class model, while the subsequent two volumes extend and deepen
the analysis by examining "many capitals" and, thus, industrial capitalism as an historical-empirical reality.[62] Marx did not discover classes in
modern society; class structure was well known to historians and political
economists. Marx's innovation was to construct a theory of how class
agency is related to particular historical epochs in the development of
the forces and relations of production in society.[63]

Ideologies

Marx's critique of ideology has been one of his most persuasive ideas.[64]
His theory of ideologies not only explains how people come to hold their
erroneous views about society; it also assigns a positive role to social
theories in the transformation process. He considered that ideologies
are both effect and cause of the reality that they purport to explain.[65]
Marx held that, in all class societies, the dominant class develops and
disseminates a web of social beliefs about how men and women relate
to one another and how society should function, which provides legitimacy for its domination. Marx's treatment of ideology, as found in *The
German Ideology*, is part of his critique of Hegelian idealism. Whereas
Hegel believed that ideas were manifestations of the spirit, Marx believed
that ideas or consciousness cannot have a life independent of practical
activity; they are generated by and embedded in human activity or praxis
like other social relations. This premise is indicated in Figure 5.1 as solid
lines. This is the meaning of the statement "The production of ideas, of
conceptions, of consciousness, is at first directly interwoven with the
material activity and the material intercourse of men, the language of real
life."[66] In this sense, the social circumstances in which productive labor
occurs both condition the perception of the society in which people live
and form the *practical consciousness* of human beings.

Marx and Engels caution that ideologies are a distortion and have the
effect of inverting human perceptions of social reality: "In all ideology men
and their circumstances appear upside down as a *camera obscura*."[67] The
claim here is that ideas are like badly prescribed lenses; while allowing a
person to view material conditions, they distort or obscure social reality.
As an example, Marx and Engels posit that the liberal ideology of the
French and American revolutionaries, proclaiming the rights of man and

equality, cannot be taken at face value and that political and legal freedoms are not eternal truths about humanity. Thus, the bourgeois ideology
could only be understood with respect to the social relations of production
in which it was embedded, that is, the pressing need of the bourgeoisie
to end feudal controls and for unfettered competition in economic life.

Marx's treatment of ideology also emphasizes that ideas do not evolve
in a social vacuum; they do so as part of the consciousness of human
beings living a particular mode of life, and, historically, they are propa-
gated to serve a given class. In this way, Marx's theorem focuses on the
connection between human consciousness, or thought, and praxis, or
labor, which differentiates his view from Hegelian philosophy. In all class
societies, the purpose of the creation and dissemination of ideas is to justify the rule of the dominant class over another class. In the words of Marx
and Engels, "The ideas of the ruling class are in every epoch the ruling
ideas: i.e., the class which is the ruling *material* force in society is, at the
same time, its ruling *intellectual* force."[68] The class that controls the means
of production also controls the means of ideological production and the
dissemination of ideas. For example, the bourgeois economic theory of
free trade is the principal ideology scaffolding capitalist globalization.

Marx's generalization that the dominant ideas of any epoch are the ideas
of the dominant class underscores the connection between the ideological
superstructure and the forces and relations of production in a given society. The acceptance of the role of class domination arguably accounts for
subordinate classes not recognizing their capacity to change society because
of ideologies that obscure injustice and inequality, but which fallaciously
appear to be natural. Marx did not use the term *false consciousness*, a term
used to explain the proletariat's general lack of interest in social revolution,
but he may have implied it.[69] Although some Marxist thinkers interpret
Marx's conception of history as *closed*, whereby ideas are of secondary
importance in the understanding of social change, others have convincingly reconstituted Marx's theory as an *open* theoretical perspective—an
interpretation that emphasizes the relative autonomy of social factors and
underscores the role of human consciousness in the shaping of history.[70]
Marx's theory of ideology is complex and controversial, but it allows
sociologists to explore the nexus among economics and culture and ideas.

Criticism

Marx's general theory provokes a cacophony of criticisms, raising issues
that are complex and not easily settled.[71] The first critique relates to
Marx's materialist account of human nature, which is predicated on a
universal human being engaged in "creative" labor. Marx's ideal has been

criticized both for being too materialistic and for being utopian—requiring an impossibly total development of the individual when an extensive division of labor is necessary to meet the ever-demanding and sophisticated needs of people.[72] Under communism, labor is free of alienation because, declares Marx, "society regulates the general production and thus makes it possible for me to do one thing today and another tomorrow, to hunt in the morning, fish in the afternoon, rear cattle in the evening, criticize after dinner, just as I have a mind, without ever becoming hunter, fisherman, shepherd or critic."[73] The question of who would collect the garbage, clean the toilets, or unblock the sewers was neither asked nor answered. Once asked who would polish shoes in a communist regime, Marx retorted, "You should." Critics rightly point to the adoption of a dehumanizing division of labor, embodied as Taylorism, in the failed Soviet Union and the Republic of China.[74] Against this criticism, it is argued that twentieth-century examples of socialized production deviate widely from what Marx envisioned and that his views on alienated free labor applied only when "world-historical" communism replaced capitalism.

Critics accuse Marx of *historical* determinism, of conceptualizing history as being causally determined by factors entirely outside human control. There is certainly evidence of this, for example, in the first volume of *Capital*, when Marx discusses social antagonism and makes reference to "*natural* laws of capitalist production ... working with iron necessity towards *inevitable* results" [emphasis added].[75] Some of the most trenchant criticism of Marx's historical theory has concentrated on its first premise, that the level of development of the productive forces will determine the nature of its social form. Critics accuse Marx of either *economic* or *technological* determinism. There is textual evidence that supports the view of Marx as technological determinist. An example is a frequently cited passage written by Marx in *The Poverty of Philosophy* (1847): "The hand-mill gives you society with the feudal lord, the steam-mill gives you society with the industrial capitalist."[76] However, others argue against this criticism, saying it is a simple-minded misinterpretation of Marx[77] that not only interprets the passage literally and in isolation, but also ignores his more thoughtful treatment of technology, as written 20 years later in the first volume of *Capital*. Marx writes: "Relics of bygone instruments of labour possess the same importance for the investigation of extinct economic forms of society, as do fossil bones for the determination of extinct species of animals.... [They] not only supply a standard of the degree of development to which human labour has attained, but they are also indicators of the social conditions under which that labour is carried on."[78] Here Marx understands that technology on its own—similar to a fossil excavated by archaeologists—allows only limited inferences to be made about the nature of society: it is not determinative. The level of technological development is a necessary but insufficient condition for the emergence of certain types of society.[79]

As we have seen, Marx himself offered an alternative to his own technological determinism, an alternative that emphasizes the primacy of class relations and class action. This alternative reading of Marx emphasizes the countless references in the texts to the idea that technology can never be separated from the economic, political, and social milieu in which it is embedded. The essence of Marx's dialectic thesis is the unity of the subjective and objective factors that are present throughout human history[80]: "Men make their own history."[81] Moreover, the view that human history is contingent on technology not only contradicts everyday experience but also is profoundly at variance with one of Marx's principal aims—to educate and politicize the proletariat. However, in *Old Gods, New Enigmas*, a systematic account of contemporary working class politics, Mike Davis argues that there is "an unprecedented crisis of proletarianization" as robots and the next generation of artificial intelligence systems displace labor, and "we can no longer rely on a single paradigmatic society or class to model the critical vectors of historical development."[82]

Although there are alternative readings of Marx's claims for the social primacy of technology or the relations of production,[83] critics agree there is a lacuna concerning gender and race. Insofar as Marx's analysis of capitalist society is a theory of exploitation and oppression, his work is rightly criticized for failing to address gender. Marx's treatment of productive labor conceptually and empirically neglects the way that gender relations, men and masculinity, and, presumably, women and femininity are socially constructed. It is not that Marx and Engels neglected non-class forms of inequality, such as gender. On the contrary, Engels developed a general historical theory of the family. The problem is rather, as feminists have argued, that Marx and Engels tended to present gender relations in class societies as "dominated by" and secondary to property relations.[84] Patriarchy is viewed as secondary and derivative from society's mode of production rather than being presented as an autonomous form of social inequality.[85] A related criticism is that Marx overanalyzes paid, productive work to the detriment of unpaid, domestic work—the sort of work performed mainly or exclusively by women. One feminist interpretation of Marx's failure to theorize female exploitation and oppression is that Marx is but one example of a European man writing about other European men and masculinity.[86] Marxist feminists argue that women's exploitation are symptoms of capitalism. In this view, the family and the gendering of paid labor and *unpaid* domestic labor are fundamentally shaped by the needs of the new industrial paradigm, and, concomitantly, the family is the site of women's oppression.[87]

Finally, as a general theory of history, his paradigmatic model is criticized for marginalizing race and slavery. Although Marx found slavery abhorrent—"The slave only works swayed by fear"[88]—critics rightly argue that he neglected the racial character of capitalism and how racial capitalist exploitation was produced by cultural ideologies. Critics argue that, driven by the need to achieve the scientific elegance demanded by theory, Marx recessed race and slavery from his discourse on human emancipation. In *Capital*, slavery is seen as the residue of a pre-capitalist mode of production—a view that disqualified slaves from historical and revolutionary agency in the era of modernity.[89]

Conclusion

Marx believed that the mode of production of material life is central to social life. Bill Clinton's 1992 campaign slogan, "It's the economy, stupid," is an excellent summing up of Marx's argument that material forces profoundly affect social, political, and intellectual life processes far beyond the workplace. For Marx, different social forms throughout the centuries are to be explained by a changing, complex interplay of the productive factors and the social and ideological spheres of society. Society is not a stable constellation of essential factors but a socially constituted structure with interconnected, contradictory tendencies and movements. Certain laws characterize human history, but it is people who ultimately build a society through purposive social activity, or *praxis*, and change it. Marx argued that class-consciousness—not the unifying self-consciousness of Hegel's dialectic—and class struggle stimulate change and social revolution. But there is nothing inevitable about progressing to a higher form of society. Marx's conception of history provides a series of interrelated structural concepts through which to interpret the development of the past and to expose contradictory social phenomena in the present.

In the twenty-first century, when grand narratives are considered passé,[90] what contribution can Marx's theory of history make to contemporary social theory? First, his theory has taught sociologists to see the current society we inhabit in historical terms. The notion of the "sociological imagination" requires us to develop a historical consciousness, that is, to relate personal biographies and troubles to the broad sweep of human history. As the eminent American sociologist C. Wright Mills (1916–62) declared,

> men do not usually define the troubles they endure in terms of historical change and institutional contradiction. The well-being they enjoy, they do not usually impute to the big ups and downs of the societies in which they live. Seldom aware of the intricate connection between the patterns of their own lives and the course

of world history, ordinary men do not usually know what this connection means for the kinds of men they are becoming and for the kinds of history-making in which they might take part.[91]

In addition, Marx's ideas about alienated labor under capitalism are extraordinarily rich and remain central to the contemporary study of work in the postmodern "new economy."[92]

The *Communist Manifesto* has been described as "without doubt the single most influential text written in the nineteenth century."[93] The text had a powerful effect on the thinking of many classical social theorists. In North America, its influence on W.E.B. Du Bois is obvious in his call to pan-African socialists: "You have nothing to lose but your Chains! You have a continent to regain!"[94] Its legacy is reflected also in *The Regina Manifesto*, adopted at the founding convention of the Canadian Co-operative Commonwealth Federation on July 20, 1933, which calls for extensive public ownership of the means of production, including all banks, communications companies, mining, and gasoline industries, and for the extension of rights for racial and religious minorities but, regrettably, not for women.[95]

Class is at the heart of Marx's concept of history. Marx rightly denied that he and Engels invented the concept of class or the notion of class struggle. What *is* unique about their contribution is that it links a theory of social class to the mode of production and provides an analysis of and an avenue toward the radical transformation of social life. Marx foresaw a steep increase in white-collar work and a decline of the working class— a remarkable achievement for a social theorist whose ideas are supposed to be archaic. Further, class remains deep in the European social psyche. And Marx's ideas still continue to provide a skeletal framework for most UK and European studies of class-based inequalities.[96] One hundred and fifty-two years after the publication of *Capital*, in every aspect of everyday life—income security, housing, quality of education, quality of health, and death rates—*class matters*. Indeed, in Europe and the United States, the observation made before the 2008 economic crisis—that "class has come to play a greater, not lesser role in important ways"[97]—has much greater significance in our current "age of austerity."

Other ideas and texts produced or elaborated by Marx remain relevant today. What is truly astonishing about *The German Ideology*, for example, is that, after more than 170 years, Marx and Engels's theory of ideology is still highly relevant in contemporary social and political theory, particularly within studies of the relationships between the realm of ideas and those of economics. Canadian writer Naomi Klein, in *The Shock Doctrine*, illustrates how the ideology of US neoliberalism serves the property-owning class. Describing the ascendancy of the ideology since the 1990s, Klein writes: "Free markets and free people have been packaged as a single ideology that claims to be humanity's best and only defense against repeating a history filled with mass graves, killing fields and torture chambers."[98] Klein describes how the business-owning class in Chile and Argentina, supported by the military elite, systematically "cleansed" society of people who believed in competing ideologies, in other words, those who believed in something other than laissez-faire capitalism and "pure profit."

In this post-Trump, post-Brexit age, Marx and Engels's base and superstructure metaphor is also compelling in understanding the prevailing consensus among the political elite. In this regard, a point from *The German Ideology* has particular resonance: "The ideas of the ruling class are in every epoch the ruling ideas." And what are the ruling ideas of our epoch? The dominant social idea is neoliberalism. The idea that privatization, deregulation, tax cuts for corporations and the wealthy, and the withdrawal of the state from welfare provision in favor of the private sector is the best way to govern society.[99] Post-2008, the richest 0.1 percent earners lobby politicians to ensure that corporate business is not hampered by "wealth-destroying" regulation and that taxes remain low. Lobbying politicians takes on a global dimension when it occurs at the annual World Economic Forum held in Davos, Switzerland. This forum's notional purpose is to allow corporate executives to debate the world economy. However, its real business takes place in private sessions with corporate peers and "amenable politicians.[100] The "Davos effect" provides context to this argument: "The bigger the share of income the rich enjoy ... the more power they have to enact policies in their own interests—and the more they do so."[101] Finally, a historical perspective reminds us that, as a form of social life, capitalism is relatively new, and it is plausible to assume, as social inequality relapses to nineteenth-century levels, that a long-term alternative to capitalist globalization will develop.

FURTHER THINKING:

Why did Marx believe that the mode of production of material life is central to social life? Is Marx's theory of ideologies useful for understanding politics today?

FURTHER READING:

For a contemporary assessment of Marx's ideas on class see Jason Barker, "Happy Birthday, Karl Marx. You Were Right!", *New York Times*, April 30, 2018, https://mobile.nytimes.com/2018/04/30/opinion/karl -marx-at-200-influence.html. Mike Savage also provides an in-depth account of why class matters in *Social Class in the 21st Century* (London: Pelican, 2015). The Canadian writer Naomi Klein provides a fascinating account of how contemporary Anglo-Saxon neoliberalism works and the role of ideology in *The Shock Doctrine* (Toronto: Knopf, 2007). See especially chapter 2, "The Other Doctor Shock: Milton Friedman and the Search for a Laissez-Faire Laboratory" (pp. 56–83). On how technological change is impacting proletarian agency, see Mike Davis, *Old Gods, New Enigmas* (London: Verso, 2018), chapter 1.

Notes

1　Quoted in the *New York Times*, November 26, 2006, and by Andrew Sayer, *Why We Can't Afford the Rich* (Bristol: Polity Press, 2016), 1.

2　Naomi Eisenstadt, an independent advisor to the Scottish Government, cited by Kathleen Nutt, "Class 'Still Dictates Children's Futures,'" *The National*, July 4, 2017, 4.

3　Jason Barker, "Happy Birthday, Karl Marx. You Were Right!", *New York Times*, April 30, 2018, https://mobile.nytimes.com/2018/04/30/opinion/karl-marx-at -200-influence.html (accessed May 17, 2018).

4　Friedrich Engels, "Speech at the Graveside of Karl Marx," in *The Marx-Engels Reader*, 2nd ed., ed. Robert C. Tucker (New York: Norton, 1972), 681.

5　Quoted in David McLellan, *Ideology* (Minneapolis: University of Minnesota Press, 1995), 10.

6　Peter Berger and Brigitte Berger, *Sociology: A Biographical Approach* (London: Penguin, 1976), 40.

7　E. Rosenfeld, "Social Stratification in a 'Classless' Society," *American Sociological Review* 16, no. 6 (1951): 766–74.

8　See Graeme Salaman, "The New Corporate Leadership," in *Leadership in Organizations*, ed. John Story (London: Routledge, 2016), 55; Editorial, "The Stamp of Ideology," *The Guardian*, May 7, 2013, 28.

9　Tucker, *Marx-Engels Reader*, 344–45.

10　Jon Elster, *An Introduction to Karl Marx* (Cambridge: Cambridge University Press, 1986), 41.

11　Tucker, *Marx-Engels Reader*, 430.

12　Tucker, *Marx-Engels Reader*, 71–77.

13　Jonathon Wolff, *Why Read Marx Today?* (Oxford: Oxford University Press, 2002), 32.

14　Tucker, *Marx-Engels Reader*, 479.

15　Tucker, *Marx-Engels Reader*, 74.

16　Tucker, *Marx-Engels Reader*, 76.

17　Quoted in Keith Grint, *The Sociology of Work*, 2nd ed. (Cambridge: Polity Press, 1998), 1.

18　Grint, *The Sociology of Work*, 78.

19　See Paul Du Gay, *Consumption and Identity at Work* (London: Sage, 1996).

20　Tucker, *Marx-Engels Reader*, 4.

21 Jon Elster, *Making Sense of Marx* (Cambridge: Cambridge University Press, 1985), 243–53.

22 Elster, *Making Sense of Marx*, 254.

23 Tucker, *Marx-Engels Reader*, 4.

24 Quoted in Peter Millican, "Introduction," in *An Enquiry Concerning Human Understanding*, by David Hume (Oxford: Oxford University Press, 2007), xlii.

25 S. H. Rigby, *Marxism and History* (Manchester: Manchester University Press, 1998), 178.

26 See Terry Eagleton, *Why Marx Was Right* (New Haven, CT: Yale University Press, 2011), a work we have drawn upon here.

27 Tucker, *Marx-Engels Reader*, 151.

28 Tucker, *Marx-Engels Reader*, 151.

29 See Friedrich Engels, "Origins of Family Property and the State," in *The Marx-Engels Reader*, ed. Tucker, 734–59.

30 Tucker, *Marx-Engels Reader*, 151.

31 Tucker, *Marx-Engels Reader*, 151.

32 Tucker, *Marx-Engels Reader*, 153.

33 Maurice Dobb, *Studies in the Development of Capitalism* (London: Routledge, 1963), 85.

34 Tucker, *Marx-Engels Reader*, 153.

35 Tucker, *Marx-Engels Reader*, 153.

36 Tucker, *Marx-Engels Reader*, 437.

37 Gareth Stedman Jones, *Karl Marx* (London: Penguin, 2017), 414.

38 Tucker, *Marx-Engels Reader*, 93.

39 Tucker, *Marx-Engels Reader*, 160.

40 Tucker, *Marx-Engels Reader*, 4–5.

41 See Gerald A. Cohen, *Karl Marx's Theory of History* (Princeton, NJ: Princeton University Press, 2000), 326–40; Jon Elster, *Making Sense of Marx*, 258–67.

42 Tucker, *Marx-Engels Reader*, 5.

43 Cohen, *Karl Marx's Theory of History*.

44 Salvador Allende, as quoted in Naomi Klein, *The Shock Doctrine* (Toronto: Alfred A. Knopf, 2007), 122.

45 See Rigby, *Marxism and History*, chap. 8, 143–74, which we have drawn upon and quoted from here.

46 See Mike Davis, *Old Gods, New Enigmas* (London: Verso, 2018), 8.

47 Davis, *Old Gods, New Enigmas*, 9.

48 Tucker, *Marx-Engels Reader*, 5.

49 Tucker, *Marx-Engels Reader*, 473–74.

50 Tucker, *Marx-Engels Reader*, 5.

51 Tucker, *Marx-Engels Reader*, 478.

52 Tucker, *Marx-Engels Reader*, 595.

53 Alex Callinicos, *Social Theory: A Historical Introduction*, 2nd ed. (Cambridge: Polity Press, 207), 92–99.

54 See Allen W. Wood, *Karl Marx*, 2nd ed. (New York: Routledge, 2004), 82–100.

55 Davis, *Old Gods, New Enigmas*, 119.

56 *Deutsche-Brüsseler-Zeitung* (November 18, 1847), quoted in Elster, *Making Sense of Marx*, 336.

57 Tucker, *Marx-Engels Reader*, 474.

58 Tucker, *Marx-Engels Reader*, 441.

59 Tucker, *Marx-Engels Reader*, 218.

60 Tucker, *Marx-Engels Reader*, 481.

61 Alan Swingewood, *Marx and Modern Social Theory* (London: Macmillan, 1975), 47; Alan Swingewood, *A Short History of Sociological Thought* (New York: St. Martin's Press, 2000), 40.

62 Swingewood, *Marx and Modern Social Theory*, 46.

63 David McLellan, *The Thought of Karl Marx* (London: Macmillan, 1980), 182.

64 Elster, *An Introduction to Karl Marx*, 168.

65 Elster, *Making Sense of Marx*, 459.

66 Tucker, *Marx-Engels Reader*, 154.

67 Tucker, *Marx-Engels Reader*, 154.

68 Tucker, *Marx-Engels Reader*, 172.

69 Larry Ray, *Theorizing Classical Sociology* (Buckingham, UK: Open University Press, 1999), 71.

70 Irving M. Zeitlin, *Ideology and the Development of Sociological Theory*, 7th ed. (Upper Saddle River, NJ: Prentice Hall, 2001).

71 Wood, *Karl Marx*.

72 See Cohen, *Karl Marx's Theory of History*; C. Tausky, "Work Is Desirable/ Loathsome: Marx versus Freud," *Work and Occupations* 19, no. 1 (1992): 3–17.

73 Tucker, *Marx-Engels Reader*, 160.

74 Craig R. Littler, *The Development of the Labour Process in Capitalist Societies* (London: Heinemann, 1982).

75 Tucker, *Marx-Engels Reader*, 296.

76 Karl Marx, *The Poverty of Philosophy* (1847), in *Karl Marx: Selected Writings*, 2nd ed., ed. David McLellan (Oxford: Oxford University Press, 2000), 219–20.

77 See Wood, *Karl Marx*, chap. 5.

78 Tucker, *Marx-Engels Reader*, 346.

79 Zeitlin, *Ideology and the Development of Sociological Theory*, 161.

80 McLellan, *The Thought of Karl Marx*, 137.

81 Tucker, *Marx-Engels Reader*, 595.

82 Davis, *Old Gods, New Enigmas*, 7.

83 Debate among philosophers and historians on the alternative readings of Marx's theory of history has produced much scholarship. Readers are directed to Cohen, *Karl Marx's Theory of History*, and Rigby's text *Marxism and History* as examples of the divergence between the two schools of thought.

84 Friedrich Engels, "The Origin of the Family, Private Property, and the State," in Tucker, *Marx-Engels Reader*, 734–59.

85 Rigby, *Marxism and History*, ix.

86 See Susan Himmelweit, "Reproduction and the Materialist Conception of History: A Feminist Critique," in *The Cambridge Companion to Marx*, ed. Terrell Carver (New York: Cambridge University Press, 1991), 196–221; and Jeff Hern, "Gender: Biology, Nature and Capitalism," in *The Cambridge Companion to Marx*, ed. Terrell Carver, 222–45.

87 See R. A. Sydie, *Natural Women, Cultured Men* (Vancouver: University of British Columbia Press, 1994), 104–21.

88 Karl Marx's *Capital*, in *Karl Marx: Selected Writings*, 512, and cited in Cedric J. Robinson, *Black Marxism* (Chapel Hill: University of North Carolina Press, 2000), xxix.

89 Cedric J. Robinson argues that Eurocentrism limits Marx's historical materialism as does the significant influence of Aristotle's view that slavery was necessary for the self-sufficiency of the *polis*. See Robinson, *Black Marxism*, xxix.

90 See, for example, David Harvey, *The Condition of Postmodernity* (Oxford: Blackwell, 1990).

91 C. Wright Mills, *The Sociological Imagination* (New York: Oxford University Press, 2000), 3–4.

92 James W. Rinehart, *The Tyranny of Work: Alienation and the Labour Process* (Toronto: Thomson-Nelson, 2006).

93 Peter Osborne, quoted in *The Communist Manifesto Now: Socialist Register*, ed. Leo Panitch and Colin Leys (New York, 1998), 190, and cited in Eagleton, *Why Marx Was Right*, x.

94 W.E.B. Du Bois, *The Autobiography of W.E.B. Du Bois: A Soliloquy on Viewing My Life from the Last Decade of Its First Century* (New York: International Publishers, 1968), 404.

95 See Gerald Caplan, "A Faith to Love, Free of Utopias," *The Globe and Mail*, July 19, 2008, A15.

96 Anthony Giddens, *Sociology* (Cambridge: Polity Press, 2009).

97 Janny Scott and David Leonhardt, "Class in America: Shadowy Lines that Still Divide," *The New York Times*, Sunday, May 15, 2005, 1; quoted by Lynn S. Chancer and Beverly Xaviera Watkins, *Gender, Race, and Class* (Malden, MA: Blackwell, 2006), 79.

98 Klein, *The Shock Doctrine*, 121.

99 David Harvey, *A Brief History of Neoliberalism* (Oxford: Oxford University Press, 2005).

100 Aditya Chakrabortty, "In an Alpine Hamlet in Switzerland, Where the Rich Plot to Get Even Richer," *The Guardian*, January 22, 2013, S5.

101 Linda McQuaig and Neil Brooks, *The Trouble with Billionaires* (Toronto: Penguin, 2011), 226.

6. Karl Marx:
Economics of Capitalism

Marx viewed capitalism as a monstrous form of existence. It was the most promiscuous regime known to human history, boundless and malformed, a freakish medley of different forms and a stranger to all measure or proportion.

—Terry Eagleton, 2018[1]

Much of what Marx said seems to become more relevant by the day.

—*The Economist*, 2017[2]

MARX'S ECONOMIC THEORIES, in contrast to mainstream orthodox economics, cannot be separated from his philosophy, history, or sociology, particularly in that his economic theory is concerned with social relations, social structure, and agency rather than with the technical relations between commodities and prices. Consequently, Marx's economic writings are deeply textured and profoundly sociological. Marx's critique of the economics of capitalist society is found in various works: *Wage Labour and Capital* (1849); *The Grundrisse: Foundations of the Critique of Political Economy* (1857–58), which was not published until 1953; and the three volumes of *Capital* (*Das Kapital*), which constitute the centerpiece of his economic writing. As previously noted, only the first volume of *Capital* (1867) was published in his lifetime, and therefore he had no opportunity to edit the completed work, eliminate inconsistencies and repetitions, and clarify ambiguities.

This chapter focuses in a simple way, at the risk of oversimplification, on Marx's analysis of the nature of capitalism. Its goal is to allow the reader to engage with the original texts and to discover the complexity, the subtlety, and the deeply social nature of Marx's economics. First we examine commodity production and Marx's notion of commodity fetishism. From this, it is a rational next step to examine Marx's development of the Ricardian labor theory of value, and, his most outstanding contribution, the theory of surplus value, which still remains a powerful critique of labor exploitation. Finally, we examine one of the most controversial areas of Marx's economics, his theories of capitalist cyclical crises.

Commodity Production

Marx's economic theory is closely interconnected to his theory of history in that it ultimately aims "to lay bare the economic law of motion of modern society."[3] The discussion in chapter 4 on dialectics and the methodology of unintended consequences apply to Marx's economic theory. For Marx, a scientific economic theory is one that adopts the principle of totality, which involves an understanding of the relations of the most simple to the more complex, the part to the social whole.[4] The principle of totality explains why Marx begins *Capital* with an analysis of a commodity. A commodity is the most basic *part* of the society that must be related to the social *whole*, a totality. Marx's holistic methodology emphasizes the need to investigate the multiple and historically changing inner connections between productive forces and all the other non-economic facets of society.

In any society, people have to *produce* by their own labor things that satisfy their basic needs. In some form or other, they also *distribute* among one another the products of their productive labor. The individual members of the society *consume* the distributed products according to their needs. In *Capital*, Marx explains how these three activities occur in a capitalist society. For Marx, the basic element of a society is a single commodity, and its wealth is "an immense accumulation of commodities." Thus, his economic theory of the capitalist mode of production begins with an analysis of a *commodity*, defined as any "object outside us, a thing that by its properties satisfies human wants of some sort or another."[5] In Marx's theory the term *commoditization* refers to a fundamental feature of capitalist modernity: a highly complex, interdependent system of commodity production for the purpose of exchange through the market, as opposed to production for the direct use by the producer.

Following Adam Smith, Marx states that every commodity has a twofold aspect: its utility or *use value* and its *exchange value*. The use value of a commodity is determined by its capacity to satisfy a human need, which cannot be quantified. Use values are specific, concrete, and ahistorical, in the sense that they exist in all societies. The exchange value of a commodity refers to the value a commodity has when offered in exchange for other commodities. The exchange has to satisfy certain properties, for example, quantity or weight. If x exchanges for y, then x is equivalent in exchange to y. For example, if a dairy farmer produces cheese, by virtue of its natural properties, part will be consumed to satisfy a need. Any surplus may be taken to a market and exchanged either by barter for another product that the farmer cannot produce (e.g., a scythe) or for money. Thus, the commodity (cheese) acquires another feature unrelated to its use value, namely exchange value. Exchange value refers to the way a quantity of one commodity, say a kilo of cheese, can be expressed in terms of another commodity, say a scythe. Every commodity has a use value, but every commodity does not have an exchange value, either because it is something freely available (e.g., air, sunshine) or it is not exchanged (e.g., something produced only for personal consumption).

Although every commodity is characterized by its particular physical or natural properties that give it its use value, the question that Marx addressed is what the determinant of a commodity's exchange value is. This had been a prime object of study by classical economists Adam Smith and David Ricardo. Adam Smith, in *An Inquiry into the Nature and Causes of the Wealth of Nations* (1776), postulates that value is conferred on a commodity by the act of labor. Smith explained it this way:

> Every man is rich or poor according to the degree in which he can afford to enjoy the necessaries, conveniences, and amusements of human life. But after the division of labour has once thoroughly taken place, it is but a very small part of these with which a man's own labour can supply him. The far greater part of them he must derive from the labour of other people, and he must be rich or poor according to the quantity of that labour which he can command, or which he can afford to purchase. The value of any commodity, therefore, is equal to the quantity of labour which it enables him to purchase or command. Labour, therefore, is the real measure of the exchangeable value of all commodities.[6]

For both Smith and Ricardo, labor adds value to a commodity. As Mike Davis points out in his astute reading of *Capital*, Marx always acknowledged that the development of the labor theory of value, usually attributed to him, was actually achieved by working class intellectuals such as the Scottish factory worker John Gray, the journalist Thomas Hodgskin, and the American-born printer John Bray.[7] Although Marx's most basic model of capitalist production incorporates both Ricardo's distinction between use value and exchange value and also Smith's labor theory of value, Marx used the economic concepts to draw very different conclusions.

Marx maintains that what creates the relationship of exchange is not a physical property derived from the use value but a historically specific social one; it is the amount of labor time embodied in the commodities of production. Thus, the property that all commodities have in common—the one that creates the relationship of exchange—is that they are the product of labor. Marx next claims that labor, like a commodity, has a dual character depending on whether it produces use value or exchange value. *Concrete labor* is labor of a particular type and purpose that creates use value. *Abstract labor*, on the other hand, creates exchange value based upon the quantity of abstract labor. Under capitalism, labor is, at the same time, both concrete and abstract, and its product is both a use value and an exchange value. Marx believed that his account of the "twofold character of labor" was one of the best points in *Capital*.[8]

Marx's abstract treatment of value does not ignore the importance of demand. Commodities do exchange above their value; the *social necessary labor time* to produce them takes into account both direct (living) labor inputs and indirect (dead) labor inputs: the social necessary labor time to produce machinery and extract raw materials, that is, the means of production. Marx, unlike mainstream economists, recognizes that demand has a class dimension: "supply and demand presuppose the existence of different classes and sections of classes which divide the total revenue of a society and consume it among themselves as revenue, and, therefore, make up the demand created by revenue."[9]

The capitalist mode of production is characterized by the production of social use values, and the exchange of the products of concrete labor is expressed, in exchange, as abstract social necessary labor. If value were determined by actual abstract labor time, it would mean that a commodity produced by a slow and incompetent worker would produce a more valuable commodity than an identical one produced in less time by a conscientious worker. This problem is avoided because of the concept of social necessary labor time, which means the average amount of time and level of skill and effort required for the production of the commodity in a particular industry.

Marx's labor theory of value embodies a social relationship that can be theoretically quantified by calculating the exchange value of a commodity in relation to the total amount of labor time expended to produce the commodity. What characterizes the capitalist mode of production is not just the exchange of commodities but the buying and selling of the worker's capacity to work, which Marx called labor power. For Marx, it is only historic abstract labor power that defines capitalism: "On the one hand all labour is, speaking physiologically, an expenditure of human labour-power, and ... it creates and forms the value of commodities. On the other hand, ... human labour-power [has] ... a definite aim, and ... it produces use-values."[10] Under capitalism, labor power becomes a commodity—the buyer is the capitalist; the seller is the worker. The price of labor power is the wage. As a commodity, labor power must have a use value: therefore, it is the creator of use values in the form of commodities and, as such, embodies abstract labor. In this process, labor power is unique as a commodity because its use value creates specific values in commodity form, and, hence, it is the creator of value for the capitalist. Marx's labor theory of value not only explains commodity production but also embodies the basic relations of production specific to capitalism. The social exchange of labor power is predicated upon the private ownership of the means of production, on the one hand, and the existence of a class of workers selling their labor power, on the other.

Capitalist Exchange Process

Having established that a commodity has a twofold nature—its use value and exchange value—and that the exchange value of a commodity is determined by the amount of labor time necessary for the production of a commodity, Marx provides a lengthy account of the genesis of money in the exchange process and of how money becomes capital. Exchange relationships between commodities predate capitalism, which develops when labor power itself becomes a commodity and money is introduced into the exchange process. Money is the most abstract of commodities. It is a means of payment, a unit of account, and a store of wealth. As a means of payment, it avoids simple bartering and mediates the process of exchange by creating a set of equivalencies among intrinsically different physical commodities (e.g., food, sweatshirts, and fuel) and labor power.

Typically, under capitalism, simple commodity exchange starts with an individual who owns some commodity (e.g., one ton of corn) that needs to be exchanged for another. First, the commodity must be exchanged for money. Marx expressed this step by C–M, where C denotes commodity and M is money. Second, the money received is exchanged for the needed commodity (e.g., fertilizer), expressed as M–C. In order to purchase other commodities, certain commodities are sold for money, which is essentially a use value. This simple exchange process is represented by C–M–C, the circulation of commodities, and is shown in Figure 6.1.

In simple commodity exchange, C denotes the two extremes of the circulation because each is in commodity form and each has the same

FIGURE 6.1 Simple Commodity Exchange: Selling in Order to Buy

C ———————————— M ———————————— C

value; however, they are *not* the same commodity. This simple commodity exchange can also illustrate the sale of the commodity of labor power, which is the wage laborer's only means for the consumption of goods and services. In this case, labor power (C) is exchanged for wages (M) and eventually for wage commodities (C).

Marx had to show how it is possible for the capitalist to make a profit and accumulate capital. A capitalist starts not with labor power but with money. Using money, the capitalist purchases particular types of commodities, raw materials, machinery, and tools—the means of production—and, of course, labor power. A prerequisite for capitalist production is the willingness of workers to exercise their "freedom" of exchange and sell their labor power. Whereas Smith and Ricardo characterize this process as two equal parties pursuing their individual interests, Marx argues that the exchange is fundamentally asymmetrical because the capitalist owns the means of production and labor power is the only commodity that labor is able to sell. The capitalist organizes the productive forces and sells the resulting commodities, or outputs, for money. The capitalist's exchange process is represented by $M–C–M_1$, the general formula for capital shown in Figure 6.2.

FIGURE 6.2 The Capitalist Exchange Paradigm: Buying in Order to Sell Higher

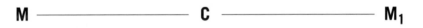

$$M \text{———————} C \text{———————} M_1$$

In contrast to simple commodity exchange, the $M–C–M_1$ circulation begins and ends with money, not commodities. The two extremes (M) are the same (money), but they are *not* of the same value. The industrial capitalist's motive of exchange is to expand value; so the money received at the end of the cycle (M_1) is greater than the money advanced at the start (M). Money used to generate more money (profit) is called *capital*, hence capitalism. The aim of the "circuit of capital" is to act as self-expanding value, that is, profit in the form of money.

Commodity Fetishism

Marx's theory of value calls attention to the social division of labor and the relationships of interdependence underlying commodity production, which are obscured by what he called fetishistic or reified commodities. "A commodity *appears* ... a very trivial thing ... it is, in reality, a very queer thing," writes Marx (emphasis added).[11] Here, Marx juxtaposes commodity production alongside a world of social illusion, a world in which value is thought to exist essentially in commodities—inanimate

Marx identifies positive aspects of technical innovation. New technology, such as the robotic arm, *potentially* frees workers from dehumanizing labor and offers the opportunity for men and women to engage in creative labor, in which they exercise their unique human capacities.

objects—instead of being added through labor. Consumers mistakenly believe that the lifeless commodity, such as an iPhone or a pair of Nudie denim jeans, has social status, while those who produce it are perceived as commodities and are treated as inanimate things.

Marx's notion of commodity fetishism is rooted in his account of alienation in *The Economic and Philosophical Manuscripts of 1844*. Under pre-capitalist modes of production, in the imagination of primitive people, inanimate objects acquire superhuman qualities and become a fetish. Paralleling his critique of religion, Marx writes that capital appears as an object (money) while social relations take on an illusory or fetish form. Whereas in primitive social forms God is the human's own creation, in capitalist modernity people also create market relationships between commodities, concealing exploitative social relations, and this is justified by the doctrine of freedom of exchange. The link between Marx's notion of commodity fetishism and his critique of religious consciousness is made explicit in *Capital*:

> There is a definite social relation between men that assumes, in their eyes, the fantastic form of a relation between things. In order, therefore, to find an analogy, we must have recourse to the mist-enveloped regions of the religious world. In that world the productions of the human brain appear as independent beings endowed with life, and entering into relation both with one another and the human race. So it is in the world of commodities with the

products of men's hands. This I call Fetishism which attaches
itself to the products of labour, so soon as they are produced as
commodities, and which is therefore inseparable from the production of commodities.[12]

Commodity fetishism describes the tendency for consumers and
capitalists alike to display excessive devotion toward material "things,"
to believe that things have an independent existence and are endowed
with extraordinary powers. Indeed, the premise of commodity fetishism is that relations between people have been substituted for relations
between things. By being granted independence as a commodity, in the
sense that it becomes endowed with the powers of human beings, things
appear to exert control, so what happens to people seems to depend upon
the movement of markets and not on the social relations of production
characteristic to capitalism. For example, in the United States after the
credit market meltdown began in August 2007, the loss of a person's life
savings or home was typically blamed on an objective, natural thing—the
credit market—rather than on the deranged logic of market fundamentalism and the imperative of maximizing shareholder value. Over the last
several decades, the effects of market fundamentalism and the so-called
Washington Consensus[13] has resulted in an increase in commodification.
Neoliberal policies of privatization and the hollowing out of government
agencies have had the effect of increasing the number of commodities
acquiring an exchange value, including water supply, pensions, education, health care, and radio and TV airwaves. These events can only be
understood in relation to the needs of capital, which we turn to next.

Theory of Surplus Value and Exploitation

So far, we have focused on Marx's economic analysis of the capitalist
system of commodity production. To understand the development of a
capitalist society, to expose Marx's "economic law of motion," we have
to examine the process of extracting a surplus from labor power. This
is Marx's second great law—referred to by Engels in his "Speech at the
Graveside"—the theory of surplus value. It is the social theory of capitalist production. Importantly, this is the theory that explains the forces that
propel the development of capitalism.

In Figure 6.2, M_1 has a greater value than M. This means that, in the
movement $C-M_1$, extra value has been created. Marx called this extra value
surplus value, the difference between the values of inputs and outputs.
That productive labor creates surplus value is not controversial; what is
contentious, however, is the premise behind Marx's theory that the source
of profit on capital comes from the exploitation of labor. The thesis that

capital exploits labor stems from a presupposition of the labor theory of value—namely, that labor power is the only commodity that produces surplus value. Marx's theory of surplus value explains the long-term future of capitalism. Marx foresaw a relative decline in workers' standard of living, the need for capitalists to transform the production process continually, and the tendency for capitalism as a whole to experience periodic crises.

Marx's theory of surplus value makes distinctions between *constant capital* and *variable capital* and between *necessary labor* and *surplus labor*, and it describes methods to increase surplus value. Constant capital refers to the part of capital that constitutes the means of production and does not, in the process of production, undergo any quantitative change of value. Variable capital, on the other hand, is "that part of capital, represented by labor power, [which] does, in the process of production, undergo an alteration of value. It both reproduces the equivalent of its own value, and it produces an excess, a surplus value, which may itself vary, may be more or less according to the circumstances."[14] The value of labor power is the cost of its purchase, which is the labor time necessary to produce a "real wage," a subsistence basket of commodities (food, shelter, clothing) necessary for its maintenance. The value labor power creates in production is the quantity of labor time exercised in return for that wage. Under capitalism, the contribution made by labor power to the value of output exceeds its cost. In *Wage Labour and Capital*, Marx writes, "The worker receives means of subsistence in exchange for his labour power, but the capitalist receives in exchange for his means of subsistence labour, the productive activity of the worker, the creative power whereby the worker not only replaces what he consumes but *gives to the accumulated labour a greater value than it previously possessed....* [I]t is just this noble reproductive power that the worker surrenders to the capitalist in exchange for the means of subsistence received. He has, therefore, lost it for himself."[15] The system compels the worker to work longer than is sufficient to embody in the product the value of his or her labor power. The rate of surplus value can be quantified by dividing the working day of the wage laborer; it falls into two parts: socially necessary labor time and surplus labor time, as in Figure 6.3.

FIGURE 6.3 The Rate of Surplus Value

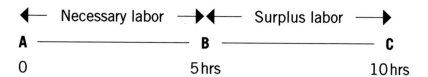

In Figure 6.3, the line A to C represents a working day of ten hours. Suppose a worker works a ten-hour day and that the socially necessary labor time to produce her wage is five hours. During the first five hours of the working day (A to B), the worker produces a value equivalent to the value of the means of subsistence necessary for the reproduction of her labor power. This is what Marx calls "necessary labour time," and the work spent during this time is *necessary labor*. The necessary labor time will vary considerably in different industries depending on the level of technology, the degree of human skill, and the cost of raw materials. The work undertaken during the second part of the working day, the line B to C, brings no advantage to the worker, and she works for "free" for the capitalist. As Marx explains, "During the second period of the labour process, that in which his labour is no longer necessary labour, the workman, it is true, labours, expends labour power; but his labour, being no longer necessary labour, he creates no value for himself. He creates surplus value which, for the capitalist, has all the charms of a creation out of nothing."[16] Thus, Marx calls this productive activity in the second period of the working day "surplus labour time," and the value produced in the second five hours is *surplus value*, which is appropriated by the capitalist.

For Marx, the appropriation of surplus value is the basis of profit, once other fixed and variable costs (e.g., rent and raw materials) have been deducted. The rate of surplus value, defined as the ratio of surplus labor time to the necessary labor time, is 5/5, in this example, which equals 1 or 100 percent. This rate can be explained as follows:

$$\text{Rate of surplus value} = \frac{s}{v} \frac{\text{surplus labor time}}{\text{necessary labor time}} = \frac{5}{5} = 100\%$$

The rate of surplus value expresses the degree of exploitation of the worker by the capitalist: "The rate of surplus value is therefore an exact expression for the degree of exploitation of labour power by capital, or of the labourer by the capitalist."[17] The rate of exploitation is $e = s/v$, where v, the necessary labor time, is called variable capital because it varies during the production, contributing more value to output than it costs as an output. For Marx, the appropriation of surplus value applied also to the pre-capitalist feudal modes of production, but it is only under capitalism that exploitation in production is veiled by the ideology of freedom of exchange. Thus, the surplus value ratio, like capital itself, embodies a particular class relation and a form of domination. The accumulation of surplus value depends directly on the total amount of labor the capitalist employs and on the rate of exploitation. For Marx, "capital is dead labour, that, vampire-like, only lives by sucking living labour, and lives the more, the more labour it sucks."[18]

As a system, capitalism imposes an imperative objective on capitalists or its agents (managers): the means of production must be operated for the purpose of valorization or profit maximizing. On the basis of existing technology, extending the length of the working day can increase the rate of surplus value. Consider, for example, the situation represented in Figure 6.3. If the capitalist extends the working day by two hours, from ten to twelve hours, that would extend the B–C portion of the line A–C by two hours, which would represent an increase in the rate of surplus value: e is 7/5 or 140 percent. Physiological and legal restrictions limit the capitalist's ability to increase absolute surplus value by extending the working day. The surplus value produced by lengthening the working day, Marx termed *absolute surplus value*.

The dynamic nature of capitalism itself generates the production of *relative* surplus value as the dominant method of increasing the rate of exploitation (or e). New technology, by cheapening labor costs, can reduce the time needed to produce commodities, in other words, the necessary labor time (or v). If, for example, machinery reduces the necessary labor time from five to four hours each day, e would be 6/4 or 150 percent. In Figure 6.3, the line A to B would be shortened, so more of the worker's total time (A–C) would produce surplus value. The surplus value produced by the reduction of the necessary labor time, Marx termed *relative surplus value*. To increase the "productiveness of labour," Marx predicts that modes of production must be revolutionized. He writes, "When surplus value has to be produced by the conversion of necessary labour into surplus labour, it by no means suffices for capital to take over the labour process in the form under which it has been historically handed down, and then simply to prolong the duration of that process. The technical and social conditions of the process, and consequently the very mode of production must be revolutionized, before the productiveness of labour can be increased."[19]

In Part 4 of the first volume of *Capital*, Marx details the many strategies for increasing relative surplus value. His analysis foreshadows the genesis of management in modern society. The first strategy to increase relative surplus value is through finer division of labor within workshops, which has the effect of giving the capitalist "undisputed authority" over the workers.[20] The second strategy to increase relative surplus value "beyond all bounds set by human nature"[21] is through investment in machinery. When controlled by capitalists, machinery cheapens commodities by increasing the pace of work, stimulating scientific innovation, and exponentially reducing the value of necessary labor time. Marx describes the effects of machinery on workers in his chapter on "Machinery and Modern Industry." Machinery, in the hands of capitalists, causes "a more intensified labour"[22] and "endless drudgery," and molds workers' behavior into "a barrack disciple," writes Marx.[23] Maximizing control over workers is seen by Marx to derive from the fact that the wage-labor exchange secures only a *potential* labor power for the production of surplus value. He calls attention to a pronounced tendency for improvements in machinery to be labor saving and, somewhat less obvious, to substitute one type of worker for another, the less skilled for the more skilled, the young for the adult, and the female for the male. He made the prescient observation that improvements in machinery led to "the separation of the intellectual powers of production from the manual labour, and the conversion of those powers into the might of capital *over* labour" (emphasis added).[24] Marx predicts a permanent pool of unemployed workers, the "industrial reserve army" of labor, which would have the designed effect of downward adjustments in wage rates.

It is false, however, to assume that Marx's analysis of machinery was totally negative. In *Capital*, he also identifies positive aspects of technical innovation: "Modern Industry, indeed, compels society, under penalty of death, to replace the detailed-worker of today, crippled by life-long repetition of one and the same trivial operation, and thus reduced to the mere fragment of a man, by the fully developed individual, fit for a variety of labours, ready to face any change of production, and to whom the different social functions he performs, are but so many modes of giving scope to his own natural and acquired powers."[25] This passage is one of the most expressive testimonials written to capitalism's achievements. It also speaks to Marx's notion that creative labor, in which men and women exercise their unique human capacities, defines what it is to be human and what the relationship is between people and paid work. Thus, technology *potentially* frees men and women from dehumanizing labor and offers the opportunity for labor to correspond to human essence.

Although new productive technology has the potential to enhance human experience and living standards, Marx's economic thesis predicts dire living conditions for the working class:

> To say that the worker has an interest in the rapid growth of capital is only to say that the more rapidly the worker increases the wealth of others, the richer will be the crumbs that fall to him, the greater is the number of workers that can be employed and called into existence, the more can the mass of slaves dependent on capital be increased. We have thus seen that: Even the *most favourable situation* for the working class, *the most rapid possible growth of*

capital, however much it may improve the material existence of the worker, does not remove the antagonism between his interests and the interests of the bourgeoisie, the interests of the capitalists. *Profit and wages* remain as before in *inverse proportion.* If capital is growing rapidly, wages may rise; the profit of capital rises incomparably more rapidly.[26]

Marx's analysis of capitalism in *Capital* speaks to the vulnerability of wage labor to capital. The relationship between the working class and the capitalist, even in the most favorable economic conditions, is one of contradiction. The capitalist has an interest in intensifying work and minimizing labor costs to maximize the production of relative surplus value. This aim of the capitalist to maximize profit has far-reaching effects, and Marx investigates these as well. Whereas, in the first volume of *Capital*, Marx analyzes the production of surplus value inside the factory, in the other two volumes he examines a whole series of capitalist phenomena occurring outside in the market, including economic crises.

Theories of Crises

Finding ways to produce relative surplus value makes capitalism highly dynamic, but the process generates three tendencies that are central to capitalist development: the accumulation of capital in fewer hands, the organization of labor into finer and more complex divisions of labor, and the creation of global markets as capital seeks new markets and cheaper labor. A central objective of Marx's economic theory was to demonstrate that, although capitalism was historically the most efficient mode of production, it was prone to chronic economic crises. In essence, Marx postulates that crises are inevitable for two reasons: insufficient demand and the falling rate of profit.

Inherent in Marx's theory of relative surplus value is a fundamental contradiction between production and consumption: on the one hand, the capitalist class is driven by the urge for wealth to increase the production of surplus value, which increases the supply of commodities that must be converted into money; on the other hand, accumulation is based on the fact that consumption by the producers of surplus value—the exploited workers—is restricted to basic necessities. In any society other than capitalism, the overproduction of commodities would be a celebration; extra commodities would mean increased individual consumption. However, for capitalism, private consumption is necessary, but not sufficient; consumption must realize a profit. In the second volume of *Capital*,

Marx points to insufficient demand or underconsumption as a causal mechanism for economic crisis: one unsold "stream of commodities" entering the market causes commodity producers to compete with one another and to sell at lower prices. Thus, a crisis breaks out when insufficient consumption causes the supply of commodities to exceed consumer demand.[27] For example, when unsold automobiles build up on dealers' lots, autoworkers are laid off, and the economy enters a crisis until the unsold automobiles are purchased and the automobile manufacturer restarts production. This illustration focuses on the breakdown of an individual capitalist producing a particular commodity, but the economy is a network of capitals that are intimately integrated with other circuits of capital. As consumption of a commodity (e.g., automobiles) falls, it triggers a decrease in investment for automobile machinery, which, in turn, causes a crisis among capitals producing the machines that build automobiles. It is this interconnected system of unplanned "commodity capital" (e.g., automobile manufacturers) and "productive capital" (e.g., robot manufacturers supplying the automobile industry) that led Marx to refer to the anarchy of capitalist production. Economic crises break out extremely often, given the anarchy of capitalist production, fluctuations in market prices, the vagaries of the credit system (e.g., the 2008 collapse of the US housing market due to subprime mortgages), and technological change.

In the last volume of *Capital*, Marx synthesizes his analysis of the production of surplus value and the realization of profit into his contentious "law" of the tendency of the rate of profit to fall. Although classical economists believed that the unavoidable tendency for the rate of profit to fall was a natural fact, Marx's treatment of the falling rate of profit was placed in the social context of capitalist relations of production. Mathematically, a theoretical demonstration of the falling rate of profit can be given, but Marx articulates this situation in a sociologically more interesting way as follows:

> Proceeding from the nature of the capitalist mode of production, it is thereby proved a logical necessity that in its development the general average rate of surplus value must express itself in a falling general rate of profit. Since the mass of the employed living labour is continually on the decline as compared to the mass of materialised labour set in motion by it, i.e., to the productivity consumed means of production, it follows that the portion of living labour, unpaid and congealed in surplus value, must also be continually on the decrease compared to the amount of value represented by the invested total

capital. Since the ratio of the mass of surplus value to the value of the invested total capital forms the rate of profit, this rate must constantly fall.[28]

In essence, Marx's argument is that, as more productive capital (machinery) is introduced into the production of surplus value, less necessary labor time is needed to produce the same quantity of commodities. As a result, the costs of "constant capital" (c) increase relative to the "variable capital" (v). Following Marx, the rate of profit (r) is defined as the ratio of surplus value (s) to the total capital employed $[c + v]$: $r = s / [c + v]$. In words, since the cost of total capital employed is increasing in relation to the rate of exploitation, the rate of profit must inevitably fall. The "breakdowns" between capitals, and a general tendency for the rate of profit to fall, account for economic booms and recessions, which characterize the capitalist business cycle.

For Marx, crises stem from the fundamental contradiction of capitalist production and consumption—from unrestrained production without regard to corresponding levels of consumption. Marx writes,

> The *real barrier* of capitalist production is *capital itself*.... This means—unconditional development of the productive forces of society—comes continually into conflict with the limited purpose, the self-expansion of the existing capital. The capitalist mode of production is, for this reason, a historical means of developing the material forces of production and creating an appropriate world-market and is, at the same time, a continual conflict between this its historic task and its own corresponding relations of social production.[29]

Marx's conception of these crises is not simply an economic concept that goes along with the theory of value; it is a sociological theory, the center of which is a particular mode of productive forces and hierarchical relations. Crises are highly probable because the anarchic nature of the capitalist mode of production is the social outcome of interactions among capitalists' individual economic actions; whereas a falling rate of profit is a social outcome that makes such economic actions inevitable.[30] Although Marx believed that crises were endemic to capitalism, nowhere in his writings does he predict an inevitable apocalyptic economic collapse. Economic crises do, however, function as a force toward equilibrium by eliminating overcapacity, and they play a crucial role in fostering revolutionary consciousness and collective action.

Criticism

Critics of Marx's economic theories have been numerous and prolific, but space permits only a brief consideration of some of the major criticisms that have the most direct bearing on the themes covered in this chapter. One set of criticisms relates to a main tenet of Marx's analysis of capitalism, his theory of value. The first major criticism is its inutility for the rational allocation of commodities and scarce resources in an economy. Marx's proposition that labor is the source of all value is "useless at best, harmful and misleading at its not infrequent worst."[31] Moreover, the limitation of the theory of value, critics argue, is glaringly apparent because it ignores the key factor of relative scarcity, which is central to determining equilibrium prices in markets and the equilibrium rate of profit. There is textual evidence that explicitly repudiates this critique. Marx's theory of value is a model of commodity production; it is "*not* meant as a general theory of relative prices."[32]

The second major criticism is of Marx's doctrine of the "progressive pauperization" of the proletariat. Marx forecast that there would be periodic recessions, the growth of colossal quasi-monopolistic corporations, and growing unemployment resulting from technological change. In this scenario, the working class would experience increasing misery as living standards underwent decline over time. The forecast is based on the premise that capitalists are impelled by a competitive imperative to increase the amount of capital invested in technology, as opposed to increasing the proportion paid to labor in wages. The received economic wisdom is that the ownership by the working classes of the ubiquitous automobile, satellite disk, flat-screen TV, and other luxury products has proven Marx wrong. In retrospect, it is easy to see why his forecast has long since appeared incorrect: Marx underestimated the effects of the rise of liberal democracy. In Western capitalist societies, at least, progressive income tax, free universal education, health care coverage, and more are now regarded as basic to postmodern liberal democracies. Marx did not anticipate "varieties of capitalism"[33] with policies that reflect local realities, local cultures, and, ironically, the political clout of local social movements. The idea of diversity is illustrated by contrasting the capitalism practiced in the Nordic states of Europe—for example in Norway, Sweden, and Finland—with the more laissez-faire capitalism of Britain and the United States.

Marx's economic theory, arguably, did not adequately take into account the growth of political democracy in the Western world, but it is also important to understand that the orthodox economic critique is based on a misreading of Marx's *Capital*.[34] Consider this statement:

"Pauperism forms a condition of capitalist production, and the capitalist development of wealth. It enters into the *faux frais* of capitalist production; but capital knows how to throw these from its own shoulders on to those of the working class and the lower middle class."[35] Here, Marx is referring not to the impoverishment of the entire proletariat but to the impoverishment of the "lowest sediment": the underclass of the unemployed, the widows, the addicts, the sick that capital is unwilling to pay for directly. After World War II, most Western governments, through the creation of more or less generous social welfare programs, have met the incidental operational costs of capitalism. They have supplied education and training, infrastructure, health care, and, increasingly, pollution management—costs that capital is all too happy to pass on to the working and middle classes. Periodically, for the capitalist system to work, the state (that is, the taxpayer) has to intervene directly in the economy. This was demonstrated plainly a decade ago when the British government rescued the financial institution Northern Rock, and the US administration intervened to save mortgage giants Fannie Mae and Freddie Mac. In such cases, the cost to the taxpayer can be huge. As *The Economist* acknowledged in July 2008, "The unpalatable truth is that by the time a financial crisis hits, the state often has to ... shoulder a large part of the losses."[36] In times of relative economic stability, neoliberal ideology propagates the myth that the economy and society are two separate realms in order to allow unfettered capital accumulation. It is at this time that we are likely to hear that business must always be "unshackled from 'wealth-destroying' regulation."[37] In times of crisis, the myth of separation is easier to expose. The logic of the "self-regulating" market, whether applied to banking or food processing, always needs the social superstructure, which is why the language of "too big to fail" simply means "so big that it can depend on society to pick it up when it topples."[38] That capital's profits are privatized but risks and losses are socialized would not have surprised Marx in the least.

A third major criticism relates to Marx's theories of capitalist crises. Marx's dialectical method commits him to foretell that certain social changes are historically inevitable. Much of his economic theory is an exposition of the mechanism that "inevitably" brings about economic crises. His model on the tendency for the rate of profit to fall has received much criticism. Critics have pointed out, for example, that if, as Marx contends, the rate of profit falls because of investment in productive forces, then, presumably, the decline should be avoided when capitalists disinvest or when stagnation in technical innovation sets in.[39] Furthermore, Marx neglects that those capitalists experiencing a fall in the rate of profit might adopt a business strategy that generates countertendencies to partly or completely offset it, for example, by entering a global market or by expanding consumption through easier access to credit. Also, it is glaringly apparent that globalization has undermined the international solidarity of the proletariat. Although in *The Communist Manifesto* Marx and Engels urge all workers of "all countries to unite,"[40] in reality, Canadian and US automobile workers identify more closely with their aggrieved employers, as Japanese automobiles made by Japanese workers dominate the North America market. In the early twenty-first century, reality is much more complex than might have been expected by a writer who died over 136 years ago.

Conclusion

The two main pillars of Marx's analysis of capitalism are the labor theory of value and the theory of crises. In opposition to classical accounts of value, Marx's labor theory of value embodies a social theory of commodity production, which makes *Capital* "unrivalled" as a work of sociological theory.[41] The theory characterizes capitalism as a fundamentally exploitative system or "an act of robbery."[42] "The work of Marx taken as a whole," writes C. Wright Mills, "is a savage, sustained indictment of one alleged injustice: that the profit, the comfort, the luxury of one man is paid for by the loss, the misery, the denial of another."[43] The subversive thesis that profit arises from the exploitation of labor was centrally important in Marx's economics because it provided the exploited with a moral and theoretical justification for taking collective action against capitalism. The central object of Marx's theory of crises was to demonstrate that the "anarchic" capitalist system was prone to periodic economic upheavals. Nowhere in his writings does Marx predict an inevitable apocalyptic economic collapse.

In spite of the fact that Marx's economic theories contain omissions, are ambiguous, and underestimate the chameleon nature of capitalism, contemporary readers of *Capital* acknowledge the sheer perspicacity of Marx, and therefore we need to balance criticisms of his theories with their not inconsiderable achievements. Perhaps the main achievement of Marx's *Capital* is its pioneering contribution to the sociological analysis of technological change and management. Marx's work on the effects of machinery pioneered the sociological analysis of the effects of technological change, particularly what is known as labor process theory, which seeks to reveal the social and class interests behind technological change. It is this perspective that Harry Braverman employed in *Labor and Monopoly Capital* to account for employers' strategies to control and de-skill workers through the application of new technology.[44] In "post-Braverman" sociological studies of paid work, labor process concepts have been applied to clerical occupations and also to a variety of Japanese management strategies.[45] Marx's work also identifies the genesis of management as an outcome of the historical development of production and power relations. Marx's analysis also centers attention on the dominant imperative of management—realizing a satisfactory degree of control over antagonistic capital-labor relations so as to obtain the efficient extraction of surplus value (what is now called labor productivity) and the levels of profitability that this extraction secures.[46]

A further achievement of Marx's economic tome is its pioneering contribution to the twenty-first-century debate on sustainable development. By the 1860s, the depletion of soil fertility was a major environmental concern in Europe. Informed by the works of the German chemist Justus von Liebig (1803–73), Marx provided a systematic critique of large-scale capitalist agriculture, centering on how soil fertility is modified by human agency. In Part 4 of the first volume of *Capital*, Marx is eloquent on the trade-offs between capitalist economics and land ecology:

> All progress in capitalistic agriculture is a progress in the art, not only of robbing the labourer, but of robbing the soil; all progress in increasing the fertility of the soil for a given time, is a progress towards ruining the lasting sources of that fertility.... Capitalist production, therefore, develops ... only by sapping the original sources of all wealth—the soil and the labourer.[47]

In this passage, Marx's central theory is that of a "metabolic rift" or contradiction between the natural environment and human agency, a rift caused by the intensive exploitation of the soil through the use of fertilizer. Marx's social theory captured the essence of sustainable development and, in terms of the classical tradition, provides important theoretical foundations for environmental sociology.[48]

Another major achievement of Marx's economics is its correct prediction of the growth of corporations and economic globalization. For Marx, the logical tendency of capitalism was the concentration and centralization of capital. The process of concentration refers to the amount of capital individual capitalists control. The process of centralization, on the other hand, refers to the merging of capital. The effect of both is to lead to giant business corporations that have substantial control over markets and are capable of destroying many of their smaller competitors and dictating contracts with smaller producers that supply the conglomerate. The effect of the giant US retailer Wal-Mart on small local retailers and their suppliers attests to this prediction. As Joel Bakan's *The Corporation* (2004) persuasively argues, an aggregate of capital is a "pathological institution" that relentlessly pursues, without exception, "its own self-interest, regardless of the often harmful consequences it might cause to others."[49] Marx's economic concepts explaining the long-term tendency of monopoly capital constitute an indispensable intellectual element of critical globalization theory.

The essence of Marx's thesis is that capitalism brought massive income and wealth inequality. In his revelatory book *Why We Can't Afford the Rich*, Andrew Sayer engagingly explains the pernicious influence of the super-rich on society. He lays bare the dyfunction mechanisms that allow the top 1 percent to get richer, even in the worse economic crisis for 80 years during which, in Britain, workers experienced the "worse pay freeze for 200 years."[50] Since 2008, the top 1 percent in United States, Britain, and Canada have been taking an increasing share of national wealth. As Sayer observes, "the less you had to do with the crisis, the bigger the sacrifices—relative to your income—you have had to make."[51] In 2018, for example, the wealth of Jeff Bezos, founder and CEO of Amazon, exceeded $129 billion, making him the world's wealthiest man. Bezos's fortune increases by roughly $302,610 per minute. In contrast, Marx would not be surprised to learn, Amazon full-time workers in the United States make an average of less than $15.00 an hour, and as little as $233 per month in India.

Can Marx's intellectual legacy contribute to our understanding of postmodern capitalism? Arguably, neoliberalism, by definition, encourages corporate "recklessness, hubris and greed." Indeed, this is the judgment of British House of Commons MPs on the collapse of the giant construction company Carillion. As the company began imploding in early 2018, the directors focused on increasing and protecting their bonuses. And, in plain English that could have been appropriated from Marx and Engels's *Communist Manifesto*, MPs declared it was "[s]ame old story. Same old greed. A board of directors too busy stuffing their mouths with gold to show any concern for the welfare of their workforce or their pensioners."[52] Today, the issues of precarious employment and income inequality are part of a public consciousness regarding the deleterious effects of globalization, but that we can find these ideas in Marx's *magnum opus* indicates what a remarkable achievement these works were in their time. Importantly, that so much of human activity today—from politics to education, health policy to culture—is "perceived principally through the prism of economics"[53] would come as no surprise to those familiar with Marx's writings. And in the context of global economic instability and deepening income inequality, it must be conceded that Marx's early realization of the effects of unfettered global expansion makes him in a certain sense more postmodern today than many of his intellectual detractors.

FURTHER THINKING:

What is meant by *relative* surplus value? Is the concept relevant in explaining the effects of robot technology?

FURTHER READING:

The British economist and journalist Paul Mason provides a readable account of Marx's theory of crisis in *Postcapitalism: A Guide to Our Future* (London: Penguin, 2016, pp. 49–78). A more rigorous and contemporary account of Marx's economics is provided by Ben Fine and Alfredo Saad-Filhocan, "Marx Economics," in *Rethinking Economics*, eds. Liliann Fisher et al. (London: Routledge, 2017, pp. 19–32). For an exposé on how economic globalization promotes inequality, see Joseph Stiglitz's book, *Globalization and Its Discontents Revisited* (London: Penguin Books, 2017).

Notes

1 Terry Eagleton, *Radical Sacrifice* (London: Yale University Press, 2018), 165.

2 Anonymous, "Labor Is Right—Karl Marx Has a Lot to Teach Today's Politicians," *The Economist*, May 11, 2017.

3 Robert C. Tucker, ed., *The Marx-Engels Reader*, 2nd ed. (New York: Norton, 1972), 297.

4 Alan Swingewood, *A Short History of Sociological Thought* (New York: St. Martin's Press, 2000), 40.

5 Tucker, *Marx-Engels Reader*, 302–3.

6 Adam Smith, *An Inquiry into the Nature and Causes of the Wealth of Nations* (1776; London: Penguin, 1997), 133.

7 Mike Davis, *Old Gods, New Enigmas* (London: Verso, 2018), 114.

8 Letter from Marx to Engels, August 24, 1867, cited in David McLellan, *Marx* (London: Fontana Press, 1975), 564.

9 Karl Marx, *Capital* (1894; London: Lawrence & Wishart, 1971), 3:194–95.

10 Tucker, *Marx-Engels Reader*, 312.

11 Tucker, *Marx-Engels Reader*, 319.

12 Tucker, *Marx-Engels Reader*, 321.

13 See, for example, Joseph Stiglitz, "A Global Lesson in Market Failure," *The Globe and Mail*, July 8, 2008, A15.

14 Karl Marx, *Capital* (1867; London: Lawrence & Wishart, 1970), 1:209.

15 Tucker, *Marx-Engels Reader*, 209.

16 Marx, *Capital*, 1:217.

17 Marx, *Capital*, 1:218.

18 Tucker, *Marx-Engels Reader*, 362–63.

19 Tucker, *Marx-Engels Reader*, 379.

20 Tucker, *Marx-Engels Reader*, 395.

21 Tucker, *Marx-Engels Reader*, 404.

22 Tucker, *Marx-Engels Reader*, 407.

23 Tucker, *Marx-Engels Reader*, 410.

24 Tucker, *Marx-Engels Reader*, 409.

25 Tucker, *Marx-Engels Reader*, 413–14.

26 Tucker, *Marx-Engels Reader*, 210–11.

27 Karl Marx, *Capital* (1885; London: Lawrence & Wishart, 1974), 2:78.

28 Karl Marx, *Capital*, 3:213.

29 Karl Marx, *Capital*, 3:250.

30 Ben Fine, *Marx's Capital* (London: Macmillan, 1975), 58.

31 Jon Elster, *Making Sense of Marx* (New York: Cambridge University Press, 1985), 120.

32 Allen W. Wood, *Karl Marx* (London: Routledge, 2004), 228.

33 See Peter A. Hall and David Soskice, *Varieties of Capitalism* (Oxford: Oxford University Press, 2001); Leslie Sklair, *Globalization: Capitalism and Its Alternatives* (New York: Oxford University Press, 2002).

34 Francis Wheen, *Karl Marx* (London: Fourth Estate, 2000), 300.

35 Tucker, *Marx-Engels Reader*, 429. In Marx's analysis of production, *faux frais* refers to "incidental operating expenses" incurred in the productive investment of capital, which alone do not add new value to output.

36 Anonymous, "Twin Twisters," *The Economist*, July 19, 2008, 15.

37 Will Hutton, "The Meat Scandal Shows All That Is Rotten about Our Free Marketeers," *The Observer*, February 17, 2013, 43.

38 See Raj Patel, *The Value of Nothing* (Toronto: HarperCollins, 2009), 19.

39 Wood, *Karl Marx*, 157.

40 Tucker, *Marx-Engels Reader*, 500.

41 Ken Morrison, *Marx, Durkheim, Weber*, 2nd ed. (London: Sage, 2006), 81.

42 Harry Schwartz, "Introduction," in *Marx on Economics*, ed. Robert Freedman (London: Penguin, 1962), xv.

43 C. Wright Mill, *The Marxists* (New York: Dell Publishing, 1962), 33.

44 Harry Braverman, *Labor and Monopoly Capital: The Degradation of Work in the Twentieth Century* (New York: Monthly Review Press, 1974).

45 See John Bratton, *Japanization at Work* (London: Macmillan Press, 1992); Tony Elger and Chris Smith, *Global Japanization?* (London: Routledge, 1994).

46 See Mike Reed, *The Sociology of Management* (London: Harvester Wheatsheaf, 1989); David Knights and Hugh Willmott, eds., *Managing the Labour Process* (Aldershot, UK: Gower, 1986).

47 Tucker, *Marx-Engels Reader*, 416–17.

48 That Marx's social theory provides an important theoretical contribution to modern environmental sociology has been a matter of some debate, however. For example, Frederick Buttel, in "Sociology and the Environment," *International Social Science Journal* 109 (1986): 337–56, wrote that, until recently, "there has been general agreement among environmental sociologists that the classical sociological tradition has been inhospitable to the nurturing of ecologically-informed sociological theory" (338). And with respect to Marx, it has been argued that he was "ecologically blind"—namely, that he was allegedly unable to perceive the exploitation of nature and the role of technology in environmental degradation. See, for example, Raymond Murphy, *Sociology and Nature* (Boulder, CO: Westview, 1996). In contrast, John Bellamy Foster, in "Theory of Metabolic Rift: Classical Foundations for Environmental Sociology," *American Journal of Sociology* 105, no. 2 (1999): 366–405, and James O'Connor, in *Natural Causes* (New York: Guilford, 1998), offer a more positive account of Marx's contribution to environmental sociology. In Foster's article, a work we have drawn upon here, Foster contends that Marx certainly argued "*as if nature mattered*" (398) and that his analysis of capitalist agriculture and, in particular, his theory of "metabolic rift" offer firm classical foundations for the development of a comprehensive sociology of the environment.

49 Joel Bakan, *The Corporation* (Toronto: Penguin, 2004), 1–2.

50 Nadia Khomami, "London TUC Rally Protests at 'Worst Pay Squeeze for 200 Years'," *The Observer*, May 13, 2018, 23.

51 Andrew Sayer, *Why We Can't Afford the Rich* (Bristol: Polity Press, 2016), 1.

52 Rob Davies, "Carillion Fall Blamed on Hubris and Greed," *The Guardian*, May 16, 2018, 1.

53 John Ralston Saul, *The Collapse of Globalism* (Toronto: Viking Canada, 2005), 18.

7. Émile Durkheim:
The Division of Labour in Society

Apart from Marx himself, there can be few social thinkers whose fate
it has been to be so persistently misunderstood.
—Anthony Giddens, 1971[1]

More than any other social theorist of the first rank, Durkheim
sought to contribute sociology as a distinct and autonomous science
with its own theoretical protocols and professional infrastructure.
—Alex Callinicos, 1999[2]

IN *THE DIVISION OF LABOUR IN SOCIETY* (1893), Émile Durkheim gives an analysis of the evolution of society from small-scale societies with little division of
labor to complex, industrial, urban societies in which he identifies a breakdown in shared norms and values. The book is also a work of theory in which
he explores the relationship between the individual and society and in which
he argues that even the idea of individualism depends upon changes in the
social structure. The moral and political problems that emerged from the
evolution of large, complex societies included questions of how to reconcile
individual freedom and social order and how to find forms of social organization that would produce both social solidarity and individual freedom. In
discussing the idea of social solidarity, Durkheim variously refers to the ties,
or social links, that bind the individual to the group and ensure social cohesion. He also refers to these ties as "social cement" because of attachments
between individuals that could have an intense emotional hold over them.[3]

Life and Works

David Émile Durkheim was born in 1858 at Épinal, the regional capital
of the Vosges in France. His father was the chief rabbi in the region, but

while still a schoolboy, Durkheim decided against following his father into the rabbinate. He was a clever pupil and obtained two baccalaureates, one in letters in 1874 and one in sciences in 1875. He spent three years preparing for entry to the École Normale Supérieure in Paris. During this period, he turned to the study of morality, society, and sociology. He was influenced by one of his teachers, Renouvier, whose interest in the scientific study of morality, views on social cohesion based on the individual's dependence on others, preference for justice over utility, and advocacy of producers' associations and secular state education later became themes in Durkheim's work.[4] Durkheim also drew from Auguste Comte's work, particularly the idea that society could be studied scientifically and that the task was to establish exactly what the subject matter of sociology should be and to show how this discipline could be used to diagnose social pathologies in order to provide a guide to future action.

After his *agrégation*—a prestigious competitive examination for the recruitment of secondary teachers in France—in 1882, Durkheim became a philosophy teacher, and, during this period, he began to focus on the ideas that were eventually to be his doctoral thesis, as well as the core of his first book, *The Division of Labour in Society*. He began to concentrate on the relations of the individual personality to social solidarity, and he came to see that the solution to the problem belonged to the new science of sociology.[5] At the time, sociology was mainly seen as being associated with Comte and was looked upon critically by philosophers in France.

In 1887, Durkheim took up a position at the University of Bordeaux and, in the following 15 years, produced three major works: *The Division of Labour in Society*, *The Rules of Sociological Method*, and *Suicide*; he also established the first sociological periodical, *L'Année sociologique*. In 1902, he moved to the Sorbonne, in Paris, and later became Professor of the Science of Education (only in 1913 did he become Chair of the Science of Education and Sociology).[6] This appointment was met with considerable hostility, especially from the Catholic Right,

Émile Durkheim was born in 1858 at Épinal, France. He is the theorist of social cohesion in which society is held together through shared values. Consequently, he became increasingly interested in religion and morality. He died in 1917.

who opposed giving the responsibility for teacher education to a secularist and advocate of the new, controversial discipline of sociology.[7] During this period, Durkheim's main sociological concern was the study of religion and morality, which led to the publication of *The Elementary Forms of Religious Life* in 1912. His work on morality was never completed, and he died in 1917 at the age of 59. Durkheim's achievement was the founding of sociology as an academic discipline. His many publications attracted scholars to work with him and to help build a body of sociological work.

Intellectual Influences

Several intellectual influences shaped Durkheim's analysis of society and his conception of sociology. An important one was Auguste Comte's discussion of scientific methodology, or positivism, as outlined in *A Course in Positive Philosophy*, published between 1830 and 1842. This methodology posits an alternative to the dominant, speculative philosophical doctrines of the eighteenth and nineteenth centuries, which it sought to replace with knowledge based upon observation.[8] As we discussed in chapter 3, Comte's "Law of Three Stages" depicts knowledge and human consciousness in three stages: the theological stage in which nature is understood in terms of the will of anthropomorphic gods; the metaphysical stage of knowledge based upon abstract, conceptual thought; and the final, positive stage based on scientific laws derived from the observation of facts. This evolutionary trajectory made speculative thought appear less developed. In addition, as Morrison points out, Comte developed a system for comparing and ranking different sciences in which he showed that the most developed sciences, such as physics and biology, were positivistic and, therefore, more successful because of their use of scientific methods. In comparison, history, philosophy, and economics appeared less advanced, and this critique provided a receptive climate for the spread of positivism in France and England. Positivism advocates the extension of scientific method to the social sciences, including the abandonment of abstract analysis in favor of the search for law-like, causal regularities and the basing of knowledge on observation. Durkheim drew upon the influence of Comte in his attempt to establish sociology as a scientific discipline during his years at Bordeaux.[9]

A second influence on Durkheim's view of society was a philosophical perspective known as realism.[10] From this perspective, social realities exist in a world that is external and independent of people's perceptions. According to realists, this external reality exists in the structures or customs of society, and these structures can restrain people by influencing how they behave, for example if they feel obliged to conform. Thus, these external structures can be seen as material objects of study; they can be observed in order to see how they affect people's behavior. These ideas will be discussed more fully in chapter 8.

A third influence on Durkheim was the perspective of individualism that was prominent toward the end of the nineteenth century.[11] The ideas of the Enlightenment and the political changes of the French Revolution raised the profile of the individual and increased individual political and legal rights. At the beginning of Durkheim's career, there was a strong sense in France that individual rights were undermining collective obligations and authority. Any perspective that viewed society as simply an agglomeration of individuals weakened Durkheim's effort to establish a discipline of sociology based upon the idea that society is an objective and constraining material reality, external to the individual. Durkheim opposed the utilitarian doctrine that was influential in the second half of the nineteenth century. The views of John Stuart Mill and Jeremy Bentham, the main advocates of utilitarianism, put the freely acting individual at the center of social life. Such individuals, it was argued, pursue their own interests, especially private economic gain, and relate to society only if required by their pursuit of private utility. Society, in this theory, is based just on rational individuals merely pursuing their private goals. In *The Division of Labour in Society* Durkheim emphasizes that social order cannot be based only on freely contracting individuals because there are social rules regarding which contracts are just and there are moral codes concerning the honoring of contacts.[12] In addition, individuals are not analytically separate from society, as they cannot exist outside a social framework. In *The Division of Labour in Society* Durkheim argues that, historically, society precedes the individual and that only under certain social structural conditions can the idea or the reality of individual autonomy exist.

Division of Labor

A central concern in Durkheim's first book is the relationship between the individual and social solidarity. He notes that there are two apparently contradictory movements—as individuals became more autonomous they became more dependent upon society—and he proposes that this contradiction can be resolved by changes in social solidarity flowing from changes in the division of labor.[13] Although Adam Smith discussed the division of labor in relation to the specialization of economic activities, Durkheim perceived it as a much broader process that affects political, administrative, judicial, and educational institutions, as well as being present in the arts, philosophy, and sciences. Debates in the study of biology extended the principle of the division of labor to organisms, as well as to societies: "It may even be stated that an organism occupies the more exalted a place in the animal hierarchy the more specialized its functions are."[14] Thus, the division of labor is placed almost at the beginning of life and is considered a fundamental process within "the essential properties of organized matter" rather than a recent product of the intelligence and will of men. In these terms, the increasing division of labor appears to be a manifestation of a general process, and Durkheim contended that it was becoming "one of the fundamental bases of the social order."[15]

In his discussion of the functions of the division of labor, Durkheim gives a much greater significance to division of labor than does Adam Smith, who attributes it to the increase in production. Durkheim argues that the division of labor is the principal source of social solidarity, which "links those co-operating together at the present time" and provides "order, harmony and social solidarity."[16] Because social solidarity is a moral phenomenon that cannot be directly observed, Durkheim argues that an external index of social solidarity, such as a type of law, has to be noted. He identifies two types of law based upon the different sanctions attached to them. The first type is penal law, which has repressive sanctions involving loss or suffering for the person who has infringed such laws. The second type includes civil, commercial, procedural, administrative, and constitutional law and has restitutive sanctions that consist in "restoring the previous state of affairs" to its normal form.[17]

Durkheim argues that, in small societies with little division of labor, there is mechanical solidarity based upon likeness, and, in such societies, there is a strong *collective* or *common consciousness* made up of the "totality of beliefs and sentiments common to the average members of society," which "forms a determinate system with a life of its own."[18] This collective consciousness continues to exist irrespective of which particular individuals live in a society at a particular time. It is separate from individual conscience, though it requires this for its continued existence. Crime, then, refers to an act that offends the collective consciousness. Durkheim states, "In other words, we must not say that an act offends the common consciousness because it is criminal, but that it is criminal because it offends that consciousness. We do not condemn it because it is a crime, but it is a crime because we condemn it."[19] In a society with a strong social likeness and a strong collective consciousness, offenses against the collective consciousness are perceived as threats to social bonds—to something greater than the individuals, the very basis of the existence of society—and such a society calls forth vengeful, penal sanctions. This reaction occurs because it is the society that "is harmed even when the harm done is to individuals, and it is the attack upon society that is repressed by punishment."[20] In societies of a mechanical nature, punishment of crime is repressive and has a quasi-religious nature because the crime offends a morality that "we vaguely feel is more or less outside and above us."[21] Revenge is extracted because crimes are against collective sentiments and are perceived as a threat to society. Penal laws reflect a type of social solidarity that is mechanical because it is based upon social likeness. People have a shared common consciousness, a shared psychic type, and a collective existence. Penal law represents mechanical solidarity wherein members of society share common states of consciousness, and the more extensively the common conscience regulates social life, the "more also it creates ties that bind the individual to the group; the more, consequently, social cohesion derives completely from this cause."[22]

In Durkheim's view, organic solidarity can be recognized when there are restitutive sanctions that are concerned with only a restoration of the normal situation rather than with punishment or disgrace. This is possible because repressive law is linked to the collective conscience, while restitutive law has feeble links with the collective conscience. Restitutive law is administered within specialized tribunals and systems of arbitration that are concerned with specific groups and specialized activities. Areas of law such as domestic law, contract law, procedural and administrative law, and constitutional law regulate the cooperation that derives from the division of labor. This body of cooperative law is restitutive and "exempt from the effects of the collective consciousness" because it governs specialized activities, ones that concern only a limited section of society, rather than being common to all. Without the central role of the collective conscience, these rules do not demand expiation and are concerned merely with regulating social relations.

The two forms of solidarity have different sanctions and types of law, and they also permit different degrees of personality or individuality. The form of solidarity that has a limited division of labor and a strong collective consciousness can be strong only if the ideas shared by all members are more intensively experienced than the ideas held by individuals. Durkheim explains the distinction: "The solidarity that derives from similarities is at its *maximum* when the collective consciousness completely envelops our total consciousness, coinciding with it at every point. At that moment our individuality is zero."[23] The individual does not exist in this type of society and, indeed, individuality is a function of a different type of social solidarity, one that assumes individual differences. There has to be an element of individual personality that is not touched by the collective conscience in order for people to pursue their special functions. In this case, individuality can flourish, but it does not undermine social cohesion:

> The more extensive this free area is, the stronger the cohesion
> that arises from this solidarity. Indeed, on the one hand each one

of us depends more intimately upon society the more labour is divided up, and on the other, the activity of each one of us is correspondingly more specialised, the more personal it is. Doubtless, however circumscribed that activity may be, it is never completely original. Even in the exercise of our profession we conform to usages and practices that are common to us all in our corporation. Yet even in this case, the burden that we bear is in a different way less heavy than when the whole of society bears down upon us, and this leaves much more room for the free play of our initiative. Here, then, the individuality of the whole grows at the same time as that of the parts. Society becomes more effective in moving in concert, at the same time as each of its elements has more movements that are peculiarly its own.[24]

Durkheim calls this form of social solidarity—that attributable to the division of labor—organic, as it is analogous with the solidarity found in the organism of higher animals, where a biological unity is based upon the specialization of individual parts. So specialization produces interdependence and cooperation among people who depend upon one another's speciality.

The basis of social order among those connected through mechanical solidarity is not just socialization, nor is the division of labor the only basis for social order among those connected through organic solidarity. The law has a role to play too. Although the law appears in Durkheim's theory as an index of solidarity, in mechanical society, it is a product of similar collective consciences, which, through the imposition of repressive measures, then "impose upon everybody uniform beliefs and practices."[25] The division of labor in advanced societies produces restitutive laws that regulate the divided functions. In addition, moral rules accompany each type of solidarity. Under mechanical solidarity, social activities are governed by extensive moral and religious rules. If a highly developed restitutive law exists and does not touch closely upon the collective conscience, there is still a need for moral rules. One source of moral rules, Durkheim believed, is the occupational morality that could be developed for each profession. Such moral rules and ideas of justice force individuals, when entering into commercial relationships, to consider the ends of others, to make compromises, and to consider ends beyond their own. Also, outside the occupational sphere in domestic or social situations, people have to consider their obligations; here, the state is increasingly "charged with reminding us of the sentiment of common solidarity."[26]

This stress on the moral nature of organic society shows how Durkheim rejects the idea that social order in advanced societies is based upon individuals pursuing their own interests through contractual relationships. He thus distances himself from utilitarian and laissez-faire nostrums. Durkheim argues that contracts cannot exist unless there is some socially derived moral force to ensure their regulation. He denies that a moral society could be replaced by one based upon the pursuit of individual economic interests. While cooperation has its moral basis, Durkheim sees the cooperative, interdependent society as one in which individual personality can become strong. Nevertheless, there is still a role for morality. Each profession has its occupational morality: among groups of workers or professionals, there are "opinions" and "usages and customs." And although these are not enforced legally, they command obedience, "which none can infringe without incurring the reprimand of the corporation."[27] People can choose their professions and the features of their personal life, and, although the rules and morals that are necessary to support organic solidarity limit individual initiative, they do not do so in the rigid way that the morality of mechanical solidarity does. The laws and morals of organic solidarity are not so repressive and are amenable to negotiation or change.

For Durkheim, there is an inverse relationship between the collective conscience and individuality. Initially, only tribal societies with mechanical solidarity existed, and because these were based upon identical groups or clans, they "comprise a system of homogenous segments similar to one another,"[28] which he called segmental societies. The structure of organic societies is different because they are made up of a system of different organs with specialized roles and they contain their own differentiated parts. Gradually, organic societies grew, and the existence of features of mechanical solidarity became more hidden, although, as Durkheim believed, they never completely disappeared. The causes of this evolution need to be examined.

In Durkheim's reasoning, the expansion of the division of labor comes about as the social segments lose their individuality, become more permeable, and combine in new ways. Such changes enable new relationships to develop among individuals who were previously separated. Individuals come into greater contact with each other as the boundaries between segments are loosened. Division of labor expands as interaction and commerce grow between segments—a process that Durkheim calls increasing "moral density." In this process, territorial segregation between segments declines, no matter whether the process occurs in a society of nomads, hunters, shepherds, or agricultural villagers. A further development is the rise of cities, which permit more intimate and intense contacts. Developments in communication and transportation also increase moral density as they reduce the gaps between segments.

Moral density also increases intra-social relations, and its effects are multiplied when the population grows, producing an increase in social volume. This dual pressure results in an increase in the division of labor because the "struggle for existence becomes more strenuous."[29] The division of labor enables people to avoid conflict by refining and specializing their tasks, and its benefits enable more people to be maintained and to survive. As a sociologist, Durkheim had a different outlook on the division of labor than did an economist: "We see how different our view of the division of labour appears from that of the economists. For them it consists essentially in producing more. For us this greater productivity is merely a necessary consequence, a side effect of the phenomenon. If we specialise, it is not so as to produce more, but to enable us to live in the new conditions of existence created for us."[30]

Durkheim theorized that, as society increases in volume, the collective consciousness becomes more abstract and cannot make specific demands upon personal conduct because the collective consciousness must then influence a larger population spread over a greater space. As society's demands become less discrete and more universal, the collective consciousness leaves greater space for individual variation. The collective consciousness in segmental society is a traditional form of authority. One factor that breaks down this traditional constraint on individuality is the growth of the city; because the city is based upon the migration of people into its ranks, the power of segmental society and its collective consciousness erodes. The city dweller becomes cut off from authority figures. New ideas, fashions, and beliefs develop in this context where individuality and rationality gain more freedom to develop. Durkheim concludes, "As society spreads out and becomes denser, it envelops the individual less tightly, and in consequence can restrain less efficiently the divergent tendencies that appear."[31] In the urban context, as moral density and volume increase, the individual is less watched and controlled, which enables the individual to escape such controls. The individual becomes increasingly free of the collective consciousness, permitting greater individuality. Therefore, the division of labor is a function of the social structure. A segmental society encloses the individual within tradition, and, as structural changes weaken its grip, individuality and the division of labor can emerge.

Lukes points out that the content of the collective consciousness changes in organic societies: because there are few collective beliefs that can take on the strength of religious character, the collective consciousness becomes more rational and secular.[32] Durkheim gives an exception to this thesis. The idea of human dignity becomes a central part of the common consciousness, allowing it to become the object of a "sort of religion" or "cult of the individual."

As we will discuss later, the place of human dignity in the collective consciousness had to be buttressed by notions of equality of opportunity, a work ethic, and social justice. The collective consciousness in organic society becomes more rational and human. Morality does not require people to obey rules inspired by powers that are outside the human group. Instead it requires people to fulfill their tasks, which should be allocated according to their talents and for which they should be justly rewarded.

In Durkheim's view, organic society does have rules, but they are concerned with the functions of each organ of society. Different parts of the division of labor have their own rules, moralities, and laws, but they do not restrict the broader freedoms of the individual. These occupational rules only invoke a small number of consciences and do not require or invoke a collective consciousness. His generally optimistic tone regarding the possibility of social cohesion within organic solidarity begins to change during his discussion of the moral nature of organic society and, especially, when he admits that there is "only reason to believe, as we shall see later more clearly, that in our present-day societies this morality has still not developed to the extent which from now onwards is necessary for them."[33]

This theme reoccurs in Durkheim's discussion of the origins of the division of labor, which he states can only occur within an existing order that has sufficient moral constraints to prevent chaos emerging.

The Abnormal Forms of the Division of Labor

Despite Durkheim's portrayal of the organic society as normal, in the last section of *The Division of Labour in Society*, he discusses some abnormal forms of the division of labor, which he represents as pathological states.

Anomie
The first example, called *anomie*, refers to industrial and commercial crises and bankruptcies that represent a lack of adjustment in the division of labor. Durkheim says that the number of bankruptcies in France rose by 70 percent between the years 1845 and 1869. The struggle between capital and labor is an example of conflict, rather than solidarity, that proceeds from increases in the division of labor.[34] Durkheim describes an industrial history in which conflict increases with successive changes in the division of labor and the organization of work. For example, the medieval workshop is described as a place of cooperation, equality, and regular interaction between the master and his workers. From the fifteenth century, Durkheim argues, a separation developed between workers and the masters, and each formed their own organizations, which would periodically come into conflict and engage in strikes and boycotts;

however, the conflicts were not perpetual. From the seventeenth century on, with the birth of large-scale industry, workers and employers became more separated, work became more specialized and regimented, revolts become more frequent, and, as Durkheim wrote, the "war has become increasingly more violent."[35]

The existence of periodic industrial crises and conflicts shows that organic solidarity has not been perfectly achieved. In Durkheim's analysis, this is not because of the decline of mechanical solidarity but because "all the conditions for the existence of the former [organic solidarity] have not been realized."[36] In particular, the regulation of different functions did not develop properly. To facilitate cooperation and avoid constant conflict, a system of regulation is needed, which, in most instances, predetermines the way in which specialized organizations relate to each other. This system of regulation is an extension of the division of labor. If specialized organs relate and interact together in a mutual way, then these actions are repeated and become habits, which, in turn, may develop into rules of conduct. Mutually beneficial transactions among the functions of the division of labor lead to repetition or customary practices, and even become obligatory, but they are not the source of organic solidarity. This regulatory system grows out of the division of labor and helps it to function.

Durkheim argued that the necessary regulation did not exist in, or was out of step with, the current stage of the division of labor, and, therefore, "this lack of regulation does not allow the functions to perform regularly and harmoniously."[37] Durkheim clearly believed that some form of regulation is necessary over and above the price mechanism that economists use as the device for regulating the relationship between supply and demand. The price mechanism cannot avoid periods of disruption and instability, and the greater the complexity of social organization the greater is the need for regulation. If the division of labor does not produce solidarity in markets or factory systems, it is because they are not regulated; this lack of regulation is what he calls anomie. The state of anomie cannot exist if specialized organs have been in regular contact over time because regulation is consolidated in this way. Anomie arises when contacts are rare or infrequent or too new, and so each situation is one of trial and error. Durkheim takes the example of economic markets. In the segmental or mechanical type of society, markets correspond to each segment. Producers are near their consumers and can easily calculate the needs of the local population. With the advent of organic solidarity, the boundaries of these segments break down, and local markets expand so that they are national or even global in scale. Producers are no longer supplying a local and known market, and they cannot easily see the market's extent or limits. Production becomes unregulated, producers tend to overestimate or underestimate demand, and crises ensue.

Modern production showing the repetitive and socially isolated work described by Durkheim as anomic.

Anomie also exists in the industrial factory system, which developed to service large markets and caused changing relations between employers and employees. The introduction of machinery to replace manufacture, the regimented discipline of the factory, the separation of the workers from their families during the working day, and the separate lifestyles of the employers and employees all required new organization and regulation. The rapid pace of growth of the industrial system meant that "the conflicting interests have not had time to strike an equilibrium."[38] Like Marx, Durkheim analyzed the effects of machinery: another manifestation of anomie is the experience of specialized workers who tend machines and perform repetitive work. This work is often performed as a monotonous routine, without interest or understanding, and the worker "is no more than a lifeless cog, which an external force sets in motion and impels in the same direction and in the same fashion."[39] One solution to this debasement of workers would be to provide them with a general education; but once they are accustomed to a concern with art or literature, Durkheim argues, they would find being treated as a machine even more offensive. Unlike Marx, however, he regarded the experience of the denatured and isolated worker as a product of the rapid development of specialization at work rather than as an inherent product of the capitalist division of labor. In its normal development, workers within the division of labor interact with their fellow workers in their different, but related, tasks. Durkheim explains that the worker need not experience work as a machine because an awareness of the goals of the task will develop, which will give the work intelligence and meaning.

Durkheim took up these issues again in his preface to the second edition of *The Division of Labour in Society*. Here, he portrays economic life as unregulated, chaotic, and anarchic, where no one knows what their roles and obligations are and where great conflict and disorder exist. Those who defend market society do so because they believe it supports individual liberty, but he argues that true liberty can only be realized when there is regulation by a superior moral force to prevent the abuse of physical or economic power.

For anomie in economic life to cease, there must be a group that can generate the rules that are needed. Durkheim thought that the state was not sufficiently involved in economic activities to be able to create adequate regulation, so he believed that each professional and occupational group, drawn from all participants in each industry and organized into a single body, should carry out this task. In general terms, such bodies would have to be capable of morally regulating national and international markets; therefore, they would have to include all members of an occupation distributed over large territories. National assemblies of elected representatives of employers and employees would head the corporations. Corporations would fix levels of production; wages and salaries; and the duties of agencies within the industry, both to each other and to the public. They would also be a source of employment law within each industry. Durkheim thought that such corporations would go beyond providing the economic and moral regulation of economic life to fulfill other needs such as education, welfare, and the cultural requirements of their members. They would establish a political organ between the individual and the state, especially because old sentiments toward local communities had weakened.

The Forced Division of Labor

A second abnormal division of labor is the forced division of labor; this point directs attention to structural inequalities and how these restrict people's opportunities and lead to oppression and, possibly, class conflict. Here, Durkheim entered the territory of class inequalities more usually associated with Marx, but, instead of seeing such structural features as endemic to capitalism, he chose to see them as temporary features of the pathological state of the division of labor. The existence of classes, he thought, not only leads to the allocation of less rewarding and satisfying work to the lower classes but also can be the source of class conflict if people cease to be satisfied with restricted opportunities and if they believe that the restrictions can be removed. Because humans have different abilities and aptitudes—and if social solidarity is to develop with the division of labor—specialized tasks have to fit the individual's natural talents. The existence of classes and castes hamper the spontaneous allocation of work to those with the appropriate aptitudes and abilities.

The inheritance of occupational positions through family ties is not in accordance with a spontaneous allocation of work. The children of those who own businesses may not inherit the needed aptitudes and abilities, and allocation along hereditary lines restricts the opportunity of others who may possess the necessary talents. Similarly, the hereditary transmission of wealth may give advantage to some, particularly in ways that are discrepant with their personal qualities. If the division of labor is spontaneous, however, "social inequalities express precisely natural inequalities." Perfect spontaneity requires "absolute equality in the external conditions of the struggle," even though this situation is never perfectly realized. In segmental societies, the collective conscience may legitimate inequalities in the way work is allocated, but in societies that have organic solidarity, contracts are central to social and economic life. In such contracts, through which people exchange equivalent values, the contract must be just, not a product of inequality. External conditions must become level:

> Every form of superiority has repercussions on the way in which contracts are arrived at. If, therefore it does not depend upon the person of individuals and their services to society, it invalidates the moral conditions of the exchange. If one class in society is obliged, in order to live, to secure the acceptance by others of its services, whilst another class can do without them, because of the resources already at its disposal, resources that, however, are not necessarily the result of some social superiority, the latter group can lord it over the former. In other words, there can be no rich or poor by birth without there being unjust contracts.[40]

Social inequalities need to be reduced to allow a modern solidarity based upon the division of labour to function. Consequently, the need of a common faith to provide social order has to be replaced by a need of justice.

In *Professional Ethics and Civil Morals*, Durkheim refers to the need to end the inheritance of wealth in order to prevent the forcing of unjust contracts upon the poor. The ending of inheritance within propertied families implies the handing over of wealth to the corporations who would become the new heirs.[41] Also, in the conclusion of the second preface to *The Division of Labour in Society*, he states his support for the socializing of production. His discussion of the need to allocate people to tasks that are commensurate with their natural abilities and aptitudes, and his reference to equalizing the external conditions in which people enter the competition for work appear to point in the direction of a meritocracy, where social inequalities would reflect natural inequalities only. Such appeals for economic justice reflect the arguments of socialists in his time.[42] Durkheim's analysis of social, structural, and moral change built upon the contrast between two types of social solidarity. His studies led him to the conclusion that a new type of social solidarity was possible based upon new forms of rights and duties, ones in which there would be more individual freedom and choice of action. However, this increased liberty requires the existence of rules and justice to regulate the more complex, specialized society. The shattered old morality cannot be resuscitated as it no longer corresponds to new conditions. Durkheim's diagnosis points to the need for a new goal—the creation of a new moral code—which cannot be created in the study of a social theorist but would have to be created in cumulative responses to emerging social strains and conflicts.

Criticisms

Durkheim was well informed regarding the ideas of Marx and other socialists, and he gave a series of lectures in 1895 in which he discussed the socialist ideology and the social conditions that gave rise to socialist ideas.[43] Durkheim did not find the class character and conflictual nature of socialist ideas attractive, and he regarded socialist ideas as a reaction to the tensions produced by the decline of social regulation and the injustice produced by class divisions. It is not surprising that his theory, which is based upon organic solidarity rather than class conflict, would be criticized by Marxist sociologists for not referring to the structural contradiction between social classes. The contrast between mechanical solidarity in simple societies and organic solidarity in complex ones is fundamental to Durkheim's theoretical position, but it has been challenged by Hunt who argues that the anthropological evidence suggests that Durkheim overemphasized the role of repressive law in primitive societies and that, although his argument about the expansion of restitutive law is strong, there is evidence that the capitalist state has expanded some repressive laws, especially in relation to offenses dealing with property.[44]

Conclusion

The Division of Labour in Society introduces several enduring themes in Durkheim's work. One of them is the idea of social evolution from simple, mechanical solidarity to a more complex organic one. The analysis of this evolution involves an analysis at the level of social structure, in which structural change, such as the increasing volume and moral density of society in its evolution from the segmental type, leads to changes in the collective consciousness as well as the differentiation of specialized organs of society. The idea of the freedom of the individual is also connected to this process of structural change. Durkheim believed that the division of labor could produce both greater independence for the individual and greater functional integration and social solidarity. In capitalist industrial society an organic division of labor occurs. However, he identified some abnormal forms that prevented this "normal" organic situation from being realized. His criticisms of capitalism revolve around the anarchy of the market, anomie, and the unjust nature of the forced division of labor.

Anomie is a key critical concept that Durkheim introduced in *The Division of Labour in Society*. It describes the breakdown of social regulation and the failure to provide a moral regulation of people's naturally limitless desires, a situation of collapse that results from rapid social change. Since the 1980s, when US President Ronald Reagan, Britain's Prime Minister Margaret Thatcher, and Canada's Prime Minister Brian Mulroney furthered the influence of neoliberal thinkers such as the economist Milton Friedman and the philosopher Friedrich August von Hayek, the discourse of free markets, individualism, and the laissez-faire state became popularized. This helped to usher in a less regulated, more market-oriented version of capitalism. One possible outcome of the *marketization* of society is that a lack of regulation (or anomie) could produce a situation that is conducive to corporate crime. In 2002, for instance, there was a wave of corporate accounting scandals that implicated top US executives at Enron, Adelphia Communications, and WorldCom. Passas has applied anomie theory in a wide-ranging analysis of globalization and neoliberalism in the developed world, where social inequalities have increased, and in the developing world, where traditional goals and constraints have weakened under the impact of Western consumerist goals. The country that has experienced the most extreme anomie, he says, is post-Soviet Russia, which underwent the transition from socialism to capitalism after its command economy collapsed and it embarked on a rapid neoliberal experiment: "In the 1990's, however, the rates of fraud, prostitution, drug trafficking and abuse, alcoholism, smuggling, white-collar crime, violence and corruption sky-rocketed."[45]

As globalization leads to the decline of the importance of manufacturing, some Western societies became more reliant on their financial sectors to produce wealth, create jobs, and provide highly paid work that can be taxed to support government spending. In the boom prior to 2008, bankers were sometimes referred to as "masters of the Universe," but a series of scandals came to light including HSBC's failure to prevent money laundering by Mexican drug cartels; the payment of millions of pounds by British banks to compensate customers for the mis-selling of personal protection insurance; and the weak controls at UBS, which failed to stop a trader, Kweku Adoboli, from losing £1.5 billion sterling. The biggest scandal, though, was the fraudulent rigging of Libor, which it is believed was carried out by about a dozen banks around the world over a period of several years. Taken together, these practices have exposed both a culture of greed and dishonesty and a lack of regulation within banks during this period of casino-style banking.

Any one of these scandals could be perceived as indicative of the existence of anomie as defined by Durkheim, but the conspiracy to fix Libor is the most worthy of a longer comment because of the scale of its economic and moral impact. Libor stands for the London Interbank Offered Rate and is the interest rate at which banks agreed to lend to each other. It was set across 15 time frames of up to one year and in ten currencies.[46] Put simply, about 20 banks submitted a daily rate at which they claimed to pay to obtain loans from other banks, and the average was used by banks to set the prices charged on transactions valued at least £300 trillion in financial contracts around the world, including contracts such as business loans and household mortgages. The Greek financier Minos Zombanakis, who is widely credited with setting up the system in the 1960s, acknowledged in an interview after the scandal had erupted that the system was built on the assumption that people would act with honesty and trust—that the people involved in the market were "gentlemen."[47] Subsequently, at least three banks were fined by the British Financial Services Authority (FSA) and the US Commodity Futures Trading Commission (CFTC). A British bank, Barclays, was fined £290 million in June 2012 and another British bank, the Royal Bank of Scotland (RBS), was fined £390 million in February 2013. The Swiss bank UBS was fined £940 million in December 2012.[48] Inadequate controls by banks over traders allowed them to manipulate submitted prices. FSA and CFTC reports into the three fined banks include examples of electronic communications between traders and brokers (who work as intermediaries between banks) which reveal how deals were done to lower rates in order to conceal that a bank was in financial difficulties or to raise rates to increase profits and bonuses. One communication from a UBS trader to a broker stated, "I need you to keep it [the six-month Japanese Libor rate] as low as possible ... if you do that ... I'll pay you, you know, 50,000 dollars, 100,000 dollars ... whatever you want."[49] Other communications reveal offers to pay £15,000 per quarter or to provide "sushi rolls" and Bollinger champagne. Between 2005 and 2009, Barclays traders made 257 requests to fix rates.

These abuses can be understood as symptoms of anomie, and they relate to one aspect of Durkheim's concept—the lack of regulation in the market. As first presented in *The Division of Labour,* though, anomie has another facet—the manner in which the specialization of tasks within industrialized factories and processing plants creates empty, repetitive tasks in which work for the worker lacks interest and meaning. The following two examples involving scandals in the meat industry in Europe and Canada can be understood, respectively, as a reflection of each of these senses of anomie. The first example is a Europe-wide scandal involving the contamination of frozen and fresh meat products, such as beef burgers and lasagne, with horsemeat. The Food Safety Authority of Ireland (FSAI) tested a range of beef burgers and ready meals from supermarkets and found horse DNA in over one-third of the beef burger samples.[50] It is not clear whether the agency looked for other species' DNA in beef products in the course of a random check or because it had been tipped off, but, because of the serious nature of the findings and their potential damage to commercial interests, the FSAI spent a further two months retesting before publishing its findings in January 2013. The FSAI found two factories in Ireland and one in the UK as the source of the contamination or adulteration. Two of these sources were subsidiaries of APB Food Group, one of the largest beef processors in Europe. APB blamed the contamination on their suppliers in the Netherlands, Spain, and Poland. The Polish government checked its horse slaughterhouses and found no irregularities in labeling. Five weeks after the outbreak of the scandal in Ireland, the source of contamination in the chain was still not clear.

Following the Irish findings, the UK FSA asked the industry to test its beef products for horse. These tests revealed that beef products made for Tesco, Aldi, and Findus by a French manufacturer, Comigel, contained up to 100 percent horse. Comigel made contaminated beef meals for supermarkets and food brands in 16 countries including Germany, Sweden, Belgium, the Netherlands, Switzerland, Ireland, and the UK, leading to the widespread withdrawal of these products across Europe. The trail of the French manufacturing scandal involved the subcontracting of ready meal production to Tavola, a factory in Luxembourg. It was supplied with meat by a company in the South of France, Spanghero, which had bought meat from a Dutch trader called Draap (which is Dutch for horse spelled backward) whose owner, Fasen, had previously been convicted for fraudulently labeling horse as beef in deals going back to 2007. The horsemeat found in ready meals exported from France was said to have been imported by Draap from Romania. The Romanian government said that this meat had been labeled correctly as horse. The French government said Spanghero was the first to label the horse as beef, though Spanghero denied doing so deliberately. Fasen claimed that Spanghero and Comigel were aware of the deception. The degree of specialization and task differentiation within these production and distribution processes, as well as the concomitant interconnectedness required by the new work environment, meant that tracking down a culprit—even at the level of a whole company—was difficult.

According to Lawrence, "The food and retail industries have become highly concentrated and globalized in recent decades. A handful of key players dominate the beef processing and supermarket sectors across Europe."[51] They have organized long supply chains, which enabled them to buy ingredients for processed food as cheaply as possible on the global commodity markets. The supply chain involved brokers, cold-storage operators, and subcontracted meat-cutting plants to supply fluctuating orders "just in time." These changes happened in a context in which supermarket buyers and food brands had driven down prices as recession-hit consumers reduced their spending. At the same time, manufacturers' costs had been increasing. Regulation of the meat industry in the UK had been reduced, as the trend had been to deregulate, reduce government-employed inspectors, and allow the industry to police itself. The number of inspectors declined from around 1,700 to around 800. A further dimension to the scandal was the growing international trade in knackered horses, including horses bred for racing and pets; and this was a trade without proper passports. Because of the number of fake passports, there was not a reliable record of which of horses had been treated with an anti-inflammatory drug called phenylbutazone or "bute," which is banned from the human food chain because it can cause aplastic anemia or bone marrow failure. Some horse-meat containing bute found its way into the human food chain.

In the following example deregulation and food contamination was also a feature of the Canadian food industry. A huge amount of meat from the XL Foods Inc. plant in Brooks, Alberta, for example, was recalled. The plant was closed for a month, and thousands of workers were laid off because of an outbreak of E. coli, which poisoned many people. This was one of Canada's largest meat processing plants, with more than 4,000 head of cattle processed per day. It processed and packed meat supplied to more than a dozen countries. Media coverage concentrated on the danger of tainted meat for the public, but also of concern were the occupational health and safety risks to the "voiceless workers—many of whom are temporary and foreign."[52] The nature of the work, which was highly mechanized with line speeds that were too fast for workers to keep up, is very reminiscent of the routinized, repetitive, mindless work characterized as anomic by Durkheim. On average, workers had to deal with 260 carcasses per hour, which did not give them time to follow safety protocols. About a third of the 2,200 employees at XL Foods were temporary foreign workers, and the company had a high rate of labor turnover. It often had insufficient workers to maintain line speeds. A list of regulation failures by the Canada Food Inspection Agency (CFIA) included "deficiencies in sanitation and maintenance; grease build-up and blood clots on the evisceration table; broken eye/handwash tap; large amounts of fat and meat build-up throughout; water pooling on the floors; a foul odour from a drain near the rendering room; condensation on the kill floor and in the offal hallway dripping onto boxed products; [and] improper airflow at the processing floor."[53] People worked in hot, humid conditions among moving equipment and often had to work on wet slippery floors. Workers had to use knives to cut carcasses that they had to process in seconds to keep up with the line. Workers were provided with protective clothing but often did not use it because it was uncomfortable or because goggles steamed up in the heat. As a result, they were at risk of inhaling airborne contaminants and being exposed to contamination when they handled carcasses stained with blood, feces, and body fluids. In this context, the inexperienced workers were not well trained in safety procedures and food safety regulations. Like Marx, Durkheim was aware that a major criticism of the division of labor was that it reduced the worker to a mere cog in a machine, to someone isolated from other workers and forced to perform a narrow activity as mere routine and with little understanding of the process as a whole. This lack of opportunity to comprehend the total process and perform the work with more understanding and not in a way that was so debasing contributed to the contamination of the product as well as to the endangerment of the health and safety of employees. The examples presented in the concluding discussion are intended to suggest that anomie is endemic in capitalist market societies in the conditions of work in many situations and, especially, in the lack of regulation in economic institutions and markets.

FURTHER THINKING:

What did Durkheim mean by anomie? Is anomie a relevant concept in contemporary capitalist societies?

FURTHER READING:

See Émile Durkheim, *The Division of Labour in Society* (1933; New York: The Free Press, 1997), 291–322. The following are also useful secondary sources on Durkheim: Ken Morrison, *Marx, Durkheim, Weber: Formations of Modern Social Thought*, 2nd ed. (London: Sage, 2006); Alex Callinicos, *Social Theory: A Historical Introduction*, 2nd ed. (Cambridge: Polity Press, 2007), 133–38.

Notes

1 Anthony Giddens, *Capitalism and Modern Social Theory* (Cambridge: Cambridge University Press, 1971), ix.

2 Alex Callinicos, *Social Theory* (Cambridge: Polity Press, 1999), 124.

3 Ken Morrison, *Marx, Durkheim, Weber: Formations of Modern Social Thought*, 2nd ed. (London: Sage Publications, 2006), 160.

4 Steven Lukes, *Émile Durkheim: His Life and Work* (Harmondsworth, UK: Penguin Books, 1973), 54–55.

5 Lukes, *Émile Durkheim*, 67.

6 Lukes, *Émile Durkheim*, 366.

7 Frank Parkin, *Durkheim* (Oxford: Oxford University Press, 1992), 5.

8 Morrison, *Marx, Durkheim, Weber*, 150.

9 Morrison, *Marx, Durkheim, Weber*, 151.

10 Morrison, *Marx, Durkheim, Weber*, 152–53.

11 Morrison, *Marx, Durkheim, Weber*, 153.

12 Émile Durkheim, *The Division of Labour in Society* (New York: The Free Press, 1997), 162.

13 Durkheim, *The Division of Labour*, xxx.

14 Durkheim, *The Division of Labour*, 3.

15 Durkheim, *The Division of Labour*, 3.

16 Durkheim, *The Division of Labour*, 24.

17 Durkheim, *The Division of Labour*, 29.

18 Durkheim, *The Division of Labour*, 38.

19 Durkheim, *The Division of Labour*, 40.

20 Durkheim, *The Division of Labour*, 48.

21 Durkheim, *The Division of Labour*, 56.

22 Durkheim, *The Division of Labour*, 64.

23 Durkheim, *The Division of Labour*, 84.

24 Durkheim, *The Division of Labour*, 137.

25 Durkheim, *The Division of Labour*, 172.

26 Durkheim, *The Division of Labour*, 173.

27 Durkheim, *The Division of Labour*, 172.

28 Durkheim, *The Division of Labour*, 131.

29 Durkheim, *The Division of Labour*, 208.

30 Durkheim, *The Division of Labour*, 217.

31 Durkheim, *The Division of Labour*, 238.

32 Lukes, *Émile Durkheim*, 156.

33 Durkheim, *The Division of Labour*, 174.

34 Durkheim, *The Division of Labour*, 292.

35 Durkheim, *The Division of Labour*, 293.

36 Durkheim, *The Division of Labour*, 301.

37 Durkheim, *The Division of Labour*, 303.

38 Durkheim, *The Division of Labour*, 306.

39 Durkheim, *The Division of Labour*, 306–7.

40 Durkheim, *The Division of Labour*, 319.

41 Irving M. Zeitlin, *Ideology and the Development of Sociological Theory*, 7th ed. (Upper Saddle River, NJ: Prentice Hall, 2001), 345.

42 Susan Stedman Jones, *Durkheim Reconsidered* (Cambridge: Polity Press, 2001), 51.

43 Zeitlin, *Ideology and the Development of Sociological Theory*, 331.

44 Alan Hunt, *The Sociological Movement in Law* (London: Macmillan, 1978), 70–72.

45 Nikos Passas, "Global Anomie, Dysnomie and Economic Crime: Hidden Consequences of Neoliberalism and Globalization in Russia and Around the World," *Social Justice* 27 (2000): 16–44.

46 Jill Treanor, "'Day of Shame' as RBS Fined £390m," *The Guardian*, January 7, 2013, 1.

47 Helena Smith, "System Was Set Up in a More Honest Age, Says Its Inventor," *The Guardian*, December 18, 2012, 23.

48 Jill Treanor, "UBS Libor Case Uncovers Tangled Web of Bank-Broker Relations at Heart of System," *The Guardian*, December 20, 2012, 29.

49 "UBS Libor Emails: 'I'll Pay You $50,000, $100,000 ... Whatever You Want' to Rig Rate Trader Told Broker," *The Telegraph*, December 19, 2012, http://www.telegraph.co.uk/finance/libor-scandal/9755021/UBS-Libor-emails-Ill-pay-you-50000–100000-...-whatever-you-want-to-rig-rate-trader-told-broker.html.

50 Felicity Lawrence, "Horsemeat Scandal: The Essential Guide," *The Guardian*, February 15, 2013, http://www.guardian.co.uk/uk/2013/feb/15/horsemeat-scandal-the-essential-guide.

51 Lawrence, "Horsemeat Scandal."

52 Jean Lian, "Silence on the Floor," OHS Canada, *Canada's Occupational Health and Safety Magazine*, January/February 2013, http://www.ohscanada.com/news/silence-on-the-floor/1001981474/.

53 Lian, "Silence on the Floor."

8. Émile Durkheim: *The Rules of Sociological Method* and *On Suicide*

Without denying the importance of his concern with "solidarity" and the conservation of societies, we have found good cause to support the view that there is an important strand of radical criticism in his work, backed by a secular reforming spirit.

—Steve Fenton, 1984[1]

Émile Durkheim taught the modern world how to think about suicide. Before him, suicide seemed a matter of purely individual despair. Durkheim saw that suicide has a social dimension. People from different religions, classes, and religious backgrounds destroy themselves in different proportions. Durkheim asked why this should be.

—Richard Sennett, 2006[2]

THE DIVISION OF LABOUR IN SOCIETY and the two other books that this chapter is devoted to represent Durkheim's endeavor to establish a scientific method of studying society, one that focuses on society as a distinct level of analysis. He was opposed to the utilitarians, such as John Stuart Mill and Jeremy Bentham, who believed that isolated individuals were free to enter into contracts in the pursuit of self-interest and, thus, owed nothing to society. In *The Division of Labour in Society*, he argues that contracts cannot exist unless there are pre-existing rules and customs surrounding contracts that both enable and restrain contractual relationships. Durkheim argues that "collective life did not arise from individual life; on the contrary, it is the latter that emerged from the former."[3] He wanted to establish a subject matter for sociology, which he believed needed to concentrate on a level of reality that is external to the individual. As a consequence of this level of focus, sociology, Durkheim argued, could be based upon the techniques of observation. He distinguished between the study of the mind of individuals, psychology, and the study of facts that are external to individuals, and thereby challenging the idea that the individual is at the center of society. He was critical of Tarde, who argued that society is no more than the transmission of acts from one person to another through imitation.[4] Durkheim was also opposed to early sociologists such as Comte and Spencer, whom he thought were still too wedded to speculative theories of evolution rather than to an objective analysis based upon the observation of social facts. A contemporary student might think that a book entitled *The Rules of Sociological Method* would contain a discussion of different ways of collecting information, such as surveys, questionnaires, or focus groups. Instead, it is a highly polemical work concerned with establishing the new discipline of sociology and challenging individualistic, psychological explanations and philosophical speculation.

Sociological Method

Social Facts

In his second book, *The Rules of Sociological Method*, Durkheim tries to make the method he developed in *The Division of Labour in Society* more explicit. To begin with, Durkheim establishes that there are *social facts* that are external to individuals and that affect how people act: "When I fulfil my obligations as brother, husband, or citizen, when I execute my contracts, I perform duties which are defined, externally to myself and my acts, in law and in custom."[5] These social facts are external because individuals do not create them and only become aware of their existence through education or socialization. Examples of social facts are the religious beliefs and practices that people hold, the language used to express thoughts, the system of currency, and professional practices; all of these function independently and exist independent of the individuals who live in a society at a particular time. He states, "Here, then, are ways of acting, thinking, and feeling that present the noteworthy property of existing outside the individual consciousness."[6]

In addition, Durkheim argues that these social facts possess a "coercive power" and impose themselves upon the individual. In many instances, people consent and conform to the type of conduct expected of them and do not experience constraint unless they try to resist these social constraints, when they become aware of their force. Also, whereas the law counters its violation with expiation or compensation for the harm done, public attitude exercises a check on morality and administers less violent (though possibly more emotionally hurtful) punishments than does the law. The breaching of conventions such as dress codes or ways of speaking may lead to ridicule or ostracism. Durkheim writes, "Here, then, is a category of facts with very distinctive characteristics: it consists of ways of acting, thinking, and feeling, external to the individual, and endowed with a power of coercion, by reason of which they control him."[7] These social facts—which contain ways of acting and their representations—are not biological phenomena, nor are they psychological phenomena: they are outside individual consciences. Because the source of these facts is not the individual, Durkheim claims to have identified a new variety of phenomena to be called social: "their substratum can be no other than society."[8] Consequently, "these ways of thinking and acting constitute the proper domain of sociology."[9] In this view, people do not completely determine themselves: rather, "most of our ideas and tendencies come from without. How can they become a part of us except by imposing themselves upon us?"[10]

Some social facts, such as legal and moral rules, religious doctrine, and financial constraints, appear to be derived from social institutions; however, people might experience other social facts as feelings derived from *social currents*, such as the emotion that can develop in a crowd. Other social currents might be currents of opinion on religious, political, or artistic affairs. Another example given by Durkheim is the socialization and education of children: "All education is a continuous effort to impose on the child ways of seeing, feeling, and acting which he could not have arrived at spontaneously."[11] Social facts might be recognized by the way they are written down, communicated, or become a moral or legal rule. They take on collective dimensions as beliefs, tendencies, or practices, even though individual manifestations have their own features. Currents of opinion may impel certain groups to certain levels of marriage, birth rate, or suicide, which can be expressed in statistics, but the details of individual cases are concealed within the statistics.[12] The domain of sociology is the study of social facts, and "a social fact is every way of acting, fixed or not, capable of exercising on the individual an external constraint; or again, every way of acting which is general throughout a given society, while at the same time existing in its own right independent of its individual manifestations."[13]

The Observation of Social Facts

Durkheim's next step was to establish some rules for the observation of social facts, which he believed could be considered things. Something has the character of a thing if it can be subject to observation—it can be treated as data—and Durkheim (as was seen earlier) identified some specifically sociological facts. Social life is imbued with values, and, although these cannot be observed directly, it is possible to study them scientifically because there is a "phenomenal reality" that expresses them. For instance, morality is expressed in the body of rules governing conduct. Social phenomena are distinct from the "consciously formed representations of them in the mind" and can be studied "objectively as external things."[14] These phenomena are objective because individuals cannot alter them with their will, and an understanding of them that reflects their nature has to be developed empirically. Laws are embodied in legal codes; statistical data are collected on social activities; fashions are preserved in clothing; and taste is developed in works of art: all of these take on an independent existence external to the consciousness of individuals. Later in the preface to the second edition, he refers to these social phenomena as "collective representations" that convey "the way in which the group conceives itself in relation to objects which affect it."[15] As Lukes says, Durkheim's sociology of knowledge and of religion involved a systematic study of collective representations.[16]

The Normal and the Pathological

Durkheim was able to find a justification for science to be a guide to practical action by making a distinction between normal and unhealthy societies: "Briefly, for societies as for individuals, health is good and desirable; disease, on the contrary, is bad and to be avoided. If, then, we can find an objective criterion, inherent in the facts themselves, which enables us to distinguish scientifically between health and morbidity in the various orders of social phenomena, science will be in a position to throw light on practical problems and still remain faithful to its own method."[17] He defines *health* as the "perfect adaptation of the organism to its environment" and *morbidity* as anything that "disturbs this adaptation." Because these arguments apply to living organisms, he thought they could be extended to societies; therefore, he needed criteria for assessing the health or morbidity of societies, that is, for evaluating the "various degrees of completeness of this adaptation."[18] A normal, healthy society is one having the social conditions that are generally found within all societies—bearing in mind the stage of the society's development, just as the young adult stage will be different from that of an old person.[19] Morbid or pathological states are ones that depart from this normal state.

Durkheim applied his definition of normality to crime, which is commonly seen as a pathological condition. Although what is deemed to be crime varies between societies, he claims that all societies identify some acts as deserving of punishment. To say that the existence of crime is normal seems a startling conclusion. Durkheim does not say that crime is ever present because all societies contain wicked people, but he asserts that it is "a factor in public health, an integral part of all healthy societies."[20] Crime is normal because all societies have it and also because it offends the collective conscience. Crime is functionally useful to society because punishment reinforces the values that a crime offends, and some criminals could be harbingers of a new and more progressive morality.[21]

Rules for the Explanation of Social Facts

In the fifth chapter of *The Rules of Sociological Method*, Durkheim makes a distinction between the functions of a fact and the cause or origin of that fact. The demonstration that a fact is useful does not explain its origins. We may have a need for things, but we cannot will them into existence. So again, Durkheim uses his discussion of social facts to stress their independent nature and force and to distinguish between individualistic and sociological explanations: "But since each one of them is a force, superior to that of the individual, and since it has a separate existence, it is not true that merely by willing to do so may one call them into being. No force can be engendered except by an antecedent force."[22] Causal and functional analyses are separate orders of analysis. However, taken together, they give a fuller understanding of a social phenomenon because a fact may need to have a function for it to survive. Durkheim was critical of Comte and Spencer's discussions of society that were ultimately teleological and psychological. Rather than looking at society as based on individual psychology, Durkheim argued that society "exercises pressure on individual consciences"; it is an external impulse to which people submit. The pressure exerted by society is the "pressure which the totality exerts on the individual": the whole is greater than the sum of its parts. Furthermore, a system formed by the association of individuals is a reality with its own characteristics. The group gives people ways of thinking, feeling, and acting that are different than those that isolated individuals would have. "Collective representations, emotions and tendencies are caused not by certain states of the consciences of individuals but by the conditions in which the social group in its totality is placed."[23] Sentiments are formed by the social group—by social organization rather than by the individual. For these reasons, sociological and psychological explanations are very different. Psychological states may be associated with social conditions, but rather than explaining social facts by psychological or innate human characteristics, sociologists explain these characteristics with reference to the preceding social facts. In other words, the sociologist is concerned with how the human milieu "exerts influence on the course of social phenomena." Durkheim refers to two aspects of the social milieu that affect social existence: the volume or size of a society and its dynamic density. This last aspect refers to the number who share a common life, the extent to which social segments are fused, and whether a society has experienced the intensification of social life so that the horizons of individual thought and action can be extended.[24]

Rules Relative to Establishing Sociological Proofs

Durkheim states that the only way to establish that a given social fact is the cause of another is to observe how one fact (the effect) varies in relation to another (its cause). In sociology, these social facts cannot be artificially produced in an experimental situation, so they must be observed as they occur in social situations by using the method of comparison, in what may be described as an indirect experiment. Because of the complexity of social phenomena, Durkheim argues that the methods of agreement and difference are not applicable, particularly as it may be impossible to isolate all but one of the causal variables. Consequently, he argues for the utility of the method of concomitant variations, a method that can test the variation or movement between two variables. From the analysis of observed data, a sociologist may be able to deduce how one of two phenomena may produce the other. This proposition will become clearer in the discussion of Durkheim's use of the comparative method in his study of suicide rates. Comparisons can then be made to test a theorized possible cause of a particular effect, and if the connection is verified through the comparison, the cause, it is said, can be proven. Durkheim suggested that, throughout history, there have been many variations in collective life, and sociologists can draw upon the evidence of this. Some evidence is present in all societies, including crime, suicide, birth rate, marriage rate, and the practice of thrift; these are manifest in different forms according to a diverse social milieu, such as geographical location, profession, or religious faith. In *The Rules of Sociological Method*, Durkheim sets out an argument for a causal science of the social world to achieve an objective analysis by treating social facts as things.

On Suicide

Suicide was perceived in the late nineteenth century as a growing social problem, and it served as a test of both Durkheim's methodology and his concept of the field of sociology. As Durkheim defines *suicide*, "the term applied to any case of death resulting directly or indirectly from a positive or negative act, carried out by the victim himself, which he was aware would produce this result."[25] Psychology concentrates on individual factors such as character, temperament, or the features of an individual's life prior to suicide, but Durkheim emphasized the centrality of the suicide rate, which he argues is an objective social fact. He provides statistics for several countries and demonstrates that each tends to have a relatively stable suicide rate over a period of years, unless there is sudden social upheaval. Suicide rates are thus seen as social facts; each society has its own tendency to produce voluntary deaths, and it is the social causes of these rates that constitute the sociological study of suicide.[26]

Durkheim criticized explanations of suicide that are based on extra-social factors such as psychopathic or mental states, race, heredity, climate, and imitation. The elimination of individual and psychological explanations enabled him to develop his original theory regarding the connection between the total rate of suicide and different social contexts. He stressed that the focus should be on the general social state that produces suicides rather than on suicidal motives, which are only the most apparent causes and are "merely the individual repercussions of a general state ... One might say that they indicate the individual's weak points, those through which the current, which comes from outside inviting him to destroy himself might most easily enter."[27] Only later in his thinking, does Durkheim consider how the general causes of suicide affect the individual in ways that produce suicidal acts.

Social Integration: Egoistic Suicide and Altruistic Suicide
Durkheim linked two types of suicide with the degree of social integration, by which he meant the feeling of attachment individuals have toward groups. He predicted that the suicide rate would vary inversely with the degree of social integration. When social groups have less of an integrative role, Durkheim argues, the individual's goals preponderate over communal ones, and the individual is more orientated to the pursuit of his or her private interests. This situation makes certain individuals susceptible to *egoistic* suicide, which originates from excessive individualism.[28] Egoism is a cause of suicide "because the link that attaches [an individual] to society has itself been relaxed,"[29] which makes life appear purposeless. In contrast, when people are strongly integrated, they feel more constrained to fulfill their duties to society and less inclined to evade them by taking their own life. If people belong to a group they love, they feel less likely to let the group down; or if they have loyalties to group goals, they feel their own private troubles less.

Religion and Egoistic Suicide
Drawing upon statistics from various sources in a range of countries and regions, Durkheim showed that, without exception, Protestants were much more likely than Catholics to commit suicide: the difference is from a minimum of 20 to 30 percent and up to 300 percent.[30] This difference

cannot be explained by reference to religious beliefs because each religion condemns suicide. The significant difference, Durkheim insists, is related to the fact that Protestantism allows "a great deal more freedom of enquiry"[31] than Catholicism which, he says, is a more traditional, hierarchical system of authority in which believers accept a ready-made faith. In contrast to Catholicism, Protestantism, Durkheim asserts, enables individuals to be more the authors of their faith and allows more scope for personal judgment, which results in its having a weaker religious influence over people's lives and, thus, in Protestants experiencing less social integration.

The Family as Protection against Egoistic Suicide

Durkheim reasoned that the family could produce greater social integration and have an effect similar to religion. The absolute figures he used show that unmarried persons were less likely to commit suicide, and this finding confirmed the common-sense view that suicide is a way of escaping the burdens of life. An unmarried person could be seen to have an easier life, with fewer responsibilities. However, Durkheim points out that a more careful examination of the statistics shows that the reality is otherwise: the absolute figures for the unmarried include all persons under 16, and this age group had a low rate of suicide. After adjusting the rate for age, Durkheim demonstrates that the suicide rate for married people was less than that of the unmarried. In France during the period 1889–91, for every million inhabitants, the suicide rate for 30- to 40-year-old unmarried men was 627, compared with 226 for the married men of that age; and the rate for 40-to 50-year-old unmarried men was 975, compared with 340 for married men in this age range.

Durkheim argues that the lower suicide among married men was related to the structure of the domestic environment. The family can be regarded as containing two different environments: the conjugal family of husband and wife and the family that includes husband and wife and their children. Quoting statistics from the French census of 1886, he demonstrates that the state of marriage had only a slight preservative effect on men aged 40 to 50, since married men without children committed suicide only a third less often than unmarried men.[32] Furthermore, he reasoned that it is not the conjugal family that had the greatest preservative power and that families with the most density (in terms of numerical size and frequency of interaction within families) had the lowest level of suicide. Thus, rather than increasing suicide by adding to the burdens of life, large families "are on the contrary, the daily bread without which one cannot survive."[33] Why does the family have this preservative value? Durkheim's answer is that larger domestic groups have greater integration because there is a more intense and continuous interaction between relatives.

Integration of the Political System and Egoistic Suicide

Typically, Durkheim begins his discussion with reference to comments of contemporary authors, who believed that, as political systems disintegrate, suicide increases. He points out that, ever since the collection of suicide statistics in European states in the nineteenth century, the evidence contradicts this view. In France, following the revolutions in 1830 and 1848, the drop in the number of suicides was about 10 percent. As the revolution spread throughout Europe, suicide declined as much as 18 percent in Denmark, Prussia, Bavaria, Saxony, and Austria. Revolutions in France produced a decrease in suicide in Paris, 13 percent fewer in 1830 and 32 percent fewer in 1832. Also, Durkheim refers to suicide statistics during political crises, election periods, and wars, in which a decline of up to 14 percent is recorded. Durkheim concludes that social upheaval and popular wars, which stimulate collective sentiments, patriotism, and national feelings, contribute to a stronger integration of society. Durkheim reasons that crises produce struggles, and "since these oblige men to cling together in order to confront a common danger, the individual thinks less of himself and more of the community,"[34] and this outlook leads to a reduction in egotistic suicide.

Altruistic Suicide

Durkheim believed that egoistic suicide was rare in tribal societies, but that three types of altruistic suicide, produced by insufficient individuation, were widespread: obligatory, optional, and acute. To describe the obligatory form of altruistic suicide, performed as a duty, he gives examples of societies in which death from old age or sickness was a disgrace, so old men would kill themselves to avoid dishonor. Such societies might reinforce these practices with the belief that those who took their own lives would enter a beautiful world or that those who had died of sickness or old age were condemned to a harsh and intolerable existence. In addition, some social customs expected a woman to kill herself on the death of her husband, and, in others, the followers and servants of a chief were expected to take their own lives after his death.[35] This type of suicide was the product of a socially defined duty, backed by religious sanctions and the loss of honor. Durkheim's explanation of this type of suicide contains references to the lack of individuality, which was first expounded in his discussion of mechanical solidarity. For altruistic suicide to exist, there has to be little concept of individual personality, and the individual has to be absorbed into a highly integrated group. In tribal societies, the group was small and the individual was easily, collectively supervised, thus preventing the emergence of individual egos as a source of resistance to a collective demand for the cessation of life.

Durkheim refers to the second type of altruistic suicide as optional, such as that which might occur in societies of Polynesia or among aboriginal people of North America. This form of suicide was not expressly imposed by society, but it might be a culturally condoned act in defense of a person's honor. In other words, it might be conventional for a person to commit suicide after offending someone or after a marital quarrel or a disappointment. Such acts, by which a person might avoid stigma or gain esteem, were enabled in cultures that placed little emphasis on individual interests. The third type, which Durkheim calls acute altruistic suicide, refers to people taking their own lives "for the pleasure of sacrifice."[36] Some religions of India furnish examples of this type of martyrdom, including the practices of seeking death in sacred rivers, allowing oneself to be crushed under the chariot wheels of the idol Juggernaut, or throwing oneself from a cliff into sulfur mines. Altruistic suicide is a product of over-integration; this occurs when individuals have a goal beyond themselves, and their own life is seen as an obstacle to achieving this goal. Egoism produces feelings of "incurable lassitude and dreary depression," but altruism is "derived from hope, because it comes from the fact that more beautiful prospects are glimpsed beyond this life."[37] In contemporary society, as individual personalities become increasingly free from the collective identity, altruistic suicide becomes very rare.

However, Durkheim identifies the army as a social context in which altruistic suicide was chronic. The statistics for several European countries and the United States that compare suicide rates in the military with those for civilians show a difference of between 25 and 900 percent: Austria, United States, and Italy had the highest incidence of suicide among their soldiers. One explanation could be that most soldiers are bachelors, but Durkheim demonstrates that suicide among French soldiers was higher than for unmarried civilians. Another explanation is the hardship of military life, but Durkheim shows that the suicide rate was higher for the longer-serving soldiers who had re-enlisted, and it was higher for officers, whose conditions were more comfortable. Thus, suicide was most associated with soldiers who chose a military career and who possessed the "acquired habits or natural predispositions that make up the military ethos."[38] Durkheim deduced that the explanation of such high suicide rates was the culture within the army, which lacks individualism, as soldiers have to follow and not question orders. This lack of individualism in the army makes it a unique institution of modern society and one characterized by the high integration and low individualism of tribal societies: "The military mind is itself in certain respects a survival of primitive morality. Under the influence of this predisposition, the soldier kills himself at the slightest disappointment, for the most trivial reasons, for a refusal to grant leave, for a reprimand, for an unjust punishment, for a hitch in promotion, for a matter of honour, for a passing fit of jealousy or even quite simply, because other suicides have taken place before his eyes or to his knowledge."[39]

Social Regulation: Anomic and Fatalistic Suicide
Anomic Suicide

In addition to integrating individuals by developing their sentiments, society regulates and controls people. Durkheim developed two more types of suicide based upon the degree of regulation of the individual. Anomic suicide is related to a lack of regulation, wherein society begins to lose its ability to set adequate restraints upon individual desires. Durkheim discussed anomie in relation to economic crises, which he demonstrated lead to increases in the suicide rate. He referred to a financial crisis in Vienna, 1873–74, that led to a 70 percent increase in suicide. The same crisis induced a 45 percent increase in suicide in Frankfurt-on-Main in 1874. A crash on the Paris Bourse in 1882 produced an increase of 11 percent in the three months closest to the time of the crash. Bankruptcies also reflect the vagaries of economic life. The average increase in bankruptcies between 1845 and 1869 was 3.2 percent; but it was 26 percent in 1847; 37 percent in 1854; and 20 percent in 1861. Suicide increased on average in this period by 2 percent per year, but, in each of the years of high bankruptcies, it increased dramatically: 17 percent in 1847; 8 percent in 1854; and 9 percent in 1861.[40]

Once again, Durkheim challenged a common-sense explanation, that suicide increases because poverty has increased and life has become more difficult. If suicide varies according to the level of poverty, the rate would be expected to decline in periods of prosperity. Durkheim provides statistical data relating to Italy during the 1870s and 1880s that indicate people were enjoying a period of economic growth, yet suicide rates increased annually in the 1870s from 29 per million during 1864–70 to 40.6 per million in 1877. Following German unification, there was commercial and industrial expansion, but suicides increased by 90 percent between 1875 and 1886. To further enhance his claim that poverty does not stimulate higher suicide levels, he cites as examples the low suicide rates of poor countries or areas, such as Ireland, Italy (Calabria), Spain, and the poorer regions of France. Poverty, he concludes, appears to be a protection from suicide. He proposes that industrial and financial crises, no matter whether they produce more poverty or greater prosperity, increase the number of suicides because they disturb the social order.[41]

Durkheim's explanation of the suicidal impetus of social disturbances involved his views on human nature and social regulation. He asserted,

"No living person can be happy or even live unless his needs are well adjusted to his means."[42] If a person's needs cannot be granted, then there is friction and dissatisfaction, which reduces the will to live. Durkheim reasoned that animals have material and instinctive needs, but, once these are satisfied, they do not ask for anything else. An animal's "power of reflection is not sufficiently developed to imagine other ends than those implicit in its physical nature."[43] It is much harder, however, to decide upon limits to the appetites, needs, and wants of human beings and such limits are not to be found in human biological or psychological nature. In Durkheim's view, the attachment to life becomes weakened when the demands of life cannot be satisfied because of insurmountable obstacles or because the pursuit of one demand just leads to another one. Hence, Durkheim writes, "For things to be otherwise, it is above all necessary that passions should be limited. Only then can they be harmonised with the faculties and then satisfied."[44] An external moral force that people feel is just, which they respect, and to which they can respond spontaneously must accomplish this limitation. This moral power is society, which is superior to the individual. Society can create laws, set limits beyond which the passions cannot go, and it "alone can assess what prospect of reward should be offered to every kind of official in the common interest."[45]

Durkheim believed that there is usually awareness, in the moral consciousness, of the worth and lifestyle appropriate to different functions within the social hierarchy and that these set limits to ambitions and expectations. These relative limitations, though, are not static; they are subject to gradual change over time and as conditions change; they "make men content with their lot, while at the same time giving them moderate encouragement to improve it; and it is this average contentment that gives rise to feelings of calm, active happiness, to the pleasure at being and living which, for societies as for individuals, is a sign of health. Each person, at least in general, is then in harmony with his condition and wants only what he can legitimately wish for as the normal reward for his activity."[46]

This superior, moral, socially derived consciousness usually governs people's behavior and normally overrides the demands and needs that are ultimately located within the nature of the human as a biological organism. When there are sudden social crises, this moral constraint may temporarily lose its effect, leading to a sudden increase in suicide because individual aspirations are stimulated. Whether these crises introduce poverty or prosperity, it takes time for the moral conscience to re-establish itself, and, for a while, people do not know what aspirations are just or unjust, what the limits are, and what demands and hopes are reasonable. In this period of anomie, passions are less disciplined. At times of upheaval such discipline is most needed because the relations within economic functions are shaken up and social conflict may arise as a result. According to Durkheim's theory, in this context, the desire to live is weakened.

Economic crises can produce fluctuations in the suicide rate, but, in Durkheim's vision, anomie is in a chronic state in the sphere of trade and industry. He argued that industrial relations became less regulated as traditional religion and the guilds lost their moral hold over the relations between employers and workers—the ability to explain and limit aspirations was lost. Markets had been extended beyond the local region, potential gains greatly increased, and expectations excited: "From top to bottom of the ladder, desires are aroused but have no definite idea on what to settle. Nothing can appease them, since the aim towards which they aspire is infinitely beyond anything they might attain."[47] The constant pursuit of new experiences, pleasures, and novelties led to a situation in which people had become disillusioned with a finally meaningless "endless pursuit" of new pleasures, sensations, and novelties. According to Durkheim, the people who worked in trade and industry in the modern economy were the least regulated by the old mechanisms of restraint, and these workers had a much higher suicide rate compared with those employed in agriculture—people who, Durkheim concludes, were still subject to some of the old forms of regulation.

Fatalistic Suicide

Durkheim confines his comment on the fourth type of suicide—fatalistic suicide—to a footnote at the end of the chapter on anomic suicide, and he only includes it for the sake of theoretical completeness. This type is the opposite of anomic suicide and is a social consequence of excessive regulation; people kill themselves whose futures are "pitilessly confined and whose passions are violently constrained by oppressive discipline."[48] Thinking it was of little contemporary significance, he gave very few examples and cited only the suicides of very young husbands and married women who were childless. Historically, the term could also be applied to the suicide of slaves, because of their excessive regulation. Pearce points out that Durkheim's formulation of fatalistic suicide is too cryptic and that the notion of over-constraint and repressive discipline could be extended to the phenomenon of the forced division of labor,[49] as discussed in the previous chapter. Inheritance and privilege influence how people are recruited or excluded from positions in the division of labor. If this inequality in the allocation of people to work is seen as unjust, and if it were perceived as an unalterable constraint, then, in Pearce's view, it could produce potentially suicidal conditions. Durkheim believed that the rapid increase in suicide in the most industrially advanced parts of

Europe was due to the rapid transformation of the social structure, which had destroyed old social institutions without putting anything in their place. He reasoned that established religions, the family, and the state were not able to provide sufficient influence over individuals, resulting in the increase in egoistic and anomic suicides. The social structure had changed in ways that reduced the ability of society to inculcate a collective morality and adequate restraint over individual desires. He returned to the idea of occupational associations,[50] which he believed could order social life at a level between that of the individual and that of the state and, thus, act as a new source of regulation and morality.

Criticisms

Durkheim referred to social or collective forces that give each society a "suicidal propensity." Society's "moral constitution ... determines at any moment the number of voluntary deaths" and each society has a collective force, "which drives men to kill themselves."[51] The suicide rate in this sociological theory does not result from individual inclinations or temperament; rather, it is the other way around. Each society possesses currents of egoism, altruism, and anomie, each with a corresponding mental state of "languid melancholy, active renunciation, or exasperated lassitude." These societal-wide tendencies "penetrating the minds of individuals make them decide to kill themselves."[52] Durkheim was convinced that suicide rates, which remain stable unless there is a sudden change in the social environment, demonstrate that society has an influence on behavior, that the study of this influence is distinct from the study of behavior (the realm of psychology), and that it is possible to study social regularities, such as suicide rates, scientifically. According to Durkheim, the reason some individuals succumb to suicidal currents (apart from insanity)[53] is that the mental constitution of the one who succumbs, "such as nature and events have made it, offers less resistance to the suicidal current."[54] Despite his argument that approaches to understanding suicide based upon individual motive or psychological analyses of individuals cannot explain the consistency of suicide rates between countries and social groups, his admission that the mental constitution of individuals can lead some to succumb to suicidal pressures opens up the role of individual psychology in the explanation of why particular people take their own lives. This might be seen as a weakness of his positivistic, sociological approach, but Parkin points out that Durkheim was concerned with differential suicide rates, not with predicting which individuals would be at risk.[55] In this regard, Durkheim's sociology shares similarities with studies of collective behavior, such as correlations between social class and educational achievement, which do not predict which individuals will succeed educationally, or correlations with etiological studies of disease, which relate lifestyle factors with ill health but cannot say who will contract the disease and who will not.

As will be seen in the later discussion of Weber, sociology is divided according to those who believe that sociology can copy the method of the natural sciences, which is positivism, and those who argue that human action is meaningful and that a proper understanding of action requires an interpretive approach that considers people's meanings and motives. Durkheim was consistent in his advocacy of the study of social facts (i.e., the social constraints that regulate collective life) as described in *The Rules of Sociological Method*, but he made assumptions about the meaning of suicide to people, which he inferred from their situations in the currents of egoism/altruism and anomie/fatalism rather than basing them upon qualitative research of actual motives. Lukes criticizes Durkheim for not including people's subjective perceptions and for making a rigid distinction between external (social) and internal (subjective) factors.[56] Durkheim was aware of the problem, but he explicitly dismissed approaches based upon motive as lacking the ability to explain variations in suicide rates. Also, his formulation of collective representations as material representations of social values puts him outside of the interpretivist tradition in sociology; however, he could be criticized for smuggling back into sociology an examination of the meanings people give to their actions through his assumptions about the feelings and motives people have in particular social milieus.

Douglas raises the issue of motives in the context of the decision-making processes of officials such as police, doctors, and coroners who decide, often when the evidence is far from conclusive, whether or not a death was a product of suicidal motives.[57] These decisions involve a reconstruction of the events leading to death and a weighing of the circumstances of and possible motives for suicide. These deliberations open up the possibility of subjective judgment at the base of the official statistics, which are the "facts" that Durkheim relies upon in his analysis. Although he was aware of these problems, Durkheim dismisses deliberations on the motives for suicide by officials as liable to error and not actually relevant to understanding the deeper causes of suicide. Douglas, however, raises some serious issues concerning how suicide statistics are socially constructed. For instance, in Catholic societies, officials may be reluctant to identify a death as a suicide because of its social stigma and its implications for the deceased's salvation in the eyes of the Catholic Church. Such deliberations would seriously compromise the statistics, quoted by Durkheim, that show lower suicide rates among Catholics, whom he deemed to be protected by their higher levels of social integration. Douglas also argues that suicide statistics are a product of negotiation. Articulate, high-status people may be able to influence the designation of the type of death by the coroner's court in a way that minimizes the total of recorded suicides for these groups. Under Douglas's critique, it appears that Durkheim's theory is based on questionable and possibly fictitious statistics. However, in his summary of this debate, Parkin points out that Durkheim found that higher educated groups were more likely to commit suicide—a finding which would not occur if Douglas's argument is correct. Douglas throws doubt on Durkheim's theory, but Parkin argues that there is insufficient evidence to establish that social groups do systematically organize themselves in a way to influence the courts.[58]

The resurgence of feminism in the 1960s stimulated the teaching of undergraduate and postgraduate courses on women's studies, as well as research and theorizing on women in society. So far in these chapters, our selection of topics from Durkheim's work has been governed by their relevance to the analysis of capitalist society—hence the discussion of economic anomie and the forced division of labor. However, in chapter 1, we referred to the impact of capitalist modernity on the experience of women, so it is necessary to discuss Durkheim's treatment of women within his sociology. Sydie, in a trenchant critique, argues that Durkheim's "analysis of sex roles is coloured by [his] understanding of natural dichotomies between the sexes. This belief in the invariable significance of biological difference means that the hierarchies of power in society, which relegate women collectively to a subordinate status to men, are taken as givens that do not require sociological analysis."[59]

Men are most likely to be affected by economic anomie, but women, who in the division of labor were more likely to be confined to family and domestic roles, suffered negatively within marriage and the family. Sydie points out how Durkheim was struck by figures that showed suicide rates varying according to marital status—with married women tending to commit suicide more often than either single women or married men, when there is no divorce. His conclusion, according to Sydie, about the societal institution of marriage's effect on a woman: it "does her less service than it does man."[60] When divorce was permitted, men were more prone to suicide due to "conjugal anomie," and they were less protected from suicide when compared to married men in societies that did not tolerate divorce. To explain why husbands and wives react differently to the marital situation, Durkheim resorted to a combination of assumptions about their different biological and intellectual capacities. He argued that marriage regulates sexual relations, but these are not just instinctive;

rather, they have accumulated aesthetic and moral characteristics that are not regulated organically:

> This is the function of marriage. It regulates all this life of the passions, and monogamous marriage more strictly than any other. By obliging the man to attach himself to only one woman, and always the same, it supplies a rigorously defined object for the need to love, and closes its horizon.[61]

So the husband has to limit his desires and "find happiness in his situation," and also his wife is duty-bound "not to fail him," providing him with pleasures which are not only "circumscribed" but also "assured and this certainty constitutes his mental bedrock."[62] In contrast, the bachelor may become prey to sexual anomie because he has no restriction on his aspirations, and his life opens up "endless new experiments raising hopes that are dashed and leaving behind them a feeling of weariness and disenchantment."[63] When divorce is allowed, the regulatory powers of marriage are weaker, as the "moral calm and tranquillity that made the husband strong are reduced"[64] and the commitment to the restraints of marriage are less heeded because marriage is not guaranteed.

In Durkheim's opinion, men need indissoluble marriage and women benefit from less severe marital bonds, as "the sexual needs of a woman are less intellectual in character, because, in general, her intellectual life is less developed."[65] Thus, biology makes her sexual needs more restrained, so she does not require such a strict social regulation as monogamous marriage. Durkheim's analysis of the different functions of marriage for men and women, and the opposing interests of men and women, which lead to more suicides for men if divorce is allowed and more for women if it is prohibited, produces a sociological impasse. He appears to prefer a solution that favors and protects men until women take up a more equal participation in social life. Yet his views about trends in the division of labor; about the greater public participation of men, which makes them more intellectual and less organically governed than women; and about the psychological differences between the sexes mean that efforts to reduce the differences between men and women will take a long time to work out and cannot be resolved by imminent legal changes alone. In answer to those who demanded that women be granted equal rights with men, Durkheim cautioned, "They are too inclined to forget that the work of centuries cannot be abolished in an instant; and that ... such legal equality cannot be legitimate as long as there is such flagrant psychological inequality."[66] Thus, Sydie argues, "Durkheim's account of the roles and functions of the sexes based on the idea of the 'natural' and therefore unchangeable dualities of physiology and psychology is no more than a continuation of a tradition in Western social theory. However, it is particularly interesting that Durkheim's sociological imagination deserted him when it came to dealing with the prejudices of his time regarding the capacities and roles of the sexes."[67]

Although Durkheim failed to transcend assumptions of his day about gender differences, there are features of his work that could be of interest to feminist sociologists, including his emphasis on the importance of social integration and individualism, which opens up the comparison of the socialization of boys and men with girls and women and the preparedness of the latter to make sacrifices for others at the expense of their own individualism.

Conclusion

Durkheim powerfully states the case for the analysis of an objective structure of society that pre-exists individuals and continues beyond their lifetimes. Of course, individuals act and develop meanings within this structure, and many of these meanings help to maintain the social structure over time. However, much of contemporary sociological theory revolves around the articulation of the ways in which structure influences human behavior, and around the degree of meaningful action or agency that can exist and would allow individuals, as Giddens puts it, "to make a difference in the world."[68] The idea of a dichotomy between structure and agency is a key one in contemporary sociological theory, and Durkheim's influence is still felt in these debates: But is Durkheim's sociology still relevant in the analysis of contemporary capitalism?

As was seen in the discussion of anomic suicide, Durkheim believes that, in stable economies, there are collective beliefs concerning the appropriate rewards that different *functions* or social classes—as we would say today—should expect for their labor. In neoliberal capitalism, there has been a rapid widening of the gap between the rich and the poor in terms of income and wealth. The extremely high incomes of the wealthiest in the population and the lack of a consensus about what are reasonable incomes and disparities in wealth can be seen in Durkheimian terms as evidence of chronic anomie. Since the 1980s in the United States, Canada, and Great Britain, income differentials have widened. Figures from Statistics Canada show that the share of the top 1 percent of income tax filers increased from 10.6 percent to 11.2 percent between 2011 and 2015.[69] Census data shows that income inequality in Canada rose between 2005 and 2015, with the highest income groups accelerating away from the broad middle class and poverty continuing to increase. Median income, before tax, rose to $34,204, which was an increase of 12.7 percent for the middle class whilst the median income of the top 10 percent rose to $93,739, an increase of 16.4 percent. The median pretax income of the top 1 percent was $234,130 in 2015, up 14.5 percent since 2005.[70] The left-leaning Canadian Centre for Policy Alternatives focused on the incomes of the 100 highest paid CEOs of companies listed in the TSX index and found that in 2016 their average compensation was $10.4 million, 200 times the income of an average worker in a year.[71] In the United Kingdom, figures produced by the Equality Trust in 2012 show that the richest 20 percent received 40 percent of total income whilst the share of poorest 20 percent amounted to 8 percent of all incomes. The average income for the top 10 percent was £83,875, but the income of the top 1 percent is much higher with an average of £253,927. The top 0.1 percent had an average of £919,882.[72] An analysis of the pay of chief executives of FTSE 100 companies undertaken by the Chartered Institute of Personnel Development and the High Pay Centre claims they were paid an average of £3.45 million in 2016. Their pay averaged £898 per hour—256 times that of an apprentice on the minimum wage.[73]

Against this backdrop, there has been a growing hostility and clearly a lack of moral consensus in regards to both the widening gap between rich and poor and the high levels of remuneration received by company executives and bankers. This last factor, in particular, can be seen, in Durkheimian terms, as a deeply embedded source of anomie. Banks in the United States and Europe have come in for much criticism concerning their remuneration policies. The British media has paid a great deal of attention to the bonuses given to bankers, especially in the period leading up to their payment. Figures published by Barclays and RBS disclosed that 523 staff were paid more than £1 million in 2012, whilst a further 2,440 Barclays staff were paid £250 thousand to £500 thousand.[74] The expression "shareholder spring," which draws an analogy with the uprisings in the Middle East, overstates the extent of shareholder dissatisfaction, but in 2018 some leading British companies (including AstraZeneca, William Hill, GVC [owners of several betting shop chains], the advertising company WPP, BT, Shell, Royal Mail, Unilever, and the builders Persimmon and Bovis) faced protest votes when around 30 percent or more of shareholders at company annual general meetings criticized the pay packages of their chief executives.[75] There has also been a global display of street-level revulsion at the increasing degree of inequality that has coincided with the neoliberal project. The Occupy movement forcefully expressed the image of the polarization between the 99 percent and the 1 percent. These conflicts over high incomes in business and finance provide examples of a lack of moral consensus; the existence of dissent and a growing desire to regulate some forms of corporate excess are indicative of what Durkheim would have regarded as anomie.

FURTHER THINKING:

Social integration and regulation are key features of Durkheim's analysis of suicide. How did Durkheim define and apply these terms to the study of suicide? Consider how these concepts might be applied to other aspects of contemporary societies.

FURTHER READING:

See Émile Durkheim, *On Suicide* (London: Penguin Books Ltd., 2006). A readable secondary source is Ken Morrison, *Marx, Durkheim, Weber: The Formation of Modern Social Thought*, 2nd ed. (London: Sage Publications, 2006), 199–230. For a modern application of Durkheim's work on suicide, see Howard I. Kushner and Claire E. Sterk, "The Limits of Social Capital: Durkheim, Suicide, and Social Cohesion," *American Journal of Public Health* 95, no. 7 (2005): 1139–43.

Notes

1   Steve Fenton, *Durkheim and Modern Sociology* (Cambridge: Cambridge University Press, 1984), 3.

2   Richard Sennett, Introduction to *On Suicide*, Émile Durkheim (London: Penguin Books Ltd., 2006), xi.

3   Émile Durkheim, *The Division of Labour in Society* (New York: The Free Press, 1997), 220.

4   Ken Morrison, *Marx, Durkheim, Weber: Formations of Modern Social Thought*, 2nd ed. (London: Sage Publications, 2006), 186.

5   Émile Durkheim, *The Rules of Sociological Method* (New York: The Free Press, 1938), 1.

6   Durkheim, *The Rules of Sociological Method*, 2.

7   Durkheim, *The Rules of Sociological Method*, 3.

8   Durkheim, *The Rules of Sociological Method*, 3.

9   Durkheim, *The Rules of Sociological Method*, 4.

10   Durkheim, *The Rules of Sociological Method*, 4.

11   Durkheim, *The Rules of Sociological Method*, 6.

12   Durkheim, *The Rules of Sociological Method*, 7–8.

13   Durkheim, *The Rules of Sociological Method*, 13.

14   Durkheim, *The Rules of Sociological Method*, 28.

15   Durkheim, *The Rules of Sociological Method*, xliv.

16   Steven Lukes, *Émile Durkheim: His Life and Work, A Historical and Critical Study* (London: Penguin Books Ltd., 1975), 6.

17   Durkheim, *The Rules of Sociological Method*, 49.

18 Durkheim, *The Rules of Sociological Method*, 50.

19 Durkheim, *The Rules of Sociological Method*, 55–57.

20 Durkheim, *The Rules of Sociological Method*, 67.

21 Durkheim, *The Rules of Sociological Method*, 67–71.

22 Durkheim, *The Rules of Sociological Method*, 90.

23 Durkheim, *The Rules of Sociological Method*, 106.

24 Durkheim, *The Rules of Sociological Method*, 114–15.

25 Émile Durkheim, *On Suicide* (London: Penguin Books Ltd., 2006), 19.

26 Durkheim, *On Suicide*, 25–27.

27 Durkheim, *On Suicide*, 154–55.

28 Durkheim, *On Suicide*, 225.

29 Durkheim, *On Suicide*, 231.

30 Durkheim, *On Suicide*, 160.

31 Durkheim, *On Suicide*, 163

32 Durkheim, *On Suicide*, 197.

33 Durkheim, *On Suicide*, 214.

34 Durkheim, *On Suicide*, 223.

35 Durkheim, *On Suicide*, 234–35.

36 Durkheim, *On Suicide*, 240–41.

37 Durkheim, *On Suicide*, 244.

38 Durkheim, *On Suicide*, 253.

39 Durkheim, *On Suicide*, 259.

40 Durkheim, *On Suicide*, 263.

41 Durkheim, *On Suicide*, 263–67.

42 Durkheim, *On Suicide*, 269.

43 Durkheim, *On Suicide*, 269.

44 Durkheim, *On Suicide*, 271.

45 Durkheim, *On Suicide*, 272.

46 Durkheim, *On Suicide*, 273–74.

47 Durkheim, *On Suicide*, 280–82.

48 Durkheim, *On Suicide*, 305.

49 Frank Pearce, *The Radical Durkheim* (London: Unwin Hyman, 1989).

50 Durkheim, *On Suicide*, 436.

51 Durkheim, *On Suicide*, 331.

52 Durkheim, *On Suicide*, 332.

53 Durkheim, *On Suicide*, 358.

54 Durkheim, *On Suicide*, 359.

55 Frank Parkin, *Durkheim* (Oxford: Oxford University Press, 1992), 25.

56 Lukes, *Émile Durkheim: His Life and Work*, 222.

57 Jack D. Douglas, *The Social Meanings of Suicide* (Princeton, NJ: Princeton University Press, 1967).

58 Parkin, *Durkheim*, 23.

59 Rosalind A. Sydie, *Natural Women, Cultured Men: A Feminist Perspective on Sociological Theory* (Milton Keynes, UK: Open University Press, 1987), 49.

60 Sydie, *Natural Women, Cultured Men*, 28.

61 Durkheim, *On Suicide*, 299.

62 Durkheim, *On Suicide*, 299.

63 Durkheim, *On Suicide*, 299.

64 Durkheim, *On Suicide*, 300.

65 Durkheim, *On Suicide*, 301.

66 Durkheim, *On Suicide*, 431.

67 Sydie, *Natural Women, Cultured Men*, 41.

68 Anthony Giddens, as cited in Derek Layder, *Understanding Social Theory* (London: Sage Publications, 1994), 5.

69 Statistics Canada, "High Income Tax Filers in Canada," https://www.150.statcan.gc.ca/t1/tbl1/en/tv.action?pid=1110005501 (accessed August 5, 2018).

70 Andrew Jackson, "Census Data Shows Income Inequality Remains a Major Challenge," *Globe and Mail*, October 8, 2017.

71 Sophia Harris, "Canada's Top CEOs Earn 200 Times an Average Worker's Salary," *CBC*, https://www.cbc.ca/news/business/ceo-income-pay-canadian-worker-1.4462496.

72 The Equality Trust, "The Scale of Economic Inequality in the UK," https://www.equalitytrust.org.uk/scale-economic-inequality-uk (accessed July 9, 2018).

73 Rupert Neate, "An Honest Year's Work? Excessive Pay in Focus on 'Fat Cat Thursday,'" *The Guardian*, January 4, 2018.

74 Jill Treanor, "Barclays and RBS Reveal 523 Staff Take Home More Than £1m a Year," *The Guardian*, March 9, 2013, http://www.guardian.co.uk/business/2013/mar/08/barclays-pay-staff-millions-libor.

75 Rajeev Syal, "UK Firms to Be Forced to Justify Pay Gap Between Bosses and Staff," *The Guardian*, June 10 2018, https://www.theguardian.com/uk-news/2018/jun/10/uk-firms-to-be-forced-to-justify-pay-gap-between-bosses-and-staff (accessed August 6, 2018).

9. Émile Durkheim: Religion and Education

> The collective effervescence of ritual life reintegrated individuals
> into the group. Thus religion was a form of social glue.
> —Bryan S. Turner, 1999[1]

THE ELEMENTARY FORMS OF RELIGIOUS LIFE (1912) is widely regarded as Durkheim's most important work. In it, he demonstrates his evolutionary approach to the study of society by choosing to study religion in its most simple form. In his analysis of the totemic religion of Australian tribes, he explains how religion is based upon the awareness of a force that genuinely exists and is a source of moral authority, although his scientific explanation goes behind the appearance of things in the eyes of believers. The work is also a theory of knowledge, as religion is seen as the first way in which human beings articulate their understanding of the world.

It has already been pointed out that Durkheim was employed at Bordeaux and Paris to lecture, primarily to trainee school teachers, and that his employment as an educationalist enabled him gradually—and against much opposition—to introduce sociology as an academic discipline within higher education. Two courses of lectures on education were published shortly after his death, and a third on the evolution of secondary education was first published in 1938. These lectures show how he regarded education as a source of morality and how he explained the evolution of education as a reflection of social structural conditions.

The Elementary Forms of Religious Life

Durkheim wished to carry out a scientific analysis of religion; so he chose to study the religion of the simplest society in order to understand people's religious nature, which he believed is an essential and permanent aspect of human culture. He argued that an institution such as religion could not rest on an error or a lie; otherwise it would flounder on the resistance to it of social reality. Primitive religions, he argues, "are rooted in reality and are an expression of it."[2] The reasons that individuals give to explain their beliefs are most likely to be mistaken, so it is the task of the scientist to "reach beneath the symbol to the reality it embodies and which gives it its true meaning."[3] The study of the religion of Australian tribes, he argues, enables the scientist to study the features of a religion in its most essential aspects, in the absence of the complexities that develop with the evolution of religion, and to relate these features to the tribe's social conditions.

Durkheim's study of religion is more than a study of the social basis of religion: he declares early in his work that religion is the original source of theories about the nature of the world and is thus the basis of science and philosophy. Furthermore, he argues that religion has shaped forms of knowledge and that basic categories of thought such as notions of time, space, genus, cause, substance, and personality—without which it would be impossible to have shared reasoning—have their basis in primitive religious beliefs. A central part of Durkheim's argument is that religious representations are collective representations that are created when the assembled group participates in rituals, which create and reinforce certain mental states. Similarly, the categories of thought that are created through religious beliefs and ceremonies are social things. Durkheim takes a position on the nature of knowledge that differs from the two opposing doctrines of *apriorism* and *empiricism*. The first views the basic categories as logical and independent of the human mind and human experience; the second views them as subjective and dependent upon the personal experience of the individual. A problem with apriorism is that categories of reason appear to have a reality of their own based upon the power of reason, the basis of which remains unaccounted for. The problem with empiricism is that, if knowledge is based upon individual experience, then the idea of reason itself, as a form of impersonal rationality, is jettisoned. Durkheim believed that he had found a solution that took into account the objections to each position, and he regarded categories of thought as products of the meeting of many minds over space and generations. Thus, individual experiences contribute to the intellectuality of the group. From the experience of the collectivity, then, an agreement emerges concerning what can be logically accepted: "This is the authority of society colouring certain ways of thinking that are the indispensable conditions of all common action."[4] A discussion of Durkheim's sociology of knowledge will be taken up again after a discussion of his sociology of religion.

The Definition of Religion

In his definition of religion Durkheim states that religious phenomena can be divided into beliefs and rites and that all religious beliefs classify the representations of material or ideal things that people devise. He presents two comprehensive, but opposing, categories—the *sacred* and the *profane*.[5] The first refers to beliefs about spirits, myths, legends, and the nature of sacred things and their powers; even a rock, a tree, or a vegetable can be imbued with a sacred character. Rites, also part of the sacred, are actions that are fixed, such as words or formulaic ways of speaking that relate to sacred beliefs and that may be said by consecrated persons. Everything else belongs to the category of the profane. The sacred and the profane are conceived as two separate worlds, with nothing in common, and may even be seen in the human mind as antagonistic. Hence, they cannot intermingle, and boundaries have to be set to demarcate when people may move between the two. Humankind and its gods have a mutual dependency, according to Durkheim: just as a people depend upon their gods, the gods depend upon people performing rites in their honor, such as offerings or sacrifices; otherwise the gods would die.[6]

Durkheim defines *religion* as "a unified system of beliefs and practices relative to sacred things, that is to say, things set apart and surrounded by prohibitions—beliefs and practices that unite its adherents in a single moral community called a church."[7]

The identification of religion's communal nature enabled Durkheim to distinguish between magic and religion. The former contains beliefs and rites as well, and it calls upon similar forces. The difference lies in the collective nature of religious beliefs, which, as Durkheim stressed, are held by a collective group of people who profess the same beliefs and practice their religious rites. Magic is different. There might be a collection of magicians who share beliefs, but they do not share them with a wider community of worshippers. The magician has a clientele, not a church, and does not have a continuous relationship with a body of worshippers.

Two existing theories of religion, *animism* and *naturism*, come under a detailed critique. The first refers to the origins of religion as being located in the experience of dreams, which leads to the religious experience of spirits, the soul, demons, and deities with a human-like consciousness and superior powers.[8] The latter locates the experience of the "great cosmic forces" of nature as the source of an inexhaustible force.[9] Durkheim's critique of each of these theories amounts to the same kind of refutation. He argues that each is based upon the notion of hallucination, but each would have been seen for what it was and could not have convinced people throughout the centuries. Prayers, chants, and feast days could rarely appear to produce the desired control over nature or protect people or produce other desired results. The all too frequent failure of these rituals would have persuaded people that their beliefs were false. Therefore, Durkheim asserts that all beliefs in religion and myth "must have some objective foundation," despite being "mistaken about the true nature of things."[10] Something else must have given man a sense of an "infinite power outside him to which he is subject,"[11] and this idea figures in Durkheim's theory of people's sense of the divine.

Totemic Beliefs

Durkheim's study draws mainly on research by anthropologists who had described and analyzed tribal societies in central and northern Australia. Durkheim divides his study into an examination of religious beliefs and rites, and, although these are interdependent, he begins by outlining the totemic beliefs of Australian tribes. Their society is based on tribes that have two exogamous groups called *phratries*, and each of these phratries contains several clans. Clans constitute a basic element of collective life, and, although clan members are not related by blood, "they regard each other as part of the same family."[12] They bear the same name, and they respect mutual obligations as recognized among kin, including vengeance, mourning, and the avoidance of intermarriage. The name of each clan is its own totem, which usually is a plant or an animal with which the clan believes it has a special relationship. Usually, individuals receive their clan names from the mother, who lives in the territory of the father, who, according to rules of exogamy, is of a different clan.

   Durkheim describes tribal life as akin to a federation of clans in which each clan has its totem. The worship of the clan totem is the most frequent level of religious experience among the Australian aboriginal people and the one that Durkheim particularly focuses on. Each phratry and tribe also has its totem, and entire tribes sometimes meet to carry out totemic ceremonies such as initiation rites. He describes how totemism is a religious system of the whole tribe.[13] Each clan has a name, such as "crow" or "white cockatoo," which Durkheim describes as an emblem, coat of arms, or flag. Images of the totem are reproduced on things owned by the clan, such as weapons, and even on the bodies of men during religious ceremonies. A totem is the name of the clan, but its use in religious ceremonies demonstrates how it is also a sacred thing. Each totem group has a collection of sacred pieces of wood or polished stone called *churingas*, which feature in their sacred rites and which have engraved drawings that represent the group's totem. Some of the wooden ones, usually referred to as bullroarers, have holes pierced in them, and, with the use of a thong, they can be swung rapidly in the air to make a loud noise during ceremonies. The *churingas* are the most sacred possession of the clan, and profane persons such as women and uninitiated young men are not allowed to touch or see them. Where they are stored between ceremonies (perhaps in a small cave) is kept hidden, and the uninitiated are not allowed near this sacred place. The *churingas* are believed to possess special qualities: touching them can cure wounds and illnesses. They can confer power on the totemic species and ensure its successful reproduction, and they can give men strength and weaken their enemies. They are not just useful to individuals, rather the "collective fate of the whole clan depends upon them."[14] The stone or wood *churingas* are similar to many other objects, except they are painted or carved with the emblem of the totem, and this marking is what makes them sacred.

A *churinga.*

The animals or plants that are related to the totem of a clan are also sacred. Restrictions surrounding the *churingas* are much greater than those related to access to the totemic animal or plant that commonly exists in the profane world. From this fact, Durkheim concludes that the images of the totemic being are more sacred than the totemic objects.[15] In fact, he identifies a hierarchy of sacredness: first the emblem of the totem, then the totem, and then each member of the clan are invested with a sacred nature. The Australian, Durkheim explains, believed that he was both a man and also an animal or plant of his totemic species. Although this belief may be hard for others to understand, Durkheim says it was made more plausible for the clan member through myths that tell of the common origins of the totemic being and the clansfolk. The emblem of the totem, the totemic species, and the clan members share elements of sacredness; however, men have more sacred dignity than women and the uninitiated young members of the clan, and old men have the greatest religious nature. Nevertheless, totemism is not the worshipping of animals or plants; both humans and their totemic beings are seen as sharing a degree of sacredness. Totemism is a shared religion of "a kind of anonymous and impersonal force that is found in each of these beings though identical with none."[16]

This anonymous and impersonal force is independent of particular individuals, and it pre-exists and survives them. While individuals die and are succeeded by new generations, this force remains constant. It is, Durkheim states, "an impersonal god, without a name, without a history, immanent in the world, diffused throughout a multitude of things."[17] The Australian, in Durkheim's view, is not aware of this force in an abstract way but sees it as a material thing, as an animal or plant, though the basis of the cult is an energy that is diffused throughout the universe. Each clan within the tribe has a notion of these forces as belonging to its totem. These forces, which have a physical aspect upon which life is seen to depend, also have a moral aspect that obliges a person to behave in particular ways toward other members of the clan, or to perform certain rites. In addition, in common with other religions, the ritual practices of totemism give man more confidence in his dealings with the world.

The Origins of Totemic Beliefs

The totem is the symbol of the god and the symbol of the clan. So Durkheim reasoned that the god of the clan, the totemic principle, must be the clan itself, "transfigured and imagined in the physical form of the plant or animal species that serve as totems."[18] In order to explain how this came about, Durkheim describes how life in the Australian clan alternated between two different phases. For most of the time, the population was scattered in small groups of hunters and gatherers providing for their needs. At agreed-upon times, people would congregate in particular places where the entire tribe or clan would meet for periods of several days or weeks to participate in religious ceremonies. This lifestyle offered a stark contrast between a mundane existence, which was the profane part of the tribe's life, compared with a time of enacting sacred rituals, during which the proximity of individuals generated a stimulating environment and a state of high exaltation. Durkheim, quoting anthropological studies, describes the excitement and tumult created during the whirling of bullroarers, the chanting and rhythmic dancing often enhanced by firelight, and the subsequent collective effervescence and unleashing of passions. In these circumstances, individuals would feel that they had entered into relations with extraordinary powers. In the Australian context, religious activity was concentrated in these periods of collective effervescence when, Durkheim believed, the religious idea was born: "Therefore it is in these effervescent social settings, and from this very effervescence, that the religious idea seems to be born. And this origin seems confirmed by the fact that in Australia, strictly religious activity is almost entirely concentrated in the times when these assemblies are held."[19]

When the clan meets, it "awakens in its members the idea of external forces that dominate and exalt them," but the clan is "too complex a reality for such rudimentary minds to picture clearly its concrete unity."[20] The native does not see that the group has generated these feelings or that the group is capable of generating new energies with the power to transform people. Furthermore, these new sensations are experienced at a time when the emblem of the group is everywhere—on the *churingas* and painted on the bodies of the assembled clan members. Later, when people see the totem's emblem again, their memories of that state of heightened emotions are revived. When people congregate, and the emblem

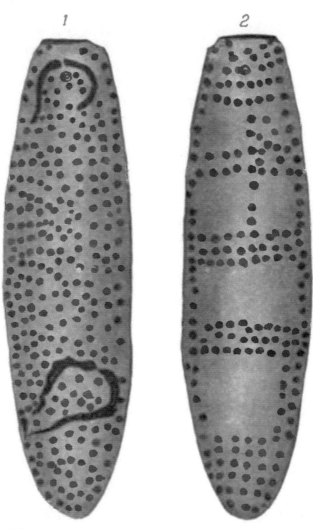

A bullroarer.

is everywhere during these gatherings, mysterious forces are generated, which the native Australian believes emanate from the clan's emblem. The totem is seen to be the source of actions that benefit or harm the clan, so the clan must take action to influence this force by performing rites addressed to this foremost of sacred things. Because of the resemblance between the clan's emblem and the animal or plant from which the clan takes its name, the actual animal or plant takes on sacred qualities, and it ranks above a human in the sacred hierarchy. Although the religious force of the totem appears to be external, it can only be realized through the active participation of clan members; they come to imagine that the totem is part of them and that they too have a religious character, though to a lesser degree.

Being in opposition to animism and naturism, Durkheim rejects the notion that religion is based upon physical or biological sensations and, therefore, is no more than a hallucination. In a key passage, he states that "the worshipper is not deluding himself when he believes in a higher moral power from which he derives his best self: that power exists, and it is society."[21] The exalted experience of the clan member is real and is "really the product of forces external and superior to the individual." It is a mistake to believe that this heightened vitality is a product of the power derived from a plant or an animal, but "there is a concrete and living reality."[22] For Durkheim, the main purpose of religion is to provide a system of thought that enables individuals to imagine the society to which they belong and their relationship with it. In particular, religion refers to "an eternal truth that something exists outside us that is greater than we are, and with which we commune ... god is merely the symbolic expression of society."[23] Rather than the act of worship strengthening the ties of the worshipper and a god, they strengthen the ties between the individual and society because "god is merely the symbolic expression of society."[24]

Totemic Rites

Durkheim identified negative and positive rites. The *negative rites* comprise various prohibitions on behavior, which serve to preserve the separation between the sacred and profane. Prohibitions on profane behavior and the suffering of privations make the individual feel more elevated and on a level with sacred and moral forces. The *positive rites* refer to bilateral relations between humans and the totemic forces. Durkheim draws heavily from the writings of anthropologists who described a ceremony of the Arunta tribe, referred to as the *intichiuma*, which appeared to be a widespread practice among other tribes as well. Among the Arunta, this ceremony starts at the beginning of the rainy season, which brings forth a sudden appearance of vegetation. The first phase of the ceremony is concerned with the preservation of the prosperity of the animal or plant species that is the clan's totem. Members of the tribe believe that their ancestors had left rocks in the places where they had disappeared into the ground. These imperishable rocks are seen as a source of life for the totemic species; because these rocks ensure the reproduction of the totemic species and allow people to continue to draw upon their powers, they must be visited annually. The ceremony of the Witchetty Grub clan, for instance, involves all the men of the tribe walking solemnly around the sacred site, stopping at rocks that are thought to represent the grub, and striking the rocks to displace some dust that is regarded as the seeds of its life. The dust is dispersed by men who wave tree branches in the belief that they are maintaining the abundant reproduction of the grub that the clan both protects and depends upon.[25]

In a second phase of the *intichiuma*, the usually strict prohibition against the eating of the totem animal is lifted for a short period of time. In the Witchetty Grub clan, the grubs are gathered, cooked, and crushed into a powder, some of which the chief and the elders consume in a solemn ceremony. Durkheim believed that this type of ceremony, which took similar forms in other tribes, contains the essence of the institution of sacrifice that can be found in many more highly structured religions.[26] Consuming the sacred totem enables clan members to incorporate its sacred principle within themselves, but because the sacred principle's powers gradually erode, it must be replenished periodically.

In the first phase of the *intichiuma*, men of the clan assist in the fecundity of the totemic species to ensure that it survives. In the second phase, "man" borrows from the species "the forces necessary to sustain and restore his spiritual being. So, we can say that it is man who makes his gods, or at least makes them endure, but at the same time it is through them that he endures."[27] Thus, the celebrations of the totemic cult bring about the renewal of belief in the gods, and they bring "internal and moral renewal" in the participants. Ritual life is circular, and so is social life, as the individual takes from society personality, culture, language, science, arts, and morality—all of what makes a person civilized. If the individual's idea of society dies and social beliefs and traditions cease to be held, then the society will die. So rites possess an efficacy, though not the one perceived by the participants. They enable the creation and perpetuation of the gods—of a moral entity that is society—making individuals and their community feel stronger. Common beliefs are strengthened, and the individual soul "is regenerated, too, by immersing itself once more in the wellspring of its life; subsequently, it feels stronger, more in control of itself."[28]

Sociology of Knowledge

Durkheim's sociology of knowledge is intricately woven into his sociology of religion. Religion, he argues, was always a cosmology as well as a theory of the divine, and thus philosophy and science grew out of religion. In addition, he argues that basic categories of understanding—ideas of time, space, genus, number, cause, substance, and personality—which are the basis of all thought, originated in religion.[29] Religious rituals are collective assemblies that produce collective representations about the relationship between humans and their gods, and, therefore, ideas about time or space, for instance, originate in these collective religious representations. Durkheim puts forward a sociological approach to knowledge that does not rely on the idea that categories are a priori in the human mind or a product of individual experience.

Durkheim argues that religions give a total representation of the world, and, within Australian totemism, all things within the universe are part of the tribe and all men and objects are allocated between the clans. Those things that are allocated to an individual's clan, whether animate or inanimate, "are parts of the body of which he is a part."[30] Durkheim gives a number of examples. For instance, the Mount Gambier tribe is divided into two phratries, the Kunmite and the Kroki, and each of these has five clans. Everything in nature belongs to one or another of these clans, so everything in nature is classified under ten totem-like species, under their own genera. While men and women may be identified with crows or white cockatoos, natural phenomena are also divided into their respective totems: rain, thunder, lightning, clouds, hail, and winter, for example, are also part of the crow totem. The way in which the notions of genus or class are formed was modeled on social organization: "Because men formed groups, they were able to group things; they classified things simply by placing them in groups they had already formed ... the social groups they belong to are themselves interdependent, and through their union form an organic whole—the tribe. The unity of these first logical systems merely reproduces the unity of society."[31] Durkheim uses this example to demonstrate that the notion of category can be a product of social organization. Initially, it could have been based on each phratry having opposing dichotomies—a white cockatoo in one phratry and a black cockatoo in the other or one clan linked to the sun and the other to the moon and stars. Categorization could also be based on similarities: the black cockatoo is linked with the moon, the white cockatoo with the sun. Durkheim writes, "Of course, we cannot always understand the obscure psychology that presides over many of these affinities and distinctions. But the preceding examples suffice to demonstrate that a certain intuition of similarities and differences evident in things has played a role in creating these classifications."[32] In Durkheim's view, the classification of categories, a genus, is a tool of thought, invented by people, that comes from society and not from some a priori existence outside us. "Society has provided the canvas on which logical thought has operated."[33] This canvas consists of a religion in which humans and natural phenomenon are linked. This system of religious thought enabled people to think that there are internal connections between things and that these can be categorized according to opposition and agreement; therefore, Durkheim insists, religion contains the basic elements of scientific thought.

Durkheim argues that the idea of a vague, anonymous force that influences men's minds and material objects was, in totemic religion, the earliest form of a later secular version found in the natural sciences.[34] Religion and science are, Durkheim insists, concerned with nature, man, and society: "Religion endeavours to translate these realities into an intelligible language that is no different in kind from the language employed by science; both involve connecting things to one another, establishing internal relations between them, classifying them, and systematizing them."[35] If religion is based on society and science originates in religion then, ultimately, knowledge is based in society, whether this reflects the way that space is divided up between social groups or how time is defined socially to enable people to meet to perform rites or participate in feasts. Similarly, Durkheim relates concepts—the material of logical thought— to society because, in order for people to communicate, concepts must be shared: thus, they are collective representations of the community. Concepts represent social ways of thinking that contain general and permanent properties and combine the collective wisdom and knowledge, accumulated over centuries, with what personal experience can teach. Systems of concepts, derived in this way from society, help people to think impersonally in ways that surpass their own experiences.[36]

Durkheim provides a critique of theories that assume that religious experience is grounded in hallucinations, which are themselves based on psychological perceptions or on the experience of nature, and he argues that, for religion to persist, there has to be some form of underlying reality, which he identifies as society. This argument supports his own version of sociological rationalism, but, to those who believe in a divine basis for religion, it must appear little different to the view that religion is based upon hallucination. Durkheim's belief that society is a moral phenomenon buttresses his view that society needs some kind of religion or system of unifying beliefs: "No society can exist that does not feel the need at regular intervals to sustain and reaffirm the collective feelings and ideas that constitute its unity and personality."[37]

This reaffirmation of morals is based on meetings or assemblies in which individuals come into close contact and reaffirm their common feelings. According to Durkheim's analysis, humanity is now in a period of transition, and it is hard to imagine what future ceremonies will be like: "The ancient gods grow old or die, and others are not yet born."[38] New cults cannot be created; they have to emerge from life. There will be new experiences of collective effervescence and new formulae will grow to serve humanity for a time; however, in an age when science is dominant, religion will have to accept its findings. As science slowly accrues knowledge, there is, according to Durkheim, still a place for religion to "run ahead of science and develop theories about living and acting."[39]

Sociology of Education

During his years in Bordeaux and Paris, Durkheim was primarily employed as an educationalist, and, although his regular lectures on education to trainee teachers may have interrupted his sociological work, they provided him with opportunities to reiterate many of his favorite themes, such as the relationship between man and society, his theory of evolution, and his views on social solidarity. Durkheim referred to a crisis in secondary education that had been felt since the second half of the eighteenth century. Economic and moral changes in society meant that the old educational ideals were inadequate; in the Middle Ages, the goal was the creation of dialecticians, and, after the Renaissance, it was the creation of humanists. However, he argued that there was no clear notion of what conception of man should be created through secondary education in late nineteenth- and early twentieth-century France.[40] Durkheim supported secular state education, and these too were matters of political contention.

Durkheim points out that a historic perspective on education shows that different periods have different educational organizational objectives, because education is shaped by custom, religion, political and economic organization, and the existing state of science. Education is the system of interaction between adults and youth in which a society attempts to create an "ideal of man" in terms of certain physical, intellectual, and moral states that each person is expected to possess. In addition, as society becomes more complex, education has to provide attributes that enable more specialized roles to be carried out. Education is a form of socialization of each new generation of asocial and egoistic beings, making people into social beings by exposing them to religious, moral, national, and other collective beliefs to enable them to lead a social life. It is a short step from this position to see education as the instrument through which society "represents the best in us" by making children into adults.[41]

In the course he taught on moral education, Durkheim's task was to provide a conception of secular moral education for state elementary schools, which he regarded as the guardians of French national character. He argued that morality is not beyond scientific analysis; to accept that it is would mean accepting that something is essentially irrational. During a period in which people were becoming more rationalistic and individualistic, religion was thought to be losing its force. It had become, Durkheim believed, necessary to separate morality from religion, though, in the process, new moral tendencies and demands for justice would emerge. The role of the teacher, he argued, was to help new generations become conscious of the new ideal and also to "excite in them a desire to add a few lines of their own."[42] Rather than teaching children a list of virtues, education's first task, according to Durkheim, was the determination of the basic elements of morality, namely, the fundamental mental states that could be adapted to particular circumstances. He believed that moral rules are a subtype of rules that are obeyed not because of tradition or personal benefit but because they are outside the person and they prescribe ways of acting that people cannot alter: an authority backs those rules and demands their respect. Obedience is a duty that is derived from a spirit of discipline. This is the first element of morality. The idea of discipline is a basic component of morality in Durkheim's argument because, drawing on his theory of human nature, he believed that there have to be constraints upon people's passions to prevent egoism and anomie. For Durkheim, discipline is a key factor in education. Convinced that it is necessary for children's appetites to be restricted, he believed these could be defined in ways that lead to happiness and moral health so that children can have realizable goals that are compatible with their abilities. This is not a static view of human aspiration. Durkheim argues that, with historical change, human nature changes and so do the boundaries of people's realizable expectations.

Durkheim further argues that moral acts are always in pursuit of impersonal ends, and once theological ideas are ruled out, the only superior entity is society. Therefore, moral authority comes from the social groups of which people are members, but the group itself is superior because it outlives the individual members. Thus, "we are moral beings only to the extent that we are social beings."[43] Durkheim refers to how society is superior to the individual, arguing that individuals owe so much to society—language, culture, and personality—and they are prepared to see society as the source of authority. Attachment to groups is the second element of morality. He states, "When our conscience speaks it is society speaking within us."[44]

The third element of morality in Durkheim's theory is autonomy or self-determination. The scientific knowledge of the natural world enables us to know how the external world works, and, because we have understanding of this, we accept its constraints and know we have no alternative. As Durkheim states, "We liberate ourselves through our understanding." If people understand the nature of moral rules and sci-entifically investigate the reasons for their existence in society, they can make rational decisions. As he puts it,

> Now we are able to check on the extent to which the moral order is founded in the nature of things—that is in the nature of soci-ety—which is to say to what extent it is what it ought to be. In the degree that we see it as such, we can freely conform to it.... Thus, on condition of having adequate knowledge of moral pre-cepts, of their causes and of their functions, we are in a position to conform to them, but consciously and knowing why. Such con-formity has nothing of constraint about it.[45]

Durkheim concedes that the science of morality is less developed than are the natural sciences, but he believed that, if people knew the reasons for moral imperatives, they would obey voluntarily and desire this obedi-ence because they would know why the moral rules exist. Science can empower people to know and influence things that exert a control over them. A third dimension of morality is thus "enlightened assent."[46] The role of a teacher in a modern secular society is to teach modern secular morality—to help the child understand the rules he should abide by and to make him "understand his country and his times, to make him feel his responsibilities, to initiate him into life and thus to prepare him to take his part in the collective tasks awaiting him."[47]

After discussing the elements of morality, Durkheim turned his atten-tion to educational psychology and the development of morality in the child. The school is a socializing agency between the family and the wider society; school rules and the social life of the classroom introduce the child to the spirit of discipline. The teacher should impress upon the child the general nature of these rules by which all people, the teacher included, are constrained. The infraction of such rules should be punished by blame and by making it clear that others disapprove of this behavior.[48] Consequently, Durkheim was opposed to corporal punishment in schools because contemporary morality is one of moral individualism based on freedom and human dignity: "One of the chief aims of moral education is to inspire in the child a feeling for the dignity of man. Corporal punish-ment is a continual offence to this sentiment."[49]

Attachment to the group is the second dimension of morality, and, in this respect, Durkheim identifies the school environment as one in which the child may experience a collective life that is more intense than the quieter life within the family. He argues that participation in this extended collective life enhances the child's being. Class life should not be sober but have a joyful aspect—which appears rather like a less intense version of the experience of some of the rites described in simple religions—and the teacher is encouraged to stimulate a sense of class identity or spirit.[50] The third level of morality in Durkheim's schema— autonomy or self-determinism within a moral system—requires people to evaluate their moral choices. Durkheim drew upon the elementary introduction of natural sciences into the school to give the child a sense of the complexity of things and the role of experimental sciences.[51] In order to make moral choices, people need to be aware of social reality, and, in view of the lack of development within the social sciences, Durkheim identified historical knowledge as being capable of making pupils aware of social forces that have shaped their society and those features of the collective consciousness that have formed French national character. The teacher should highlight those historical events and instill in children a sense of how they are a product of what has gone before them. Durkheim thought that teaching the history of the child's society would strengthen his or her attachment to society and imbue the child with a sense that each individual is part of the "complex of ideas and sentiments, ways of seeing and feeling, a certain intellectual and moral framework distinctive of the entire group. Society is above all a consciousness of the whole. It is, therefore, this collective consciousness that we must instill in the child."[52]

In the course of his lectures in 1902, Durkheim gave a structural and historical analysis of the development of secondary education in France from the early Middle Ages. Because the Christian church had a mission to shape the individual, schools grew up as moral communities attached to cathedrals and gradually became secondary schools and universities. The church was the link between the Roman and Germanic societies, and it initiated people into "the only culture which then existed, namely classi-cal culture."[53] However, because there was a tension between Christianity and the classical culture that was the product of pagan Greco-Roman society, Durkheim discussed how classical education selected features from that culture. He argued that, in the early Middle Ages, the stress was on grammatical formalism, which was followed by a dialectical formal-ism. Changes in social class and educational philosophy in the sixteenth century ushered in a preference for the study of classical literature as the best way to mold pupils' minds. The closing of the wealth gap between the leisured classes and the nobility made the former desire to imitate the politeness of aristocratic society. Durkheim has been criticized for neglecting the relationship between social class and education, but, in this regard, he does describe the educational philosophy of the humanists as an ideology based on the values of aristocratic and leisured classes, which neglected the educational needs of masses of people "for whom education should have raised their intellectual and moral standards and improved their material condition."[54]

Conclusion

This chapter has provided a summary of Durkheim's ideas on religion, knowledge, and education. There have been criticisms of his ideas on religion from anthropologists who argue not only that societies simpler than that of the Australian natives existed and did not have a totem, but also that Durkheim did not discuss the negative effects of religion on society.[55] The discussion of this key part of his work shows that Durkheim provides a perspective that relates consciousness to the structural organization of society: the tribe is the basis of totemism, or social organization is basic to categories of thought and education.

Durkheim insists that religious beliefs are not based upon some kind of hallucination; however, to argue that religious experience is a product of the membership of society seems to be not much different to those who have faith. As Rosati puts it, "Durkheim's approach highlights how the believer, worshipping a transcendental and superior being that he identifies with god or with some mysterious force, is both right and wrong. He is wrong insofar as the content of what he represents to the mind through religious belief is not what he imagines it to be (God or another extra-social force); he is right in that the content is something that is transcendent and superior to him, namely society."[56]

Religion has social causes in Durkheim's theory, and all life has a material context, but religion is not just a product of the brain or of economic conditions. Rather, Durkheim stresses how the collective consciousness "must be produced by a *sui generis* synthesis of particular consciousnesses," which

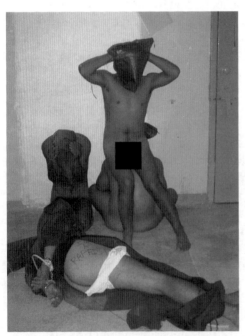

A lack of rules relating to the treatment of prisoners in Iraq has been seen as a sign of anomie in a contemporary war situation.

have "the effect of unlocking a whole world of feelings, ideas and images that once born, obey their own laws."[57] Durkheim's analysis of religious beliefs and rites suggests that collective representations and the experience of a collective effervescence have a powerful role as a basis of feelings and beliefs. As explained previously, Durkheim thought that the old religions had lost their powers, but he was aware that any new religion—even one based upon the cult of the individual—and human dignity require some kind of assembly of the community to reinforce beliefs. Thus, Durkheim's sociology presents possible new insights into the study of culture; social bonding and regulation; the reworking of social solidarity; and, as his discussion of corporations shows, the role of civil society in maintaining social solidarity.[58]

In modern terminology the cult of the individual, which was discussed earlier in this chapter and in chapter 7, would be referred to as a discourse of human rights. Joas points out that Durkheim was the first person to discuss, during the political upheavals of the Dreyfus scandal, how the *human person* had become the most sacred object in society:[59]

> This human person, the definition of which is like the touchstone which distinguishes good from evil, is considered sacred in the ritual sense of the word. It partakes of the transcendent majesty that churches of all time lend to their gods; it is conceived of as being invested with that mysterious property which creates a void about sacred things, which removes them from vulgar contacts and withdraws them from common circulation. And the respect which is given it comes precisely from this source. Whoever makes an attempt on a man's life, on a man's liberty, on a man's honour, inspires in us a feeling of horror analogous in every way to that which the believer experiences when he sees his idol profaned.[60]

Because offenses against the individual offend this new collective conscience, Joas discusses its impact on criminal and civil law and the resultant changes in eighteenth-century penal policy. It is possible to see that the sacralization of the person has its roots in Judeo-Christian traditions, but Durkheim regards these religious roots as no longer important. Individuals may become increasingly included in political and legal rights, but, as Joas states, the rights are not universally upheld because there are counter forces, even in the West.

The concept of anomie provides a critical concept for the exposure of irrational and unjust features of contemporary society. The previous chapters have shown how this concept can be used to explain corporate crime and the malaise of neoliberal market societies. Anomie has also been effectively used to explain the systematic abuse of human rights and the torture at Abu Ghraib prison in Iraq. US government reports and the analysis of testimony given at the court-martial trials, held at Fort Hood, Texas, relating to the abuse at Abu Ghraib show that anomie—defined by Durkheim as *dérèglement* (derangement)—that is a "rule that is a lack of rule"—was ubiquitous at a range of levels within the US government and the US army. Low-ranking soldiers were blamed for the torture and abuse, although chaotic and inconsistent views about interrogation techniques and prisoners' rights prevailed at all levels of command, internationally, nationally, and locally.[61]

FURTHER THINKING:

What is the role of collective representations in the formation and re-affirmation of religious belief in Durkheim's theory of religion? In the sense that late modernity is often experienced as "free market" individualism, and people pursuing personal identity projects of "self-fulfillment," is collective representation salient today?

FURTHER READING:

See Émile Durkheim, *The Elementary Forms of Religious Life* (Oxford: Oxford University Press, 2001). The following are useful secondary sources on Durkheim: Raymond Aron, *Main Currents of Sociological Thought, Durkheim, Pareto, Weber*, vol. 2 (London: Routledge, 2017); Ken Morrison, *Marx, Durkheim, Weber: Formations of Modern Social Thought*, 2nd ed. (London: Sage Publications, 2006), 231–39.

Notes

1 Bryan S. Turner, *Classical Sociology* (London: Sage, 1999), 196.
2 Émile Durkheim, *The Elementary Forms of Religious Life* (Oxford: Oxford University Press, 2001), 4.
3 Durkheim, *The Elementary Forms*, 4.
4 Durkheim, *The Elementary Forms*, 19.
5 Durkheim, *The Elementary Forms*, 36.
6 Durkheim, *The Elementary Forms*, 38.
7 Durkheim, *The Elementary Forms*, 46.

8 Durkheim, *The Elementary Forms*, 47.
9 Durkheim, *The Elementary Forms*, 66.
10 Durkheim, *The Elementary Forms*, 70–72.
11 Durkheim, *The Elementary Forms*, 74.
12 Durkheim, *The Elementary Forms*, 88.
13 Durkheim, *The Elementary Forms*, 119–20.
14 Durkheim, *The Elementary Forms*, 98.
15 Durkheim, *The Elementary Forms*, 104.
16 Durkheim, *The Elementary Forms*, 140.
17 Durkheim, *The Elementary Forms*, 141.
18 Durkheim, *The Elementary Forms*, 154.
19 Durkheim, *The Elementary Forms*, 164.
20 Durkheim, *The Elementary Forms*, 164.
21 Durkheim, *The Elementary Forms*, 170.
22 Durkheim, *The Elementary Forms*, 170.
23 Durkheim, *The Elementary Forms*, 171.
24 Durkheim, *The Elementary Forms*, 171.
25 Durkheim, *The Elementary Forms*, 247.
26 Durkheim, *The Elementary Forms*, 248.
27 Durkheim, *The Elementary Forms*, 253.
28 Durkheim, *The Elementary Forms*, 259.
29 Durkheim, *The Elementary Forms*, 11.
30 Durkheim, *The Elementary Forms*, 109.
31 Durkheim, *The Elementary Forms*, 112.
32 Durkheim, *The Elementary Forms*, 113.
33 Durkheim, *The Elementary Forms*, 115.
34 Durkheim, *The Elementary Forms*, 151, 168.
35 Durkheim, *The Elementary Forms*, 324.
36 Durkheim, *The Elementary Forms*, 330.
37 Durkheim, *The Elementary Forms*, 322.
38 Durkheim, *The Elementary Forms*, 322.
39 Durkheim, *The Elementary Forms*, 326.
40 Émile Durkheim, *Education and Sociology* (New York: The Free Press, 1956), 141.
41 Durkheim, *Education and Sociology*, 72–76.
42 Émile Durkheim, *Moral Education* (New York: Dover Publications, 2002), 14.
43 Durkheim, *Moral Education*, 64.
44 Durkheim, *Moral Education*, 90.
45 Durkheim, *Moral Education*, 117.
46 Durkheim, *Moral Education*, 120.
47 Durkheim, *Moral Education*, 124.
48 Durkheim, *Moral Education*, 180–82.
49 Durkheim, *Moral Education*, 183.

50 Durkheim, *Moral Education*, 241.

51 Durkheim, *Moral Education*, 260–61.

52 Durkheim, *Moral Education*, 277.

53 Émile Durkheim, *The Evolution of Educational Thought* (London: Routledge & Kegan Paul, 1977), 25.

54 Durkheim, *The Evolution of Educational*, 206.

55 Kenneth Thompson, *Émile Durkheim* (London: Tavistock Publications, 1982).

56 Massimo Rosati, "Inhabiting No-Man's Land: Durkheim and Modernity," *Journal of Classical Sociology* 8 (May 2008): 241.

57 Durkheim, *The Elementary Forms*, 319.

58 Kenneth Thompson, Introduction to *Durkheim Today*, ed. W.S.F. Pickering (Oxford: Berghahn Books, 2002).

59 Hans Joas, "Punishment and Respect: The Sacralization of the Person and Its Endangerment," *Journal of Classical Sociology* 8 (May 2008): 169–75.

60 Émile Durkheim, "Individualism and Intellectuals," in *Émile Durkheim on Morality and Society*, ed. R. Bellah (Chicago: University of Chicago Press, 1973), 43–75, quoted in Joas, "Punishment and Respect," 170.

61 Stjepan G. Mestrovic and Ronald Lorenzo, "Durkheim's Concept of *Anomie* and the Abuse at Abu Ghraib," *Journal of Classical Sociology* 8 (May 2008): 179–85.

10. Max Weber: Methodology

Weber's resolutely anti-philosophical sociology aimed
to release empirical social science from the tutelage of
speculative metaphysics.

—Alex Law, 2015[1]

One way to appreciate Max Weber's extraordinary achievement as
a methodologist ... is to understand him historically, in relation to
his own intellectual field. Seen in that way, Weber perfectly typifies
the clarifying critic who restates, rationalizes, and thus partly
transcends the assumptions of his own culture.

—Fritz Ringer, 1997[2]

SO FAR WE HAVE EXAMINED how classical social theory understands society in terms of materiality, through the works of Marx and Engels, and morality, through the works of Durkheim. Like Marx and Durkheim, Max Weber is widely recognized for his substantive analysis of Western capitalism and modern forms of life. In Weber's writings, as is the case with Durkheim, the subject matter of sociology, its method of human inquiry, and its relationship to other disciplines is accorded significant attention. For Weber, a society is constituted through rationally calculated and goal-directed human action, and wholesale rationalization comes to dominate Western culture and institutions. Weber is also recognized as a pillar of sociological thought, but his identity as a sociologist is a complex topic. Although he engaged with sociologists and was a co-founder of the *Deutsche Gesellschaft für Soziologie* (the German Society for Sociology), Weber conceived of himself first and foremost as a political economist, as is evident from his texts. Whereas Durkheim's work was influenced by Comteian positivism and his early studies were rather abstract and philosophical, by contrast, Weber employs the notion of interpretive understanding, *Verstehen*, in his discussion of methodology, and his early works are meticulous historical studies. Among Anglo-Saxon scholars, Max Weber's role as a founding figure of sociology has alternated since the 1980s between "in doubt" to "resurrection."[3] More recently, Weber and Georg Simmel have been considered the most contemporary of the sociological canon, even representing the first signs of postmodernism.[4] And others posit that "Weber is one of the sources of our culture."[5] *The Methodology of the Social Sciences* and his later work on methodology, which this chapter will consider, are highly polemical works that still inform modern sociology. They discuss analytical procedures and provide sociologists with an appreciation of the central unresolved problem of values and objectivity in social research. Weber's *Methodology* was heavily influenced by his intellectual heritage and written in response to his immediate circumstances; therefore, a contextual understanding of his work is necessary. This chapter examines both the intellectual genealogy that shaped Weber's methodology and his key pronouncements on method.

Life and Works

Max Weber was born on April 21, 1864, in Erfurt, a small city in the southeastern region of Germany. Shortly after his birth, the Weber family moved to Berlin. Weber's parents were polar opposites. His mother, Helene Fallenstein Weber, was a devout Calvinist, a woman of culture and piety who led an ascetic life, and it was her austere Puritanism that came ultimately to shape Max Weber's personal ethics.[6] His father was a lawyer and politician who led a hedonistic lifestyle, in contrast to his wife. He was also allegedly a stereotypical Victorian: a disciplinarian to his children, arrogant and insensitive to his wife. The dissonance between his father's values and lifestyle and his mother's orientation to life negatively affected Weber's psychological development and shaped his intellectual direction. The family home attracted local artists, intellectuals, and business and political elites, so the young Weber was exposed to the educated "chattering class." After taking his *Abitur* and completing high school, Weber entered the University of Heidelberg and chose to study law, his father's profession. He also chose to follow his father's social life: drinking and partying a lot and studying a little. After a 12-month stint in the military, he returned to his parents' home and resumed his academic studies at the University of Berlin, moving later to the University of Göttingen. As a student, Weber was financially dependent on his father, a situation he progressively grew to resent. And, in the eight years living with his parents, he gravitated toward his mother's values and orientation to life while his antipathy to his father increased. Young Weber became a disciplined and conscientious student. In 1889, he completed his doctoral dissertation on medieval trading companies, and, in 1891, he presented his postdoctoral thesis (*Habilitationsschrift*) on Roman agrarian history. This formally qualified him for an academic university position, and he was appointed as a lecturer in law at the University of Berlin. In 1892, he married Marianne Schnitger, a scholarly interlocutor who supported her husband's academic career. After teaching economics at the University of Freiburg, in 1896 Weber accepted an appointment as professor at the University of Heidelberg. He was 32. His contemporaries considered him very young to be appointed professor at such a prestigious German university.

Max Weber was born in Erfurt, Germany, in 1864. In 1892, he married Marianne Schnitger, an academic. Weber's circle of friends included the philosopher Georg Lukács, as well as the sociologists Robert Michels and Georg Simmel. Weber died of pneumonia in 1920, at the age of 56.

It was at the University of Heidelberg that Weber suffered a nervous breakdown in 1898, and he resigned from the university. His mental illness occurred soon after the death of his father. It is a matter of conjecture whether quarreling with Weber senior caused the mental illness. Shortly before his father died, Max had a violent argument with him, which culminated in his ordering his father from the house. Father and son were never to speak to each other again. On hearing of his father's unexpected death, Max Weber was consumed by guilt and remorse. Unable to concentrate on his academic life, he traveled widely, especially around southern Europe. It was not until 1903, at the age of 39, that he was able to resume his academic career, which provided him with extended sabbaticals. In 1904, while traveling in the United States, he delivered his first lecture in more than six years. It is reported that he was enamored of the US democratic processes and captivated by the pace and mayhem of life in the large cities. Traveling around the United States appeared to have a cathartic effect on Weber, for, on returning to Germany, he produced some of his most important work on methodology and religion and capitalism. As did

Émile Durkheim, Weber contributed to the development of the nascent discipline of sociology. He helped establish the German Society for Sociology, and, in 1903, he accepted a position as associate editor of the prestigious *Archiv für Sozialwissenschaft und Sozialpolitik* (Archive for Social Science and Social Policy). His circle of friends included philosopher Georg Lukács, as well as sociologists Robert Michels and Georg Simmel.

Weber wrote more than ten books and numerous scholarly papers on a range of topics, including *The Methodology of the Social Sciences* in 1904 and his best-known work, *The Protestant Ethic and the Spirit of Capitalism*, during 1904 and 1905. He taught himself Russian and became proficient enough in reading contemporary Russian sources to write an article on the 1905 Russian Revolution. World War I interrupted his scholarly productivity. Too old for active service, much to his regret, he worked as a hospital administrator for a short period before serving on an obscure government commission to examine tariff-related problems. After 1916, most of his time was devoted to writing about his lifelong interests: religion, political economy, and society. Shortly thereafter, he published his important studies of world religions: *The Religion of China: Confucianism and Taoism* (1916); *The Religion of India: The Sociology of Hinduism and Buddhism* (1916); and *The Sociology of Religion* (1921). After the war, he became politically active, joined the newly formed *Deutsche Demokratische Partei* (German Democratic Party), and was shortlisted as the party's candidate for a Frankfurt constituency. He failed to get the nomination and was apparently deeply disappointed by the decision.[7] For sociology, at least, his rejection was all to the good because Weber was able to continue working on his major project, the three volumes of *Economy and Society* (published posthumously in 1921). A sociological treatise, it has become an integral part of the sociological imagination.[8] Weber's publications are clearly many, diverse, complex, and possess a fragmentary character, which has had the effect of generating a variety of interpretations of his work.[9]

Weber's personality was full of paradoxes. On the one hand, he cultivated a puritan lifestyle, but, on the other hand, he himself gave no sign he was a believer.[10] Though an academic mandarin, he craved to be a man of action and wrote, "I am not really a scholar; scientific activity is for me primarily an occupation for the leisure hours.... The feeling of being active in a practical way is entirely indispensable to me, and I hope that the pedagogic side of the teaching profession will satisfy this craving."[11] This contradiction within Weber's personality is summed up by Reinhard Bendix: "He continuously engaged in the simultaneous effort to be a man of science with the strenuous vigour more common in a man of action, and to be a man of action with all the ethical rigor and personal detachment more common in a man of science."[12] Though Weber is now recognized as a member of the sociological canon, his work contains paradoxes and ambiguity that have generated multiple and conflicting interpretations. Though he did not have a conception of society as a social system, he famously warned about the "iron cage" of industrial capitalism. His methodological ideas are ambiguous, and grappling with them has been characterized as "handling a bar of wet soap."[13] Weber died of pneumonia on June 14, 1920, at the age of 56.

Intellectual Influences

Max Weber's social theories were shaped by the specific historical context of his time and by several intellectual sources. An appreciation of these contexts is necessary in understanding Weber's substantive ideas on the methodology of the social sciences and his analysis of the origins and nature of modernity. Weber was writing during a period of profound political and intellectual uncertainty, and his sociology is hollow once divorced from the political context in which it is embedded.[14] As a member of the German educated middle class, Weber possessed political and cultural values reflective of this social group's commitment to nationalism, so his work addresses the problem of the economic retardation of Germany and of the country's position in global politics. In his inaugural address at the University of Freiburg in 1895, Weber emphasized the need for a strong, united Germany. He declared, "The object of our work in social policy is not to make the world happy, but to unify socially a nation surrounded by economic progress."[15] Following Bismarck's resignation in 1890, debates on the weakness of the German middle classes, the stifling effect of state bureaucracy, the leadership vacuum, and the perceived external threat of Britain, Russia, and the United States fashioned Weber's theories on bureaucracy, leadership, and class structure.[16]

The influence of Marx's ideas on Weber's intellectual apparatus has been the topic of considerable debate and scholarship. It was the American sociologist Talcott Parsons, in *The Structure of Social Action* (1937), who first introduced Weber's work to Anglo-Saxon sociologists. From Parson's reconstruction of Weber, it became common parlance that Weber intended *The Protestant Ethic and the Spirit of Capitalism* and *Economy and Society* as a "refutation" of Marx's thesis on capitalism. It is not difficult to support this incorrect view when, for example, Weber makes reference to "naïve historical materialism."[17] In Marx's conception of history, the change in the economic base had come first—from feudalism to capitalism—followed by changes in the superstructure, such as variations in religious beliefs. In identifying the influence of religious ideas on

Weber argued that sociologists can understand social action by penetrating to the subjective meanings those humans themselves attach to their own behaviors, a method called *Verstehen*. This contemporary photograph shows a homeless person spending the night in the public space of the metropolis. Weber's methods suggest that researchers cannot understand the homeless, for example, unless they examine how the homeless themselves view and explain their situation.

the development of capitalism, Weber's analysis in *The Protestant Ethic* appears to reverse the base-structure assumption of Marx. Weber explicitly denies this interpretation: "We have no intention of defending any such foolishly doctrinaire thesis as that the 'capitalist spirit' ... let alone capitalism itself, *could only* arise as a result of certain influences of the Reformation."[18] Weber calls Marx a "great thinker"[19] and acknowledges the importance of a society's economic conditions. One study of Marx and Weber shows that, despite very different political standpoints, their social theory shares a central interest in the dehumanizing effect of industrial capitalism.[20] Thus, both classical theorists reveal a convergence in their critique of capitalism, and there are substantive affinities between Marx and Weber.[21] Marx's theory of alienation and Weber's concepts of rationalization and disenchantment, as in the iron cage, for example, exhibit significant similarities.[22]

The hypothesis of the "debate with the ghost of Marx," as an intellectual milieu for understanding Weber's work, has been replaced by the thesis that the German philosopher Friedrich Nietzsche (1844–1900) was a decisive intellectual influence on Max Weber.[23] Nietzsche is acknowledged as the principal philosopher responsible for the dethronement of Enlightenment reason and the celebration of the irrational. According to Nietzsche, people must understand that the social world is replete with ambiguity, absurdity, cruelty, and injustice and that unconscious impulses and strivings dominate human behavior, not rational principles. As a late-modern philosopher, Nietzsche believed that there exist no absolute moral standards whose truth can be demonstrated by reflective reason: nothing is true. Christianity, said Nietzsche, smothered human's true essence, the spark of life. In proclaiming that "God is dead" and Christian morality is defunct, Nietzsche believed that traditional moral values had lost their authority and binding power in late-capitalist societies. His writings are riven with contradictions that inspire multiple interpretations, controversy, and conjecture.[24]

Nietzsche's philosophy shaped the development of Weber's sociology in several important ways. Like Nietzsche, Weber emphasizes the primacy of power in social life. In *Economy and Society*, Weber writes, "Domination in the most general sense is one of the most important elements of social action."[25] Furthermore, Nietzsche's views on the loss of authority of traditional moral values, with his "God is dead" and his criticism of absolutist notions of truth, profoundly influenced Weber's ideas about the ability of the social sciences ever to establish, unambiguously, the "truth" in the social world. A legacy of Nietzsche's philosophy was that truth exists only from a particular standpoint or perspective. Thus truth is always contingent. There are no meta-narratives. Weber's critical observations on the moral basis of intellectual inquiry and his pessimistic analysis of modern bureaucracy's capacity to eliminate "love, hatred, and all purely personal, irrational, and emotional elements"[26] can be traced back to Nietzsche.

In addition to Marx and Nietzsche, a third intellectual force influencing Weber's encyclopedic writings is neo-Kantianism, particularly the works of Wilhelm Dilthey (1833–1911), Wilhelm Windelband (1848–1915), and Heinrich Rickert (1863–1936).[27] In the 1880s, the natural sciences, with their positivist thinking, were pre-eminent in discovering truths about the natural world, and this raised questions about the intellectual authority of the philosophical sciences. The dispute about the relationship between the natural sciences (*Naturwissenschaften*) and human sciences (*Geisteswissenschaften*) initiated what is known as the *Methodenstreit* debate. The German neo-Kantian movement was an expression of dissatisfaction with the dominance of positivist thinking and the crisis in philosophical sciences. In education, realistic, or modern, schools challenged the pre-eminence of classical studies, while utilitarian, or technical, schools gained strength. Among German mandarins, there was widespread revulsion against positivism; it was considered "a kind of intellectual acid, a potentially disastrous dissolvent of holistic concepts, traditional beliefs, and socially integrative certainties."[28] The neo-Kantian movement aimed to secure the intellectual authority of the humanities and social sciences.

The Dilthey-Windelband-Rickert triumvirate addressed two central issues: subject matter and the theory of knowledge. According to Dilthey, the natural sciences and the social sciences studied different objects. He also challenged the secular sobriety of French positivism and instead emphasized humanity's creative and meaningful commonality, which was unmasked by hermeneutics approaches, a process of understanding, interpretation, and explanation. In Dilthey's words, "Everything in which the mind has objectified itself contains something held in common between I and thou. Every square planted with trees, every room in which seats are arranged, is intelligible to us from our infancy because human planning, arranging and valuing—common to all of us—have assigned a place to every square and every object in the room."[29] Dilthey's hermeneutics work to understand social life has been described variously as a declaration of war against positivism[30] or as a declaration of independence on behalf of humanities.[31] He never abandoned his conviction that empathy is an element in interpretation, but, in a 1907 essay on descriptive psychology, Dilthey developed the concept of *Verstehen* to capture human meanings from social experience. Georg Simmel articulated aspects of Dilthey's *Verstehen* as early as 1892. Like Dilthey, Simmel emphasized the relationship between inner movements of the soul and their outward manifestations. This point is important because Simmel influenced Weber more directly than Dilthey.[32]

By contrast, Wilhelm Windelband held that the subject matter of the human sciences seeks fully to describe a single event in its "unique actuality" at a particular location in time. He argued that, methodologically, the natural sciences pursue nomothetic knowledge (*Gesetz*) in the form of universal laws and the human sciences strive for an ideographic knowledge (*Gestalt*) of single patterns or actions. The younger Rickert refined Windelband ideas. Heinrich Rickert believed that the principal distinction between the natural and human sciences was between their respective methods. For Rickert, the natural sciences generalize, the human sciences individualize. He also conceived of human cultures as systems of values. Facts, argued Rickert, are constituted out of experience and given form by cognitive activity, which connotes selection and judgment. Rickert's belief was "first we judge and then we know."[33] While the natural sciences explain phenomena in terms of causal arguments, the human sciences are concerned with understanding the significance and importance of cultural phenomena. Thus, both physics and anthropology are sciences but they require different methods of inquiry. Whereas physics can be studied within the framework of laws and causes, in anthropology the emphasis is with hermeneutics and the problem of how to *Verstehen*—understand, interpret, and make judgments about—the meaning of ritual acts and customs with reference to values, which are embedded in the cultural context of the researcher.

Weber and the *Methodenstreit*

Although the genealogy of Weber's methodological essays is complex,[34] Nietzsche's philosophy and the neo-Kantian view of concept formation undoubtedly influenced Weber's writings on the methodology of social research. Weber's contribution to the Methodenstreit debate was his integration of two divergent positions.[35] Weber agreed with the anti-positivists that the application of general laws to study social reality in its totality is problematic. However, Weber argued that rational scientific methods should be applied to the human sciences and should not be reserved exclusively for the natural sciences. Whatever the object under investigation, scientific criteria are always the aspiration; the specificity of the human sciences, the motives and values that guide human inquiry, necessitate special consideration.[36] The problem of values, of normative judgments and empirical knowledge, or of truth is addressed in *The Methodology of the Social Sciences*. Weber distinguishes between value freedom and value relevance. He recognizes that, in the initial research stage, personal and cultural values cannot be exorcized, and, consequently, what is selected for investigation mirrors the researcher's values. However, Weber insists that social science be value-free in the analysis stage. Weber writes, "*An attitude of moral indifference* has no connection with *scientific* 'objectivity.'"[37]

For Weber, objectivity involves a moral commitment to the pursuit of knowledge, that is, truth. Although sociologists recognize the value of knowledge from "one-sided points of view," objectivity in research and scholarship demands "the insistence on the rigorous distinction between empirical knowledge and value-judgements."[38] For many years, Weber's position on objectivity has been widely misinterpreted to mean value freedom (*Wertfreiheit*), implying a simple objectivity that requires researchers to free themselves of all values in the course of their research. Weber intended the term *objectivity* to mean that researchers have an obligation to be aware of the ideologies and values that dominate their own perspectives and observations and to strive to go beyond their own individual views.[39]

Weber emphasizes that the direction of the social scientist's personal worldview and the values in the prism of her or his mind give direction to the selection of subject matter, theoretical assumptions, and methodology. In other words, he underscores that human inquiry involves moral choices, and the implication is that sociologists need to explain the moral choices that they make.[40] Like Rickert, Weber conceived of culture as a value concept. This quotation is typical of his argument: "The *significance* of a configuration of cultural phenomena and the basis of this significance cannot ... be derived and rendered intelligible by a system of analytical laws ... since the significance of cultural events presupposes a value-orientation towards these events."[41] The social scientist must abstract sufficiently unambiguous conceptualizations from the infinite complexity of social reality. But what is the criterion by which a segment of social life is selected for investigation? Weber, influenced by Rickert, formulates what he believes to be the decisive feature of social sciences methodology, the principle of *value orientation*. Social sciences analyze segments of social action in terms of their *significance*; but importantly, these are only the segments that have become significant to the scientist because of their value relevance. As Weber writes,

> Only a small portion of existing concrete reality is coloured by our value-conditioned interest and it alone is significant to us. It is significant because it reveals relationships which are important to us due to their connection with our values. Only because and to the extent that this is the case is it worthwhile for us to know it in its individual features.... The focus of attention on reality under the *guidance of values* which lend it significance and the selection and ordering of the phenomena ... is entirely different from the analysis of reality in terms of laws and general concepts. [emphasis added][42]

Weber argues that, given the infinite variety of empirical reality, only a chaos of judgment would result from any serious attempt to analyze segments of social reality "without presuppositions." For instance, a Canadian researcher investigating the social barriers facing young women entering higher education may assume there is a potential connection between social class and university access. On the other hand, a social scientist is likely to have a different presupposition if the same study is conducted in Turkey, a predominantly Muslim country. Weber's position is clear: what is deemed meaningful is a cultural construct. The social scientist is confronted with a chaos of "existential judgements" about myriad individual actions. Direction, however, is brought into this chaos because only an *element* of concrete reality is interesting and significant to the researcher, and this, in turn, is guided by the values with which she or he approaches the subject matter.

For Weber as for Rickert, in the human sciences, judgments of relevance and meaning will be developed with reference to cultural values. Further, where the uniqueness of a social phenomenon is concerned, causality is not a matter of abstract general laws but of specific, concrete, causal relationships. For Weber, an objective analysis of social reality that proceeds according to the ideal of laws is meaningless.[43] Weber's preoccupation with such topics as ethical neutrality in teaching and objectivity in social inquiry was driven by the practical circumstances related to academic freedom in Germany's universities and inspired by Nietzsche's critique of the Enlightenment's absolutist notions of truth. Weber accepted Nietzsche's argument that truth is always contingent upon the perspectives of the inquiring scholar. If God is dead, the "freedom" of a social science means that there is no grounding by which any one perspective could have legitimacy over other perspectives. Weber's deliberations on the problem of objectivity in the social sciences, and particularly on the problem of understanding human action, were attempts to address this issue of legitimacy.[44]

Definition of Sociology and Methodologies

The *Methodenstreit* controversy underpins Weberian sociology. In *Economy and Society*, Weber refers to the science of society as interpretive sociology (*Verstehend Soziologie*), and he defines sociology as "a science concerning itself with the interpretative understanding of social action and thereby with a causal explanation of its course and consequence."[45] Sociology is concerned with investigating social action, which includes both the failure to act and a passive acquiescence that may be oriented to the past, present, or future behavior of others. However, not every kind of human action is social action. Here, Weber makes a distinction between behavior and action. Behavior is an observable act or movement that humans do without attaching a meaning to it. For example, if a person coughs or faints, the act can be understood as the result of a physical cause rather than meaningful action.

Social Action

Sociology investigates meaningful social action or reaction, whether meaning is attributed to the actions of a single individual; to those prevailing, on average, within a particular group; or to those attributed to a hypothetically constructed, typical actor.[46] His well-known definition of *social action* states: "The acting individual attaches a subjective meaning to his behaviour—be it overt or covert, omission or acquiescence. Action is 'social' insofar as its subjective meaning takes account of the behaviour of others and is thereby oriented in its course."[47] Weber's definition makes a distinction in that sociology is concerned only with meaningful *social* action that is affected by or oriented toward others. The example Weber uses to show this distinction is an accident between two cyclists. The collision may be looked at as a natural event, a result of a causal chain of physical events: Although the cyclists are engaged in meaningful action, neither intended the collision to occur. On the other hand, if an altercation or an apology follows the collision, either would constitute meaningful social action in which an individual is directing her or his action toward the other. Weber also insists that actions conditioned by crowd psychology or the imitation of the action of others do not constitute social action. Weber's theorizing of human action is significantly different to that of Marx or Durkheim. For Marx, economic forces, of which people often have little or no understanding and to which they do not attribute a subjective meaning, constantly affect human action. For Durkheim, the notion of social consciousness implies that meaning itself is socially constructed: people are socialized into ways of thinking. Weber's meaningful social action might be described as norm-following, and, by definition, norms reflect or embody a culture's values and are always backed by sanctions of one kind or another: norms are cultural constructs.

Weber identifies four types of social action: traditional, affectual, value-rational, and instrumentally rational. *Traditional action* is rooted in a body of cultural beliefs, customary habits of thought, and practices, which produce almost automatic action following habitual stimuli, as, for example, with showering, eating, walking, or a priest following church doctrine. The great mass of everyday action approaches this type of action and is on a borderline between pre-social (non-reflective) and social (meaningful). *Affective* or *emotional action* is designed to capture the diverse emotional states of individuals by means of empathy. Such empathy is easier, writes Weber, "the more we ourselves are susceptible to such emotional reactions as anxiety, anger, ambition, envy, jealousy, love, enthusiasm, pride, vengefulness, loyalty, devotion, and appetites of all sorts, and to the 'irrational' conduct which grows out of them."[48] This type of action is also on the borderline of what can be considered meaningfully oriented action, for it is not primarily goal directed. An example might be an individual leaping with joy during a religious service.

Value-rational action (*Wertrational*) is anchored in a conscious belief in the ultimate value of achieving some substantive goal (e.g., salvation) by calculated—rational—means (e.g., pursuing an ascetic lifestyle). Value-rational actions are those of individuals who, regardless of personal cost, put their convictions into practice to do what seems to them to be required because of a religious call, personal loyalty, duty, or the importance of some cause. An example would be Martin Luther King Jr., who strove for racial equality in the United States in the 1960s but who advocated non-violent means of achieving the movement's goal. *Instrumentally rational action (Zweckrational)* takes into account the ends, the means, and the secondary outcomes; in this form of social action, the goals themselves have also been rationally chosen. This type of action is the most rational and, in Weber's words, is determined by "expectations as to the behaviour of objects in the environment and of other human beings; these expectations are used as 'conditions' or 'means' for the attainment of the actor's own rationally pursued and calculated ends."[49] Instrumentally rational action involves calculated consideration of alternative means to the end, of the relations of the end to the secondary consequences, and of the relative importance of different possible ends. Weber's typology is an abstraction, and actual social action, as in the case of the actions of the ascetic Protestant sects described in *The Protestant Ethic and the Spirit of Capitalism*, is likely to involve all four types—that is, non-rational (traditional and affective types) and rational (value and instrumental types)—in different degrees.[50]

The significance of Weber's interest in legal philosophy is seldom factored into his methodological writings. In German civil law cases, the problem facing legal experts is that they must attribute effects to causes in particular circumstances and thus engage in the doctrine of singular causal analysis. For example, in assessing the role of negligence in an accident, legal opinion compares the sequence of events or actions that actually occurred with what could have been expected if normal caution or action had prevailed. According to Weber, sociology is concerned with causal explanation of social action, and his suggested method relies heavily upon the doctrine of singular causal analysis.[51] In his essay "Critical Studies in the Logic of the Cultural Sciences," Weber examines the methodological foundations of singular causal claims. He writes, "For the meaning of history as a *science of reality* can only be that it treats particular elements of reality not merely as heuristic *instruments* but as *objects* of knowledge, and particular causal connections not as premises of knowledge but as *real* causal factors."[52] The social scientist has to exclude the reproduction of the totality of concrete conditions in order to conceptually isolate complex antecedent conditions that more or less favor the outcome to be explained. Therefore, to achieve adequate causation, the *judgments of possibility*—that is, propositions regarding what *would* happen in the event of the exclusion of certain conditions—are "a matter of isolation and generalization" and involve "the continuous reference to empirical rules [*Erfahrungsregeln*]."[53] Weber writes, "The 'knowledge' on which such a judgement of ... 'significance' rests is ... on the one hand, knowledge of certain 'facts' ('ontological' knowledge), 'belonging' to the 'historical situation' ... and on the other ... knowledge of certain known empirical rules, particularly those relating to the ways in which human beings are prone to react under given situations ('nomological knowledge').[54] Weber's formulation of the causal explanation of varieties of social action is a representation of causal relationships that deals in *trajectories* of actions and in the divergences between trajectories and outcomes. Weber's creative reformulation and application of singular causal analysis set him apart from other participants in the *Methodenstreit* debate.

Understanding Social Action

According to Weber's definition, sociology concerns itself with the subjective meaning of social action. But what does Weber mean by the term *subjective*? How do sociologists truly grasp meaningful social action? Developing the work of hermeneutic philosopher Wilhelm Dilthey, Weber argues that social scientists can understand, *Verstehen*, types of social action by penetrating to those subjective meanings that humans attach to their own actions and to the action of others. Whereas the natural sciences examine the *outer states* of the natural world, the human sciences are concerned with the interpretation of the subjective *inner states* of actors. All interpretations of meaning, argues Weber, "strive for clarity and verifiable accuracy of insight and comprehension."[55] However, because social actions range from the highly rational to the highly emotional, the basis for accuracy in understanding may be rational, emotional, empathic, or artistically appreciative. Accordingly, Weber is amenable to using two types of understanding: direct and explanatory. Table 10.1 indicates the relationship Weber sees between the types of understanding and the types of evidence. He focuses primarily on explanatory (rational) understanding. Types I and II represent *direct understanding*, which involves comprehending the meaning of an action by virtue of the physical or symbolic characteristic of the act, such as observing that certain facial or body movements indicate anger, boredom, and so forth. These are understandings in which the directly observable evidence is sufficient to establish an interpretation, such as why someone moves her hand away from a hot stove or chops wood for winter fuel.

Weber's own example of direct understanding is the Pythagorean theorem in reasoning and the proposition $2 \times 2 = 4$. Types III and IV represent *explanatory understanding*, which entails comprehending the meaningful connection between an action and the likely reasons and motives underlying that act. For example, chopping wood may be part of a fitness routine for a person in a sedentary occupation, or it may be a therapeutic exercise if a person is angry after a quarrel with his or

TABLE 10.1 Types of Understanding and Evidence

TYPE OF UNDERSTANDING	TYPE OF EVIDENCE	
	Intuitive	Rational
Direct	I	II
Explanatory	III	IV

SOURCE: Adapted from Sven Eliaeson, *Max Weber's Methodologies* (Cambridge: Polity Press, 2002), 42.

her boss. For Weber, the fact that an interpretation cannot be derived directly from the action observed and empathized with suggests that, for valid knowledge of individual subjective motives, some method is required that involves assessing interpretative hypotheses as causes. Weber writes that the method of explanatory understanding is "not normative correctness, but rather, on the one hand, the conventional habits of the investigator ... in thinking in a particular way, and on the other, as the situation requires, his capacity to 'feel himself' empathically into a mode of thought which deviates from his own and which is normatively 'false' according to his own habits of thought."[56] Explanatory understanding requires the investigator to engage in a mode of thought that is sensitive to the context in which the researched and the researcher are located. For example, if we were informed of a statistical correlation between the numbers of students attending university and the polar bear population, we would regard the causal relationship as meaningless. On the other hand, if we were informed of a correlation between the numbers of students attending university and family income, we would likely consider the causal connection plausible. Why? Because we are members of the society that generated the data, we have experience of tuition fees, and we can follow the likely motives and reasoning underlying the social action. Explanatory understanding differs from direct understanding in that it requires more intellectual effort, it strives to understand social action within a context on the basis of the relevant facts and experiences, and it involves judgment. For Weber, interpretive sociology accomplishes something that is never attainable in the natural sciences: the capacity to confer intelligibility on the social action of the component individuals.

Ideal Type as a Logical Construct
Weber's methodology is primarily about conceptualization and the challenge of generating meaningful selections from an infinite and

multifarious reality. In order to strive for scientific precision on the meaning of social phenomena and to arrive at a *causal explanation* of observed reality, Weber developed his *ideal type*, defined as a "one-sided emphasis and intensification of one or several aspects of a given event."[57] The concept is borrowed from neoclassical economic theory. In empirical research, the ideal type has only one function: "Its function is the comparison with empirical reality in order to establish its divergences or similarities, to describe them with the *most unambiguously intelligible* concepts, and to understand and explain them causally."[58] An ideal type is not a description of reality; neither is it an average of something nor a normative exemplar to be achieved. Ideal types are logical hypothetical constructs. Weber's conception of the ideal type is central to his method because it simplifies the multiple complexes of social reality: "An ideal type is formed by the one-sided *accentuation* of one or more points of view and by the synthesis of a great many diffuse, discrete, more or less present and occasionally absent *concrete individual* phenomena, which are arranged according to those one-sidedly emphasized viewpoints into a unified *analytical* construct [*Gedankenbild*]. In its conceptual purity, this mental construct [*Gedankenbild*] cannot be found empirically anywhere in reality. It is a *utopia*."[59] The more precisely an ideal type is constructed, that is, the more abstract it is, the better it can perform its function in formulating terminology and potentially useful hypotheses. Ideal types are indispensable as cognitive means to the extent that they lead to knowledge of concrete social phenomena in their interrelatedness, their causes, and their significance.[60] Ideal types also possess substantial heuristic as well as expository value. In that they are constructed to project a hypothetical *progression* of observable action that *could* be explained in terms of understandable motives, ideal types are an integral part of Weber's triadic model of singular causal analysis. In the analysis of *real* social action, ideal-type projections become the basis for the causal ascription of deviations from the rationally understandable progression of actions. A diagrammatic representation of ideal-type analysis is shown in Figure 10.1.

The line A–B represents the external progression of rational actions that would have occurred if the individual had acted as specified in the ideal type. The line A1–B1 is the actual progression of actions observed by the investigator. The positing of the ideal type allows the investigator to compare A1–B1 with A–B and thus "quantify" the deviation B–B1 that must be attributed causally to the difference between A, the "motives" hypothetically ascribed to the ideal, typical individual, and A1, the "motivation" of the actual individual or individuals studied. For example, in a pure ideal-type form, bureaucracy has certain traits,

FIGURE 10.1 Weber's Ideal-Type Analysis of Social Phenomena

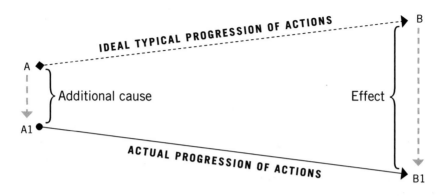

such as its performance of specialized tasks, continuity, formal procedures and rules, clarity, strict subordination, unified control, the allocation of positions on the basis of technical qualifications, and a defined hierarchy. Weber's ideal type of bureaucracy is compared with the observed conduct or processes of a bureaucratic organization.

A problem faces the researcher, though: How do we know we have constructed an ideal-type conception of the social phenomena we wish to study? Weber's criterion for evaluating the usefulness of an ideal type is matter of fact. Weber notes in the canonical text, "*Theory*-construction can never be decided *a priori*. There is only one criterion, namely, that of success in revealing concrete cultural phenomena in their interdependence, their causal conditions and their *significance*. The construction of abstract ideal-types recommends itself not as an end but as a *means*."[61] Examples of what Weber means by ideal-type constructs include Marx's capitalist modes of production, Durkheim's mechanical and organic solidarity, Ferdinand Tönnies's *Gemeinschaft* and *Gesellschaft*, as well as Weber's own typology of social action. Ideal types can also be constructed for developmental stages, such as feudalism, or historical particularities, such as the industrial city. As Weber posits, "all specifically Marxian 'laws' and developmental constructs—insofar as they are theoretically sound—are ideal types."[62] For Weber, the construction of ideal types has three main functions in social theorizing: they help to conceptualize the multifarious mosaic that is social life in modernity, they help to formulate empirical research questions and *suggest* potential causal relationships, and they underscore the active role of the researcher in the interpretation of social action.

Criticism

There have been several criticisms of Weber's methodology.[63] The first criticism questions the fact-value dichotomy and the notion of value neutrality. Weber's position is criticized on the grounds that, because human science operates within a moral universe, it is naïve to believe that it can avoid moral judgment of its data; moreover, in conditions of "irrational power politics" (e.g., fascism), so-called impartiality may be an abdication of responsibility. The second criticism relates to Weber's ideal types, which, critics argue, are located in the context of asymmetrical power relations. For feminists, a critical issue is the relationship of women to the process of power. Weber's key methodological tool occurs in the context of a "natural inequality" between the sexes. Although Weber posits that all knowledge of social reality is always knowledge from particular standpoints, when he actually applies his concept of power to forms of domination, it is obvious that he regards men's access to power and male domination as natural and inevitable. A contemporary iconoclastic feminist affirms that the "ideal type patriarchy assumes that the domination of women is a 'natural' phenomenon."[64] The third criticism is that Weber's conception of instrumental rational social action is limited to a relationship between means and ends, with each step leading on to the next in a linear fashion, until the desired end is achieved. Critics consider this conception of rationality as one that is more concerned with domination: the control and exploitation of the natural world.[65]

The fourth criticism relates to Weber's approach to understanding, *Verstehen*. Even though *Verstehen* calls for the investigator to be perceptive of meaningful connections between actions and context, it creates only causal hypotheses that do not constitute knowledge per se, however plausible an interpretation may appear. In other words, the validity of the relationship needs to be established empirically. Another critique relates to relativism, which is raised by the notion of interpretation. For Weber, the meaning of any social action is deeply embedded in its cultural context. This argument appears to be relatively clear, but, if meaning is specific to the local, how is any *general* knowledge of society as such possible? If, for example, the strategies of multinational companies have to be interpreted within the context of national spaces and values, can there be a universally relevant sociology of work? Finally, Weber's notorious typology has been critiqued because it poses problems of validation, which Weber attempted to resolve with judgments of plausibility and empirical evidence. As others have pointed out, this approach raises questions. How does the researcher know that the central traits of a social phenomenon have been thoroughly abstracted from reality? And, once an ideal type has been abstracted, how much deviation from it is scientifically acceptable before the researcher must conclude that it bears too little resemblance to social reality to be useful? Although the ideal type was central to his sociological work, Weber was never able to provide a satisfactory definition of the ideal-type rational social action. His quest for objective social science and his extreme form of constructivism, critics argue, reflects his "ontological insecurity," which is rooted in his pessimistic view of humans in modernity.

Conclusion

Max Weber made an immense contribution to social research discourse. Neo-Kantian thinkers such as Nietzsche, Dilthey, Simmel, Windelband, and Rickert heavily influenced his writings. Weber extended the *Methodenstreit* debate in several important ways by emphasizing that the subject matter of the social sciences was made up of individuals whose social action was based on values; that, in both natural and social sciences, facts never speak for themselves, they require interpretation; and that research methods are always shaped by the researcher's cultural values and ideologies. Weber's value-freedom/value-relevance dichotomy, as well as his use of singular causal analysis, his theory of social action, his application of *Verstehen* as a distinct mode of understanding, and his account of the nature and purpose of ideal-type constructs are among his central conceptual and procedural contributions to methodology. Weber laid the foundations for the furtherance of testable procedures in social research. Weber's essays, charting the boundary between judgments and epistemological neutrality, have been given canonical status in most introductory texts on social research methods.[66]

What emerges from Weber's work on social inquiry is that historical understanding is always interpretative. Indeed, his methods foreshadow postmodernist thinking, in particular the multiple challenges to meta-narratives. Moreover, his methodological legacy still provides researchers with concepts and practices—and with a deep appreciation of the problem of values and meaning in research. Weber's status as a classical sociologist affirms his own argument that science does not stand outside ideology. Talcott Parsons misinterpreted Weber's *The Protestant Ethic* and his methodological essays as a refutation of Marx's thesis on capitalism and as a support for "value-free" research. And the context that shaped this theoretical interpretation of Weber's work was global politics that eventuated in the Cold War. Although the central metaphor for much of modern human inquiry is the crystal—with its infinite variety of shapes, patterns, colors, and transmutations—rather than the ideal type, Weber's work is a vivid reminder that the interpretive process of studying social phenomena involves a complex interaction among the conceptual world of the researcher, the situational constraints under which research takes place, and the reality of the people and culture the researcher seeks to understand. It is a reflection of his legacy that, within the matrix of contemporary uncertainty, his ideas remain remarkably relevant in epistemology considerations, and his insights on the complexity of interpretive understanding still resonate with social scientists today.

FURTHER THINKING:

"In both natural and social sciences facts never speak for themselves, they require interpretation." How does Weber's contribution to the debate about the nature of the natural and the human sciences lead to this conclusion?

FURTHER READING:

See Max Weber, *The Methodology of the Social Sciences,* trans. E. Shils and H. Finch (Glencoe, IL: The Free Press, 1949); Alex Callinicos, *Social Theory: An Historical Introduction* (Cambridge: Polity Press, 2007), 153–59; and Kieran Allen, *Max Weber: A Critical Introduction* (London: Pluto Press, 2004), 68–80.

Notes

1   Alex Law, *Social Theory for Today* (London: Sage, 2015), 75.

2   Fritz Ringer, *Max Weber's Methodology* (Cambridge, MA: Harvard University Press, 1997), 168.

3   Keith Tribe, ed., *Reading Weber* (London: Routledge 1989); Bryan S. Turner, *For Weber* (London: Sage, 1996).

4   Ian Craib, *Classical Social Theory* (Oxford: Oxford University Press, 1997), 43.

5   Stephen Turner, ed., *The Cambridge Companion to Weber* (New York: Cambridge University Press, 2000), 1.

6   Reinhard Bendix, *Max Weber: An Intellectual Portrait* (New York: Anchor Books, 1962), 1.

7   Marianne Weber, *Max Weber: A Biography* (New York: Wiley, 1975).

8   Guenther Roth, introduction to Max Weber's *Economy and Society*, ed. Guenther Roth and Claus Wittich (Berkeley: University of California Press, 1968).

9   Turner, *For Weber* (London: Sage, 1996).

10 Sven Eliaeson, *Max Weber's Methodologies* (Cambridge: Polity Press, 2002), 3.

11 Bendix, *Max Weber*, 4–5.

12 Bendix, *Max Weber*, 6.

13 Eliaeson, *Max Weber's Methodologies*, 126.

14 Turner, *For Weber*, 74.

15 Quoted in Anthony Giddens, *Capitalism and Modern Social Theory* (Cambridge: Cambridge University Press, 1971), 190–91.

16 Turner, *For Weber*.

17 Max Weber, *The Protestant Ethic and the Spirit of Capitalism* (London: Penguin, 2002), 13.

18 Weber, *The Protestant Ethic*, 36.

19 Max Weber, *The Methodology of the Social Sciences*, trans. E. Shils and H. Finch (Glencoe, IL: Free Press, 1949), 103.

20 Karl Löwith, *Max Weber and Karl Marx* (London: George Allen & Unwin, 1982), translated from "Max Weber and Karl Marx," *Archiv für Sozialwissenschaft und Sozialpolitik* 66 (1932): 53–99 and 175–214, and cited in Bryan S. Turner, *Classical Sociology* (London: Sage, 1999), 51–55.

21 Irving M. Zeitlin, *Ideology and the Development of Sociological Theory*, 7th ed. (Upper Saddle River, NJ: Prentice-Hall, 2001), 196.

22 Bryan S. Turner, *Classical Sociology* (London: Sage, 1999).

23 In addition to primary sources, this section draws from Alex Callinicos, *Social Theory: A Historical Introduction* (Cambridge: Polity Press, 2007); Turner, *Classical Sociology*.

24 See John Ralston Saul, *Voltaire's Bastards* (Toronto: Penguin, 1993); see also J. Lavin, *Nietzsche* (New York: Scribner, 1971), who argues that all the fascist theories can find some support in Nietzsche's philosophy.

25 Max Weber, *Economy and Society* (1921; Berkeley: University of California Press, 1978), 941.

26 Weber, *Economy and Society*, 975.

27 This section draws from Ringer, *Max Weber's Methodology*; Eliaeson, *Max Weber's Methodologies*; Ken Morrison, *Marx, Durkheim, Weber* (London: Sage, 2006); Callinicos, *Social Theory*; and Turner, *Classical Sociology*.

28 Ringer, *Max Weber's Methodology*, 22.

29 Wilhelm Dilthey, "Awareness, Reality: Time," in *The Hermeneutic Reader*, ed. Kurt Mueller-Vollmer (Oxford: Blackwell, 1985), and quoted in Larry Ray, *Theorizing Classical Sociology* (Buckingham, UK: Open University Press, 1999), 118.

30 Morrison, *Marx, Durkheim, Weber*, 332.

31 Ray, *Theorizing Classical Sociology*, 125.

32 Ringer, *Max Weber's Methodology*, 29.

33 Morrison, *Marx, Durkheim, Weber*, 336.

34 Giddens, *Capitalism and Modern Social Theory*, 133.

35 Ringer, *Max Weber's Methodology*, 1.

36 Eliaeson, *Max Weber's Methodologies*, 18.

37 Weber, *Methodology of the Social Sciences*, 60.

38 Weber, *Methodology of the Social Sciences*, 49.

39 See Weber, *Methodology of the Social Sciences*, 20–21, 82.

40 Craib, *Classical Social Theory*, 52.

41 Weber, *Methodology of the Social Sciences*, 76.

42 Weber, *Methodology of the Social Sciences*, 76.

43 Weber, *Methodology of the Social Sciences*, 80.

44 Turner, *Classical Sociology*, 61.

45 Weber, *Economy and Society*, 4.

46 Ringer, *Max Weber's Methodology*, 101.

47 Weber, *Economy and Society*, 4.

48 Weber, *Economy and Society*, 6.

49 Weber, *Economy and Society*, 24.

50 Turner, *Classical Sociology*.

51 Ringer, *Max Weber's Methodology*.

52 Weber, *Methodology of the Social Sciences*, 135.

53 Weber, *Methodology of the Social Sciences*, 173.

54 Weber, *Methodology of the Social Sciences*, 174.

55 Weber, *Economy and Society*, 5.

56 Weber, *Methodology of the Social Sciences*, 41.

57 Michel S. Zouboulakis, "From Mill to Weber: The Meaning of the Concept
    of Economic Rationality," *European Journal of Economic Thought* 8, no. 1
    (2001): 30.

58 Zouboulakis, "From Mill to Weber," 34.

59 Weber, *Methodology of the Social Sciences*, 90.

60 Ringer, *Max Weber's Methodology*, 112.

61 Weber, *Methodology of the Social Sciences*, 92.

62 Weber, *Methodology of the Social Sciences*, 103.

63 These criticisms are largely drawn from Turner, *Classical Sociology*; Anthony
    Giddens, *The Consequences of Modernity* (Cambridge: Polity Press, 1990);
    Eliaeson, *Max Weber's Methodologies*; and Ringer, *Max Weber's Methodology*.

64 R.A. Sydie, *Natural Women, Cultured Men* (Vancouver: University of British
    Columbia Press, 1994), 84.

65 See Turner, *Classical Sociology*.

66 See, for example, Allan Bryman and James Teevan, *Social Research Methods*
    (Don Mills, ON: Oxford University Press, 2005).

11. Max Weber: Capitalism and Modernity

To understand modernity is to understand Weber.
—Bryan S. Turner, 1992[1]

It is rationalization, then, not capitalism *per se,* which for Weber lies at the root of the modern world order, and the reasons for this are to be found in various peculiarities of "the West."
—Derek Sayer, 1991[2]

THOUGH THERE HAVE BEEN SEVERAL FORAYS into Weber's writings with the purpose of discovering a principle of thematic unity, scholars widely acknowledge that it is difficult to impose a single unifying theme on his work. The quest for an organizing theme has been complicated by problems connected to the transmission of his ideas through translation, publication, and fragmentation.[3] Much contemporary Anglo-Saxon Weberian scholarship argues that Weber's theory of modernity centers on the primacy of rationality and the process of rationalization. Weber used the term *rationalization* to describe a set of interrelated social processes by which nature, individuals, culture, and institutions have been systematically transformed by rational human action. It is important to note that, like his writings on social methodology, Weber's critique of capitalism was fashioned from many intellectual sources. A number of translated texts have tended to be identified as constituting the core of Weber's sociological writings. Prominent among these are his best-known and influential work *The Protestant Ethic and the Spirit of Capitalism* and the assortment of manuscripts posthumously published under the title *Economy and Society.* His writings are ambiguous, fragmented, and full of paradoxes. Though he did not have a conception of society as a social system, he famously warned about the iron cage of industrial capitalism.

Reinhard Bendix notes the paradoxes of his scholarly work: "His lifetime study [the development of rationalism] revealed not only the complexity of its antecedents, but the precariousness of its achievements."[4] The aim of this chapter is to elucidate his study of the complex connections between capitalism and religious beliefs, his idea of Western rationalization, and his ambivalent evaluation of modern capitalism. In so doing, we shall identify some major differences between Marx and Weber.

Rationalization Thesis

An overarching theme in Weber's social theory is the concept of rationalization. The term appears repeatedly in *The Protestant Ethic* and in *Economy and Society*, but the most extensive treatment of the concept appears in his *Sociology of Religion*.[5] Whether the rationalization thesis is Weber's pivotal theoretical core or whether it is one of several crucial concepts he used to analyze modern life is a matter of protracted debate.[6] Challenging the orthodox reading of Weber, Wilhelm Hennis, for example, argues that Weber's "central question" (*Fragestellung*) is a concern with the nexus between forms of life conduct (*Lebensführung*), the ways in which individuals attempt to give meaning to their lives, and the universal constraints imposed by the differential distribution of power.[7] Attempts at a "correct" reading of Weber to explain or reject his rationalization thesis are not helped by the ambiguity and inconsistency in his technical use of the term. However, no complete understanding of Weber's sociology is possible without examining this important concept. Weber sees a systematic process of rationalization underlying Western industrial capitalism. The term is complex and multifaceted, but, at the risk of oversimplification, *rationalization* describes a constellation of ubiquitous interrelated processes that systematically transformed Western European societies by a long-run tendency to bring order and perfection to what, in its "natural" state, is less ordered and imperfect. The following passage by a Weber scholar offers a lucid picture of Weberian rationalization:

> Weber's rationalization is ... the product of scientific specialization and technical differentiation peculiar to Western culture ... sometimes associated ... with the notion of intellectualization. It might be defined as the *organization of life through a division and coordination of activities on the basis of an exact study of men's relations with each other, with their tools and their environment, for the purpose of achieving greater efficiency and productivity.* Hence it is a purely practical development brought about by man's technological genius.

> Weber also described rationalization as a striving for perfection ... as an ingenious refinement of the conduct of life and the attainment of increasing mastery over the external world ... he analyzed its evolution in all major branches of human activity—religion, law, art, science, politics, and economics—while being careful not to go beyond the limits of what is objectively ascertainable.[8]

The essence of the concept consists of three facets: secularization, calculability, and rational action. The process of rationalization involved the decline of magical interpretations and explanations of the world, the decreasing authority of the church, the erosion of the social status of the clergy, and the general secularization of the modern world. The tsunami of rational calculation in all spheres of life has created the phenomenon that Weber identified as the *disenchantment* or *de-enchantment* of modernity. What he meant by these terms is a process by which enchantment becomes expunged from everyday life through a progressive loss of faith in the invisible but enchanted shapers of the human theater, in the magical or divine presences provided by folk beliefs as well as by organized religions.[9] The regimented forms of thought and social action had, for Weber, virtually replaced religion as the unquestioned, motivating creed across much of Western civilization.[10] Within the legal system, rationalization involves the decline and erosion of ad hoc legal decision making in favor of law making, such that, "in both substantive and procedural matters, only unambiguous general characteristics of the facts of the case are taken into account."[11] In the political sphere, rationalization is associated with the decline of traditional domination and the rise of legal-rational systems of authority. Rationalization in the sphere of human labor involves the explicit, systematic design of paid work from the point of view of calculability, efficiency, predictability, and profitability. The notion of timed labor epitomizes rationalization and modernity. A contemporary of Weber explained modern factory work and the need to calculate tasks precisely: "The idea [is] that man must have every second necessary but not a single unnecessary second."[12] In social terms, generally, rationalization involves the extension of scientific rationality to the conduct of social life itself, including modern systems of surveillance and the rise of bureaucratic forms of administration.

Weber's rationalization thesis is closely interlinked with his notion of rationality, which occupies a central place in *Economy and Society*. Rational action is differentiated from other forms of social action. The former involves submitting social action to constant calculative scrutiny by weighing up the means and ends prior to action, which produces a continuous drive toward change. In his writings, Weber identifies four types of rationality: practical, theoretical, formal, and substantive.[13] *Practical rationality* assumes no external mystical causes affecting the outcome of human actions and sees reality in terms of what is given. *Theoretical* or *technical rationality* involves a cognitive effort to master the world through causality and logical deduction and induction. This type of rationality allows individuals to understand the meaning of life by means of abstract concepts and conceptual reasoning. *Formal rationality* refers to the application of technically appropriate modes of calculation (means) that go into decisions to ensure consistency of outcome and efficiency in attaining specific goals (ends). *Substantive rationality* refers to the degree to which human action is guided or shaped by a value system regardless of the outcome of the action. Accordingly, formal rationality involves a practical orientation of social action in relation to goals or ends, and substantive rationality involves an orientation to values.

Religion and Capitalism

Marx, Durkheim, and Weber studied religion, and in their respective conceptions of religion, they are in some ways compatible. Marx believed that religion has ideological implications that serve to justify social inequality. Durkheim emphasizes the role of religion in supporting social cohesion. Weber's study of the "economic ethics" of major world religions examines the link between religion and cultural development. These studies form the context of what is a very complex argument concerning the significance of Western rationality. If we frame Weber's theory in terms of Marx's base and superstructure schema (see Figure 5.1), the direction of influence and emphasis is reversed. Rather than emphasizing how class relations at the base influence an institution (namely religion), Weber's analysis calls attention to how religion affects the dynamics of class relations at the base. Weber notes, "To the natural uncertainties and resistances facing every innovator, religion adds powerful impediments of its own. The sacred is the uniquely unalterable."[14] His study of Chinese religion identifies the importance of the ancestor as an impediment to rationalism. Weber's study of Hinduism and Buddhism refers to a "magical garden" from which rationality could not develop.[15] Weber emphasizes the affinities between Judaism and Puritanism.[16] In Western Europe, some sects of Protestantism did prove to be amenable to rational capitalism, to be alterable, which brings us to Weber's classic work on the Protestant ethic.

In *The Protestant Ethic*, Weber aims to discern the significance of ascetic Protestantism—in relation to other formative elements of culture—to the growth of modern capitalism in the West and to illustrate the process by which ideas become a force for social change.

> The task before us is to indicate the significance of ascetic rationalism for the content of the *ethic* of the *social* economy, that is, for the type of organization and the functions of social communities, from the conventicle to the state. Then its relationship to humanist rationalism and its ideals and cultural influences, to the development of philosophical and scientific empiricism, and to technological development and the arts must be analyzed ... [I]t must be shown in what way Protestant asceticism itself was influenced in its growth and character by the totality of the cultural, and especially *economic*, conditions of society.[17]

As we have seen, Weber asserts that a high degree of formal rationality characterizes capitalism as a modern phenomenon and that the process of rationalization affects all dimensions of social life. Weber's thesis, in brief, proposes that a new attitude to work and the pursuit of wealth, in which work becomes a means of demonstrating godliness, was linked to the rise of Calvinism and that this cultural shift was associated with the rise of *rational* capitalism.

Weber's investigation begins by focusing on the significant cultural differences between European Protestants and Catholics. Comparing the two denominations, he posits that Catholic school students, unlike Protestant, were averse to studying commerce, which, he argues, helps explain "the low participation rate of Catholics in capitalist business life."[18] Further, Protestant skilled workers tended to migrate to the new factories where they formed the "upper echelons of skilled workers and management," whereas Catholic journeymen showed a "greater inclination to remain in craft work."[19] Weber held that "the choice of occupation and future career has undoubtedly been determined by the distinct *mental characteristics* which have been instilled in them."[20]

A surface-level comparison of Protestantism and Catholicism might conclude that the latter induces its followers to an ascetic lifestyle while the former, by secularizing every dimension of life, induces its followers to a hedonistic lifestyle. To illustrate this perception, Weber cites a popular adage: "Protestants like to eat well, while Catholics want to sleep well."[21]

Weber held that, on the contrary, this is not the case. The English, Dutch, and American Puritans were characterized by "the very opposite of enjoyment of life," argues Weber.[22] Indeed, Weber contends that

Protestants had an "inner affinity" toward an ascetic lifestyle that made them especially receptive to the rational capitalist culture.

To support his elusive principal thesis—the ideal type—Weber extensively quotes Benjamin Franklin, who, although no Calvinist, personified the new capitalist ethos. Franklin, an eighteenth-century version of contemporary management guru Tom Peters (*In Search of Excellence*), is important to Weber's thesis because Franklin's writings emphasize the link between religiosity and entrepreneurship.[23] Franklin enumerates what Weber regards as the ideal-type "spirit" of capitalism:

> Remember, *time is money*. He that can earn ten shillings a day by his labour, and goes abroad, or sits idle, one half of that day, though he spends but sixpence during his diversion or idleness, ought not to reckon *that* the only expense; he has really spent, or rather thrown away, five shillings besides.
>
> Remember, that *credit is money*. If a man lets his money lie in my hands after it is due, he gives me the interest, or so much as I can make of it during that time.
>
> Remember, that money is the *prolific, generating nature*. Money can beget money, and its offspring can beget more, and so on.
>
> Remember this saying, *the good paymaster* is lord of another man's purse. He that is known to pay punctually and exactly to the time he promises, may at any time, and on any occasion, raise all the money his friends can spare. This is sometimes of great use.
>
> The most trifling actions that affect a man's credit are to be regarded. The sound of your hammer at five in the morning, or eight at night, heard by the creditor, makes him easy six months longer, but if he sees you at a billiard table, or hears your voice at the tavern, when you should be at work, he sends for his money the next day.... It shows, besides, that you are mindful of what you owe; it makes you appear a careful as well as an *honest* man, and that still increases your *credit*.[24]

For Weber, the importance of Franklin's mantra is the notion that the individual has a *duty* to accumulate wealth, which is assumed to be an end in itself. Franklin also acknowledges that this spirit is more than a case of purely "egocentric maxims"; the actions constitute a religious conviction and search for salvation. Here is Weber's summation of Benjamin Franklin's words:

> The "*summum bonum*" (great good) of this "ethic" is the *making of money* and yet more money, coupled with a strict avoidance

of all uninhibited enjoyment. Indeed, it is so completely devoid of all eudaemonistic, let alone hedonist, motives, so much purely thought of as an end *in itself* that it appears as something wholly transcendent and irrational, beyond the "happiness" or the "benefit" of the *individual*. The aim of a man's life is indeed money making, but this is no longer merely the means to the end of satisfying the material needs of life. This reversal ... of what we might call the "natural" state of affairs is a definite leitmotiv of capitalism, although it will always be alien to anyone who is untouched by capitalism's aura.[25]

Whereas Marx understood the same phenomenon in terms of the subordination of "use-value" to "exchange-value," capital accumulation, and a change in the relations of production, Weber understood it as resulting from a change in ethical orientation toward the world.[26]

Weber explains that Calvinism as such did not foster the capitalist spirit; rather, it was Calvin's followers and the doctrine of predestination that infused the social ethic of capitalist culture. But Catholics, according to Weber, believed they could secure their place in heaven through, among other things, good works on behalf of the poor or by performing acts of faith on earth. For example, the premodern Christian interpretation of the sermon "It is easier for a camel to go through the eye of a needle than for a rich man to enter the kingdom of God"[27] made the renunciation of wealth for the sake of the poor a primary condition of avoiding being "cast into hell." On the other hand, Weber asserted that Calvinism had developed a set of beliefs around the concept of predestination that broke the hold of tradition. Followers of Calvinism came to believe that their predestined future left them with no means of knowing or altering their ultimate destination. This uncertainty led anxious Calvinists to search for signs from God that they were among the "elect" to have a place in heaven. Wealth was taken as a manifestation of being among God's elect, thereby encouraging believers to apply themselves rationally to acquire wealth through their ascetic lifestyles. Thus, Protestant preaching stressed that followers had "a duty to *regard* themselves as elect, and to dismiss any doubts as a temptation from the devil.... The exhortation of the apostle to 'make one's own calling sure' was interpreted as a duty to strive for the subjective certainty of one's election and justification in daily struggle.... And ... *tireless labour in a calling* was urged as the best possible means of *attaining* this self-assurance. This and this alone would drive away religious doubt and give assurance to one's state of grace."[28]

According to Weber, this set of beliefs led to the emergence of what he calls an "ethic of inner conviction" (*Gesinnungsethik*) in which the external observance of holy law is displaced by a more dynamic and intense cultivation of an inner religious state.[29] Herein lies the ultimate source of ascetic Protestantism's social-transforming potency:

> Wherever the power of the Puritan philosophy of life extended, it always benefited the tendency toward a middle-class [*bürgerlich*], economically *rational* conduct of life, of which it was the most significant and only consistent support. This is, of course, far more important than merely encouraging the formation of capital. *It stood at the cradle of modern "economic man."* [emphasis added][30]

Weber recognized that asceticism provided a religious legitimacy for the exploitation of human labor. A look at the textual evidence supports this point of view: "Protestant asceticism ... did add tremendous depth to the view and created the psychological *drive* for this norm to achieve its effect by interpreting such work as a *calling*, and as the *sole* means of making sure of one's state of grace. It also legalized the exploitation of this characteristic willingness to work by interpreting the employer's moneymaking as a 'calling' too."[31] Protestant asceticism transformed the world when it "moved out of the monastic cells and into working life, and began to dominate inner worldly morality," writes Weber. And in a prophetical observation, he speculates that "this mighty cosmos determines ... the style of life not only of those directly involved in business but every individual who is born into this mechanism, and may well continue to do so *until the day that the last ton of fossil fuel is consumed*" (emphasis added).[32] Although Weber did not believe Calvinism was *the* cause of the transformation of society, he did believe rational capitalism, in part, grew from Calvinism. In contrast to Marx, Weber argues that the growth of Western capitalism cannot be explained through wholly material and structural forces: it was embedded in the process of rationalization. The Protestant ethic thesis is often incorrectly interpreted as a refutation of Marx, but, as we explained in chapter 10, this debate has become passé, archaic, and discredited.

The Characteristics of Modern Western Capitalism

In Weber's view, there is nothing capitalistic in the pursuit of profit or financial gain; both have been sought in many different ways and in all parts of the world. What defines modern Western capitalism is the striving for *profit* in the course of continuous, rational, capitalistic enterprise, for *more and more* profits, and for 'profitability.'"[33] Weber goes on to define a capitalist act as one which "rests upon the expectation of profit through the exploitation of opportunities for *exchange*, that is, on (formally) *peaceful* opportunities for acquisition."[34] In the new capitalistic order, where capitalist acquisition is rationally pursued, an enterprise has to take advantage of its opportunities for making profit in the market or face extinction, and decisions are made according to the "*calculation* of capital*,*" with modern bookkeeping methods as a device to ascertain the balance of profit, in monetary terms, that has been made over a period of business.[35]

Various kinds of capitalism have existed in many parts of the world, but, for Weber, a different kind of capitalism developed uniquely in the West, namely, the "rational, capitalist organization of (formally) *free labor.*"[36] Weber identified other factors that also made rational capitalism possible in the West. The first one is the separation of business from the household (which separates corporate and personal property), and the second is rational bookkeeping. In addition, a rational system of law and administration was necessary so that reliable formal rules were available to govern business activity, and this system developed only in the West. Each of these factors facilitated the precise calculation of profit and the rational organization of formally free labor. All of them are important conditions for rational capitalistic enterprise. However, it is worth stressing also the key significance of a strong cultural drive to constant application in work, which, after all, as Weber pointed out in *The Protestant Ethic*, was itself irrational from the point of view of achieving happiness.

For Weber, modern capitalism and the market society are characterized by formally rational economic action "that is rationally oriented by deliberate planning, to economic ends."[37] Economic action is formally rational when the "provision for needs ... is capable of being expressed in numerical, calculable terms."[38] This does not mean that the production of a certain amount of profit or the production of certain utilities as cheaply as possible is ethically good or bad. Any such evaluation would consider the substantive rationality of economic action in terms of its ultimate ends or values, which may be political, ethical, religious, egalitarian, or whatever. Socialistic standards would involve considerations of social justice and equality, but, whatever ultimate ends are considered, such a criteria of rationality goes beyond formal calculability, however rational the means that may be applied to the chosen ends. Weber accepted that the pursuit of calculability within modern capitalism might produce results that are objectionable when assessed by some ethical standard. He identified some "substantively irrational" consequences of modern capitalist production (to be discussed later), such as the growth of managerial authority in the workplace and the growing inequalities of income due to the bargaining superiority given to property ownership in the market.[39]

Modern Capitalism and the "Iron Cage"

Although Weber's metaphor for how the market and material goods in modern capitalism constrain individuals—the "iron cage"[40]—has become well known, Weber is not usually seen as a critic of capitalism. Also, as already stated, he saw socialism as less rational and more bureaucratic than capitalism. Socialism, to him, represented not the dictatorship of the proletariat but the dictatorship of the official.[41] He saw modern capitalism, and its orientation to the market, as more rational than any other system, but his ambivalence toward modern, market capitalism can also be seen in his awareness that rationality can lead to irrationality, in ways that will become clear as we look at his concluding remarks in *The Protestant Ethic* and his comments on capitalist discipline, the ethos of bureaucracy (discussed more fully in the following chapter), and rational law.

Weber's methodology, as we have seen in the previous chapter, rests on the analysis of individual, purposeful social action, and, in *The Protestant Ethic*, Weber provides an analysis of how a Protestant-influenced motivation toward economic action produced a uniquely Western capitalism, which submits the individual to its demands. In the following passage, Weber describes how capitalism has become a constraint upon the individual:

> Today's capitalist economic order is a monstrous cosmos, into which the individual is born and which in practice is for him, at least as an individual, simply a given, an immutable shell [*Gehäuse*] in which he is obligated to live. It forces on the individual, to the extent that he is caught up in the relationships of the "market," the norms of its economic activity.[42]

The market society also demands that the employer submits to its rules: "The manufacturer who consistently defies these norms will just as surely be forced out of business as the worker who cannot or will not conform will be thrown out of work."[43] The rules once grounded in both an ethical-religious orientation to work and a rational economic system, then, seemed to take on a life of their own. Hennis believes that Weber was concerned with the cultural problem of the age in terms of the ability of people to choose their conduct in life, on the one hand, and the impact of rational institutions on the personality of those who live in them, on the other. This problem is particularly acute when, under material and technical constraints, the choice of life conduct is "rationalised away, discipline is enough."[44]

Over time, the original religious motives for performing dedicated work in a calling fell away, and, in the concluding pages of *The Protestant Ethic*, Weber reflected on the unintended effects of this change:

> The Puritans *wanted* to be men of the calling; we, on the other hand, *must* be. For when asceticism moved out of the monastic cells and into working life, and began to dominate innerworldly morality, it helped to build that mighty cosmos of the modern economic order (which is bound to the technical and economic conditions of mechanical and machine production). Today this mighty cosmos determines, with overwhelming coercion, the style of life *not only* of those directly involved in business but of every individual who is born into this mechanism, and may well continue to do so until the day that the last ton of fossil fuel has been consumed.... In Baxter's view, concern for outward possessions should sit lightly on the shoulders of his saints.... But fate decreed that the cloak should become a shell as hard as steel (*stabhartes Gehäuse*).[45]

The fate of the "savage," in Weber's view, was to live in the belief that life is controlled by magical or mysterious forces that could not be completely controlled. Despite the potential for liberation provided by rational thought, science, and technology, the fate of men and women in modernity, then, is one in which technology, the market, and "the outward goods of this world gained increasing and finally inescapable power over men as never before in history."[46] How is it that Weber is still discussing the fate of people in modernity and their lack of control despite society having attained a high level of rationalization and intellectualization, which enables the realization that everything is potentially understandable, humanized, and disenchanted—in other words, allowing people to perceive that social and economic arrangements are humanly created artifacts that have the potential to be changed? The answer lies in Weber's view of capitalist modernity, which he believes is complex and ambiguous.[47] There is a paradox in Weber's conception of the fatefulness of modernity for, as Kronman points out, "modernity means enlightenment and greatly enhanced possibilities of human control, but it also means the increasing domination of fateful forces, among which he includes reason itself."[48]

What kind of irrationalities does rationalization produce? An answer to this question can be found in Weber's discussion of the irrationalities produced in rational systems such as the factory, bureaucracy, and the modern legal order. For Marx, the division of labor and mechanization are inextricably bound up with de-skilling workers, alienation, and issues of power. Here, Weber concurs with Marx, recognizing that one of the "substantively irrational" consequences of modern capitalism is produced by the imposition of factory discipline. In *Economy and Society*, Weber explains that factory work is organized and administered with military precision and discipline. It is so designed as to provide a high degree of measurement with the goal of maximizing profitability of the individual worker. The centerpiece of the means of production is the separation of tasks into their simplest constituent elements—the routinization of work. The logic of work fragmentation and routinization became the founding principles of "scientific management" pioneered by the American Frederick W. Taylor (1856–1915). The major principles of scientific management were adopted by Henry Ford (1863–1947) to assembly-line production of motor vehicles, known as Fordism. Concomitant with routinization was the separation of planning and doing, close supervision, the timing and measurement of tasks (which allowed "speed-up"), and the minimization of skill requirements to perform a task, which inexorably reduced the individual worker's control over the labor process. The process of rationalization means that the worker has to attune to the new rhythm of routine work, which diminishes the importance of individual creativity and charisma, with negative psychological repercussions.[49]

Mirroring Marx's analysis, Weber provides a powerful critique of the ways in which a rationalized system of production makes the individual worker conform to the demands and pace of the machines and how tasks and skills are appropriated by "experts" who calculate the most efficient ways of performing routine tasks. The fate of the industrial worker is a loss of autonomy and control over the labor process. As explained in the following chapter, bureaucracy ubiquitously spreads across all forms of work organization because of its efficiency, calculability, and rationality. Further, within bureaucracies where the authority and function of the bureaucrat is bound by rules set by those who occupy the upper levels of the hierarchy, Weber argues, the bureaucrat is equally controlled by the organization. These points echo Marx's discussion of the alienated workers' loss of control over the work process, which he presented in the *Paris Manuscripts*, although Weber does not extend his argument, as Marx does, to the loss of control over the commodities produced by labor or the alienation of workers from their "species being."

The rationalization of the legal order has produced a similar loss of control.[50] The development of a rational legal system removes the sacred and magical elements of primitive law and comes to be perceived as a superior technical legal apparatus analogous to superior modern technology. The law has become increasingly technical so that those not trained in its intricacies have to rely increasingly on specialists and experience a

For Marx, machinery is inextricably bound up with alienation and power. Here Weber concurs with Marx, recognizing that one of the "substantively irrational" consequences of modern capitalism is produced by the imposition of factory discipline.

loss of control. The processes of rationalization and intellectualization, in Weber's vision, have led to a situation in which, theoretically, the inhabitants of modernity dwell in a disenchanted world, are liberated from the control of gods or magic, and collectively have more control over their material and social circumstances. At the same time, paradoxically, their fate is to live in a new form of "bondage"—in a "shell" constructed by the institutions that humans have made. This critique of modernity as "irrational" is built on the tension between formal and substantive rationality. The discussion so far raises this question: What are the values that Weber draws on to criticize the lack of individual control embodied in modern institutions? In order to answer this, we must take the discussion a stage further and consider Weber's ambivalence toward modernity in more depth, especially in his analysis of bureaucracy and political leadership discussed in the following chapter.

Criticism

Almost every aspect of Weber's Protestant asceticism thesis has been subject to criticism by economic historians and sociologists.[51] Weber was well informed regarding Marx's materialist conception of history, and he believed that Marx's major analytical concepts were "extraordinarily fruitful." Weber seems to repudiate the importance of economic processes and assigns primacy to ideologies in governing human action. This interpretation leads to the criticism that Weber illegitimately replaced

Marx's materialist thesis with an idealistic one. Weber explicitly denies this aim: "It cannot be our purpose," writes Weber, "to replace a one-sided 'materialist' causal interpretation of culture and history with an equally one-sided spiritual one."[52] This statement has not stopped Marxist sociologists from criticizing Weber for his apparently subjectivist and individualist approach to social change.[53]

A second criticism is that Weber neglected the fact that capitalism predates Calvinism. Evidence that capitalism took shape well before the 1780s, and before the influence of Calvinism began, is part of a postmodernist debate that disputes whether or not the British Industrial Revolution occurred or if it is, in fact, a myth. The British historian Eric Hobsbawm comments: "It has become fashionable ... to deny that objective reality is accessible.... I believe that without the distinction between what is and what is not so, there can be no history."[54] Weber's account of the connection between Calvinism and capitalism does not obviate the pre-existence of capitalism in the early modern period. By 1850, however, there was abundant evidence of rational capitalism on an unprecedented scale that counts as an Industrial Revolution, so, for Weber, Calvinism did *not* cause capitalism, but it did help shape the qualitative formation and the quantitative growth of the social revolution. Weber's account of the trajectory of modernity is Eurocentric and excludes most women and non-whites from the "community of moderns."[55]

A third criticism is Herbert Marcuse's analysis of Weber's theory of industrialization and capitalism. Marcuse takes issue with Weber's concept of formal rationality, which he believes Weber "turns into *capitalist* rationality."[56] The irrational "acquisitive drive" was transformed, Marcuse argues, into a rationally controlled motivation via a religious "inner-worldly asceticism" that then became the crucial economic motor of modern capitalism—an engine that can be defined as the orientation to continuous and ever-renewed gain within the rationally organized capitalist enterprise. This capitalist enterprise involves a systematic measurement of profitability using methods of accounting so that reason becomes a technical matter of the mastery of individuals and materials in a system of calculable efficiency (factories and bureaucracies). But, asks Marcuse, "*to what purpose* does it control them?" Formal rationality appears to be an abstract value-free concept, but it is bound by the fact that economic activity to satisfy human needs is restricted by the framework of private enterprise and the calculation of profit for the entrepreneur or enterprise. The category of reason (or what is deemed rational) reflects the values of the economic class that owns the means of production. The measure of rationality is based on the calculations of the entrepreneur and the separation of the worker from the means of production, on the buying and selling of *free* labor; both buyer and seller are essential to this measure, as already discussed. These two features of capitalism are presented as technological necessities for the existence of a formally rational calculative capitalism, which is contrasted with the sort of rational action that is imbued with substantive value.

Marcuse rejects this dichotomy into two types of rational action and argues that the idea of formal rationality contains an implicit substantive rationality:

> The very concept of technical reason is perhaps ideological. Not only the application of technology but technology itself is domination (of nature and men)—methodical, scientific, calculated, calculating social control. Specific purposes and interests of domination are not foisted upon technology "subsequently" and from the outside; they enter into the very construction of the technical apparatus.... Such a "purpose" of domination is "substantive."[57]

Thus, technical reason reflects a political agenda, and, in a different political culture, it could contribute to the liberation rather than the domination of people. While Weber sees such liberation as utopian, Marcuse intimates that Weber was, perhaps, ambivalent toward technical reason:

> It is difficult to see reason at all in the ever more solid "shell of bondage" which is being constructed. Or is there already in Max Weber's concept of reason the irony that understands but disavows? Does he by any chance mean to say: And this you call "reason"?[58]

A fourth criticism of Weber's analysis of capitalism is linked to his deterministic "iron cage" thesis, particularly its incessant pessimism. Although Weber and Marx's views are grounded in a similar philosophical anthropology, Weber, as we have seen, was pessimistic about the effects of domination on human liberation and about the likelihood of our escape from the iron cage. Weber never recognized the human agency to exploit *inherent* potential within capitalism and to shape alternatives. Marx, on the other hand, was optimistic about the opportunity for liberation. The difference in their views has been summed up succinctly: "Marx proposes a therapy while Weber has only a diagnosis to offer."[59] These contrasting views of Weber and Marx might help us to understand why Marx, not Weber, still has a following in the liberation movement. The reappraisal of Weber's work, however, points to the possibility of taking advantage of "rusting iron cages" and to the potential for "breaking vicious circles" within the dynamics of late modernity.[60]

Conclusion

Along with the controversy over "value freedom" in research, *The Protestant Ethic* debate has been one of the longest-standing disputes in modern sociology.[61] According to Weber, ascetic Protestantism accelerated the process of rationalization, and this, in turn, affected the trajectory of modernity. In contrast to Marx's, Weber's narrative of development avers that the development of Western capitalism cannot be explained through wholly material and structural forces: it was embedded in the interconnected process of rationalization. The concept of "elective affinity" (*Wahlverwandtschaft*) is an analytical tool used by Weber for interpreting human history.[62] According to Weber, there is an elective affinity between ascetic Protestantism and the capitalist spirit. Similarly, there is an active relationship or elective affinity between rational capitalism and rationally designed bureaucracies (discussed in the following chapter).

George Ritzer's discussion of McDonaldization[63] provides an excellent example of Weber's theory of rationalization and of the irrationality of rationality. Ritzer claims that the McDonald's fast food restaurant has surpassed bureaucracy in the process of rationalization identified by Weber. Although McDonaldization has many advantages, which the organization is perfectly capable of promoting, Ritzer takes on the task of highlighting the negative side, which is not so widely disseminated.

According to Ritzer's thesis, the spread of McDonaldization to many other organizations across the world is due to four features of the McDonald's model. First, efficiency: it provides the fastest way to achieve a particular goal, such as moving to having a full stomach from the state of being hungry. Second, McDonald's offers its customers food that can be easily quantified and calculated, hence the stress on big servings, value for money, and rapid service. Third, McDonald's offers predictability, as the food is identical in each outlet. Finally, McDonald's epitomizes control over employees, especially through technology. Like Weber, Ritzer is concerned with the ways in which irrationalities may limit or undermine rational forms. The main irrationality of McDonaldization, in Ritzer's view, is its dehumanization. The work is routinized and de-skilled, leading to low staff morale and high turnover rates among the workers, who are not allowed to think or be creative. This tension between the process of rationalization and the attendant loss of human control, initiative, and creativity clearly resonates with Weber's notion of the "iron cage" of rationalization.

The economic and cultural driving forces behind McDonaldization are too strong, in Ritzer's view, to be stopped. Like Weber, he takes a pessimistic view, seeing rationalization as an unavoidable fate: what will bring it to an end will probably be an even more rational social form. At best, Ritzer believes, the situation can be slowed down only by those consumers who feel the need to resist rationalization by subverting the rationalized and standardized provision of services. They might, for example, order a rare hamburger or patronize small local enterprises. In truth, this last decision is not totally irrational in the context of the high transportation costs induced by the increasing price of oil or by the taxation of carbon emissions, both of which will have the effect of encouraging more sustainable business practices. Inarguably, Weber's rationality and irrationalities concepts are highly relevant to the contemporary reader. Weber was aware of the achievements of a rational society, but he was also deeply concerned with its limitations—so much so that he feared a rationalized future would usher in a "polar night of icy darkness and hardness."[64]

FURTHER THINKING:

What key aspects of Calvinism does Weber believe contribute to the development of modern capitalism? Why does Weber portray modern capitalism as exercising control over people?

FURTHER READING:

See Max Weber, *The Protestant Ethic and the Spirit of Capitalism* (New York: Penguin, 2002); Kieran Allen, *Max Weber: A Critical Introduction* (London: Pluto Press, 2004), 32–46; and Ken Morrison, *Marx, Durkheim, Weber: Formations of Modern Social Thought*, 2nd ed. (London: Sage Publications, 2006), 313–29.

Notes

1   Bryan S. Turner, *Max Weber: From History to Modernity* (London: Routledge, 1992), vii.

2   Derek Sayer, *Capitalism & Modernity: An Excursus on Marx and Weber* (London: Routledge, 1991), 134.

3   Keith Tribe, *Reading Weber* (London: Routledge, 1989); Bryan S. Turner, *For Weber* (London: Sage, 1996).

4   Reinhard Bendix, *Max Weber: An Intellectual Portrait* (New York: Anchor Books, 1962), 9.

5   Max Weber, *Sociology of Religion* (Boston: Beacon Press, 1964).

6   The thesis that rationality and rationalization constitute the key to Weber's work is associated with Bendix's early work, *Max Weber: An Intellectual Portrait*, and Friedrich H. Tenbruck, "The Problem of Thematic Unity in the Works of Max Weber," *British Journal of Sociology* 31, no. 3 (1980): 316–51. For an alternative reading of Weber, see Wilhelm Hennis, "Max Weber's Central Question," *Economy and Society* 12, no. 2 (1983): 136–80; Hennis, *Max Weber: Essays in Reconstruction*, trans. Keith Tribe (London: Allen & Unwin, 1988); Hennis, *Max Weber's Central Question*, trans. Keith Tribe (Newbury, UK: Threshold Press, 2000); and Keith Tribe, ed., *Reading Weber*. For an extended discussion on the merits of the argument, see Turner, *Max Weber*.

7   Hennis, *Max Weber's Central Question*.

8   Julien Freund, *The Sociology of Max Weber*, trans. M. Ilford (New York: Random House, 1968), 18, and quoted by Alan Sica, "Rationalization and Culture," in *The Cambridge Companion to Weber*, ed. Stephen P. Turner (Cambridge: Cambridge University Press, 2000), 48.

9   Stewart R. Clegg, "Max Weber and Contemporary Sociology of Organizations," in *Organizing Modernity*, ed. L. J. Ray and M. Reed (London: Routledge, 1994), 46–80.

10 Sica, "Rationalization and Culture," 42–58.

11 Max Weber, *Economy and Society*, ed. G. Roth and C. Wittich (Berkeley: University of California Press, 1978), 2:656–57.

12 Henry Ford, quoted in Huw Beynon, *Working for Ford* (Harmondsworth, UK: Penguin, 1984), 33.

13 Ken Morrison, *Marx, Durkheim, Weber* (London: Sage, 2006), 285.

14 Weber, *Economy and Society*, 1:406.

15 Ian Craib, *Classical Social Theory* (Oxford: Oxford University Press, 1997).

16 John Love, "Max Weber's Ancient Judaism," in *The Cambridge Companion to Weber*, 200–20.

17 Max Weber, *The Protestant Ethic and the Spirit of Capitalism*, ed. Peter Baer and Gordon C. Wells (1905; New York: Penguin Books, 2002), 121–22.

18 Weber, *The Protestant Ethic*, 3.

19 Weber, *The Protestant Ethic*, 4.

20 Weber, *The Protestant Ethic*, 4.

21 Weber, *The Protestant Ethic*, 5.

22 Weber, *The Protestant Ethic*, 5.

23 Irving M. Zeitlin, *Ideology and the Development of Sociological Theory* (Upper Saddle River, NJ: Prentice-Hall, 2001).

24 Weber, *The Protestant Ethic*, 9–10.

25 Weber, *The Protestant Ethic*, 12.

26 Craib, *Classical Social Theory*, 251.

27 See the Bible: Matthew 19:23–24; Mark 10:24–25; Luke 18:24–25; and the teachings of Saint John the Baptist.

28 Weber, *The Protestant Ethic*, 77–78.

29 Love, "Max Weber's Ancient Judaism," 199.

30 Weber, *The Protestant Ethic*, 117.

31 Weber, *The Protestant Ethic*, 119.

32 Weber, *The Protestant Ethic*, 120–21.

33 Weber, *The Protestant Ethic*, 359.

34 Weber, *The Protestant Ethic*, 359.

35 Weber, *The Protestant Ethic*, 362.

36 Weber, *The Protestant Ethic*, 28.

37 Max Weber, *The Theory of Social and Economic Organization* (New York: The Free Press, 1964), 158.

38 Weber, *The Theory of Social and Economic Organization*, 185.

39 Weber, *The Theory of Social and Economic Organization*, 248.

40 Use of the "iron cage" metaphor in English literature on Weber became widespread following Talcott Parsons's 1930 translation of *The Protestant Ethic and the Spirit of Capitalism*. However, in the 2002 translation of *The Protestant Ethic and the Spirit of Capitalism*, edited by Peter Baer and Gordon C. Wells, which is also quoted in this chapter, the German *stalharte Gehäuse* is translated as "a shell which is as hard as steel." The earlier translation has been retained in this section because of its common use.

41 Max Weber, "Speech for the General Information of Austrian Officers in Vienna, 1918," in *Max Weber: The Interpretation of Social Reality*, ed. J.E.T. Eldridge (London: Michael Joseph, 1971), 209.

42 Weber, *The Protestant Ethic*, 13.

43 Weber, *The Protestant Ethic*, 13.

44 Hennis, *Max Weber's Central Question*, 97.

45 Weber, *The Protestant Ethic*, 120–21.

46 Weber, *The Protestant Ethic*, 121.

47 Anthony T. Kronman, *Max Weber* (London: Edward Arnold, 1983), 169.

48 Kronman, *Max Weber*, 170.

49 See Weber, *Economy and Society*, 2:1148–58, for a full description of the characteristics and impact of the factory on the worker.

50 Kronman, *Max Weber*, 175.

51 Larry Ray, *Theorizing Classical Sociology* (Buckingham, UK: Open University Press, 1999).

52 Weber, *The Protestant Ethic*, 122.

53 See "Weber and Late Capitalism," in Turner, *For Weber*, 352–68.

54 Eric J. Hobsbawm, *On History* (London: Weidenfeld & Nicholson, 1997), viii.

55 Larry Ray and Michael Reed, eds., *Organizing Modernity* (London: Routledge, 1994).

56 Herbert Marcuse, "Industrialization and Capitalism in the Work of Max Weber," in *Negations* (London: Penguin University Books, 1972), 201–26, see page 204.

57 Marcuse, "Industrialization and Capitalism in the Work of Max Weber," 224.

58 Marcuse, "Industrialization and Capitalism in the Work of Max Weber," 226.

59 Bryan S. Turner, *Classical Sociology* (London: Sage, 1999), 52.

60 Ray and Reed, *Organizing Modernity*.

61 Ray and Reed, *Organizing Modernity*.

62 Callinicos, *Social Theory*, 163.

63 George Ritzer, *The McDonaldization of Society* (Thousand Oaks, CA: Sage, 2013).

64 Max Weber, "Politics as a Vocation," in *From Max Weber*, eds. H. H. Gerth and C. Wright Mills (London: Routledge & Kegan Paul), 128.

12. Max Weber:
Social Classes and Legitimate Domination

Fully 83 percent of jobs paying less than $20 per hour face the threat of automation in the near future. As a direct corollary, the "precariat" has a brilliant future.

—Mike Davis, 2018[1]

I was not born with an opinion of the world but it clearly seemed that the world had an opinion of people like me. I did not know what race and class supposedly were but the world taught me very quickly.

—Akala, 2018[2]

WEBER'S DISCUSSION OF CLASS and legitimate domination share the theme of power. In the context of late modernity, class can seem intellectually passé, but in reality class continues to shape life experience. Though class inequalities persist in most countries, by North American and European standards the British class system is still particularly pernicious. For Weber, the class position a person occupies depends upon their location in modern market capitalism where people are formally free to utilize their capital, if they own any, or to sell their labor at whatever price their knowledge or skills command. Those who have the power to access and obtain experience, skills, or knowledge can command higher remuneration and enjoy superior life-chances. The way Weber conceptualized power and how it is legitimated is introduced in the section of this chapter on power and legitimation in the context of Weber's three ideal types of domination.

Social Class and Status

In his writings on class, Weber finds much common ground with Marx and Engels. Weber agrees with Marx and Engels that industrial capitalism is predicated on a reservoir of formally free labor. There must be a sufficient pool of individuals who are in a state of extreme economic dependence and compelled to sell their labor power to employers. Weber writes, "The development of capitalism is impossible, if such a property-less stratum is absent, a class compelled to sell its labor services to live."[3] In his theory of class, Weber clearly builds upon the analysis developed by Marx. In *Economy and Society*, Weber explicitly makes reference to Marx: "The unfinished last part of Karl Marx's *Capital* apparently was intended to deal with the issue of class unity in the face of skill differentials."[4] Weber and Marx both regard society as characterized by conflicts over resources and power. Sounding distinctly Marxist, Weber argues that the ownership of property constitutes a "positively privileged property class"[5] and that the factor producing class derives from the "relative control" within "a given economic order."[6]

In an oft-quoted passage, Weber identifies three conditions for a class to exist: "We may speak of a class when (1) a number of people have in common a specific causal component of their life chances, insofar as (2) this component is represented exclusively by economic interests in the possession of goods and opportunities for income, and (3) is represented under the conditions of the commodity or labor markets. This is the 'class situation.'"[7] Thus, Weber sees a class emerging when a large number of people share similar life chances in the commodity or labor markets. By *life chances*, he means the ability to gain access to scarce and valued goods and services such as property, education, and training. The ownership of property confers power on the propertied classes. For Weber, as for Marx, social class in a modern capitalist society is more complex than a simple two-class model of capitalist and proletariat. Although Marx in his later work refers to "three big classes," he also recognizes the existence of a "middle and intermediate strata."[8] Weber, too, identifies a variety of social classes: "The working class as a whole—the more so, the more automated the work process becomes, the petty bourgeoisie, the propertyless intelligentsia and specialists (technicians, various kinds of white-collar employees, civil servants—possibly with considerable social differences depending on the cost of their training), the classes privileged through property and education."[9]

In their 1848 *Manifesto*, Marx and Engels predicted that the petty bourgeoisie would "decay and finally disappear"[10] and "sink" into the working class in the face of modern industry. Over a quarter-century after the death of Marx, Weber noted the enduring presence of the petty bourgeoisie. He also witnessed the unprecedented growth of the new middle class: technicians, supervisors, and civil servants. Weber's class analysis closely overlaps with his theory that rationalization comes to dominate the modern world. As an economic process, rationalization is associated with mass production and a highly specialized division of labor. This process is vividly demonstrated by 1914–18 trench warfare, which, according to Weber, "means the world-wide triumph of this form [rationalization] of life."[11] Trench warfare battles of 1914–18 were battles of materials (*Materialschlacht*). During the battle of Jena in 1806, Napoleon expended fewer than 1,500 rounds of artillery to defeat the Prussians. In 1914, France planned for 10,000–12,000 shells

For Weber, the access that people have to societal resources, such as education, is crucial in determining people's life chances. This photograph of "ragged children" with their teacher was taken in the 1890s in England. Notice that the children are not wearing shoes, and contrast this image with that of "public" (private) boarding schools for children of the Victorian social elite.

of artillery *a day*; by 1918, production had reached 200,000 shells a day.[12] The mass slaughter of human lives on the Western Front required mass production of hitherto inconceivable quantities of military products, which, in turn, accelerated rationalization, specialization, and the bureaucratic modes of control essential for the mobilization of resources. This rationalization of war caused a burgeoning of white-collar technicians, managers, and civil servants.

For Marx, the class stratum is determined according to people's common relationship to the means of production, the means by which a large-scale grouping of people gain a livelihood. Weber's class theory, by contrast, was predicated on an economic struggle to control particular markets: money, commodities, or various job markets, for example. For Weber, control over a profitable market is the chief basis of class differences: "'Class situation' and 'class' refer only to the same (or similar) interests which an individual shares with others. In principle, the various controls over consumer goods, means of production, assets, resources and skills each constitute a *particular* class situation."[13] For example, the elite, privileged upper class typically comprises those who succeed in gaining a monopoly on some lucrative market; the less privileged classes, such as the shrinking old "working class," typically comprise those who fail to achieve a monopoly on their bundles of skills and are subject to the leveling forces of the free market. Weber continues, "A *uniform* class situation prevails only when completely unskilled and propertyless persons are dependent on irregular employment. Mobility among, and stability of, class positions differs greatly; hence the unity of a social class is highly variable."[14] Here Weber's view of social class emphasizes that skill may constitute a form of property. Thus, Weber distinguishes between *property* classes, typically comprising "rentiers" receiving income from the ownership of land, mines, factories; *commercial classes*, typically comprising "entrepreneurs" offering services on the market, such as bankers and financiers; and *professionals*, who are typically lawyers and physicians. These social classes are "positively privileged." In contrast, paupers and the unskilled who have neither property nor specialized skills constitute the "negatively privileged."

For Marx and Engels, social class and class consciousness are inextricably bound up with class struggle. Here Weber differs sharply from Marx, recognizing that Marx's notions of a "class for itself" and class solidarity did not resonate among the new white-collar managers, intelligentsia, and government mandarins. Whereas Marx refers to the specter of class antagonisms and class struggles, Weber emphasizes that social conflict and demands for radical changes to the economic system need not occur simply because of the differentiation of classes. The following passage explains his argument:

> The mere differentiation of property classes is not "dynamic," that is, it need not result in class struggles and revolutions. The strongly privileged class of slave owners may coexist with the much less privileged peasants or even the declassed, frequently without any class antagonism and sometimes in solidarity (against the unfree). However, the juxtaposition of property classes *may* lead to revolutionary conflict between ... landowners and the declassed or ... creditors and debtors.... These struggles need not focus on a change of the economic system, but may aim primarily at a redistribution of wealth. In this case we can speak of "property revolutions" [*Besitzklassenrevolutionen*].[15]

As an example of the absence of class conflict, Weber cites the relationship of the "poor white trash" to the plantation owners in the southern United States. The former were, he argues, "far more anti-Negro than the plantation owners, who were often imbued with patriarchal sentiments."[16] Weber believed that his multiple-class model of class meant that there is no simple relationship between class position and class consciousness. Importantly, the mere differentiation of class is not dynamic, as Marx had thought. For Weber, class constitutes a vital objective factor in the formation of consciousness, affecting "life chances" in the market in a variety of ways; but, significantly, economic and class interests are not automatically transposed to "solidaristic" class consciousness.[17]

Weber recognized that class is not purely an economic and market phenomenon. Alongside the objective aspect of social class is a subjective aspect whereby individuals are located hierarchically in society by virtue of status (*Stände*). "In contrast to the purely economically determined 'class situation,'" Weber writes, "we wish to designate as a *status situation* every typical component of life of men that is determined by a specific, positive or negative, social estimation of *honour*."[18] In modern society, argues Weber, status came to be typically founded on style of life, that is, formal education or hereditary or occupational prestige. Symbols of status, including education, manner of speech, apparel, and occupation, all have the effect of shaping an individual's social status in the eyes of others sharing the same culture.

Weber adds complexity to the ideas of class promulgated by Marx and Engels by introducing the notion of "status group," which he defines as "a plurality of persons who, within a larger group, successfully claim (a) a special social esteem, and possibly also (b) status monopolies."[19] Weber explains that status groups are created by virtue of lifestyle or occupation, through hereditary charisma (e.g., members of a European royal family), or through the monopolistic appropriation of political powers. His approach is often seen as antagonistic to Marx and Engels's sociology, but, in *Economy and Society* (first published in 1921), Weber discusses the developing "solidarity" of the various classes, which is close to Marx and Engels's view of the working class. Weber also discusses social classes in terms of "privileged" education. This concept would imply that each status group has a distinctive culture and the propensity to see the world in a particular way. The cultural milieu of each status group has ideas that reflect its members' own interests and also the social conditions that surround these interests.

It is plausible to argue that each status group defends its monopoly and position in society and, for this reason, may be considered an economic network. The lifestyle of the status group depends and draws upon its economic resources and wealth. The dominant upper classes, for example, buy education for their children from private schools such as Eton in England—elitist bastions of privilege—as a process of turning education and social capital into economic capital. The concepts of class and status group have been a subject of debate among readers of Weber, and Weber himself is hardly eloquent on the point. On the one hand, he defines *class* in terms of relative control over income-producing resources and material wealth, but he also maintains that status groups are founded on non-economic "style of life."

In practice, suggests Weber, class and status tend to correspond, but he is adamant that this need not necessarily be the case. An individual can have class without status and status without class. For example, in the latter category would fall a junior professor whose income may not differ very much from the salary of a customer service manager at a bank. On the other hand, the professor's position may confer more status in society at large. Weber explains the disjuncture between class and status as follows:

> Status *may* rest on class position of a distinct or an ambiguous kind. However, it is not solely determined by it: Money and entrepreneurial position are not in themselves status qualifications, although they may lead to them; and the lack of property is not in itself a status disqualification, although this may be reason for it. Conversely, status may influence, if not completely determine, a class position without being identical with it. The class position of an officer, a civil servant or a student may vary greatly according to their wealth and yet not lead to a different status since upbringing and education create a common style of life.[20]

For Weber, status may vary independently of class position. The term *genteel poverty*[21] refers to the conferment of high status to an individual with little or no economic wealth. A *status group* refers to a plurality of individuals who are socially distinct and exclusive in terms of consumption patterns and lifestyle, and, as such, asserts Weber, "the status group comes closest to the social class."[22] He further explains, "With some oversimplification, one might thus say that classes are stratified according to their relations to the production and acquisition of goods; whereas status groups are stratified according to the principles of their *consumption* of goods as represented by special styles of life."[23]

There is a dynamic dimension to social stratification that results from struggles between different classes and status groups in production and markets. Power constitutes an expression of the distribution of interests within society and is an integral dimension of social stratification. Power may be valued for the economic rewards it confers but also for the social status it bestows on itself. For Weber, classes, status groups, and political parties, which represent interests determined either through class or status positions, are "phenomena of the distribution of power within a community."[24] Weber's writings on the complex interplay of class, status, and party offer a foundation for analyzing social stratification. In multicultural societies, for example, a disjuncture between class and status positions may occur because of racial or ethnic status. For instance, a wealthy African American or Asian entrepreneur might not be situated in the same subjective or status hierarchy as a member of the majority population who, in pure economic terms, has an identical class position. In part because of his multifaceted approach to determining status, Weber's work has had a considerable influence on American sociology, as status and social mobility are central to the "American dream,"[25] and status forms part of the structural functionalist theory of social stratification. The Weberian influence is also evident in W.E.B. Du Bois's discussion of class and status in African American history (see chapter 15).

Power, Domination, and Bureaucracy

Reinhard Bendix explains that Weber, in his sociology of religion, gives greater weight to ideology and interests than to the theme of power (*Macht*) and domination (*Herrschaft*), which has also been translated as "authority." This emphasis is reversed in his sociology of politics.[26] At the center of Weber's political sociology are his theories of power, domination, and the state. He does not define *power* in terms of class economic interests but in terms of social action as "the chance of a man or a number of men to realize their own will in a social action even against the resistance of others who are participating in the action."[27] He emphasizes that, in this general sense, power is an aspect of virtually all social relationships. Men can exercise power in the family unit, at social events, in public discourse, and in the market. However, the underlying premise of his analysis is that power per se is an insufficient basis for ordering social action. Weber defines *domination* as "the probability that certain specific commands (or all commands) will be obeyed by a given group of persons."[28] Domination, according to Weber, can be legitimate or illegitimate (coercive). Weber was primarily interested in legitimate forms of domination or power, or what he called legitimate authority, that allocates the right to command and the duty to obey. He argues that every form of rule attempts to establish and cultivate the belief in its legitimate authority. The starting point for his theories is his classification of legitimate domination into three types: traditional, charismatic, and legal-rational. These typologies are related to Weber's social action, and they are also ideal types, as discussed in chapter 10.

Traditional domination is based on the sanction of immemorial traditions and on belief in the legitimacy of those who exercise authority. The pure form of traditional domination is *patriarchy*, literally translated as "rule of the father," which describes domination by male heads of household. Weber suggests that the feudal system of monarch, nobles, and serfs is a form of patriarchal domination. This patrimonial authority will be based on personal loyalty and obligation to the ruler: "The obedience is owed to the *person* of the chief who occupies the traditional sanctioned position of authority and who is (within its sphere) bound by tradition."[29] In such regimes the exercise of power is highly personalized and discretionary in a variety of ways, for instance, by eating at the ruler's table, by rights of land use in return for services, and by bestowing or receiving fiefs.[30]

Charismatic domination is based on devotion to the exceptional sanctity, heroism, or exemplary character of an individual person, whose authority will typically be theocratic. The English word *charisma* derives from the Greek *kharisma*, meaning "favor" or "grace." Weber defines the term *charisma* as "a certain quality of an individual personality by virtue of which he is considered extraordinary and treated as endowed with supernatural, superhuman, or at least specially exceptional powers or qualities. These are such as are not accessible to the ordinary person, but are regarded as of divine origin or as exemplary, and on the basis of them the individual concerned is treated as a 'leader.'"[31] Weber believes that charismatic domination involves four related elements: an individual of exceptional powers or qualities, a social crisis, a radical solution to the crisis offered by the individual, and devoted followers. Ancient and modern history offers many examples of charismatic power. Thus, presumably, the disciples obeyed Jesus Christ because he possessed charisma; leaders such as Mahatma Gandhi in India and Ayatollah Khomeini in Iran were also charismatic. Weber posits that charismatic power, unlike traditional domination, is a powerful force for social change, which abandons traditional rules: "Charismatic belief revolutionizes men 'from within' and shapes material and social conditions according to its revolutionary will," writes Weber.[32]

Winston Churchill and, more recently, Margaret Thatcher provide alternative examples of charismatic domination. Based on Marx's analysis of Napoleon Bonaparte's coup, Durkheim's notion of collective effervescence, and Weber's insistence that charismatic leaders emerge only during periods of a crisis or "moments of distress,"[33] an alternative understanding of charismatic power emerges. It can be seen as a quality conferred on a "supernatural" leader by virtue of particular situations and crises rather than as a quality or individual trait.[34] Thus, in 1940 following the evacuation of the British Expeditionary Force at Dunkirk, the British Prime Minister Winston Churchill demonstrated charisma. In the United States, writes the Canadian historian Margaret Macmillan, "the cult of Winston Churchill" evokes his stirring speeches—"Britain shall never surrender"[35]—in his stand against appeasing the charismatic, demonic Adolf Hitler. But Churchill's charisma melted away like fresh snow in late spring after the war. Although it might seem surprising, Ken Loach's 2013 film *The Spirit of '45* contains a clip from a newsreel showing Churchill campaigning for re-election on an open platform being booed by the audience, which seems to contain many demobbed soldiers and sailors. Indeed, in 1945, the Labour Party defeated Churchill's Conservative government in the general election. In Britain, Churchill is also remembered as a politician who had his share of failures and controversial views: as architect of the disastrous Gallipoli campaign in 1915; for his rabid anti-union views, for example when he advocated a "shoot them down" policy toward strikers during the labor unrest of 1910–14;[36] for his strongly imperialist position; and for his notorious comment about Mahatma Gandhi, "this malignant subversive fanatic."[37]

In the 1980s, it appeared that Margaret Thatcher also possessed charismatic powers during the Malvinas (Falklands) War with Argentina, and this view was later reinforced, for some, with her government's victory in the coal miners' strike of March 1984 to March 1985. A twist in Weber's thinking is his argument that the influence of a situation may lie not in the presence of a moment of crisis but in its *absence*. The absence of crisis, uncertainty, and fear, argues British academic Keith Grint, may generate a need on the part of some people for an exciting alternative to the routine boredom of everyday life.[38] Importantly, charismatic power is conferred upon a leader by his or her followers, but it can also be retracted. Weber devotes time to discussing how charismatic power, in its pure form, is foreign to the routines of everyday life and involves the "routinization of charisma."[39] Once a crisis has passed, charismatic leaders must transform themselves back into everyday life, but, when they do so, their power or qualities begin to fade. Charisma will, therefore, tend to develop into either traditional or legal-rational domination.

Legal-rational domination refers to "a belief in the legality of enacted rules and the right of those elevated to authority under such rules to issue commands (legal authority)."[40] In modern democratic political systems, obedience is owed to the legally established impersonal laws. The *pure* type of legal-rational domination rests on the acceptance of the validity

Joan of Arc (1412–31) is a national heroine of France. She led the French army to several major victories during the Hundred Years' War. She is a good example of Weber's charismatic authority.

of several mutually interdependent ideas: the legal norms are established by agreement or by imposition on grounds of expediency or value-rationality or both; every body of law is part of a consistent system of abstract rules; the leader is subject to the same body of law; the followers obey in their capacity as members of a community, organization, or state; and followers obey only what is the law.[41]

Legal-rational domination may take several structural forms, but generations of sociology students have come to know this type of power through Weber's ideal-type bureaucracy. For Weber, bureaucratic administrations are "the purest type of exercise of legal authority."[42] Under a formal legal system, a bureaucracy is both a *form* of domination and a way of describing the *location* of domination. A bureaucracy is governed by the following key principles:

1. Official conduct is bound by written *rules*;
2. The bureaucracy is structured in a clearly defined *hierarchy* in which lower offices are controlled by higher ones;
3. Each office holder has a clearly defined sphere of *competence*;
4. Each member is appointed, not elected, on the basis of technical *qualifications*, and promotion is based on seniority or merit as judged by superiors;
5. Members are compensated by fixed *salaries* in money; and
6. *Ownership* of the means of production or service is separate from the office holder.

As we noted in the preceding chapter, a bureaucracy is an example of an ideal type, and Weber depicts bureaucratic administrations as highly efficient in the sense that a purely bureaucratic organization is the most rational means of exercising discipline and authority over its members.

A bureaucracy is also superior because its structure and mechanisms offer a high degree of measurement of outcomes for the leaders of the organization. The increasing spread of bureaucracy in modern capitalist societies may be explained by the systematic rationalization of economic and social life. That is, bureaucratic organizations are *technically* superior over non-bureaucratic structures. The division of labor, the compartmentalization of knowledge and expertise, speed, continuity, reporting mechanisms, and discipline create machine efficiency.

Weber viewed the power exercised through modern bureaucracies with some apprehension, and he discusses at length the potential negative aspects of bureaucracies. He states that the more perfectly bureaucracy is developed, "the more it is dehumanized,"[43] as it "reduces every worker to a cog in this [bureaucratic] machine and, seeing himself in this light, he will merely ask how to transform himself from a little into a somewhat bigger cog."[44] He believed that, once such bureaucratic structures are established, the calculus of self-interest within the system of legal-rational domination "is practically indestructible."[45] The individual bureaucrat cannot squirm out of specialized activity and is only a small cog in the total organizational machine. The masses, for their part, cannot abolish the bureaucratic apparatus once it exists, for it is predicated upon an attitude set on habit and expert knowledge, and thus the idea of dismantling this apparatus becomes more utopian. Bureaucratic regimes were a threat to individual initiative because of the irresistible force of "rational discipline," which amounts to nothing less than consistently rationalized, methodically prepared, and exact execution of the received order. Mired in with bureaucratic regimes, personal autonomy and creativity are suspended, and, argues Weber, the mandarin is unswervingly and exclusively set for carrying out commands. Likely under the influence of Nietzsche, Weber assigns substantial weight to charismatic leaders as an antidote to the antidemocratic ethos of bureaucracies.[46] And Weber's writings reveal a symmetry in his thinking if his pure types of domination are placed alongside his typology of social action: traditional action/traditional authority; affectual action/charismatic authority; and instrument-rational action/legal-rational authority.[47]

Weber's Critique of Politics in a Bureaucratic Age

In 1917, Weber published a political treatise that involved a long discussion of German politics and political institutions, which he generally assessed negatively because of their tendency to permit a bureaucratic domination of politics and their failure to allow politicians of high caliber to emerge into leadership positions. He immediately stressed that this political discussion could not "claim the protective authority of any science,"[48] a position that is consistent with his ideas on the separation of political views from scientific ones. In this essay, Weber makes revealing statements regarding the dangers of the expansion of a rational, bureaucratic organization of social life. His argument is that, given that power is exercised through bureaucratic routines, career civil servants—rather than elected politicians—make decisions that impact on our everyday needs and problems.

Weber argued that if private capitalism were to be eliminated, then "the top *management* of the socialized or crown corporations would become bureaucratic" and bureaucracy would be extended without the checks provided by the existing private bureaucracies in the economy. Weber anticipated a bureaucratic "shell of bondage" based on discipline imposed by machines and the rational, specialized, and hierarchical nature of bureaucracy.[49] Weber portrays the advance of bureaucracy as "an 'inescapable' fate" and as "irresistible," but, at the same time, he argues that bureaucracy has "inherent limitations" in the context of both government and the private economy because of the struggle for power among and between entrepreneurs, directors, politicians, and civil servants.

It is the "irresistible advance of bureaucratization"[50] that makes responsible leadership rare. Weber's vision involves the process of rationalization (as a kind of fate), which puts in ever-increasing positions of power officials who lack the vision and responsibility of "real leaders."[51]

To lead in a responsible way, Weber thought, a man has to be not only a leader "but a hero as well, in a very sober sense of the word.... Only he has a calling for politics who is sure that he shall not crumble when the world from his point of view is too stupid or too base for what he wants to offer. Only he who in the face of all this can say 'In spite of all!' has the calling for politics."[52] But the rationality of science undermines value standpoints, namely, the ultimate ends that the leader might draw upon to give his actions meaning. The disenchantment of the world implies that religion, in particular, has lost its authority because, as science and technology show, there are no mysterious forces that can be invoked—everything, in theory, can be calculated and known. At the same time, science cannot tell us how to live, and science does not give the world any meaning.[53] Science can lend clarity in the sense that it can tell us which means will produce a particular result, even if it cannot tell us which ends to choose.[54] This is why the political leader has to be sober and responsible, considering the possible means and results as well as deciding which "is God for him and which is the devil."[55]

Weber discussed how it had become the fate of people to be controlled by rational institutions, which he described as forming an "iron cage,"

a "steel shell," or a "shell of bondage." The ways in which the system of
capitalist factory discipline and the strength of bureaucratic rules reduce
the freedom and creativity of the worker and the official were outlined
in the previous chapter, as was the domination of the law over the person
not qualified in legal matters. Weber states this critique, which has Marxist overtones, sympathetically "without ever actually endorsing it."[56]

Weber's second critique of modernity stems from a critique of German
politics and its institutions. Weber argues that modern society provides
little scope for the emergence of real politicians capable of being serious
leaders and exhibiting a form of independent, committed, disciplined,
and responsible leadership—the kind of leadership that goes beyond
the duties and morality of the legally constrained official. This sort of
detached and sober but committed leader makes claims to legitimacy
that go beyond the equality-based legitimacy of the bureaucratic and
legal order. Such a leader inspires obedience and makes demands upon
people based upon his or her claim to possess special individual qualities
of leadership (charisma). The first critique implies changes to social and
economic arrangements so that the egalitarian ideals of the legal-rational
and bureaucratic order can be achieved. The second critique is based
upon a fundamentally different view, which is more antidemocratic and
elitist. If the first critique suggests that Weber is quite close to Marx,
the second one points to the influence of Nietzsche's writings. Weber
refers to the same personal qualities in a leader as does Nietzsche—
courage, passion, responsibility. Weber also references the antidemocratic
implications of using these qualities as a basis for claiming legitimacy.
These two positions are contradictory and stand fundamentally opposed,
with egalitarian ideals, on the one hand, and the idea that some people
possess special qualities that make them stand apart, on the other. Each
of these critical positions with their notions of the "fate" of people in a
rationalized modernity indicates that Weber was not simply a spokesper-
son for the superiority of Western institutions. Nevertheless, in Kronman's
view, "there was an oscillation between irreconcilable perspectives that
helps to explain why he has found supporters as well detractors on both
Left and Right."[57]

Weber's historical sociology has at its center a conflict between
the process of technical rationalization and the creative individual or
"cultured man." There could be no turning back from the long cultural
development and embrace of rationalization, and, at times, Weber showed
great pessimism, forecasting a bleak future in which people would be as
dominated as they were in ancient Egypt—especially if private capitalism
were eliminated. Also, when discussing the capitalist system that the religious motivation to work had helped to create, he referred to dominant

capitalism as a "mighty cosmos" that binds people to the demands of "the technical and economic conditions of machine production." Weber describes the situation in this way:

> No one yet knows who will live in that shell in the future. Perhaps new prophets will emerge, or powerful old ideas and ideals will be reborn at the end of this monstrous development. *Or* perhaps—if neither of these occurs—"Chinese" ossification dressed up with a kind of desperate self-importance will set in. Then, however, it might truly be said of the "the last men" in this cultural development "specialists without spirit, hedonists without a heart; these nonentities imagine they have attained a stage of humankind never before reached."[58]

The dialectic between bureaucracy and individual freedom, between individuality and rationality, was essential to maintain a dynamic society and central to Weber's world view. Weber hoped that an element of economic and political freedom and creative leadership in the form of responsible leaders in a free market capitalism—however small their chances of survival in the face of rational, technical bureaucracies—would prevent social ossification. This "attitude was one of heroic pessimism."[59]

Criticisms

Several features of bureaucracy suggest that employment in such work organizations would be stable and full time. In addition, it was stated that the stability and permanence of a bureaucracy were "predicated upon an attitude set on habit and expert knowledge."[60] Changes instituted by neoliberalism since the 1970s created a globalized economy in which companies became increasingly flexible, especially in their patterns of employment of labor. Guy Standing,[61] for example, argues that the only groups who could be said to be employed in the type of bureaucracies described by Weber form a "salariat" located in large organizations, in public sector administration, and in a "shrinking 'core' of manual employees, the essence of the traditional 'aristocracy' of labor."[62] A key question is how do these new patterns of employment affect social class? Standing identifies a new "class-in-the-making" (though not yet a "class-for-itself" in the Marxist sense), which he calls the "precariat"—a term that involves a linkage of the class's precarious state and its similarities with the proletariat. The precariat has been created as companies impose flexible ways of employing labor and aspire to "travel light."[63]

If Standing's discussion of the precariat is correct, then rational economic decisions within multinational corporations, to enable them to maximize return for shareholders, have changed the social structure and made social stratification more complex.

A second criticism of Weber is that he viewed charismatic leaders purely positively and disregarded despotism.[64] As we have pointed out, Weber assigned considerable weight to the role of "superhuman" individuals in history. He believed that charisma could be an antidote to the inexorable advance of bureaucracy. Weber was personally committed to authoritarian citizenship, and his view of German politics is definitely elitist, which sits somewhat uncomfortably with his commitment to Western liberal tradition.[65] Although Weber considered that the unrestrained will of the German working classes and their demands for equality posed a threat to Western liberal democracy, by contrast he "regarded as comparatively negligible the danger that the rule of the *Führer*, legitimized through personal plebiscite, could turn into a dictatorial (or even fascist) regime."[66] Undoubtedly, Weber's theory of charismatic political leaders reveals the pending threat to liberal democracy from the rise of German fascism in the 1930s, headed by the charismatic but malignant Adolf Hitler. Given that Weber was well aware of the political weakness of the German middle class, it is incomprehensible "why he failed to anticipate the possibility of an antiliberal fusion of the charismatic and bureaucratic principles."[67]

Conclusion

Bureaucracy was understood by Weber to be the most efficient means of administration, but he also thought it produced unintended consequences for the overall functioning of rational institutions. The idea that rational systems could produce irrationalities such as the dehumanization of those within them as well as a threat to creativity and leadership placed Weber in an ambiguous relationship with modernity, a position that anticipated postmodernist challenges to the narrative of modernity. It also presents contemporary sociologists with an important perspective on social trends and institutions, which can be seen globally and no longer in the West only.

Weber's thesis on rationalization informs his theories of social class, politics, and bureaucracies. Weber believed that class divisions derive not only from control of the means of production and property but also from access to resources such as training and education, which affect an individual's position in the labor market and, in turn, strongly influences overall life chances. The approaches of Weber and Marx have been combined into an influential theory of class by the American sociologist Erik Olin Wright.[68] At the center of Weber's political sociology are his theories of power, domination, and the state. He focuses on legitimate forms of power or what he calls legitimate authority, which allocates the right to command and the duty to obey. For Weber, bureaucracies are the purest form of legal-rational authority.[69]

In *The Protestant Ethic*, Weber pessimistically warns of the tendency of people in the modern world to experience an iron cage. His stark image of modernity is that of individual autonomy being suffocated by the pervasive process of rationalization in all spheres of modern life. Informed by nineteenth-century scholars such as Alexis de Tocqueville, and by Weber's intellectual contemporary Simmel, the "iron cage" metaphor Weber created features prominently in his analysis of bureaucracy and is one of the most influential metaphors among the general critiques of modernity. The process of rationalization, then, is unremittingly paradoxical. The way large organizations are designed is predicated on rational calculation that appears to function very efficiently, yet, at the same time, large organizations can reduce white-collar workers to inanimate cogs in a bureaucratic machine.[70] Weber's dire warnings of creeping rationalization in all dimensions of Western culture have inspired artists and sociologists alike. In literature, Aldous Huxley's *Brave New World*, George Orwell's *1984*, and Margaret Atwood's *The Handmaid's Tale* are examples of popular expressions of ubiquitous bureaucratization. In the early twenty-first century, Weber's rationalization and bureaucratization theories also resonate with Naomi Klein's notion of the "McMilitary," specifically, the danger to civil liberties that results from the outsourcing of massive state surveillance by increasingly authoritarian regimes, a policy that is said to be fully justified by the so-called War on Terror.[71] Finally, contemporary sociologists draw on Weber's ideas to make the argument that ecological problems cannot be understood without making the ideological connections between Christianity, Western rationalism, and environmental domination. The work of Ulrich Beck and others, for example, represents a renaissance of Weberian historical sociology.[72] This intellectual genre recognizably draws upon the tradition founded by Weber in arguing that global capitalism and contemporary social change are caused by the interaction of several irreducibly distinct forms of power and domination.[73]

To examine the applicability of Weberian sociology to a specific modern socio-economic trend, we need look no further than academia. Weber's idea that an individual can have class without status and status without class fits well with recent contemporary changes in the academic labor process.[74] In the United Kingdom, according to the latest data from the Higher Education Statistics Agency, more than one-third of academics experience precarious employment, teaching on temporary, fixed-term contracts as British universities "casualize" their workforces. A similar trend has occurred in Canadian and US universities. This insecurity is not confined to teaching; the data show that 68 percent of research-only staff members are on fixed-term contracts, which typically last as long as the research grant. The union representing university professors claims that university "education has become one of the most casualised sectors in the UK—second only to the hospitality industry."[75] A Weberian analysis of contemporary university employment would posit that, although junior professors have status founded on the possession of relatively scarce formal education, their class position is not valued by society at large in a way that is commensurate with this status. Thus, one might argue that, unlike other professions, teaching-only university professors have failed to protect their monopoly over scarce social knowledge, and, as a consequence, they have been subject to the leveling forces of the open market and have fallen into the emerging "precariat class."[76] The men and women undertaking precarious, short-term university work have minimal trust relationships with the university, and, therefore, like the precariat, are distinctive in class terms. They also have a peculiar status position, as they do not fall neatly into high-status professional occupations. That the Weberian concepts of class and status can be applied to the employment of academics further illustrates classical social theory in action.

FURTHER THINKING:

What are the characteristics of charismatic, traditional, and legal-rational forms of domination? Think about your own contemporary political system. To what extent, if at all, does it possess any features of these three forms of domination?

FURTHER READING:

See Max Weber, *Economy and Society,* vol. 1 (Berkeley: University of California Press, 1978), 212–65; Kieran Allen, *Max Weber: A Critical Introduction* (London: Pluto Press, 2004), 97–116; and Derek Sayer, *Capitalism & Modernity: An Excursus on Marx and Weber* (London: Routledge, 1991).

Notes

1 Mike Davis, *Old Gods, New Enigmas* (London: Verso, 2018), 3.

2 Akala, *Natives: Race and Class in the Ruins of Empire* (London: Two Roads, 2018), 5.

3 Max Weber, *General Economic History*, trans. F.H. Knight (1927; New York: Dover, 2003), 277.

4 Max Weber, *Economy and Society* (Berkeley: University of California Press, 1978), 1:305.

5 Weber, *Economy and Society*, 1:303.

6 Weber, *Economy and Society*, 1:302.

7 Weber, *Economy and Society*, 2:927.

8 Robert Tucker, ed., *The Marx-Engels Reader* (New York: Norton & Company, 1978), 441.

9 Weber, *Economy and Society*, 1:305.

10 Tucker, *Marx-Engels Reader*, 482.

11 Weber, *Economy and Society*, 2:1400.

12 Eric J. Hobsbawm, *The Age of Extremes, 1914–1991* (London: Abacus, 1995), 45.

13 Weber, *Economy and Society*, 1:302.

14 Weber, *Economy and Society*, 1:302.

15 Weber, *Economy and Society*, 1:303–4.

16 Weber, *Economy and Society*, 1:304.

17 Alan Swingewood, *A Short History of Sociological Thought* (New York: St. Martin's Press, 2000).

18 Weber, *Economy and Society*, 2:932.

19 Weber, *Economy and Society*, 1:306.

20 Weber, *Economy and Society*, 1:306.

21 The term is used by Anthony Giddens, *Sociology* (Cambridge: Polity Press, 2009).

22 Weber, *Economy and Society*, 1:306–7.

23 Weber, *Economy and Society*, 2:937.

24 Weber, *Economy and Society*, 2:937.

25 For an interesting perspective on the so-called American Dream as it applies to the sociology of work, see David E. Guest, "Human Resource Management and the American Dream," *Journal of Management Studies* 27, no. 4 (1990): 377–97.

26 Reinhard Bendix, *Max Weber: An Intellectual Portrait* (New York: Anchor Books, 1962), 290.

27 Weber, *Economy and Society*, 2:926.

28 Weber, *Economy and Society*, 1:212.

29 Weber, *Economy and Society*, 1:216.

30 Weber, *Economy and Society*, 1:235–41.

31 Weber, *Economy and Society*, 1:241.

32 Weber, *Economy and Society*, 2:1116.

33 Weber, *Economy and Society*, 2:1111.

34 Ian Craib, *Classical Social Theory* (Oxford: Oxford University Press, 1997).

35 Margaret Macmillan, *The Uses and Abuses of History* (Toronto: Penguin, 2008).

36 Alan Hutt, *British Trade Unionism* (London: Lawrence & Wishart, 1975), 60.

37 Arthur Herman, *Gandhi and Churchill* (New York: Random House, 2008), 359.

38 John Bratton, Keith Grint, and Debra Nelson, *Organizational Leadership* (Mason, OH: Southwestern, 2005).

39 *Weber, Economy and Society*, 1:246–54.

40 *Weber, Economy and Society*, 1:215.

41 *Weber, Economy and Society*, 1:217–20.

42 *Weber, Economy and Society*, 1:220.

43 *Weber, Economy and Society*, 2:975.

44 *Weber, Economy and Society*, 1:lix.

45 *Weber, Economy and Society*, 2:987.

46 Irving M. Zeitlin, *Ideology and the Development of Sociological Theory* (Upper Saddle River, NJ: Prentice-Hall, 2001).

47 Larry Ray, *Theorizing Classical Sociology* (Buckingham, UK: Open University Press, 1999).

48 Weber, *Economy and Society*, 2:1381.

49 Weber, *Economy and Society*, 2:1402.

50 Weber, *Economy and Society*, 2:1403.

51 Weber, *Economy and Society*, 2:1448.

52 Max Weber, "Politics as a Vocation," in *From Max Weber: Essays in Sociology*, ed. H.H. Gerth and C. Wright Mills (London: Routledge, 1970), 77–128, see page 128.

53 Weber, "Science as a Vocation," in *From Max Weber: Essays in Sociology*, ed. H.H. Gerth and C. Wright Mills (London: Routledge, 1970), 143.

54 Weber, "Science as a Vocation," 151.

55 Weber, "Science as a Vocation," 148.

56 Anthony T. Kronman, *Max Weber* (London: Edward Arnold, 1983), 183.

57 Kronman, *Max Weber*, 185.

58 Max Weber, *The Protestant Ethic and the Spirit of Capitalism*, ed. Peter Baer and Gordon C. Wells (1905; New York: Penguin Books, 2002), 121.

59 Wolfgang Mommsen, "Max Weber's Political Sociology and His Philosophy of World History," in *Max Weber*, ed. Dennis Wrong (Englewood Cliffs, NJ: Prentice-Hall, 1970), 193.

60 See chapter 11 of this text.

61 Guy Standing, *The Precariat: The New Dangerous Class* (London: Bloomsbury Academic, 2011).

62 Standing, *The Precariat*, 8.

63 Standing, *The Precariat*, 58.

64 Zeitlin, *Ideology and the Development of Sociological Theory*.

65 See Larry Ray and Michael Reed, eds., *Organizing Modernity* (London: Routledge, 1994); Alex Callinicos, *Social Theory: A Historical Introduction* (Cambridge: Polity Press, 2007).

66 Wolfgang Mommsen, *The Political and Social Theory of Max Weber* (Cambridge: Polity Press, 1989), 34, and quoted in Zeitlin, *Ideology and the Development of Sociological Theory*, 238.

67 Zeitlin, *Ideology and the Development of Sociological Theory*, 238.

68 See Erik Olin Wright, *Classes* (London: Verso, 1985); Erik Olin Wright, *Class Counts: Comparative Studies in Class Analysis* (Cambridge: Cambridge University Press, 1997).

69 See Paul du Gay, *In Praise of Bureaucracy* (London: Sage, 2000), for an alternative view of the conventional critique of bureaucracy.

70 Weber, *Economy and Society*, 1:lix.

71 See Naomi Klein, "Shock Therapy in the U.S.A.," in *The Shock Doctrine* (Toronto: Alfred A. Knopf Canada, 2007), 341–69.

72 Callinicos, *Social Theory*.

73 See Ulrich Beck, *What Is Globalization?* (Cambridge: Polity Press, 1999); Ulrich Beck, "Living Your Own Life in a Runaway World: Individualism, Globalization and Politics," in *On the Edge: Living with Global Capitalism*, ed. Will Hutton and Anthony Giddens (London: Jonathan Cape, 2000), 164–74; Anthony Giddens, *The Consequences of Modernity* (Cambridge: Polity Press, 1990); and Michael Rustin "Incomplete Modernity: Ulrich Beck's Risk Society," *Radical Philosophy* 67 (1994) 3–12.

74 See, for example, Callinicos, *Social Theory*, and Frank Donoghue, *The Last Professors: The Corporate University and the Fate of the Humanities* (New York: Fordham University Press, 2008).

75 Anna Fazackerley, "Casual, Part-Time ... Where Did the Proper Jobs Go?" *The Guardian*, February 5, 2013, 35.

76 Standing, *The Precariat*.

PART III
EXPANDING THE CANON

13. Gender and Social Theory

Women persecuted as witches in the early modern period were typically those who existed outside male control, such as unmarried older women ... Fast forward 350 years and their equivalent is Hillary Clinton, maligned by arch Republicans ... fans who used the slogan "Burn the witch."

—Rebecca McQuillan, 2017[1]

Rosa Luxemburg was one of the first socialist intellectuals to pay careful attention to the grassroots processes of proletarian radicalization.

—Mike Davis, 2018[2]

THE INTELLECTUAL LEGACY OF ENLIGHTENMENT ideology is a masculine vision of the process of human history and of social life. This is despite the fact that women wrote and published philosophy in the eighteenth century. In the process of European industrialization, new occupations and new ways of doing paid work had a profound impact on public attitudes toward gender roles, on everyday relationships, and on patterns of family life. Feminist writers have focused on the canonical writers' acceptance of the "natural" differences between the sexes based on the reproductive capacity of women and on their justification for hierarchical relations of female subordination. Moreover, the iconic founders of sociology constructed the social through a masculine prism. This notable deficiency means that the traditional members of the sociological canon offer an inadequate framework for understanding many important aspects of modernity.

We have seen throughout this text that Marx, Durkheim, and Weber largely neglect the gender dimension of the process of modernity. In Marx and Engels's *German Ideology*, the anatomy of civil society is to be found in political economy. But Marx's account of the labor process both conceptually and empirically obscures the way that gender roles, patterns of family life, and conceptions of sexuality are socially constructed. Likewise, Durkheim's *Division of Labour in Society* offers a dichotomized, hierarchical perspective of the sexes.[3] A critical issue for feminists in Weber's *Methodology of the Social Sciences* is the use of ideal types as he examines the relationship of women to the process of power. Weber's analysis of social life occurs in the context of "natural inequality" between the sexes.[4] This did not augur well for women's freedom and equality.

It is our objective in this chapter to expand the traditional canon by reviewing the work of a small group of early feminist thinkers in England, Germany, and the United States. While mindful that the genesis of feminist discourse can be traced back to the Levellers' movement in seventeenth-century England and eighteenth-century America, we explore early feminist social theory through the work of four of its best-known theorists: Mary Wollstonecraft, Harriet Martineau, Rosa Luxemburg, and Charlotte Perkins Gilman. Had there been more space, we would have included many others, especially those who provide a standpoint based also in their experience of racial inequality.[5] As did the founding fathers, the "founding mothers" engaged with issues of materiality, morality, rationality, and emancipation. Moreover, they challenged the rationality and morality of capitalism that does not give *all* human beings an equal opportunity to develop their inner potential and to take part in social progress.

Mary Wollstonecraft (1759–97)

A product of the European Enlightenment, Mary Wollstonecraft was one of the earliest bourgeois feminist thinkers who was able to publish her thoughts on the organization of society. She lived long before social science had a distinct existence, but she believed that the Enlightenment values of equality, rationality, and freedom ought not to be restricted by gender or race. Although these ideas found expression among elements of the educated elite, Wollstonecraft articulated her ideas in a particularly forceful way. She is recognized as a feminist contributor to the early development of a rational, empirically based sociological theory.

Wollstonecraft's Life and Works

Mary Wollstonecraft was born in London, England, in 1759. Her father inherited wealth but handled it badly, so Wollstonecraft had to support herself. At first, she attempted to live from professions considered suitable for women: governess, lady's companion, and principal of a small school. In 1787, she found her lifetime mentor, the publisher Joseph Johnson. In 1793, she moved to France where she observed at first hand the turmoil and bloodshed of the French Revolution. Although appalled by the violence, she criticized those such as Edmund Burke who rejected the Revolution on the basis of sentiment about the past.[6] In the context of eighteenth-century England, it is not surprising that Wollstonecraft was largely home-educated. A number of intellectual influences informed her feminist analysis of society. She had access to the writings of Mary Astell (1666–1731), described as the first English feminist.[7] She was also aware of the aspirations of the English working-class movement known as the Levellers, who campaigned for the equality of women and universal suffrage in the seventeenth century.[8] Another possible source of inspiration was her involvement in a group of Unitarian Rational Dissenters who believed, among other things, in the perfectibility of the conditions of life through applied conscience and reason, as opposed to hierarchy and tradition. Her major work, *A Vindication of the Rights of Woman* (1792), was widely and internationally read, translated, and publicly discussed in her time. She died in 1797 while giving birth to her second daughter.

Gender Equality

Theorizing about society is intimately connected with the European Enlightenment and the birth of modernity. As we discussed in chapter 3,

the Enlightenment movement was not a unified body of thinking but was internally fractured and riddled by contradictions. The eighteenth-century public debate on women's emancipation and rights is an example of its intellectual silences and anomalies. Mary Wollstonecraft's *Vindication* is a product of this debate. The book is a rebuttal of Edmund Burke's *Reflections on the Revolution in France* (1790) and of the views of Jean-Jacques Rousseau. However, it

Mary Wollstonecraft was born in London, England, in 1759. She was one of the earliest feminist thinkers to publish her thoughts on the differences between Enlightenment thought and social realities. She died in 1797.

was Burke's notion that women's beauty is to be attributed to their "little-ness and weakness" that Wollstonecraft found particularly abhorrent. In her view, women are not actually equal to men, but they deserve social equality with men and should be given the education necessary to compete on an equal basis.

> Should experience prove that they [women] cannot attain the same degree of strength of mind, perseverance, and fortitude, let their virtues be the same in kind, though they may vainly struggle for the same degree; and the superiority of man will be equally clear, if not clearer; and truth, as it is a simple principle, which admits of no modification, would be common to both. Nay, the order of society as it is at present regulated would not be inverted, for woman would then only have the rank that reason assigned her, and arts could not be practised to bring the balance even, much less to turn it.[9]

For Wollstonecraft, women's isolation in domestic activities and their socially engendered need to be physically attractive to men spoil them for full partnership in the making of a new world:

Mary Wollstonecraft argued that young women should be given the education necessary to compete with men on an equal basis. This photograph taken around 1910 of working-class girls in a London school shows the slow pace of equality in education. For a working-class girl, training on how to wash clothes was part of the school curriculum to prepare her for the role of housewife or maid to the rich.

Strength of body and mind are sacrificed to libertine notions of beauty, to the desire of establishing themselves—the only way women can rise in the world—by marriage. And this desire making mere animals of them, when they marry they act as such children may be expected to act: they dress; they paint, and nickname God's creatures. Surely these weak beings are only fit for a seraglio!—Can they be expected to govern a family with judgment, or take care of the poor babes whom they bring into the world?[10]

A look at the textual evidence shows that Mary Wollstonecraft never questioned the assumption that motherhood is a natural condition for women or that some professions are unsuitable for them. "Women might certainly ... be physicians as well as nurses," she writes, adding

And midwifery, decency seems to allot to them.... They might also study politics.... Business of various kinds, they might likewise pursue, if they were educated in a more orderly manner, which might save many from common and legal prostitution. Women would not then marry for a support, as men accept of places under Government, and neglect the implied duties; nor would an attempt to earn their own subsistence, a most laudable one! Sink them almost to the level of those poor abandoned creatures who live by prostitution.[11]

Wollstonecraft's arguments largely focus on the family and education. An example of this is her response to Rousseau's instructive tale, *Emile*.[12] In book five of *Emile*, Rousseau describes how "Sophy, or Woman" is to be educated so that the hero, Emile, will be a family man without sacrificing his right to freedom. Sophy needs only the education, mainly sexual, that will keep her husband in a state of mind such that he wants to be at home. Wollstonecraft rejects sexuality as the basis for marriage and argues that women's education should give them as much knowledge of the world as men's. She writes, "'Educate women like men,' says Rousseau, 'and the more they resemble our sex the less power will they have over us.' This is the very point I aim at. I do not wish them to have power over men; but over themselves."[13]

Wollstonecraft argues that women deserve social equality with men, but, in her analysis, she connects the oppression of white women and black slaves.[14] In likening woman's historically subjugated position to that of slaves, she writes, "When, therefore, I call women slaves, I mean in a political and civil sense."[15] Thus she posits that, if rationality is essentially human, it is irrational not to apply it to both women and slaves.

Harriet Martineau (1802–76)

Harriet Martineau was a beneficiary of Enlightenment thinking, and she believed that the study of society ought to be methodologically rigorous. She agreed that the new American Republic demonstrated that people had the ability to govern themselves and that the Declaration of Independence embodied the principles of universal justice, but she also recognized that class split apart the society of the Republic. Further, like Alexis de Tocqueville, she recognized that slavery and democracy contradict each other and that this contradiction was similar to the illogicality of excluding women from the democratic process. And, like Wollstonecraft, she identified certain parallels between the status of white women and the status of black women slaves. Although she recognized Wollstonecraft's pioneering influence, Martineau did not agree with Wollstonecraft's way of approaching the woman question. She writes, "Every allowance must be made for Mary Wollstonecraft herself, from the constitution and singular environment which determined her course: but I have never regarded her as a safe example, nor as a successful champion of Woman and her Rights."[16] A strong-minded, cigar-smoking, unmarried, and outspoken woman, Martineau did not escape criticism in her own right.

Harriet Martineau was born in Norwich, England, in 1802. Despite the threat of violence and social exclusion, she was a fervent abolitionist and became prominent among anti-slavery circles. She died in 1876 at Ambleside, England.

Martineau's Life and Works

Harriet Martineau was born into an upper-middle-class Unitarian family in Norwich, England. Her father was owner of an import house and a member of an elite intellectual circle. Her mother was literate but lacking in formal education. Martineau loved to write, but when callers came, she had to hide her writing, which was considered unsuitable for a woman.[17] By 1828, her family faced extreme financial difficulties when the family business dissolved. Showing an attitude that took her through life, she writes, "Being thrown, while there was yet time, on our own resources, we have worked hard and usefully, won friends, reputation and influence, seen the world abundantly ... and truly lived instead of vegetated."[18]

By 1829, she had made a precarious transition to a writing career. When her hearing loss became severe, she required a trumpet hearing aid. By 1834, however, she was financially secure, and she had become a regular participant in a London literary circle that included Charles Dickens, William Wordsworth, Charlotte Brontë, and Charles Darwin. From 1834 to 1836, Martineau traveled through the United States, practicing sociological observation. A fervent abolitionist, she became prominent among anti-slavery circles, despite the threat of violence and social exclusion that was aimed at women abolitionists of the time.[19] Martineau's first publications were in the Unitarian periodical *The Monthly Repository*. One of these, "On Female Education" published in 1822, was a protest against the injustice of the exclusion of women from higher education.[20]

Her reputation was established by her series of *Illustrations of Political Economy*.[21] These popular booklets explain the principles of political economy in a simplified form. Her engaging writing style carried on into her sociological works, such as *How to Observe Morals and Manners* (1838),[22] *Society in America* (1837),[23] and *Retrospect of Western Travel* (1838).[24] In 1855 she became desperately ill,[25] after which she did not leave her home. She died on June 27, 1876, at Ambleside, England.

Intellectual Influences

Harriet Martineau was profoundly influenced by Unitarian ideas and values during her youth. The Unitarians favored rational democratic individualism and human responsibility for social conditions. This doctrine included *necessarianism*, which held that "all the workings of the universe are governed by laws which cannot be broken by human will."[26] These ideas helped her to develop the notion that identifying universal laws and adjusting social life to them would bring progress.[27] Another of her major influences was the utilitarian belief of Jeremy Bentham that the purpose of life is to increase the amount of happiness in the world.[28] For Martineau, policies that enhanced happiness were deemed progressive. An example of this can be found in her explanation that higher forms of charity are those that alleviate and prevent the most unhappiness.

> The lowest order of charity is that which is satisfied with relieving the immediate pressure of distress in individual cases. A higher is that which makes provision on a large scale for the relief of such distress; as when a nation passes on from common

alms giving to a general provision for the destitute. A higher still
is when such provision is made in the way of anticipation, or for
distant objects; as when the civilization of savages, the freeing of
slaves, the treatment of the insane, or the education of the blind
and deaf mutes is undertaken. The highest charity of all is that
which aims at the prevention rather than the alleviation of evil.[29]

Morality, Slavery, and Politics

In Martineau's *How to Observe Morals and Manners*, morals are
described as widely shared values that are demonstrated through texts
such as the Declaration of Independence, the songs and writings that
everyone knows, and gravestone epitaphs. Manners are defined as actual
practices. Manners can be empty formulas for courtesy, or they can be
deeply rooted customs. Wide differences between morals and manners, and areas of great unhappiness, are *anomalies* that require action.
Slavery and the oppression of women are anomalies in a society that
claims equality in the pursuit of happiness, and inequality of wealth is
an anomaly in a republic of equals. Fear of public opinion is an anomaly
in a nation that values freedom of expression.[30] Published in 1838, *How
to Observe Morals and Manners* is the first systematic methodology and
theory treatise in sociology. It outlines the mechanics of unbiased data
gathering, corroboration, and the practice of theorizing based in concrete
observations. In this, Martineau envisions the reader as a traveler, who
should use informed "sympathetic understanding" as a research tool.[31]

She understands that, in every observation, there are at least two sides,
the observer and the observed, and that "the mind of the observer, the
instrument by which the work is done, is as essential as the material to
be wrought."[32]

Martineau's traveler searches for what is representative in the way
that people talk (discourses), the way that they act (practices), and the
records of these thoughts and activities (things). *Things* are the most
important of these. The number and kind of suicides and the number
and kind of criminals are things that reveal the ideas and problems of the
time. She observes that "in England almost all the offences are against
property, and are so multitudinous as to warrant a stranger's conclusion
that the distribution of property among us must be extremely faulty,
the oppression of certain classes by others very severe, and our political
morals very low."[33]

Martineau's *Society in America* reflects her method of comparing
stated morals to actual practices. The American Declaration of Independence, which embodied John Locke's theory of natural rights, declared
that government derives its power from the consent of the governed and

that it is the duty of a government to protect the rights of its citizens. What so appalled Martineau was the advocacy by some leading proponents of democracy, such as Thomas Jefferson, for dominant masculine suppositions, the "political non-existence of women,"[34] and the exclusion of slaves from full citizenship in representative democracy. Thus, she holds up the American documents that claim government gets its legitimacy from the consent of the governed and compares them with the actual condition of women (and slaves) in American society. Women were granted indulgence, not enfranchisement. She would later describe this method as flawed by "the American theory which I had taken for my standpoint."[35] The topic needed to be treated in a more concrete way, she said.[36] By this, she meant that social change should be found among the people themselves rather than within the ideologies of government. It is on this basis that she criticized what she called the "Wollstonecraft crowd" who agitated for legal reforms.[37]

Martineau's later works show the continuation of her interest in social theory. *Eastern Life, Present and Past* (1848), a study of the evolution of religion, was received mainly as a travel book about the Near East.[38] Reviewers expressed shock at her position that religion is both socially constructed and outdated. Her best-known contribution to the development of sociology is her edited translation of Auguste Comte's six-volume *Cours de philosophie positive* into *The Positive Philosophy* (1853), a version Comte so approved that he translated it back into French and substituted it for his original edition.[39] The years between the 1850s and her death saw a prodigious output of her newspaper columns and articles on contemporary women's issues, including education and discriminatory laws. She also wrote or revised two historical texts, *History of the Peace: Being a History of England from 1816 to 1854* (1864–65) and the *History of England, A.D. 1800 to 1815* (1865), and engaged in extensive political lobbying on social issues.

Rosa Luxemburg (1871–1919)

A product of European revolutionary politics, Rosa Luxemburg was one of the most creative Marxists in the early twentieth century.[40] In her time, she was best known as a Marxist theorist and antiwar activist. She was active in radical politics while still in high school. In 1889, she moved to the University of Zürich, Switzerland. There she studied political economy and law, receiving a doctorate in 1898, at a time during which women rarely even attended university. Luxemburg was imprisoned for her opposition to World War I. In 1913 she published her magnum opus, *The Accumulation of Capital*, in which she offers a critical exposition of the economic and social consequences of capitalism.

Luxemburg's Life and Works

Rosa Luxemburg was born on March 5, 1871, into a lower-middle-class Jewish family in the small town of Zamość in Russian-occupied Poland. Her father was a timber merchant, and her mother was descended from a distinguished line of rabbis and scholars. Anti-Semitism, discrimination, and exclusion, all endemic in daily life, inevitably affected the young Luxemburg. Between 1880 and 1887, she attended grammar school in Warsaw, where she gained excellent grades. She became fluent in four languages, and it was at this time that she became active in progressive politics. Context is always important. Luxemburg was politically engaged at a time when women did not have the vote and, moreover, when politics was overwhelmingly a male domain. Luxemburg's independence of mind is illustrated by the fact that although she was not married, she enjoyed an active love life, a point that was considered highly provocative and conflicted with European morals of the period.

After finishing high school, Luxemburg went to the University of Zürich, transferring from the study of natural sciences and philosophy to political economy. In 1897, she completed a doctoral degree, the only woman to have done so among the sons of landlords and state officials. During this time, she maintained a close, personal relationship with the Lithuanian socialist Leo Jogiches. While Luxemburg challenged many social mores, she was not a "new woman" by modern-day standards. When a Dutch friend fell off her bicycle, Luxemburg wrote to commiserate, joking about her own repugnance of women riding bikes. And in 1917, she told her long-standing admirer of her "helplessness in 'earthly matters.'"[41]

In the 1890s, Luxemburg challenged both the Russian and the Polish Socialist Party because of their support of Polish independence. The national issue became one of Luxemburg's main themes. To her, nationalism and national independence were regressive concessions to the bourgeoisie. Her critics argue that she consistently underrated nationalist aspirations. This became one of her major points of disagreement with the Russian leader, Vladimir Lenin, and his theory of national self-determination. In 1898, Luxemburg moved to Berlin, where she married Gustav Lübeck to obtain German citizenship. In Berlin she entered into the debate that divided the Social Democratic Party of Germany—reform or revolution. Eduard Bernstein argued that socialism in advanced capitalist countries could best be achieved through a gradualist approach, using parliament and militant trade unionism. Luxemburg

profoundly disagreed.
In *Reform or Revolution*
(1889), she defended Marxist orthodoxy, arguing that
parliament was a bourgeois
imitation of democracy.
Karl Kautsky, a leading
political theoretician, agreed
with Luxemburg.

In 1906 Luxemburg was
arrested and released for
taking part in the revolution
in Russian-occupied Poland.
Moving back to Berlin, she
studied the implications of
the 1905 Russian Revolu-
tion for the German work-
ing classes, and defended
political mass strikes as an
instrument of radical social
change. In 1907, Luxem-
burg helped develop an
anti-war program for the

Rosa Luxemburg was born in Zamość, Poland, March 5, 1871.
She produced a major critique of Marx's theory of capitalist
reproduction She was assassinated in Berlin, Germany, on
January 15, 1919.

international labor movement. Between 1907 and 1914, she lectured at
the Social Democratic Party's school in Berlin. World War I (1914–18)
divided the European labor movement.

Luxemburg was prone to ill health, but was principled, brave, quick-
witted and funny, and, above all, thoroughly committed to socialist revolution.[42] Her intellectual endeavors grew directly out of her life experiences
and political activism. Her most important publications include *Reform or
Revolution* (1889), *The Mass Strike, the Political Party and Trade Unions*
(1906), *The National Question* (1909), *The Accumulation of Capital*
(1913), and *The Junius Pamphlet* (1915). Although she supported the 1917
Russian Revolution, in the posthumous publication of *The Russian Revolution* (1918) she gave a prescient warning against the dictatorship of the
Bolsheviks. Before World War I began, Luxemburg called for a preemptive
general strike to stop the war happening.[43] In 1914, at the outbreak of
war, she was arrested and remained in prison almost continuously until
1918. *The Junius Pamphlet,* written in prison, was described as "one of the
weightiest documents against the crime of war."[44] Released from prison on
November 9, 1918, Luxemburg and Karl Liebknecht were assassinated by
a proto-fascist militia on January 15, 1919.

Intellectual Influences

An early intellectual influence on Rosa Luxemburg was the nineteenth-century Romantic writer Adam Mickiewicz, who challenged the oppression of the Polish people and made common cause with Russians defying the tsar.[45] During the 1880s, she was aware of Polish and Russian women being imprisoned and executed for their part in the revolutionary underground. Luxemburg joined small reading circles to study the literature by Marx and Engels smuggled into the country. In addition to formal academia at the University of Zürich, Luxemburg's intellectual development was shaped by debating, in the student circles she was part of, topics such as Darwinism, Marx, Bakunin, Tolstoy, the emancipation of women, and the demoralization of the bourgeoisie. Her own scholarly writings reflect a deep theoretical understanding of Marxist economics. Like Marx, she believed that capitalism is a historical phenomenon, that the growth of capital necessitated increased exploitation of labor and natural forces, and that concomitant with the accumulation process there develops a reserve army of unemployed. However, she believed that Marx had created only a very general, abstract formula that did not fully examine the future economic limits of capitalist development.

Interestingly, Luxemburg recognized both the limits and the power of academia. Of university education, she wrote, "The social, historical, philosophical, and natural sciences are today the ideological products of the bourgeoisie and expressions of its needs and class tendencies."[46] But, for the development of the working class, she posited, knowledge is power and "a lever of class struggle."[47] Luxemburg championed the cause of prostitutes who were imprisoned[48] and supported the suffragettes, but she never herself identified with the feminist movement of her day, and always avoided being categorized as a "woman." Her reasoning was political. She did not wish to be marginalized within the Social Democratic Party,[49] and regarded women's liberation "as a diversion at a time when humanity as a whole confronted gigantic tasks."[50] Works on Rosa Luxemburg paint a complex woman, "a genuine dialectician," who juggled complex and often opposing realities. Her life work, however, remains "richly relevant" in the era of global neoliberal capitalism.[51]

Capital and Its Global Setting

Rosa Luxemburg wrote *The Accumulation of Capital* while teaching at the Social Democratic Party of Germany's school in Berlin. She critiques Marx's theory of capitalist reproduction, and in so doing she produced the first modern theory of under-consumption.[52] The essence of her critique was provoked by Marx's assumption of capitalist accumulation. She argues:

Marx's diagram of enlarged reproduction cannot explain
the actual and historical process of accumulation. And why?
Because ... the diagram [assumes] that the capitalists and workers are the sole agents of capitalist consumption ... and assumes
the universal and exclusive domination of the capitalist mode of
production ... Under these conditions, there can be ... no other
classes of society than capitalists and workers.[53]

The affinity between Marx and Luxemburg clearly consists in the common emphasis on the means to increase surplus value. But whereas
Marx identified the transformation of rural peasants into an urban-
based proletariat class, as well as the appropriation of human (e.g.,
slaves) and material (e.g., cotton) resources from colonial countries,
Luxemburg argues that Marx treats these processes as "incidental"—the
travails by which the capitalist mode of production emerges from a
feudal society.

Her critique was that these processes are indispensable for capital
accumulation. She writes:

Since capitalist production can develop fully *only* with complete
access to all territories and climes, it can no more confine itself
to the natural resources and productive forces of the temperate
zone than it can manage with white labour alone. Capital needs
other races to exploit territories where the white man cannot
work. (emphasis added)[54]

The essence of Luxemburg's polemic is that mature capitalism needs to
constantly expand across the globe for "untrammelled accumulation,"
and this impulse is the economic motivation for the colonial wars
between the super powers. For Luxemburg, the outcome is the dialectical phenomenon that mature capitalist countries provide ever-larger
markets for, and become increasingly dependent upon, one another,
yet they compete ruthlessly for trade relations with non-capitalist
countries.

Luxemburg's thesis takes it as axiomatic that long-term capital
accumulation can only be understood in the context of wider socio-
economic, political, and cultural factors that shape these processes. The
conditions for capital accumulation means "[c]apitalism must ... always
and everywhere fight a battle of annihilation against every historical form
of natural economy that it encounters, whether this is slave economy
... or patriarchal peasant economy."[55] Luxemburg's insight is that, to
develop, capitalism had to "set free" labor power from "primitive social

conditions,"[56] and she stresses the importance of consciousness influencing the women's liberation movement.[57] Luxemburg argued that the doctrine of free trade, rather than ensuring harmony between competing states, brought historical antagonism to the fore. Luxemburg writes:

> In reality, political power is nothing but a vehicle for the economic process. The conditions for the reproduction of capital provide the organic link between these two aspects of the accumulation of capital. The historic career of capitalism can only be appreciated by taking them together ... and thus capitalism prepares its own downfall under ever more violent contortions and convulsions.[58]

Luxemburg's reinterpretation of Marx's model wrongly supposed that capitalism must collapse once the entire globe had been colonized, indigenous societies annihilated, and capitalism installed. Her theory underestimated capitalism's ability to mutate within its own system, not just by boosting the workers' spending power, but by transforming non-market activities (e.g., health care, leisure, personal communications) into market ones.[59] Luxemburg's analysis remains relevant to current debates on the invasions of Iraq and Afghanistan and regime change, global inequality, the vulnerability of precarious labor in the digital economy, and the still unfolding story of a new arms race and international antagonism caused by free trade rivalries between the United States, China, Russia, and the European Union.[60]

Charlotte Perkins Gilman (1860–1935)

Charlotte Anna Perkins was born July 3, 1860, in Hartford, Connecticut. Through her father, Frederic Beecher Perkins, she was related to the reform-minded Beecher family, including Isabella Beecher Hooker, a famous suffragist, and Catharine Beecher, a writer and supporter of women's education.[61] Her father was a librarian, and her mother was a cultivated, musically gifted woman. Her father abandoned the family in 1859. The family became "charity relatives" who had to move often to get ahead of their unpaid bills.[62] To finance her education at the Rhode Island School of Design during the years 1878 to 1883, Perkins painted advertisements and gave drawing lessons. In 1884, she married fellow artist Charles Walter Stetson. Their daughter Katharine was born a year later. During this period, Charlotte experienced a "severe and continuous nervous breakdown leading to melancholia—and beyond."[63] In 1887, her condition worsened, and she decided that it was "better for that dear child to have separated parents than a lunatic mother";[64] she left Stetson and moved to California. Her mental breakdown is vividly portrayed in "The Yellow Wallpaper" (first published in January 1892).

In California, she became involved with politics, found emotional support with women, and developed a reputation as a writer and public speaker. In 1896, she was invited to Hull House. Her main contributions to social theory are found in *Women and Economics: The Economic Relation between Men and Women as a Factor in*

Charlotte Perkins Gilman was born in Hartford, Connecticut, in 1860. Like Friedrich Engels, she believed the nuclear family and home to be a site of women's oppression. Suffering from terminal breast cancer, she committed suicide in 1935.

Social Evolution (1898),[65] which was subsequently published in nine editions and translated into seven languages; *The Home: Its Work and Influence* (1903), also published in nine editions and translated into seven languages; *Human Work* (1904); and *The Man-Made World* (1911). In 1902, Perkins married Houghton Gilman, a New York lawyer, who supported her writing and speaking career. A year after her husband's death, and suffering with terminal breast cancer, she ended her own life on August 17, 1935.[66]

Perkins Gilman's Intellectual Influences

Perkins Gilman's writing reflects a unique intertwining of concepts from Marx, Engels, Darwinism, Durkheim, eugenics, Fabian socialism, the social gospel, Lester Ward's gynecocentric (woman-centered) theory, Bellamy nationalism, populism, progressivism, and, of course, feminism. Like Marx, she believes human labor defines what it means to be human, and social power is based on the male control of economic resources. Like Engels, she believes the nuclear family and home to be a site of women's oppression. Like Durkheim, she draws on the work of Herbert Spencer and adopts biological imagery to analyze the organization of society. More problematically, her interpretation of social Darwinism informs her racist views on African Americans[67] and underlies her many calls to improve the race by reforming social institutions. Eugenics, both positive and negative, underlies her call for women to choose partners who are most suited to breed fit children and her recommendation that defective criminals be sterilized. Her views on race and eugenics buttress the overt racism that was ubiquitous among the Anglo-American and European social elite in the 1880–1945 period.[68] Aspects of Fabian socialism and the social gospel also merge as she imagines that Christianity evolved into a socialist form, shorn of its patriarchal trappings. Perkins Gilman saw herself as a sociologist and was influenced by sociologists. Among these, Lester Ward was particularly important. Ward's theory of androcentric society, she writes, was "the most important that has been offered the world since the Theory of Evolution; and without exception the most important that has ever been put forward concerning women."[69] Jane Addams and the women of Hull House also influenced her, although she found their immersion in the lives of immigrants and the poor to be distasteful.

Work, Gender, and Family

Perkins Gilman emphasizes the centrality of human labor and women's subordination in the economic process. In her most scholarly work, *Women and Economics*, she presents her feminist analysis of capitalism. The following tour de force contains the most succinct statement of her thought:

> The general course of life shows the inexorable effect of conditions upon humanity. Of these conditions we share with other living things ... the material universe.... What we do, as well as what is done to us, makes us what we are. But beyond these forces, we come under the effect of a third set of conditions peculiar to our human status; namely, social conditions. In the organic interchanges, which constitute social life, we are affected to a degree beyond what is found even among the most gregarious of animals. This third factor, the social environment, is of enormous force as a modifier of human life. Throughout all these environing conditions ... economic necessities are most marked in their influence.... Under all the influence of this later and wider life, all the reactive effect of social institutions, the individual is still inexorably modified by his means of livelihood ... the daily processes of supplying economic needs.... In view of these facts, attention is now called to certain marked and peculiar economic conditions affecting the human race, and unparalleled in organic life. We

are the only animal species in which the female depends on the
male for food, the only animal species in which the sex-relation
is also an economic relation. With us an entire sex lives in a relation of economic dependence upon the other sex, and the economic relation is combined with the sex-relation.[70]

On the importance of human labor, she writes: "To do and to make not
only gives deep pleasure, but it is indispensable to healthy growth."[71] This
thought is a partial echo of Marx's, except that, for Perkins Gilman, a
change in women's economic relationships would transform their social
status and enable them to fulfill their creative potential. Such a change
would rectify the situation she described in which the social status of
women in society was achieved through the paid work of their men rather
than because of women's own labor.

Perkins Gilman is best known for her critique of the nuclear family,
and Engels and Durkheim influenced her thinking here. Like Engels,
she puts the nuclear family at the center of women's subordination and
exploitation. In *The Origins of the Family, Private Property, and the State*
(1884), Friedrich Engels wrote the following:

The modern individual family is based on the open or disguised
domestic enslavement of the woman; and modern society is a
mass composed solely of individual families as its molecules.
Today, in the great majority of cases the man has to be the earner,
the breadwinner of the family, at least among the propertied
classes, and this gives him a dominating position which requires
no special legal privileges. In the family, he is the bourgeois; the
wife represents the proletariat.[72]

Although Engels's analysis has been criticized for its "one-sided economic determinism," it appears to have shaped Perkins Gilman's thought
on the issue. Applying Durkheimian concepts to unpaid domestic labor
and childcare, Perkins Gilman argues that the specialization of labor
is the basis of female emancipation and human progress. She argues
that most women are essentially unskilled, unpaid laborers. Traditional
housekeeping practices based on custom produce inefficient households.
She argues that specialized occupations and training exist for cooking,
cleaning, childcare, and health care, and, therefore, housekeeping should
be professionalized too: "done by trained specialists with proper organization and mechanical conveniences, we could release the labor power
of 80 percent of our women."[73] She also advocates community childcare.

Charlotte Perkins Gilman is best known for her critique of the nuclear family, which, she argues, is the center of women's subordination and exploitation. Taken during Perkins Gilman's lifetime, this photograph shows a British coal miner washing after a shift and his wife pouring warm water in a metal bath. The life of a miner's wife was hard: unremitting housework, childbearing, and providing for husbands and children on a subsistence wage took a physical toll.

In other words, Perkins Gilman argues for the family to be socialized.[74]

Her journal *The Forerunner* (1909–18) was used to propagate her views on racial progress through increased procreative fitness. For Perkins Gilman, the ideal marriage, in accordance with the laws of evolution, occurs when a woman who has developed herself mentally and physically chooses a male who will be the best father for her child.

When men do most of the choosing, she notes, they tend to select women who are weak and good looking rather than racially fit to produce and raise children.[75] In lines that echo Wollstonecraft's discussion of excessive sex differentiation, Perkins Gilman argues "our civilized 'feminine delicacy'" should be seen as "less delicate when recognized as an expression of sexuality in excess." She writes, "The degree of feebleness and clumsiness common to women, the comparative inability to stand, walk, run, jump, climb, and perform other race-functions common to both sexes, is an excessive sex-distinction; and the ensuing transmission of this relative feebleness to their children, boys and girls alike, retards human development."[76]

Like Wollstonecraft, Perkins Gilman believed that women should be educated to take their place as leaders in society. A really feminine society, she argued, would accord women "freedom and knowledge; the knowledge which is power."[77] She expressed many of her ideas by inventing parallel worlds that satirically exposed social problems.[78] In the first of these, *Moving the Mountain* (1911), the narrator is a male who has come back to the United States after being lost in Tibet for 30 years. He finds a society in which men and women work just two hours a day. Meals are ordered from a specialized kitchen instead of made at home. Childcare is shared. Women are not willing to marry sexually promiscuous, abusive, or drunken men, and so those vices have been wiped out. When asked how this wonderful change came about, he is repeatedly told that it happened because of a change in women's consciousness: "the women woke up."[79] As with Martineau and Addams, Perkins Gilman endeavored to reach the public with accessible materials that would challenge existing social practices.

Criticism

Classical feminist social theory may have been subject to some of the weaknesses of "male-stream" classical theorizing. The first weakness is that, in their concern to reveal the social sources of women's subordination, some of the early feminists tended to neglect the effect of class inequality. It's argued, for example, that in a society in which men monopolize paid work and women lack economic independence, the call for gender equality in education leads to what has been called "Wollstonecraft's dilemma."[80] That is, equality enables women to be treated and valued equally only to the extent that they can behave like men. This, of course, ignores the ways in which women's domestic responsibilities restrict their ability to compete for employment and how patriarchal strategies have historically excluded women from certain occupations,[81] which leaves women dependent on the goodwill of men to "snap their chains."[82] The classical "liberal" feminist theorists have also been criticized for their uncritical acceptance of an inherently male model of rationality and their portrayal of women's subordination as universal, when in reality their perspective reflects middle-class, white, Anglo-American women's experiences of subordination. More specifically, Perkins Gilman's work has been criticized for its ethnocentricity, elitism, and racism.[83]

Perhaps with the exception of Rosa Luxemburg and Perkins Gilman, the early feminists' analysis of man-made obstacles facing women does not take into account agency, that is, the creative potential of all members of society, irrespective of class, gender, or race, to understand, learn, adapt, and transform their social context. This perspective leads to a third criticism: that they underplayed the effects of power relationships and social structures in capitalist societies, which limit choice and, importantly, perpetuate inequality.[84] Postmodernists are familiar with the notion that some voices are more equal than others, particularly those in positions of power. If we want to know, then, why female contributions have been written out of histories of classical social theory, we should examine not the content of the theory but the politics of class and gender and the resources with which the theory is disseminated. By this account, it's unsurprising that early feminist thought was erased from popular consciousness for many decades.

Conclusion

Our selection of pioneering works by early feminist thinkers extends the classical social canon—and challenges all theorizing about and research on modernity that neglects gender relations. Theoretically, one of the most important corollaries of feminist sociological theorizing on modernity is its power to question the adequacy of perspectives that neglect exploitation, inequality, conflicts, and contradictions that cannot be readily subsumed under class. These early feminist theorists developed a sophisticated analysis of the nature of society and the interplay between gender relations and power. Mary Wollstonecraft, applying Enlightenment principles, emphasizes that the historical subjugation of women is connected to male desire for social power. Harriet Martineau highlights contradictions in the American Declaration of Independence, demonstrating how gender- and race-based inequality in education have resulted in the exclusion of women and African Americans from full participation in society. Through her analysis of mature imperialism, Rosa Luxemburg emphasizes the importance of consciousness for the feminist movement. Charlotte Perkins Gilman challenges the romantic view of the nuclear family, explaining how it obscures the oppression of women. Early feminist thought has helped successive generations of feminist thinkers to critically examine the position of women in modernity.

It is arguable that our choice of Wollstonecraft, Martineau, Luxemburg, and Perkins Gilman simply maintains a bias that has already begun. Certainly there are many other founding mothers of social theory.[85] There are also the contributions of men, such as Friedrich Engels's *Origins of the Family* and W.E.B. Du Bois's (1868–1963) Hegelian analysis of the distinctive life experience of black men *and* women. There is little doubt, however, that the female writers discussed in this chapter helped to develop the structural perspective on social problems and had impact on the overall development of sociological theory in a critical, often pragmatic, way. It is also possible that their marginalization from mainstream sociology restricted that impact. One hundred years after some women in Britain secured the right to vote, many of these feminist thinkers have been rediscovered, and their intellectual endeavors have become a recognized model in the field.[86]

FURTHER THINKING:

What is the meaning of the term "Wollstonecraft's dilemma"? In the light of the #MeToo movement, to what extent does Wollstonecraft's dilemma remain a feature of gender relations today?

FURTHER READING:

Reliable introductions to the study of feminist theorizing and gender are Victoria Robinson and Diane Richardson's *Introduction to Gender and Women's Studies*, 4th ed. (London: Palgrave, 2015); and Valerie Bryson's *Feminist Political Theory* (Basingstoke, UK: Palgrave, 2003). For a very contemporary exploration of Wollstonecraft's Dilemma, showing how neoliberalism can actually act in tandem with cultural conservatism to shape social order where traditional gender norms are reasserted and impair parity of participation, see Ayse Bugra's "Revisiting the Wollstonecraft Dilemma in the Context of Conservative Liberalism: The Case of Female Employment in Turkey," *Social Politics: International Studies in Gender, State & Society* 21, no. 1 (2014): 148–66. Finally, an accessible introduction to the works of Rosa Luxemburg is Helen Scott, *Rosa Luxemburg: Reform or Revolution* (Chicago: Haymarket Books, 2008). The film *Rosa Luxemburg* (1986), directed by Margarethe von Trotha, traces Luxemburg's political and moral development from journalist, Marxist economist to revolutionary leader and imprisoned pacifist. The film is available online with English subtitles at http://archive .org/details/RosaLuxemburg. A review of the film is available at https://www.nytimes.com/1987/05/01/movies/film-rosa-luxemburg -new-light-on-early-leftist.html.

Notes

1 Rebecca McQuillan, "Women at the Top: The Truth about the Sexist Backlash," *The Sunday Herald*, July, 9, 2017, 23–24.

2 Mike Davis, *Old Gods, New Enigmas* (London: Verso, 2018), 65.

3 See R.A. Sydie, *Natural Women, Cultured Men* (Vancouver: University of British Columbia Press, 1994), 13.

4 Sydie, *Natural Women, Cultured Men*, 54.

5 Among others we could have included are Mary Astell, Ida B. Wells, Anna Julia Cooper, Mary McLeod Bethune, Rosa Parks, Daisy Bates, Septima Clark, Ella Baker, Nellie McClung, Marianne Weber, and Beatrice Potter Webb.

6 Mary Wollstonecraft, *A Vindication of the Rights of Woman*, ed. Miriam Brody (London: Penguin, 2004).

7 Valerie Bryson, *Feminist Political Theory* (Basingstoke, UK: Palgrave, 2003), 9.

8 See Tony Benn, "The Levellers and the English Democratic Tradition," in *Tony Benn: Arguments for Socialism*, ed. Chris Mullin (London: Jonathan Cape, 1979), 29–39.

9 Wollstonecraft, *A Vindication of the Rights of Woman*, 48.

10 Wollstonecraft, *A Vindication of the Rights of Woman*, 15.

11 Wollstonecraft, *A Vindication of the Rights of Woman*, 183.

12 Jean-Jacques Rousseau, "Sophy, or Woman," *Emile*, trans. Barbara Foxley (1762; London: Dent, 1911), Bk. 5, http://www.gutenberg.org/ebooks/5427.

13 Wollstonecraft, *A Vindication of the Rights of Woman*, 81.

14 Moira Ferguson, *Colonialism and Gender Relations from Mary Wollstonecraft to Jamaica Kincaid* (New York: Columbia University Press, 1993), 22.

15 Wollstonecraft, *A Vindication of the Rights of Woman*, 167, and quoted in Ferguson, *Colonialism and Gender Relations*, 22.

16 Harriet Martineau, *Harriet Martineau's Autobiography*, ed. Maria Weston Chapman, 3 vols. (1877; Boston: James R. Osgood & Company, 2007), 1:305.

17 Martineau, *Harriet Martineau's Autobiography*, 1:99.

18 Martineau, *Harriet Martineau's Autobiography*, 1:126.

19 Martineau, *Harriet Martineau's Autobiography*, 1:126.

20 Martineau, *Harriet Martineau's Autobiography*, 1:113.

21 Harriet Martineau, *Illustrations of Political Economy*, 3rd ed., 9 vols. (London: Charles Fox, 1832), http://oll.libertyfund.org/title/1686.

22 Harriet Martineau, *How to Observe Morals and Manners* (1838; New Brunswick, NJ: Transaction Books, 1989). Original publication available online: Harriet Martineau, *How to Observe Morals and Manners* (London: Charles Knight, 1838), http://www.archive.org/details/howtoobservemor00martgoog.

23 Harriet Martineau, *Society in America*, ed. S.M. Lipset (1837; Garden City, NY: Doubleday Anchor 1962). Original publication available online: Harriet Martineau, *Society in America*, 2 vols. (New York: Saunders and Otley, 1837), http://www.archive.org/details/societyinameric02martgoog.

24 Harriet Martineau, *Retrospect of Western Travel*, 3 vols. (London: Saunders and Otley, 1838), http://oll.libertyfund.org/title/1876.

25 Martineau, *Harriet Martineau's Autobiography*, 3:457–58.

26 Martineau, *Harriet Martineau's Autobiography*, 1:85.

27 Martineau, *Harriet Martineau's Autobiography*, 1:127.

28 Jeremy Bentham, *The Works of Jeremy Bentham*, 11 vols., published under the Superintendence of his Executor, John Bowring (Edinburgh: William Tait, 1843), Section 8: "The greatest happiness of the greatest number requires—that such original draught, being the work of a single hand, be known to be so. Hand, known to be but one." http://oll.libertyfund.org/title/1925/116886 (accessed March 22, 2008).

29 Martineau, *How to Observe Morals and Manners*, 214.

30 Martineau, *Society in America*, 2:155–86.

31 Martineau, *How to Observe Morals and Manners*, 13.

32 Martineau, *How to Observe Morals and Manners*, 11.

33 Martineau, *How to Observe Morals and Manners*, 129.

34 Martineau, *Society in America*, 1: Section 7; see also http://xroads.virginia.edu/~hyper/detoc/fem/martineau.htm.

35 Martineau, *Harriet Martineau's Autobiography*, 1:405–6.

36 Martineau, *Harriet Martineau's Autobiography*, vol. 2.

37 Martineau, *Harriet Martineau's Autobiography*, 2:305.

38 Harriet Martineau, *Eastern Life, Present and Past* (New York: Kessinger Publishing Company, 2007).

39 Patricia M. Lengermann and Gillian Niebrugge, "Early Women Sociologists and Classical Sociological Theory: 1830–1930," in *Classical Sociological Theory*, 5th ed., ed. George Ritzer (New York: McGraw-Hill, 2008), 301.

40 Tariq Ali, *The Dilemmas of Lenin* (London: Verso, 2017), 348.

41 Sheila Rowbotham, "The Revolutionary Rosa N," *The Guardian*, March 5, 2011, https://www.theguardian.com/books/2011/mar/05/rosa-luxemburg-writer-activist-letters.

42 Helen Scott, *Rosa Luxemburg: Reform or Revolution* (Chicago: Haymarket Books, 2008), 2.

43 Ali, *The Dilemmas of Lenin*, 130.

44 Quoted in Scott, *Rosa Luxemburg: Reform or Revolution*, 25.

45 Rowbotham, "The Revolutionary Rosa N."

46 Scott, *Rosa Luxemburg: Reform or Revolution*, 5.

47 Scott, *Rosa Luxemburg: Reform or Revolution*, 5.

48 Ali, *The Dilemmas of Lenin*, 288.

49 Rowbotham, "The Revolutionary Rosa N."

50 Ali, *The Dilemmas of Lenin*, 270.

51 Scott, *Rosa Luxemburg: Reform or Revolution*, 30.

52 Paul Mason, *Postcapitalism: A Guide to Our Future* (London: Penguin, 2016), 61.

53 Rosa Luxemburg, *The Accumulation of Capital* (1913; London: Routledge, 2003), 328.

54 Luxemburg, *The Accumulation of Capital*, 342–43.

55 Luxemburg, *The Accumulation of Capital*, 349.

56 Luxemburg, *The Accumulation of Capital*, 343.

57 Rowbotham, "The Revolutionary Rosa N."

58 Luxemburg, *The Accumulation of Capital*, 433.

59 For a more detailed review of Luxemburg's argument, see Paul Mason, *Postcapitalism*, 58–63; Anthony Brewer, *Marxist Theories of Imperialism: A Critical Survey* (London: Routledge, 1980), 61–76.

60 Mikhail Gorbachev, "Mikhail Gorbachev: A New Nuclear Arms Race Has Begun," *The New York Times*, October 25, 2018, https://www.nytimes.com/2018/10/25/opinion/mikhail-gorbachev-inf-treaty-trump-nuclear-arms.html.

61 Catharine Esther Beecher, *A Treatise on Domestic Economy for the Use of Young Ladies at Home and at School* (New York: Harper, 1834). Digital version available from www.gutenberg.org/etext/21829.

62 Charlotte Perkins Gilman, *The Living of Charlotte Perkins Gilman: An Autobiography* (1935; New York: Harper & Row, 1975), 8–9.

63 Charlotte Perkins Gilman, "Why I Wrote the Yellow Wallpaper," *The Forerunner* (October 1913): 19–20, http://www.nlm.nih.gov/literatureofprescription/exhibitionAssets/digitalDocs/WhyIWroteYellowWallPaper.pdf.

64 Gilman, *The Living of Charlotte Perkins Gilman*, 97.

65 Charlotte Perkins Gilman, *Women and Economics: The Economic Relation Between Men and Women as a Factor in Social Evolution* (1898; New York: Harper & Row, 1966), http://digital.library.upenn.edu/women/gilman/economics/economics.html.

66 Denise D. Knight, "The Dying of Charlotte Perkins Gilman," *American Transcendental Quarterly* 6, no. 1 (1999): 137–59.

67 Kenneth H. Tucker, *Classical Social Theory: A Contemporary Approach* (Malden, MA: Blackwell, 2002), 240.

68   See, for example, Robert A. Nye, "The Rise and Fall of the Eugenics Empire: Recent Perspectives on the Impact of Bio-Medical Thought in Modern Society," *The Historical Journal* 36, no. 3 (1993): 687–700.

69   Charlotte Perkins Gilman, *The Forerunner*, vol. 1 (1909–10), www.fullbooks.com /The-Forerunner-Volume-1-1909-1910-2.html.

70   Gilman, *Women and Economics*, 1–5.

71   Gilman, *Women and Economics*, 157.

72   Robert C. Tucker, ed., *The Marx-Engels Reader*, 2nd ed. (New York: Norton, 1972), 744.

73   Gilman, *The Living of Charlotte Perkins Gilman*, 127.

74   Tucker, *Classical Social Theory*, 247.

75   Gilman, *The Forerunner*, 1:9.

76   Gilman, *The Forerunner*, 1:9.

77   Gilman, *The Forerunner*, 1:9.

78   Minna Doskow, ed., *Charlotte Perkins Gilman's Utopian Novels: Moving the Mountain, Herland, and With Her in Ourland* (Madison & Teaneck, NJ: Fairleigh Dickinson University Press, 1999).

79   Quotation is from Gilman's *Moving the Mountain*; see Doskow, *Charlotte Perkins Gilman's Utopian Novels*, 17, 65.

80   See Carole Pateman, "The Patriarchal Welfare State," in *Democracy and the Welfare State*, ed. Amy Gutmann (Princeton, NJ: Princeton University Press, 1988), 231–60, and cited in Bryson, *Feminist Political Theory*, 18.

81   See David Knights and Hugh Willmott, eds., *Gender and the Labour Process* (Aldershot, UK: Gower, 1986).

82   Wollstonecraft, *A Vindication of the Rights of Woman*, 263, and quoted in Bryson, *Feminist Political Theory*, 18.

83   Alys Eve Weinbaum, "Writing Feminist Genealogy: Charlotte Perkins Gilman, Racial Nationalism, and the Reproduction of Maternalist Feminism," *Feminist Studies* 27, no. 2 (2001): 201–19.

84   See, for example, R.W. Connell, *Gender and Power* (Cambridge: Polity Press, 1987).

85   Mary Jo Deegan, ed., *Women in Sociology: A Bio-Bibliographical Sourcebook* (New York: Greenwood Press, 1991).

86   For more recent assessments of the place of early feminist social theorists, see the American Sociological Association Task Force on Institutionalizing Public Sociologies, *Public Sociology and the Roots of American Sociology: Re-Establishing Our Connections to the Public* (Washington, DC: American Sociological Association Council, 2005), http://www.asanet.org/images/asa/docs /pdf/TFonPSRpt(54448).pdf; John L. Gillin, "The Development of Sociology in the United States," Presidential Address, presented at the annual meeting of the American Sociological Association, St. Louis, December 1926, http://www.asanet. org/images/asa/docs/pdf/1926PresidentialAddress(Gillin).pdf; *Marxists Internet Archive Library of Feminist Writers*, http://www.marxists.org/subject/women /feminists.htm; and Harry Perlstadt, *Sociology as Translational Research: A One Hundred Fifty Year Voyage*, unpublished paper available from Michigan State University, www.msu.edu/~perlstad/History_Applied_Sociology_H_Perlstadt _Jun_05.pdf.

14. W.E.B Du Bois on Race

The intellectual who best understood his times, and who created new methods for analyzing race and racism, was W.E.B. Du Bois.
—Manning Marable (2011)[1]

Soul music is based on suffering and sorrow. I don't know anyone who has had more of those two devils than the Negro.
—Aretha Franklin (1970)[2]

IN MAY 2018, TWITTER BUZZED TWO PHRASES, #RoyalWedding and #BlackExcellence about the British ritual—a wedding of the Queen's grandson—that would have been unthinkable in the age of the classical theorists. At this wedding of Prince Harry and Meghan Markle, talented black people were more than decoration. The presiding bishop of the US Episcopal church, Michael Curry, a campaigner for racial justice and LGBT rights, delivered the sermon, which entwined the legacy of slavery with African American culture into the heart of the British establishment. A black gospel choir sang a rendition of Ben E. King's "Stand By Me," and the couple chose 19-year-old cellist Sheku Kanneh-Mason to perform at the pageant. However, after the TV crews drive off and the confetti is swept away, race and racism still divide Britain and the United States. A 2017 UK government audit on race equality revealed "deeply ingrained disparities across the country,"[3] and a separate report concluded there is "overt racial prejudice in the [British] criminal justice system."[4] On the other side of the Atlantic, civil rights protestor Heather Heyer was killed in 2017 when a car driven by a neo-Nazi activist rammed into a group of people protesting against a white supremacy rally in Charlottesville, Virginia. Since Donald Trump became president of the United States, overt displays of white supremacy and racism have intensified, prompting a UN committee to urge the Trump administration to "unequivocally and unconditionally" reject racial discrimination.[5] African Americans are far more likely than white Americans to be stopped, arrested, jailed, shot, and executed by the state.[6] The United States does not have a monopoly on racism in society, however. For example, in 2012, the Ontario Human Rights Commission reported the persistence of racism in Canadian society. In releasing its annual report, the chief commissioner, Barbara Hall, said, "There's some really persistent issues: anti-black racism and discrimination towards aboriginal peoples."[7] Although the history of black people in Canada and Britain has followed a different trajectory to that of the United States, issues concerning racial discrimination, racial inequality, and racial strife have a powerful urgency in the early twenty-first century.

This chapter further extends the sociological canon to make society intelligible in terms of race, through the writings of American's pre-eminent African American scholar, William Edward Burghardt Du Bois (1868–1963). His social theory brings to prominence the issue of race that is largely invisible in sociology's classical canon drawn up by white men. He exposed deep-seated racism in American society and the close relationship between race, slavery, and capitalism through an enormous body of work spanning six decades, including books, sociological studies, autobiography, poetry, essays, short stories, and political commentary. Du Bois is best known in sociology for his early works, *The Philadelphia Negro* (1899/1996) and *The Souls of Black Folk* (1903/1994), in which he discusses the interplay of race and class in American society. However, Du Bois was a social theorist, a political activist, and a prominent member of the early black protest intelligentsia largely responsible for analyzing race and racism and envisioning a new social order.[8] As such, he was an iconic leader who influenced other black intellectuals and activists in the Black Freedom Movement. Du Bois's sociology is multifaceted and remains influential within contemporary sociology as well as other disciplines. The chapter begins by examining the context that shaped his life and works and proceeds by examining some of his central concepts, in particular his analysis of the interplay between capitalism, race, and racism and his work on the double consciousness and cultural hybridity.

His Life and Works

W.E.B. Du Bois was born in 1868 in rural Great Barrington, Massachusetts. He was the only son of Mary Silva Burghardt, a domestic servant, and Alfred Du Bois, a barber and itinerant laborer of Haitian descent. Although he had a privileged education compared to the vast majority of African Americans, at an early age he experienced rampant racism. He studied at Fisk University and later at Harvard University, with a spell at the Friedrich Wilhelm University in Berlin in 1892 and 1893. He was the first African American to receive a PhD from Harvard. His sophisticated analysis of race and racism was controversial; he was excluded from the canonized process in sociology and, despite his distinctive contribution to sociological theory at a time when the university system in American was expanding at an unparalleled rate,[9] he was denied a full-time academic position at the Ivy League schools. Du Bois died, with ironic timing, in Accra, Ghana, in 1963, just hours before Martin Luther King, Jr. delivered his historic "I Have a Dream" speech at the March on Washington, DC. His career problems were, in addition to racial discrimination, partly due to his tireless political activism. In 1905, Du Bois co-founded the Niagara Movement, a civil rights organization, which challenged the more accommodating and subservient policies of black educator Booker T. Washington. In 1910, when the National Association of Colored People (NAACP) was established, he edited its monthly publication, *The Crisis*, the most influential Black political journal of its time.[10] Over the years, Du Bois visited the Soviet Union and joined the Communist Party of America.

His passport was revoked for years, his books were widely banned from American libraries, the FBI harassed him, and he was arrested for "subversive" activities in 1951. Despite being vilified by American social elites, Du Bois attained international recognition for his intellectual and political leadership in Western Europe, the former Soviet Union, Africa, and China.

We have followed the traditional approach among British (e.g., Giddens, 1971), Canadian (e.g., Zeitland, 1968), and American (e.g., Nisbet, 1970)

W.E.B. Du Bois was born in 1868 in Great Barrington, Massachusetts, USA. His books were widely banned from American libraries. An intellectual leader in the American black movement, in 1944, he was forcibly retired at Atlanta University. He moved to Accra, Ghana, where he died in 1963.

sociologists to contend that social theory was in large part a response to the historically unique chemistry of economic and social transformations in Western Europe. In Du Bois's case, his social theory was written during what are arguably the three most significant socio-economic crises in the history of America: the internal migration of black workers from the rural southern states to the urban North in the decades following the Civil War (1861–65); the industrialization of the economy along with the mass influx of European immigrants; and the growth of the Civil Rights movement. In addition, his sociology is indubitably related in complex ways to global events such as the rise of socialism in Europe and the Bolshevik Revolution in Russia in 1917 that inspired the development of radical politics inside America, and to national events such as legalized racial segregation and the growth of membership of America's most notorious "terrorist organization," the Ku Klux Klan.[11]

Through racial vignettes and poetry Du Bois showed that racism took different forms: bigotry and discrimination in the North and disenfranchisement and mob lynching in the South. The virulence and horror of racism in the South is illustrated by one statistic: between 1900 and 1935 there were an estimated 1,374 lynchings, that is, an average of 39 per year.[12] During his long life, the United States was involved in four global wars: World War I (1914–18), World War II (1939–45), the Korean War (1950–53), and the Vietnam War (1959–75). Assessing these developments, Manning Marable wrote, "These turbulent social currents impacted Du Bois as an intellectual and as an important leader of opinion of an oppressed people."[13]

As an academic and opinion leader, Du Bois authored more than 1,900 works of one sort or another including books, essays, poems, and opinion pieces.[14] In 1896, he was appointed as assistant instructor at the University of Pennsylvania to do research on the black community in Philadelphia. The research resulted in his first book, *The Philadelphia Negro* (1899/1996), a classic ethnographic study that established the field of urban sociology. From 1897 to 1910, he taught sociology at Atlanta University. During this period he published the first of his autobiographical memoirs, *The Souls of Black Folk* (1903/1994). From 1910 to 1943, he edited *The Crisis*, and in its pages authored many essays on a wide range of issues on the state of African Americans. He also authored the second of his autobiographical memoirs, *Darkwater: Voices from Within the Veil* (1920/1999). After 33 years editing *The Crisis*, he returned to Atlanta University and published *Black Reconstruction in America 1860–1880* (1935/1998), which offered a revision of Marx's theory of class consciousness and class struggle. Du Bois stayed at Atlanta University until 1944, when he was forcibly retired by senior administration.

Du Boisian sociology is multidimensional, historical, and socioculturally sensitive. For Du Bois, a social problem transcends its immediate locale but is ever intertwined in complex ways between history, social condition, and social action. In 1898 he wrote: "It is not *one* problem, but rather a plexus of social problems ... and these problems have their one bond of unity in the act that they group themselves about those Africans whom two centuries of slave-trading brought into the land."[15] Thus, his classic analysis of the African diaspora in America made the distinction between the personal problems of milieu and the societal issues of social structure. In this sense, Du Bois possessed what C.W. Mills (1959/2000) legendarily called a "sociological imagination."[16] His scholarship is grounded in his experience of life in America within "the Veil," the famous metaphor he used to symbolize the specter of American apartheid and racism. In *Souls*, he wrote: "And, finally, need I add that I who speak here am bone of the bone and flesh of the flesh of them that live within the Veil?"[17]

Intellectual Influences

Du Bois studied with leading scholars at Harvard University and the Friedrich Wilhelm University in Berlin. During his time at Harvard, he describes how the intellectual milieu caused him to "turn ... back from the lonely but sterile land of philosophic speculation, to the social sciences as the field for gathering and interpreting that body of fact which would apply to my program for the Negro."[18] At Harvard, Du Bois had little exposure to Marx's work.[19] After his appointment with the NAACP, he began to read Marx's work. He wrote, for example, "I believe in the dictum of Karl Marx, that the economic foundation of a nation is widely decisive for its politics, in art and its culture."[20] The influence of Marx, in particular *The Communist Manifesto*, is evident in the following declaration to the Africa and Pan-African Movement: "You have nothing to lose but your Chains!"[21] The mature Du Bois adopted a Marxian view that, ultimately, "without the overthrow of capitalist monopoly the Negro cannot survive in the United States as a self-respecting cultural unit."[22]

The radicalization of Du Bois, from a cautious critic to a militant activist, is attributed to William M. Trotter (1872–1934), Du Bois's Harvard class peer.[23] As was the fashion in the late nineteenth century among other early American sociologists, however, Du Bois visited European universities, and his early scholarship does reflect his sojourn at the Friedrich Wilhelm University. As a student of Gustav Schmoller (1838–1917), Du Bois drew from the philosophical tradition of Hegelian phenomenology[24] and adopted Durkheimian positivism. He wrote, "I ... began to grasp the idea of a world of human beings whose actions, like those of the physical world, were subject to law."[25] Another intellectual influence was Max Weber. Like Weber, Du Bois recognizes the importance of "value-free" research. However, as a leader of African American intellectual thought, his work had origins independent of the impulses of Western liberal and radical thought.[26] Thus, the majority of his essays did not exhibit a value-free perspective, a feature he shared with Marx. The mature Du Bois denounces the "wicked conquest" of "darker" races by white races, but "with the purpose of saving both them and world civilization from themselves."[27] As Lewis opines, although Du Bois "professed a commitment to objective social science, he was temperamentally incapable of neutrality."[28]

American Capitalism, Ideology, and Race

The transformation of the United States, from an agrarian frontier society to an industrial and military global superpower that dislodged Britain as the world's hegemonic industrial nation, provided the empirical backdrop to Du Bois's analysis of race and his sociology. In 1840 America was predominantly an agricultural society with less than 10 percent of the labor force employed in manufacturing.[29] Over four decades, a period when "Dead Indians are a common feature,"[30] the "frontier" was privatized, a national railroad system was established, and aboriginal peoples were relocated on reservations as white settlers developed the West. As one observer put it, "in less than fifty years an isolationist, agrarian society transformed itself into an internationally aggressive, economically imperialist, industrial nation."[31] Economic growth served to reinforce the idea that America was the "land of opportunity" for all, regardless of class. The national ideology was popularized by terms such as "the American Dream," in spite of its contradiction. As Edgell (2000) argues, "Notwithstanding ... this 'dream' was flawed from the outset by the virtue of the ethnic cleansing of the continent's native peoples in less than four centuries and the institution of slavery, and can be shown to be empirically suspect."[32] That race and racism played a central role in early US modernity cannot be overemphasized.

    With the exception of Thorstein Veblen (1857–1929), early sociologists in America tended to celebrate rather than critique the triumph of American capitalism.[33] Like Marx, Du Bois was highly critical of colonialism that, in essence, believed "[i]t is the duty of white Europe to divide up the darker world and administer it for Europe's good."[34] *Darkwater* emphasized that colonialism and racial inequality cannot be understood without analyzing the role of ideology. The ideology of "white supremacy" was a relatively recent social construct associated

with legitimizing colonialism and slavery. The ideas among the dominant
and oppressing elite were that

> [d]arker peoples are dark in mind as well as in body; of dark,
> uncertain, and imperfect descent; of frailer, cheaper stuff; they
> are cowards in the face of mausers and maxims; they have no
> feelings, aspirations, and loves; they are fools, illogical idiots—
> "half-devil and half-child."[35]

This leads Du Bois to assert that these ideas have penetrated into the
national psyche with a thoroughness that few realized: "Everything great,
good, efficient, fair, and honorable is 'white'; everything mean, bad, blun-
dering, cheating, and dishonorable is 'yellow'; a bad taste is 'brown';
and the devil is 'black.'"[36] In *Black Reconstruction in America,* Du Bois
identified the fundamental contradiction in American history:

> From the day of its birth, the anomaly of slavery plagued a nation
> which asserted the equality of all men, and sought to derive pow-
> ers of government from the consent of the governed.[37]

For Du Bois, American slavery was a subsystem of world capitalism.[38]
Although Du Bois privileged race, as Lemert (2003) rightly observes, his
most distinctive theoretical conviction was that race never stands alone,
separate from economic realities.[39]

In *The Philadelphia Negro* Du Bois built up a meticulous picture of
how African Americans survived the social effects of mass immigration,
industrialization, and race discrimination. Importantly, he directly linked
the low economic class and status of African Americans to mass immigration, world capitalism, and racism. In his prose:

> Every one knows that in a city like Philadelphia a Negro does
> not have the same chances to exercise his [sic] ability or secure
> work according to his talents as a white man ... work open to
> Negroes are not only restricted by their own lack of training but
> also by discrimination against them on account of their race.[40]

Weber's influence is most evident in Du Bois's analysis of African
Americans' "life chances." He argued that African Americans are disadvantaged because they lacked the relevant training and skills for the
new factory work. For Du Bois, economic exploitation was difficult to
disentangle from racial oppression. The economic exploitation facing
African Americans was rooted in the legacy of enslavement.

The ideas of Du Bois provide theoretical space for examining the interplay of class and race, the intersection of racial segregation and poverty. According to Du Bois, black Americans' exclusion from the new industries was mostly attributed, explicitly and implicitly, to white Americans' prejudice and structural racism, but Du Bois develops a more structural theory of class, race, and poverty. Whereas in *Conditions* Engels saw the Industrial Revolution developing "a definite class," in *Capital* Marx envisioned the new working-class developing a "class consciousness," and in *Economy and Society* Weber called attention to the distinction between class and status, in *The Philadelphia Negro* Du Bois pioneered the way toward further "complexifying" class by emphasizing that race-based discrimination divides the working class, which results in economic self-harm and acts as a barrier to developing liberating social movements. Race-based discrimination took different forms, in some cases by direct discrimination when, for example, "white" was listed as a qualification for entry into a particular trade. In other cases, black workers were excluded from manual trades because white workers simply refused to work alongside non-union men but they also refused to let black workers join the union. In most cases, writes Du Bois, unions "invariably fail to admit a colored applicant except under pressing circumstances."[41]

In *Black Reconstruction in America* Du Bois analyzed the interlocking constructs of class exploitation, class struggle, and racism. For Du Bois, the American "white" class struggle had been effectively distorted and thwarted by the ideological power of racism and the seductiveness of the myth of the "American Dream."[42] He argued that race never stands alone, and exclusion therefore had an economic motive that impacted the labor market. Du Bois observed:

> So today the workmen plainly see that a large amount of competition can be shut off by taking advantage of public opinion and drawing the color-line. Moreover, in this there is one thoroughly justifiable consideration that plays a great part: namely, the Negroes are used to low wages—can live on them, and consequently would fight less fiercely than most whites against reduction.[43]

In this anarchy, working-class African Americans are reduced to laboring for a pittance or abject poverty when unemployed. It is in *Souls*, however, that we find one of the most powerful statements on the interplay of class exploitation and race. Here, Du Bois cites the ruminations of an old Southern black man: "White man sit down whole year; Nigger work day and night and make crop; Nigger hardly gits bread and meat; white man sittin' down gits all. *It's wrong*."[44] That race-based discriminations and class-based exploitation are central to an understanding of early American capitalism is another of Du Bois's contribution to social theory. He was among the first sociologists to document that the economic progress of the American working class as a whole was held back because of racism; that racist constructs thwart working-class consciousness and organization. Du Bois offers a complex model of class. In Weberian sociology, African Americans exemplify the interplay of class and status but Du Bois's pioneering contribution was to emphasize the historical embeddedness of racial status, which is entwined with but distinct from class.

Race and the Classic Veil

In contrast to the other classical theorists we have discussed, Du Bois's sociology privileged race. Race was, of course, at the root of what he famously called the "Negro Problem," or the antipathies and frictions between white and black Americans resulting from the social segregation—the "color-line"—of the races. In *Souls* his focus was the rupture of nearly all social relations between black and white in the United States in general, and in the South in particular, which, despite some changes in economic and civil affairs, left that "frightful chasm at the color-line across which men pass at their peril" to remain.[45] Du Bois, however, came to see racial segregation as a global phenomenon and called for "the British Negro, the French Negro, and the American Negro to rise."[46] His broader international focus on race led to an increasing number of polemical essays on world human rights.[47]

For Du Bois, "race" as a deeply historical and social construct functioned as a key part of his sociology and political writings, from the struggle against segregation and structured racism to class exploitation to self-identity to Pan-African politics. As we discussed in chapter 1, race is a multidimensional concept. According to Sundquist (1996), Du Bois never quite discarded the prevailing nineteenth-century view that race alluded to biological distinctions and nationhood. In an early polemical essay, "The Conservation of Races" (1897), Du Bois speaks of the universal prevalence of the "race spirit" and its importance for nation building, arguing that the "history of the world is the history, not of individuals ... but of races."[48] This is followed by his definition of race: "a vast family of human beings, generally of common blood and language, always of common history, traditions and impulses, who are both voluntarily and involuntarily striving together for the accomplishment of certain more or less vividly conceived ideals of life."[49] However, in an essay published 40 years later, Du Bois acknowledges that his earlier ideas of race contained "irreconcilable

tendencies" and discusses his own intellectual evolution on the conception
of race, which emphasized the cultural aspects of race.[50]

Du Boisian sociology is grounded in his formative experience growing
up in racially polarized America. In *Souls* he presents new theoretical constructs for interpreting African American identity: "the Veil," "Two-ness,"
and "Double-Consciousness." In the opening pages, he describes that first
childhood epiphany that race difference matters and makes mention for
the first time of "the Veil," the most famous figure of speech he used to
symbolize American apartheid. He wrote:

> It is the early days of rollicking boyhood that the revelation
> first burst upon one, all in a day, as it were. I remember well
> when the shadow swept across me. I was a little thing, away up
> in the hills of New England, where the dark Housatonic winds
> between Hoosac and Taghkanic to the sea. In a wee wooden
> schoolhouse, something put it into the boys' and girls' heads to
> buy gorgeous visiting cards—ten cents a package—and exchange.
> The exchange was merry, till one girl, a tall newcomer, refused
> my card, refused it peremptorily, with a glance. Then it dawned
> upon me with a certain suddenness that I was different from the
> others; or like, mayhap, in heart and life and longing, but shut
> out from their world by a veil. I had thereafter no desire to tear
> down that veil, to creep through; I held all beyond it in common
> contempt, and lived above it in a region of blue sky and great
> wandering shadows.[51]

His goal is to raise the veil or venture behind it, in order to allow white
Americans to "listen" to the souls of African Americans. He writes, "Leaving, then, the world of the white man, I have stepped within the Veil,
raising it that way you may view faintly its deeper recesses, the meaning
of its religion, the passion of its human sorrow, and the struggle of its
greater souls."[52] In *Darkwater*, he wrote this canonic passage:

> And then—the Veil. It drops as drops the night on southern
> seas—vast, sudden, unanswering. There is Hate behind it, and
> Cruelty and Tears. As one peers through its intricate, unfath-
> omable pattern of ancient, old, old design, one sees blood and
> guilt and misunderstanding. And yet it hangs there, this Veil,
> between Then and Now, between Pale and Colored and Black
> and White—between You and Me. Surely it is a thought-thing,
> tenuous, intangible; yet just as surely is it true and terrible and
> not in our little day may you and I lift it. We may feverishly

unravel its edges and even climb slow with giant shears to where its ringed and gilded top nestles close to the throne of God. But as we work and climb we shall see through streaming eyes and hear with aching ears, lynching and murder, cheating and despising, degrading and lying, so flashed and flashed through this vast hanging darkness that the Doer never sees the Deed and the Victim knows not the Victor and Each hate All in wild and bitter ignorance. Listen, O Isles, to these Voices from within the Veil, for they portray the most human hurt of the Twentieth Cycle of that poor Jesus who was called the Christ.[53]

There is broad consensus that the "Veil" is a metaphor for racial division that divides and separates white and African Americans, as a symbol for structured racism and social exclusion, which profoundly shape the dynamic of perceptions and interactions between those divided.[54] Du Bois constantly reasserts the importance of the veil to understand the psychological and social effects on African Americans of the myriad forms of racial stigmatization and racial injustice. Foremost, it figured prominently in his early theory of race relations and underscored more vividly his premise that "the problem of the Twentieth century is the problem of the color-line."[55] The imagery of the veil is one of a transparent membrane through which blacks collectively view whites across the racial divide. Despite the transparency of the veil, despite the ease with which each race can see through it, the racial vortex acts to deafen the voices from within the veil and acts to separate the races.

The veil is better conceived as a "thought-thing" or as a collection of ideas, rather than as an artifact. In this sense, it filters and organizes information that is communicated across the divided societies, a process in which whites and blacks act to exchange perceptions, to shape their own identities, and ultimately to dictate the course of their education, their employment aspirations, their lives. It is through this socialization process, of course, that white and blacks learn to become members of society, both by internalizing societal mores, norms, and values, and also by learning to perform their social roles at each side of the racial divide. As a cognitive process, consisting of discourse, thoughts, and metaphors of culture, the veil is clearly a social construct, invented or made rather than naturally given, that is inherited during childhood and that during formative years deeply affects what they think of themselves and the "other." In *Souls* Du Bois explains through a myriad of racial vignettes that what characterizes whites "without the Veil" is a "blindness" to the inveterate effects on blacks "within the Veil" of the "color-line" drawn by the collective complicity, whether active or passive, of American whites.[56]

Du Bois's veil is a metaphor for racial division that divides white and African Americans, as a symbol for structured racism, which profoundly shapes the dynamic of perceptions and human interaction between those divided.

Finally, because the veil is an intangible, emotional, deep-rooted "thought-thing," it is a social phenomenon that is not easily lifted. Although it will not happen anytime soon or without struggle, Du Bois believes that the worlds within and outside the veil are undergoing change, and someday America shall shear the veil and "the prisoned shall go free."[57]

Race and the Double-Consciousness

Du Bois's most influential sociological concept is the "Double-Consciousness," the reality that the African American self is complexly constituted and has a duality to it. The African American sees herself or himself through the eyes of others, and this reflective self has two souls, two thoughts in one body. For African Americans, therefore, the self is divided, and each individual experiences "Two-ness"—the dual life of "an American, a Negro" but rooted in a complex sensibility, that is, double-consciousness. Closely related to the concept of the veil, it is the underlying theme in *Souls*. The black person of his or her era knows how he or she is perceived—the objectified and excluded Other—and who she or he truly is—the knowing and agential self. The two may coexist divided from each other, but ultimately they come together to define his or her identity. The seminal concept of the double self with a double-consciousness is embedded is this passage:

> After the Egyptian and Indian, the Greek and Roman, the Teuton and Mongolian, the Negro is a sort of seventh son, born with a veil, and gifted with a second-sight in this American world,—

a world which yields him no true self-consciousness, but only lets him see himself through the revelation of the other world. It is a peculiar sensation, this double-consciousness, this sense of always looking at one's self through the eyes of others, of measuring one's soul by the tape of a world that looks on in amused contempt and pity. One ever feels his two-ness—an American, a Negro; two souls; two thoughts, two unreconciled strivings; two warring ideals in one dark body, whose dogged strength alone keeps it from being torn asunder.[58]

The passage reveals a complex paradox about Du Bois's double-consciousness. On the one hand, the first sentence portrays the African American's double-consciousness as a gift. In folklore in many cultures, a "seventh son" or child is especially lucky. The phrase "born with the veil" or "born with a caul" refers to a baby born with a part of the membrane of the amniotic sac covering its face. Since medieval times the appearance of a caul at birth was superstitiously regarded as a lucky sign: it endowed the child with special powers. African Americans were therefore gifted, not afflicted, with "second-sight," meaning they could see things denied to others, see through guise and guile. Thus, double-consciousness gave African Americans not insignificant power by affording them unique insight into stratified societies as a whole.[59] Black Americans were "outsiders" looking in. Separated by the veil, they were both inside and outside of the dominant white society. Du Bois posits that whites have limited understanding of blacks, whereas blacks have a profound understanding of the cultural architecture that whites employ to oppress and exclude them.[60]

Du Bois's narrative in *Souls* resonates with Hegel's master-slave dialectic, a tension between bodily and spiritual selves.[61] Parallel with Hegel's *Phenomenology*, he suggests that the virulence of racism constricts white self-consciousness, but, by contrast, the effects of racism strengthen and shape African American identity and self. The concluding sentence, on the other hand, make it clear that blacks bear the burden of two-ness and conveys the affliction and despair arising necessarily from the degradations visited upon African Americans in the post-emancipation era.[62] A sense of underachievement, of "being torn under," prevents the double self developing into a better and truer self.[63]

Du Bois contends that a black American male strives "to attain self-conscious manhood, to merge his double self into a better and truer self. In this merging he wishes neither of the older selves to be lost ... He simply wishes to make it possible for a man to be both a Negro and an American, without being cursed and spit upon by his fellows, without having the doors of Opportunity closed roughly in his face."[64] The double struggle of African Americans, on the one hand to escape white contempt and hatred and on the other hand to do only low-paid remedial work, generates tension that manifests itself in all kinds of social pathologies within the black community. He puts it like this: "This waste of double aims, this seeking to satisfy two unreconciled ideals, has wrought sad havoc with the courage and faith and deeds ... has sent them often wooing false gods and invoking false means of salvation, and at times has even seemed about to make them ashamed of themselves."[65] Structured racism meant that compared to other New World emancipation, African Americans in the southern states gained least from the abolition of slavery.[66] Du Bois was highly critical of early sociologists on the "other side" of the veil, suggesting they problematized the characteristic and behavior of blacks: "But alas! While sociologists gleefully count his bastards and his prostitutes, the very soul of the toiling, sweating black man is darkened by the shadow of a vast despair."[67] It is plausible to conclude that the despairing passage on the double self is a guiding thread weaving throughout the sociological projects that occupied much of Du Bois's work over his lifetime.

The intellectual roots of Du Bois's veil and double-consciousness are widely debated. It is suggested that between 1892 and 1894, Weber helped forge intellectual bonds between Du Bois and George Herbert Mead and Georg Simmel.[68] There are evident similarities between *Souls* and early contributions to the self-theory found in Charles Cooley's *Human Nature and Social Order* (1902), George Herbert Mead's *Mind, Self and Society* (1934), and Georg Simmel's (1908/1971) essay on the Stranger. In *Human Nature*, Cooley proposes that people are not socially real unless someone is actually conscious of them. He posits that if a person went into a foreign country and hid himself or herself so well that no one knew he or she was there, he or she would have no social existence for the inhabitants. This ethereal view of society is the essence of the veil—figuratively it renders blacks nonexistent in the collective minds of white Americans.

At Harvard, Du Bois was a student of the social psychologist William James. In *The Principles of Psychology* (1890), James' own double-self theory uses the *I/me* distinction that is popularly associated with Mead. It is plausible to conclude that James had a "direct" influence on Du Bois's double self, although he refined it and took it in a different direction. From the white side of the veil, in *Mind, Self and Society* (1934), Mead writes, "The unity of and the structure of the complete self reflects the unity and structure of the social process as a whole."[69] For Mead, the self is something that is reflexive. The Du Boisian double self concept is sensitive to history and to the primacy of power.

In *The Philosophy of Money* (1900/1990), published three years before *Souls*, the German sociologist Georg Simmel produced a much more fluid self. This quote captures his argument: "The enigmatic unity of the soul cannot be grasped by the cognitive process directly, but only when broken down into multitude of strands, the resynthesis of which signifies the unique personality."[70] For Simmel then, the metropolis and the self are intimately bound up with the conditions of the money economy. From a Du Boisian perspective, structured racism adds a complexity to the "multitudes of strands" that signify the self. There are clear parallels between Du Bois's social theory of the self and Simmel's essay on the stranger. In every human relationship, proposes Simmel, there is a pattern: "the distance within this relationship indicates that one who is close by is remote, but this strangeness indicates that one who is remote is near."[71] The African American, then, like the Stranger, is in a paradoxical position: physically near to the white group but psychologically and culturally distant at the same time.

Du Bois's distinctive theory of the self offers a more nuanced conception of the inner life of African Americans; it suggests a tapestry consisting of multiple strands of the self, a multidimensional perspective embedded in its historical-cultural foundation. For self-theory scholars, Du Bois's double self is conceptually powerful: "There is no universal self. There are only selves. White sociology has been looking under the dim light of its own cultural blindness, looking thereby in the wrong place for some universal social thing that, from Du Bois' point of view, does not exist."[72] If Du Bois had been included into the sociology canon, self-theorists would surely have concluded that Simmel's stranger likely suffered from double consciousness. To African Americans, social hierarchy and white power are exactly the sources of racism from which double-consciousness manifested.

Criticisms

Although Du Bois made a distinctive contribution to our understanding of the role race played in the dehumanization of African Americans, and provided a much more nuanced and complex picture of the components of the social self in particular, his uncompromising language and political activism exposed him as an easy target for his professional peers. As he himself acknowledges to the reader, "I who speak here am bone of the bone and flesh of the flesh of them that live within the Veil."[73] If we leave aside the intellectual climate stoked by the Bolshevik Revolution in 1917 and, later in his career, by the Cold War and the politics of "McCarthyism," many contemporary white reviewers were deeply disturbed by his early publication, *Darkwater*. One reviewer opined that, "Dr. Du Bois is too close to the struggle to see clearly the problems involved. His work is a creation of *passion* rather than intelligence" (emphasis added). One reviewer found in *Darkwater* "a remarkable example of that elemental race-hatred which [Du Bois] himself so fiercely denounces." [74] Eric Sundquist has suggested that Du Bois's prose was "culturally coded, almost subliminal language" that challenged the ability of his readers, whether white or black, to comprehend his work.[75]

Du Bois's position, however, is aligned with contemporary feminist and postmodernist thinking, which rejects the notion of "value-free" thinking as an illusion. Contemporary feminists argue that social researchers are deeply implicated with the values and the communities from which they emanated and with which they empathize. For example, although her academic training was designed to alienate her from her community, American sociologist Patricia Hill Collins writes, "Instead of viewing the everyday as a negative influence on my theorizing, I tried to see how the everyday actions and ideas of the Black women in my life reflected the theoretical issues I claimed were so important to them."[76] An oft-made criticism is that much of Du Bois's scholarship can be interpreted as elitist. This allegation is buttressed by his declaration in *The Philadelphia Negro* that the "aristocracy of the Negro population" are key actors within the African American community that must lead people in a rational direction.[77] He appears uncritically to embrace ideas of expert knowledge as a cure for deleterious social consequences of racial segregation and racial prejudice, not recognizing the limits of expertise for contributing to final emancipation when detached from democratic social movements. By the 1930s, however, Du Bois understood his earlier position to be "ideologically reactionary."[78]

In *The Philadelphia Negro*, Du Bois provides the first survey of African American working-class conditions, but, written at the beginning of his academic career, it lacks the general analysis of capitalism found in Engels's *Conditions*. He tends to believe that the white business class should initiate "social reform" in order to diversify black employment and to afford "escape from remedial employment."[79] When Du Bois declares that it is wrong "to make scullions of engineers" he can be criticized for advancing a moral argument and failing to develop a theory of American capitalism. However, Du Bois made an important contribution to Marx's concept of contradiction. In *Black Reconstruction in America*, rather than analyzing the rise of American capitalism through Marx's theoretical prism—that is, the contradiction between the modes and relations of production—Du Bois argued that capitalism and slavery were related systemically, "made possible by the ideologies of racism."[80] Moreover, from the vantage point of an African American, the absence of a study of racism in Marx's theory of history "left a monumental gap in the analysis of capitalism."[81]

Conclusion

We have examined Du Bois through white eyes, and filtered through the lenses of our greater familiarity with European, compared with classical American, writers and sensibilities. His early social theory is irrefutably related in complex ways to its sociocultural context. Most important, the personal orbit in which he experienced structured US racism and his leadership role in the Black Radical movement is undoubtedly relevant to understanding Du Bois's sociological legacy. The idea that humanity was divided by "race" penetrated the dominant ideology of the period almost as deeply as "progress" itself. Sven Lindqvist, for example, observes that nineteenth-century intellectual thought served the European imperial project, which, without doubt, shaped American modernity.[82]

Du Bois's social theory illuminates the interplay of class and race, the intersection of racial segregation and social inequality and injustice. The *leitmotif* of *Souls* is to unmask American racism and its effects on metropolitan black identity. His early sociology focuses on microsocial interactions and differentiation based on race, rather than on "meta-narratives" promulgated by Marx, Durkheim, and Weber. From this perspective, Du Bois's intellectual lineage can be located within the distinctly American "micro-interactionist tradition" (see, for example, Collins, 1994).[83] The veil and the double self concepts are Du Bois's best-known contributions to social theory and, arguably, he played a disproportionately influential role in developing the twentieth-century definition of race as a "fundamental axis of social organization in the US."[84] Applying Hegel's master-slave dialectic, Du Bois argues that African Americans develop a greater understanding of their own identity because of the life experience of racism behind the veil.

The effect of excluding *Souls* from the sociological canon caused blindness among white sociologists for they, too, did not see clearly beyond the veil. Indeed, as others have argued, the exclusion of Du Bois's intellectual thoughts, so long obscured by white academics, invites reconsideration of sociology's research and teaching on race and cultural identity in North America.[85] In the early twenty-first century, Du Bois's pioneering insights are highly relevant to theories of social construction, critical race theory, and contemporary studies of social exclusion and racial inequality.[86] It is a tribute to Du Bois's work that black American feminists have drawn from his sociological vision. Patricia Hill Collins' epistemological approach, for example, is clearly consistent with the Du Boisian tradition, and her work on "the outside within" has strong resemblances to Du Bois's thinking on double consciousness.[87] One hundred and twenty years after *The Philadelphia Negro* was published, "racial terror and violence" continue to be a central part of the African American story.[88] On both sides of the Atlantic, black, Asian, and minority ethnic (BAME) communities continue to call for society to be free of racial discrimination, a political phenomenon we discuss in the final chapter.

FURTHER THINKING:

What did Du Bois mean by "double-consciousness"? To what extent does this remain a feature of racial identities today?

FURTHER READING:

For a reliable introduction to the concepts of race and ethnicity, see Nasar Meer's "Recognition" in *Race and Ethnicity: Key Concepts* (London: Sage, 2014), 130–35. For further insight into Du Bois's concept of double-consciousness, see the original text in Du Bois, chapter 1, "Of Our Spiritual Strivings" in *The Souls of Black Folk* (1903; New York: Dover Publications, 1994), 1–7. Finally, for commentary see Paul Gilroy, chapter 4, "'Cheer the Weary Traveller': W.E.B. Du Bois, Germany, and the Politics of (Dis)placement" in *The Black Atlantic: Modernity and Double Consciousness* (London: Verso, 1993), 111–45.

Notes

1 Manning Marable, "Black Intellectuals and the World They Made," in *The New Black History*, ed. M. Marable and E.K. Hinton (New York: Palgrave Macmillan, 2011), 1–16, see page 3.

2 Aretha Franklin, *Jet Magazine*, 1970, and cited by Dorian Lynskey, "Musical Revolutionary: Flawless Voice That Gave the US Its Heart and Soul," *The Guardian*, August 17, 2018, 4–5. Aretha Franklin died as we were completing this manuscript and in tribute to her, we reproduce, from the same source, a joint statement issued by Barack and Michelle Obama:

> Every time she sang, we were graced with a glimpse of the divine. Through her compositions and unmatched musicianship, Aretha helped define the American experience. In her voice, we could feel our history, all of it and in every shade—our power and our pain, our darkness and our light, our quest for redemption and our hard-won respect. She helped us feel more connected to each other, more hopeful, more human. And sometimes she helped us just forget everything else and dance.

3 A. Asthana and H. Bengtsson, "Racial Equality Audit Reveals Deep Divides," *The Guardian*, October 10, 2017, 6.

4 O. Bowcott and V. Dodd, "Exposed: 'Race Bias' in British Justice System," *The Guardian*, September 8, 2017, 1.

5 H. Siddique and O. Laughland, "UN Sounds the Alarm over US Racial Tensions," *The Guardian*, August 24, 2017, 1.

6 Gary Younge, "Never Forget that Trump Understands the Depth of American Bigotry," *The Guardian*, September 26, 2017, 33.

7 Colin Perkel, "Despite Equality Progress, Race and Sex Discrimination Persist: Ontario Rights Chief," *The Globe and Mail*, July 18, 2012, www.theglobeandmail.com/news/national/despite-equality-progress-race-and-sex-discrimination-persist-ontario-rights-chief/article4424984/.

8 Marable, "Black Intellectuals and the World They Made."

9 The white sociologist Thorstein Veblen (1857–1929) also experienced problems gaining employment because of his political views. See Stephen Edgell, *Veblen in Perspective: His Life and Thought* (Armonk, NY: M.E. Sharpe, 2001).

10 Cedric J. Robinson, *Black Marxism* (Chapel Hill: University of North Carolina Press, 2000), 185.

11 Henry Louis Gates, Jr., *Life Upon These Shores* (New York: Alfred A. Knopf, 2011), 151.

12 A. Johnson "The Black Experience," unpublished paper (School of Social Work, University of North Carolina, Chapel Hill, 1999), and quoted in Judith R. Blau and Eric S. Brown, "Du Bois and Diasporic Identity: The Veil and the Unveiling Project," *Sociological Theory* 19, no. 2 (2001): 219–33, see page 225.

13 Manning Marable, "Introduction," *Darkwater* (New York: Dover Publications, 1999), v–viii, see page vi.

14 Henry Louis Gates (1989) estimated that Du Bois wrote on average one paper every 12 days from the age of 30 to his death at 95. Cited by Charles Lemert, "A Classic from the Other Side of the Veil: Du Bois' *Souls of Black Folk*," *The Sociological Quarterly* 35, no. 3 (1994): 383–96, see page 384.

15 Quoted in Tukufu Zuberi, "W.E.B. Du Bois's Sociology: The Philadelphia Negro and Social Science," *Annals of the American Academy of Political and Social Science* 598 (September 2004): 146–56, 147.

16 C. Wright Mills, *The Sociological Imagination*, with an afterword by Todd Gitlin (1959; New York: Penguin, 2000).

17 W.E.B. Du Bois, *The Souls of Black Folk* (1903; New York: Dover Publications, 1994), vi.

18 W.E.B. Du Bois, *The Autobiography of W.E.B. Du Bois: A Soliloquy on Viewing My Life from the Last Decade of Its First Century* (posthumous) (New York: International Publishers, Inc., 1968), 148.

19 In *The Autobiography,* Du Bois recalls, "Karl Marx was mentioned but only incidentally and as one whose doubtful theories had long since been refuted" (133). In 1904, however, he taught seminars on Marx; see Robinson, *Black Marxism*, 380.

20 W.E.B. Du Bois, "My Evolving Program for Negro Freedom," in *W.E.B. Du Bois: A Reader*, ed. David Levering Lewis (1944; New York: Henry Holt, 1995), 610–18, see page 610.

21 Du Bois, *The Autobiography,* 404.

22 W.E.B. Du Bois, "The Present Leadership of American Negroes," in *W.E.B. Du Bois: A Reader,* ed. David Levering Lewis (1957; New York: Henry Holt, 1995), 354–57, see page 357.

23 Robinson, *Black Marxism*, 195.

24 Blau and Brown, "Du Bois and Diasporic Identity," 219–233; David Levering Lewis, *W.E.B. Du Bois: Biography of a Race, 1868–1919* (New York: Henry Holt, 1993).

25 Du Bois, *The Autobiography*, 205.

26 Robinson, *Black Marxism*, 186.

27 Marable, "Introduction," *Darkwater*, vi.

28 Levering Lewis, *W.E.B. Du Bois: A Reader*, 151.

29 S. Lebergott, *Manpower in Economic Growth: The United States Record Since 1800* (New York: McGraw-Hill, 1964), 510.

30 Thomas Powers, *The Killing of Crazy Horse* (New York: Vintage Books, 2010), xi.

31 Michael Rose, *Industrial Behaviour: Theoretical Developments since Taylor* (London: Allen Lane, 1975), in Craig R. Littler (1982), *The Development of the Labour Process in Capitalist Societies* (London: Heinemann, 1982), 161.

32 Edgell, *Veblen in Perspective*, 366.

33 Edgell, *Veblen in Perspective*, 8.

34 W.E.B. Du Bois, *Darkwater* (New York: Dover Publications, 1999), 23–24.

35 Du Bois, *Darkwater*, 24.

36 Du Bois, *Darkwater*, 25.

37 W.E.B. Du Bois, *Black Reconstruction in America, 1860–1880* (New York: Harcourt Brace, 1935), 3.

38 Robinson, *Black Marxism*, 200.

39 Charles Lemert, "W.E.B. Du Bois," in *The Blackwell Companion to Major Classical Social Theorists*, ed. George Ritzer (Malden, MA: Blackwell Publishing, 2003), 333–54, see page 345.

40 W.E.B. Du Bois, *The Philadelphia Negro* (1899; Philadelphia: University of Pennsylvania Press, 1996), 98.

41 Du Bois, *The Philadelphia Negro*, 128.

42 Robinson, *Black Marxism*, 314.

43 Du Bois, *The Philadelphia Negro*, 129.

44 Du Bois, *The Souls of Black Folk*, 92.

45 Du Bois, *The Souls of Black Folk*, 59.

46 Du Bois, *Darkwater*, p. 35.

47 W.E.B. Du Bois, "The Case for the Jews" and "The Negro and the Warsaw Ghetto," in *The Oxford W.E.B. Du Bois Reader*, ed. Eric J. Sundquist (New York: Oxford University Press, 1996), 461–64, 469–73.

48 Du Bois, "The Conservation of Races," in *The Oxford W.E.B. Du Bois Reader*, ed. Eric J. Sundquist (New York: Oxford University Press, 1996), 38–47, see page 40.

49 Du Bois, "The Conservation of Races," 40.

50 Du Bois, "The Concept of Race," in *The Oxford W.E.B. Du Bois Reader*, ed. Eric J. Sundquist (1940; New York: Oxford University Press, 1996), 76–96.

51 Du Bois, *The Souls of Black Folk*, 1–2.

52 Du Bois, *The Souls of Black Folk*, v.

53 Du Bois, *Darkwater*, 143–44.

54 See Lemert, "A Classic from the Other Side of the Veil"; Blau and Brown, "Du Bois and Diasporic Identity."

55 Du Bois, *The Souls of Black Folk*, v.

56 Lemert, "A Classic from the Other Side of the Veil," 386.

57 Du Bois, *The Souls of Black Folk*, 163.

58 Du Bois, *The Souls of Black Folk*, 2.

59 James Scott, *Domination and the Arts of Resistance* (New Haven, CT: Yale University Press, 1990).

60 Blau and Brown, "Du Bois and Diasporic Identity," 219–33.

61 Blau and Brown, "Du Bois and Diasporic Identity," 221.

62 Lemert, "A Classic from the Other Side of the Veil," 388.

63 Critical discussion of this passage are too numerous to list here, but see, for example, Levering Lewis, *W.E.B. Du Bois: Biography of a Race, 1868–1919*, 280–83; Adolph L. Reed, *W.E.B. Du Bois and American Political Thought: Fabianism and the Color Line* (New York: Oxford University Press, 1997), 91–99; W. Siemerling, *The New American Studies: Culture, Writing and the Politics of Re/cognition* (New York: Routledge, 2005), 31–58; Doris Sommer, "Choose and Lose," in *Multilingual America: Transnationalism, Ethnicity, and the Languages of American Literature*, ed. Werner Sollors (New York: New York University Press, 1998), 297–311, see pages 301–3; Shamoon Zamir, *Dark Voices: W.E.B. Du Bois and American Thought* (Chicago: Chicago University Press, 1995), 114, 139–40. These works provide an analysis of the veil in terms of the master-slave struggle, and with reference to this theme in later post-colonial genre (e.g., Frantz Fanon's *Black Skin, White Mask*, published in 1967).

64 Du Bois, *The Souls of Black Folk*, 2–3.

65 Du Bois, *The Souls of Black Folk*, 3.

66 Robin Blackburn, *The American Crucible: Slavery, Emancipation and Human Rights* (London: Verso, 2011), 462.

67 Du Bois, *The Souls of Black Folk*, 6.

68 Lewis Coser, *Masters of Sociological Theory* (New York: Harcourt Brace, 1971), 326–27, 346.

69 G.H. Mead, *Mind, Self and Society* (Chicago: University of Chicago Press, 1934), and cited by Lemert, "A Classic from the Other Side of the Veil," 389.

70 Georg Simmel, *The Philosophy of Money*, ed. David Frisby (1900; London: Routledge, 1990), 296.

71 Georg Simmel, *Georg Simmel on Individuality and Social Forms*, ed. D. Levine (1908; Chicago: University of Chicago Press, 1971), 143, and quoted in Ian Craib, *Classical Social Theory* (Oxford: Oxford University Press, 1997), 167.

72 Lemert, "A Classic from the Other Side of the Veil," 390.

73 Du Bois, *The Souls of Black Folk*, vi.

74 Du Bois, *Darkwater*, vii.

75 Eric Sundquist, *To Wake the Nations: Race in the Making of American Literature* (Cambridge, MA: Harvard University Press, 1993), 537–38.

76 Patricia Hill Collins, *Black Feminist Thought*, 2nd ed. (New York: Routledge, 2000), viii.

77 Du Bois, *The Philadelphia Negro*, 316.

78 Robinson, *Black Marxism*, 197.

79 Du Bois, *The Philadelphia Negro*, 141.

80 Robinson, *Black Marxism*, 229.

81 Robinson, *Black Marxism*, 237.

82 Sven Lindqvist, *"Exterminate All the Brutes": One Man's Odyssey into the Heart of Darkness and the Origins of European Genocide* (New York: The New York Press, 2007).

83 Randall Collins, *Four Sociological Traditions* (Oxford: Oxford University Press, 1994).

84 Michael Omi and Howard Winant, *Racial Transformation in the United States: From the 1960s to the 1990s*, 2nd ed. (New York: Routledge, 1994), 13.

85 Lemert, "A Classic from the Other Side of the Veil," 383–96.

86 See Roberta Garner, "W.E.B. Du Bois" in *Social Theory: Continuity and Confrontation, A Reader*, ed. Roberta Garner (Peterborough, ON: Broadview Press, 2000), 198–202. Also, see Derrick A. Bell, *Faces at the Bottom of the Well: The Permanence of Racism* (New York: Basic Books, 1992). Bell asserts that neither wealth accumulation nor education achievements can elevate African Americans into the upper rungs of the class stratum as long as "whiteness" dominates as an ultimate caste determinant. See also Michael Hughes and Melvin E. Thomas, "The Continuing Significance of Race Revisited: A Study of Race, Class, and Quality of Life in America, 1972 to 1996," *American Journal of Sociology* 63 (1998): 785–95. Using data from the General Social Survey (GSS) for the period 1972 to 1996, Thomas and Hughes show that quality of life continues to be worse for African Americans than it is for whites, although racial disparities do not vary by and are not explained by socio-economic status. See William Julius Wilson, *The Declining Significance of Race: Blacks and Changing American Institutions* (Chicago: University of Chicago Press, 1987). See also William Julius Wilson, *When Work Disappears: The World of the New Urban Poor* (Chicago: University of Chicago Press, 1996). Wilson, like Du Bois, analyzes the changing dynamics of class as it relates to labor market shifts that further marginalize African Americans.

87 Patricia Hill Collins, *Black Feminist Thought*.

88 Natalie Y. Moore, "Overt Racists Are Easy to Spot. America's Insidious Racism Is a Greater Challenge," *The Observer*, August 20, 2017, 29.

15. G.H. Mead on Self and Society

While symbolic interactionism takes inspiration from Mead it does
so selectively.

—Hans Joas, 1985[1]

The interest Mead had in the idea of society runs parallel to the
interest that he had in the idea of the self.

—Jean-François Côté, 2015[2]

IN HIS CONTRIBUTION TO *A HANDBOOK OF SOCIAL THEORY*, Hans Joas, a
leading German sociologist, observed that Mead's work is the "bridge
between pragmatism and sociology," and goes on to state that Mead is
recognized "beyond dispute" as a classical social theorist.[3] Mead's main
intellectual legacy, posthumously published as *Mind, Self and Society,*
is the development of "a pragmatist analysis of social interaction and
individual self-reflection."[4] Mead developed a theory of self-formation
through symbols and, simultaneously, a developmental theory of society.
After Mead's death, however, it was his theory of the social self that
became a prominent piece of conceptual architecture in the Chicago
school of "symbolic interactionism." While Mead's articulation of the
social self contains an explicit link to the way he conceptualizes society, it is surprising that few sociologists have "paid serious attention
to his ideas of society."[5] Indeed, to emphasize the point, George Ritzer
confidently asserts, "Mead has relatively little to say about society."[6] In
sharp contrast, Canadian sociologist Jean-François Côté compellingly
argues that the concept of society is "fundamental" to Mead's sociological
understanding of the self.[7] This chapter, of necessity, is a highly selective
interpretation of Mead's theory of the social self and his concept of
society. It begins with a review of his life and work, and the intellectual
context informing his thinking and work.

Life and Work

George Herbert Mead was born in South Hadley, Massachusetts, USA, on February 27, 1863. His childhood and youth were spent in the intellectual milieu of Oberlin College, Ohio, where his father went in 1869 to take up a professorship in homiletics. Mead's generation was exposed to Darwin's theory of evolution, and his student years at Oberlin College witnessed the sciences gaining more space in American curricula, and thus coming into conflict with dogmatically religious claims to explain modernity.[8] In response to Darwin's thinking, the young Mead asked the question: How could the moral values of socially committed American Protestantism be preserved without outdated theological dogma?

Mead graduated from Oberlin College in 1883, and, after moving between jobs, he entered Harvard University in 1887 to study philosophy. But Mead soon became disillusioned with philosophy, regarding it as inadequate and aloof from the sciences and the social problems of American life. In 1888, Mead switched to the study of psychology because, unlike classical German idealism, it offered greater intellectual independence and promised an empirical clarification of philosophical problems. From 1888 to 1891, Mead worked in Germany on a doctoral thesis (that remained unfinished), first in Leipzig with Wilhelm Wundt, and then in Berlin under Wilhelm Dilthey. At the time, Dilthey was working on his conception of "empathy," that is, the ability to understand an author by putting the interpreter in his or her position. It is speculated that this had an influence on Mead's view of being able to "take the role of the other" in the ontogenetic development of self-consciousness.[9] As part of his doctoral research, Mead studied

George Herbert Mead was born in South Hadley, Massachusetts, USA, in 1863. Evaluating Mead's contribution to sociology has been controversial, not least because his best-known work is a posthumous compilation and publication of his lectures. He died in 1931.

the psychology of children's early moral development and the perception and constitution of space.

In 1891, Mead moved back to America to take a position teaching psychology at the University of Michigan. In 1894, he moved to the newly established University of Chicago. The new university had two major goals: to combine research and teaching more closely, but also to ensure that both were strongly focused on practical tasks, preferably in the local community. Mead became part of an interdisciplinary network of Chicago academics who involved themselves in progressive social reform projects. Jane Addams was a close friend, and Mead supported her work at Hull House. Prior to World War I (1914–18), Mead's academic work focused on developing an anthropological theory of communication and a related social psychology. After the war, his work for social reform largely receded, and his academic work turned to various questions in the philosophy of science and of nature. At the University of Chicago, his "highly influential" course in social psychology provided the foundation of Mead's intellectual enterprise. Mead died on April 26, 1931.

Though there is much evidence that there was considerable respect for Mead's ideas among his colleagues and peers, assessing his contribution to the field of sociology and his writings has been controversial, not least because Mead never systematized his thoughts in book form during his lifetime. An illustration of the problem, the "green bible" of early sociology edited by Park and Burgess published in 1921 under the title *Introduction to the Science of Sociology*, did not include any text by Mead. As Côté observes, one can only speculate about Mead's own reaction to this act of "exclusion" from such a foundational text, one with such importance for the early development of the discipline.[10] Tracing the journey of Mead's ideas and concepts in sociology was made difficult by the fact that his best-known work, *Mind, Self and Society* (1934), is a posthumous compilation of his lectures, through a stenographic copy of the 1927 social psychology course, two sets of student notes on the same course, and personal experience. With the publication of *Mind, Self and Society* comes the problem of editorship. The order and interpretation of Mead's thought by Charles W. Morris—a student of Mead—was challenged by Ellsworth Faris (1936), presenting an earlier problem of interpretation that continually arises when examining Mead's insights or appropriation of his social psychology, whether in sociology or philosophy.[11] The ten articles Mead published between 1898 and 1930 in, among others, the *American Journal of Sociology, Journal of Philosophy*, and the *International Journal of Ethics* provide further insight into his thoughts.[12] Debate and controversy about Mead's ideas and ambivalence on legacy illustrates that membership of the classical social canon is a social matter.

Intellectual Influencers

Several major intellectual schools of American and German thought associated with social behaviorism, pragmatism, and dialectics shaped Mead's
analysis of the social self and society. At Harvard, his most important
influence was Josiah Royce, a leading American authority on classical
German idealism, a philosophy of human society that interpreted the
"Kingdom of Heaven" as the historical realization of a community of all
human beings in which there is universal communication among them.[13]
Mead also experienced the intellectual milieu of German philosophy.
The debate on the merits of *Geisteswissenschaften* (Human Sciences) or
Kulturwissenschaften versus the *Naturwissenschaften* (Natural Sciences)
led to "scientific" analysis of society with different epistemological, theoretical, and analytical devices. At the universities of Leipzig and Berlin,
Wilhelm Wundt and Wilhelm Dilthey tutored Mead. It is Wundt's theory
of gestures that must be credited for helping Mead to arrive at the idea
of internalization of the external social experience.[14]

The work of American psychologists John Dewey (1859–1952) and
John B. Watson (1878–1958) also influenced Mead's thinking. Dewey and
Watson are associated with social *behaviorism*, an approach to the study
of the individual based almost exclusively on observable and measur-
able data on human behavior, which excludes ideas, emotions, and the
consideration of inner mental experience and activity. In his 1896 article
"The Reflex Arc Concept in Psychology," Dewey proposes an integrative
perspective of the relation between perception, sensibility, human action,
and showing their total integration into the whole.[15] Social behaviorism
is strongly associated with John Watson. In 1913, Watson published the
"Behaviorist Manifesto," which put the emphasis on external behavior of
people and their reactions to a given situation, rather than on the inner,
mental state of people. Watson's social behaviorism rejected the study of
human consciousness; he believed that, because it was not observable, it
could not be scientifically studied. Mead, in theatrical language, captures
Watson's view: "John B. Watson's attitude was that of the Queen in *Alice
in Wonderland*—'Off with their heads!'"[16] In contrast, Mead believes that
consciousness can be studied from a behaviorist perspective, providing
the perspective is not narrowly conceived. Mead writes:

> The opposition of the behaviorist to introspection is justified.
> It is not a fruitful undertaking from the point of view of psy-
> chological study ... What the behaviorist is occupied with ... is
> the actual reaction itself. It is not necessary for psychology to
> get into metaphysical questions, but it is of importance that it

should try to get hold of the response that is used in the psychological analysis itself.[17]

For Mead, consciousness is broadly conceived and becomes the location
of a pattern of relations that are constituted within subjective experience in the course of interaction with the social world.[18] Mead explicitly
incorporates both Dewey's and Watson's reflections into his own, to study
the social self.

The American philosophy of *pragmatism* influenced Mead's intellectual
development. Although pragmatism has different strands, its principal
feature is that it rejects the idea of absolute truths in favor of regarding
all ideas as provisional and subject to change by concrete experiences and
empirical research. Pragmatism is a "down-to-earth" philosophy, concerned with plausible scientific explanations that make sense of practice
and solving social problems in the real world. Charles Peirce (1839–1914)
is credited with founding pragmatism. For Peirce, the triumph of the
scientific method demonstrated practical relevance, precision, and plausibility of theoretical concepts. Peirce neatly summed up his perspective:
"My point is that the meaning of a concept ... lies in the manner in which
it could conceivably modify purposive action, and *in this alone*."[19] William
James (1842–1910) popularized Peirce's work. For James, pragmatism is
distinguished above all by its focus on "the concrete ways of seeing."[20] The
root of Mead's intellectual formation can be traced through his relation to
Wilhelm Dilthey. Arguing against the metaphysical foundations of earlier
attempts at studying human societies, Dilthey writes:

> For the analysis of human society *man himself* is given as a living
> unit, and the analysis of his psychophysical life-unit is therefore
> our fundamental task ... The second task of the human sciences
> is to study both the *cultural systems* that intermesh with each
> other in society and the external organization of that society.
> [emphasis added][21]

Dilthey puts much emphasis on self-consciousness as the most important content for psychological studies. Mead only identified himself as a
pragmatist late in his career, but in most of his work consciousness and
social processes mutually inform one another in a dialectical way.[22]

The ideas of the prominent German scholar Georg Simmel (1848–
1918) can be detected in Mead's work. For Simmel, the individual is not
an individual observer of the physical world but a *participant* in society
whose personality is formed through the affiliation and interaction of
others. He writes: "Just as the essence of the physical organism lies in

the fact that it creates the unity of the life-process out of the multitude of material parts, so man's inner personal unity is based upon the interaction or connection of many elements and determinants."[23] This addressing idea has evident parallels with Mead's theory of the development of the social self, and Charles Horton Cooley's 1902 account of the "looking glass self."[24] Though Mead, in Mind, Self and Society, did review Simmel's book, Simmel is not referenced and it's difficult to determine how much Mead borrowed Simmel's ideas on individual personality.

As a doctoral student in Germany, Mead was strongly influenced by the philosophy of Hegel, especially his dialectics. (We examined dialectics in chapter 4 on Marx's philosophy.) Dialectics as a feature of our thinking about the social world and dialectics as a feature of the social world itself are manifest in important ways in Mead's theory of the social self and the development of society. There is conflict, antagonism, or contradiction between Mead's the "I," the "Me," and the "Self," and at the societal level between "individuals," "institutions," and "society" itself, which culminates for Mead in an understanding of society's development as a self-transforming entity. Hegel's philosophy proposed the self-development of "spirit" through a dialectical method grounded in the "idea," which results in an exposition of what spirit is: the human mind. In terms of the development of the social self, one can interpret Mead's work in terms of a "dialectical" (Hegelian) process, as explained below. While not often recognized as such, Mead can be regarded as a dialectical thinker, and an understanding of dialectics certainly enhances the comprehension of Mead's work.[25]

Pervasive in all Mead's work is his insistence on the "social" character of psychology. Yet, curiously, Mead avoids explicit reference to sociology in Mind, Self and Society. Mead appeared to consider that sociology did not meet the criterion to be "scientific." Mead confidently wrote:

> Social science in anthropology, in sociology, pure and impure, dynamic and static, has not yet found its scientific method. It is not able to satisfactorily define its objects, nor to formulate their laws of change and development.[26]

Unsurprisingly, therefore, debate surrounds Mead's legacy in sociology. Mead was familiar with the writings of Simmel and Cooley, although the work of Durkheim or Weber seems to have "escaped his attention."[27] Mead appeared "reluctant" to fully endorse any sociological theory, in particular the writings of his colleagues at the University of Chicago.[28] A more serious allegation is that Mead appropriated Cooley's conception of the reflexive self "in order to bolster his [own] reputation."[29] The interpretation of Mead's work in terms of the journey from his social psychology to sociology should be at the center of our evaluation as to whether symbolic interactionism is Mead's enduring legacy.

To conclude our discussion of important intellectual influences into Mead's thinking, it is important that we acknowledge the influence of pragmatism on Mead's thoughts on social reform. We have already noted Mead's involvement in the work of Jane Addams and Hull House. For Mead, social psychology could not only theoretically define its objects, but also be instrumental in social change. He foresaw the further development of theoretical and applied disciplines to help in reforming society. Mead writes:

> Eugenics education, even political and economic sciences, pass beyond the phase of description and look toward the formation of the social object. We recognize that we control the conditions that determine the individual. His errors and shortcomings can be conceivably corrected. His misery may be eliminated. His mental and moral defects corrected. His heredity, social and physical, may be perfected ... The contribution that I wish to suggest ... arises out of the psychological theory of the origin of language and its relation to meaning.[30]

The reference to eugenics, which is considered abhorrent today because of its use in Nazi Germany, was, in the early twentieth century, quite "en vogue" among social elites and among some academics. The quoted passage, by contemporary experience, would also attract considerable criticism for its overt aim at social re-engineering. That language and its relation to meaning, its role in the development of the self, to others and to institutions would find expression in Mead's theory of the social self, to which we now turn.

Mead's Theory of Self

In his work Mead analyzed in much detail how social processes create the human self, emphasizing that it is impossible to understand the individual except as he or she can be understood in his or her social context. In this project, Mead gives primacy to the social world in understanding social experience. He starts not from the behavior of the individual organism but from the activity or behavior of the individual within a cooperating group: "the behavior of an individual can be understood only in terms of the behavior of the whole social group."[31] For Mead, adopting the behaviorist's approach, the individual starts not from an atomized "Robinson

Crusoe-like actor" who must first form social relationships and collective binding values, but from the complex activities or behaviors of three or more individuals; from what Mead called the "social act": "We attempt ... to explain the conduct of the individual in terms of the organized conduct of the social group, rather than ... in terms of the conduct of the separate individuals belonging to it."[32]

For Mead, the social group leads to the development of self-conscious mental states. The body is not a self; it "is essentially a social structure and it arises in social experience."[33] Dialectically the self is related to the human mind. Mead argues that, on the one hand, the self arises only when the mind has developed. On the other hand, the self is vital to the development of the mind. For Mead, the human mind is defined not as a thing but as a process, as an inner conversation with one's self. He posits, "It is absurd to look at the mind simply from the standpoint of the individual human organism ... it is *essentially a social phenomenon* ... We must regard mind ... as arising and developing within the social process, within the empirical *matrix of social interactions*" (emphasis added).[34] Mind and self are therefore conjoined because the self is both a mental process and a social process: "It is impossible to conceive of a self arising outside of social experience," writes Mead.[35]

Drawing on Wundt's concept of the gesture, Mead considered the gesture the basic mechanism in the social act and in the social process more generally.[36] Mead analyzed an expressive gesture in social terms and, from such gestures, traces the development of language communication. Mead also regarded as crucial to the internalization of such gestures: "Only in terms of gestures as significant symbols is the existence of the mind or intelligence possible; for only in terms of gestures which are significant symbols can thinking—which is simply an internalized or implicit conversation of the individual with himself by means of such gestures—take place."[37]

It is the development of vocal gestures, especially in the form of language, that require concomitant thought on the part of the actor before a response, which distinguishes humans from animals. Mead writes, "Vocal gestures ... [have] been responsible, ultimately, for the origin and growth of present human society."[38] Mead's understanding of language also incorporates the crucial condition of "reflexiveness" within the social process, for the development of the human mind. Mead writes:

> The evolutionary appearance of mind or intelligence takes place when the whole social process of experience and behavior is brought within the experience of any one of the separate individuals implicated therein, and when the individual's adjust-

ment to the process is modified and refined by the awareness or consciousness which he thus has of it. *It is by means of reflexiveness*—the turning-back of the experience of the individual upon himself—*that the whole social process is thus brought into the experience of the individuals* involved in it; it is by such means, which enable the individual to take the attitude of the other toward himself, that the individual is able consciously to adjust himself to that process, and to modify the resultant of that process in any given social act in terms of his adjustment to it. *Reflexiveness ... is the essential condition*, within the social process, *for the development of the mind*. [emphasis added][39]

This sociocultural analysis of the development of the mind provides the key concepts of Mead's social psychology. Mead's intellectual enterprise is to demonstrate that "mind and the self" are uncontested "social emergent," and that the language process provides the basic mechanism for their emergence.

For Mead, therefore, the self is not initially formed at birth, but arises in the dialectical process of social experience and activity. The self develops in the given individual as a result of her or his relations to that complex process as a whole and to other individuals within that process. The self internalizes as a result of lived experiences and social intercourse, which also translates as inner conversation or reflexivity and social attitude of the other assumed within the self. Thus, the individual takes the form of self-consciousness "only to the extent that he or she internalizes a set of social relations in which he or she is situated (as an object) with respect to other selves."[40] Otherwise, this individual remains "unconscious" of herself or himself—in other words, is deprived of self-consciousness.

The genesis of Mead's theory of the social self is represented in the developmental activities of two forms of children's behaviors: "play" and the "game." At the "play" stage, children play out all the roles of an invisible, imagined interaction among companions, in which the child uses gesture and response. For example, a child plays at being a mother, at being a teacher, at being a firefighter; that is, the child is taking different roles. Thus, the other's behavior is directly represented and complemented by the child's behavior. The child takes this set of gestures and responses and "organizes them into a certain whole."[41] In contrast, at the "game" stage, the child must be guided by the conduct of all other participants; anticipation of an imaginary companion's gesture and response is no longer sufficient. As Mead states: "The child who plays in a game must be ready to take the attitude of everyone else involved in the game,

1877 image of a women's baseball team. Mead's theory of the social self is represented in the developmental activities of two forms of behaviors: "play" and the "game." Each member of this baseball team must be oriented by a goal that is valid for all the other group members, which yields a unity of self or the "generalized other."

and ... these different roles must have a definite relationship to each other."[42] Thus, in an organized social group the child must orient herself or himself by a goal that is valid for all the other group members, which yields a "unity of self" or what Mead calls the "generalized other."

The generalized other, which is one of Mead's best-known concepts, is the attitude of the whole community or, in the example of a hockey game, the attitude of the entire team. The ability to take the role of the generalized other is essential to fully develop a self. Mead continues, "Only in so far as he takes the attitudes of the organized social group to which he belongs toward the organized ... does he develop a complete self."[43] The behavioral expectations of this generalized other are, for instance, the rules of the game, or more generally, the norms, values, and mores of a social group.[44]

Similar to Freud's internally divided model of psychic life (the Ego, Id, and Superego), none of the concepts that Mead uses (the "I," the "Me," and the "Self") can be located in the human organism. They are the symbolic expressions of the different phases of the relations between the nervous system and the environment.[45] The "I" refers to the principle of creativity and spontaneity. The "Me" refers to the individual's perception of how others see her or himself at a more primal level, to the individual's internalization of what the other "expects me to do or be."[46] The "Me" forms within the individual from a reference other, and is a basic element of an individual's developing self-image. While it may appear that creativity is stymied as individuals are busy conforming to the generalized other, Mead explains that there is not simply one grand generalized other but multiple generalized others in society. When an individual encounters several significant generalized others, these become references for an individual who must internalize and synthesize to form a new self. As Joas observes: "If this synthesization is successful, the 'self' comes into being: that is a unitary self-evaluation and action-orientation which allows interaction with more and more communicative partners; and at the same time, a stable personality structure develops which is

FIGURE 15.1 Elements of the Self

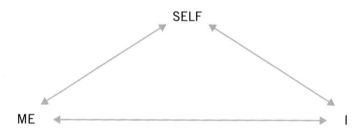

certain of its needs."[47] Mead's conceptualization of the three elements of the self is represented in Figure 15.1:

As mentioned above, Mead insisted that the self "arises in social experience ... it is impossible to conceive of a self arising outside of social experience."[48] Mead defines the "I" and the "Me" in the following way:

> The "I" is the response of the organism to the attitudes of the others; the "me" is the organized set of attitudes of others, which one himself assumes. The attitudes of the others constitute the organized "me," and then one reacts toward that as an "I." ... And it is due to the individual's ability to take the attitudes of these others in so far as they can be organized that he gets self-consciousness. The taking of all of those organized sets of attitudes gives him his "me": that is the self he is aware of ... That is, the self that immediately exists for him in his consciousness. He has their attitudes, knows what they want and what the consequences of any act of his will be, and he has assumed responsibility for the situation.

Now, it is the presence of those organized sets of attitudes that constitute that "me" to which he as an "I" is responding.[49]

The "I" represents the immediate and creative response while the "Me" represents self-conscious control and reflexivity. For Mead, consciousness is not located in the brain, but rather it is accounted for within the social process. It is only when the "Me" is taken as an object by the "I," a process made available through its relation to "generalized others," that the social self is said to embody the formation (and transformation) of self-consciousness. People are constantly reaching to organized social communities as a way not of asserting themselves, but of expressing themselves. The attitudes involved are gathered from the group, but the individual in whom they are organized has the opportunity of giving them a new expression. Mead writes:

> One appeals from fixed conventions which no longer have any meaning to a community in which the rights shall be publicly recognized, and one appeals to others on the assumption that there is a group of organized others that answer to one's own appeal— even if the appeal be made to posterity. In that case there is the attitude of the "I" as over against the "me."[50]

The realization of the self in the social situation in which it arises is a dialectical process. Mead posits that the individual, in relationship to others in the community, is "constantly reacting" to the social attitudes and changing in a cooperative process the very community to which she or he belongs. There are thus conflicts or contradictions such as between the "I" and the "Me," the need to conform to the generalized other, and the drive also to be creative and change society, which appear to proximate to Hegel's philosophy and dialectics. Importantly, it is language that allows for this continuous reaction and response from the self. Here, Mead emphasizes the symbolic nature of the social process: "The process of communication is ... in one sense more universal ... It is the medium through which ... cooperative activities can be carried on in the self-conscious society."[51] The key question, therefore, and one largely unexplored by Mead scholars, is: What is the process of self-conscious for organized society?

Mead's Theory of Society

For Mead, it is only when the "Me" is taken as an object by the "I," a dialectic process made possible through its relation to "others," that the social self is said to embody the formulation and transformation of self-consciousness. In Mead's model, it is only when an "Institution" (or

FIGURE 15.2 Structure of Society

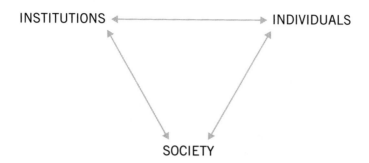

generalized social attitudes) is taken as an object by the "Individuals" in their relation to "Society" that it is said to embody a self-conscious society.[52] Figure 15.2 is a diagrammatic representation of Mead's conception of society, consisting of three elements: Institutions, Individuals, and Society.

The "Institutions" of society are "organized forms of group or social activity—forms so organized that the individual members of society can act adequately and socially by taking the attitudes of others towards these activities."[53] For Mead, social institutions, like individual selves, are developments within, and formalized manifestations of, the social life-process.[54] "Individuals" appear as mediations between their respective own "selves" and their existence as "citizens" or "individual members" within a society.

"Society" itself represents all its individual members within a universal unity, at a particular evolutionary stage of development. Mead explicitly argues that the evolution of society is decisive for both the self-conscious development of society and the self-conscious development of social selves. The evolutionary process in Mead's concept of society can be construed as a passage from "past" to "present" and to "future" in the dynamics of society. In Mead's social psychology, "institutions" and social "habits," together with what he calls the "generalized other," represent social elements involved in the dialectic development of society and of the self. Mead expresses it like this:

> There are, then, whole series of such common responses in the community in which we live, and such responses are what we term "institutions." The institution represents a common response on the part of all members of the community to a particular situation. This common response is one which, of course, varies with the character of the individual.... There is a common response in varied forms. And these variations ... have an organization,

which gives unity to the variety of the responses.... When we arouse such attitudes, we are taking the attitude of what I have termed a "generalized other." Such organized sets of response are related to each other; if one calls out one such set of response, he is implicitly calling out others as well.[55]

Institutions, habits, and the generalized other all belong to the group or "phylogenetic" development of society; thus, they have to be understood as being produced by the "self-evolution and self-transformation" of society.[56] Societal shifts, trade unions, and the suffragist movement in the twentieth century and identity politics and the #MeToo movement of the twenty-first century are examples of how the self-transformation of society occurs within mass democracy.[57]

In these forms, they are presented as "organized" and defining the social, or "socially responsible, patterns of individual conduct in only a very broad and general sense, affording plenty of scope for originality, flexibility, and variety of such conduct."[58] Similar reactions and responses among individuals are yielded through institutions, habits, and the generalized other of human behavior; the meanings that are attached to practices (e.g., traffic signals dictate driver behavior because of the meaning associated with "stop" signs); and forms of public discourse (e.g., human rights). For Mead, the self is formed by its participation in the social process of which it is part; importantly, if self-consciousness is dialectically developed in individuals as a microsocial process, it will be the result of the general macrosocial process that takes place in the development of society. Unlike Marx, Mead did not precisely explain the developmental "stages," so to speak, of human history that take societies from one form to the next; he only observed that so far as the development of human society is concerned, "the process itself is a long way from its goal."[59] However, he does make reference to some features of human society that demonstrate crucial differences in its development:

One difference between primitive human society and civilized human society is that in primitive human society the individual self is much more completely determined, with regard to his thinking and his behavior, by the general pattern of the organized social activity carried on by the particular social group to which he belongs, than he is in civilized human society. In other words, primitive human society offers much less scope for individuality—for original, unique, or creative thinking and behavior on the part of the individual self within it or belonging to it—

than does civilized human society; and indeed the evolution of civilized human society from primitive human society has largely depended on or resulted from a progressive social liberation of the individual self and his conduct, with the modifications and elaborations of the human social process which have followed from and been made possible by that liberation.[60]

Thus, in modern or "civilized" societies the "I" predominates and there is greater creative individuality in contrast to "primitive" societies where the controlled "Me" prevailed over the creative "I." As others have observed, however, Mead's evolution of the self is predicated on a dubious assumption when so much social theory—from, for example, Michel Foucault to Antony Giddens—envisages the reverse process where the creative "I" is subordinated to the discipline and self-restraint of the "Me."[61] Mead argues that the two processes—the self-conscious development of society and the self-conscious development of social selves—are parallel in that they participate in an understanding of ourselves that can only be attained as collective effort, formally transcribed and interpreted by historians.

Interestingly—and parallels can be drawn here with Marx's theory of history—Mead points out that the historical process, in order to take place under specific circumstances, relies on particular individuals who emerge as "leaders" with rhetorical skills and appear to have developed a higher level of consciousness of themselves and of their own society. As Mead states:

Occasionally a person arises who is able to take in more than others of an act in process, who can put himself into relation with whole groups in the community whose attitudes have not entered into the lives of the others in the community. He becomes a leader. Classes under a feudal order may be so separated from each other that, while they can act in certain traditional circumstances, they cannot understand each other; and then there may arise an individual who is capable of entering into the attitudes of the other members of the group. Figures of that sort become of enormous importance because they make possible communication between groups otherwise completely separated from each other. The sort of capacity we speak of is in politics the attitude of the statesman who is able to enter into the attitudes of the group and to mediate between them by making his own experience universal, so that others can enter into this form of communication through him.[62]

In this passage, Mead appears to be echoing Weber's work on "pure" charisma, and the important capacity of leaders to channel pathos to make the leaders' "own experience universal."

FIGURE 15.3 The Micro and Macro Process of Self and Society

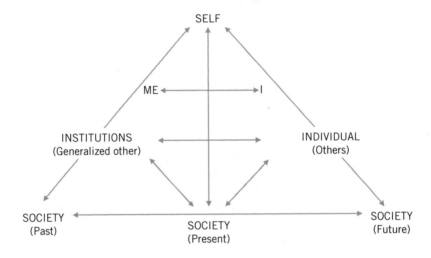

The multidimensional reality of the social self (an "I" and a "Me") and society ("Individuals" and "Institutions") each represent "mediation" between these forms. The topology of the concept of the self (Figure 15.1) and the concept of society (Figure 15.2) can be integrated to show two sets of triangles representing how the self and society are "integral parts of each other, interdependent realities that continuously interpenetrate each other,"[63] as shown in Figure 15.3.

The upper triangle depicts the microprocess of self, particularly through the "Me," which, as explained, represents the internalization of organized relations to others, as well as the generalized other. The lower triangle represents the macroprocess of society, particularly through "others," representing "individuals" in their external forms, and "institutions" as the objective form of the generalized other.

This topology of Mead's concept of self and society depicts individuals as members of society, and society embodied in individuals, as reflected in the two integrated triangles. For Mead, the "social self" is understood according to self-consciousness, which implies a reciprocal relation to other social selves. However, social selves also exist in relation to institutions and society as a whole. As he puts it:

We must recognize that the most concrete and most fully realized society is not that which is presented in institutions as such, but that which is found in the interplay of social habits and customs, in the readjustments of personal interests that have come into conflict and which take place outside of court, in the change of social attitude that is not dependent upon an act of legislature. In the society which is closest to that of the primitive man we find the reality of all that is prefigured and set out in the institutions, and while problems that are not and cannot be solved through the readjustments of the individual's habit and the immediate change in social attitudes have to be dealt with in the halls of legislature and the rooms of our high courts, they are only brought there to enable men to envisage them more clearly and especially to become conscious of interests which could not appear immediately in their reactions to each other. When, however, this has taken place and the essential meaning of the problem has been grasped, its solutions lies in the action of common citizens with reference to the common goods which our institutions have brought to their view and so analyzed that they can react to these new interests as they have to those to which they are already adjusted.[64]

This reconstruction of Mead's concept of self and society takes into account his understanding of society's evolution: "past societies" (which go back to animal societies in Mead's thought) and, conversely, "future society," which deals primarily with the "Me."

Selves and societies are understood in their mutual relations, which develop in a dynamic, evolutionary way: From past societies to future society. In other words, there is dialectic at work between Self and Society, one that is mediated by "mind," as it develops over time, from past societies to future society. Mead's conception of society is dynamic, as seen when he states:

The changes that we make in the social order in which we are implicated necessarily involve our also making changes in ourselves. The social conflicts among the individual members of a given organized human society, which, for their removal, necessitate conscious or intelligent reconstruction and modifications of that society by those individuals of their own selves and personalities. Thus the relations between social reconstruction and self or personality reconstruction are reciprocal and internal or organic; social reconstruction by the individual members of any

organized human society entails self or personality reconstruction in some degree or other by each of these individuals, and
vice versa, for, since their selves or personalities are constituted
by their organized social relations to one another, they cannot
reconstruct those selves or personalities without also reconstruct-
ing, to some extent, the given social order, which is, of course,
likewise constituted by their organized social relations to one
another.... [I]n short, social reconstruction and self or personality
reconstruction are the two sides of a single process—the process
of human social evolution.[65]

For Mead, it is the development of society per se, however, that has the
power to open up the minds of individual selves and inspire an understanding of social reform. Mead states:

Human society, we have insisted, does not merely stamp the pattern of its organized social behavior upon any one of its individual members, so that this pattern becomes likewise the pattern of
the individual's self; it also, at the same time, gives him a mind,
as the means or ability of consciously conversing with himself
in terms of the social attitudes which constitute the structure of
his self and which embody the pattern of human society's organized behavior as reflected in that structure. And his mind enables
him in turn to stamp the pattern of his further developing self
(further developing through his mental activity) upon the structure or organization of human society, and thus in a degree to
reconstruct and modify in terms of his self the general pattern
of social or group behavior in terms of which his self was originally constituted.[66]

This reciprocal relation between self-consciousness in individuals and
self-conscious society, also incorporating "time" through the categories of
"past" and "future," represent "the complete topological view of Mead's
concept of society."[67]

Writing at a time of social unrest, particularly in Western Europe prior
to World War I, post-1917 revolutionary Russia, and the growing interest
in communism across Western Europe, Mead discusses the processes
by which societies transform. Past societies were based on religion or
economic social organization. For Mead, the future society is different,
and involves universal social processes with free, open communications
as its core foundation. As he puts it:

If evolution were to take place in such a society, it would take place between the different organizations, so to speak, within this larger organism. There would not simply be a competition of different societies with each other, but competition would lie in the relationship of this or that society to the organization of a universal society....

The human social ideal—the ideal or ultimate goal of human social progress—is the attainment of a universal society in which all human individuals would possess a perfected social intelligence, such that all social meanings would each be similarly reflected in their respective individual consciousness—such that the meanings of any one individual's acts or gestures (as realized by him and expressed in the structure of his self, through his ability to take the social attitude of other individuals toward himself and toward their common social ends or purposes) would be the same for any other individual whatever who responded to them.[68]

Like Marx, Mead does envisage an "ideal society," but his ideal state has to be understood in the context of the political context in Western Europe and Mead's views on the primacy of education. Importantly, for Mead education "provides the crucial link between the ontogenetic process in the present in the child and the phylogenetic process of the evolution of society ... it is by reforming education that society at large can eventually be reformed."[69]

The most well-known accomplishment of Mead's work, the theory of the self, necessarily involves a relation to society. Mead's understanding of the dialectic process at work in the development of self-consciousness, both for the individual and for society, is a significant contribution to sociological theory, even though he seemed reluctant to endorse the discipline in his writings.

Criticism

At a theoretical level there are several aspects of Mead's theory of self that have drawn criticism. The first criticism relates to the ambivalence of Mead's definition of the "Self," which has been long debated with respect to what the "I" and "Me" elements mean. At times Mead considers the "I" as part of the social experience, but at other times he apparently considers it as an ever-elusive "transcendental entity" that stands "behind" the "Me" but reacts to it (and to reference others), and at still other times he considers the "I" as the phase of the self representing the mind in a biological sense (driven by "impulses"). As a result, Mead appears to shift from the sense of an "I" that is part of the social intercourse to the contradictory sense of an "I" defined prior to this social experience.[70]

The second criticism relates to the neglect and need to elucidate the concept of the "Me" in a society with a racial divide—how the other (African American) sees the white American or to the internalization of what the other expects "Me" to do or be. Although Mead discusses obstacles to the development of the "ideal society" and draws attention to caste systems, which, because they are restrictive, "cut down the possibility of the full development of the self."[71] Mead appears oblivious to the obstacles in apartheid America (let alone to the work of Du Bois), even though he acknowledges that the development of the democratic society "implies the removal of castes as essential to the personality of the individual."[72] Such an observation acknowledges that widespread race discrimination denied the development of the personality of African Americans.

A third criticism relates to Mead's understanding of politics and, in particular, the influences of corporations on shaping public discourse and education. It is a striking omission that these powerful actors, which by the 1900s were determining life experiences for millions of workers and influencing politicians, were so little mentioned, let alone studied, by a pragmatist thinker such as Mead.[73] Relatedly, Mead's sociocultural analysis of the self and society neglects the whole issues of "power" as it is objectively structured in society, which is puzzling, to say the least, given the importance he attached to the role of selves in the transformation of society through the remodeling of institutions, fueled by the activism of charismatics and by the activity of social movements.

The fourth criticism relates to gender and language and class and language. For Mead, vocal gestures define mind as they define human society, which means that human communication is central to social interaction and the development of the self. This being said, it seems that Mead did not pay much attention to the way communication differs between genders. There appear to be important differences between conversation styles of men and women, which affect social relationships.[74] Mead does not analyze gender. To do so, particularly in an American society deeply segregated by race and shaped by a history in which white upper-class men were at the top of the social hierarchy, would have better captured the nuances of self and societal self-development. Furthermore, there is a paucity of thinking in Mead's conceptualization of society for the intersection of language and social class. Research shows that children growing up in working-class families receiving welfare benefits in the United States hear a far less rich vocabulary during their early years than do children in professional families,[75] and, generally, social class has major effects on children's cognitive and language development.[76] Although Mead does discuss social classes in terms of "enriching" social relations, a consideration of the explicit link between class, social inequality, and language would have better enhanced our understanding of the development of the self.

The fifth criticism relates to Mead's concepts of "universality" and the notion of the "ideal society." Postcolonial theory has critiqued his "ultimate goal of human progress ... a universal human society." Cultural transmission is implicit in Mead's theory and vision of an "ideal society" when it is embedded in the formation and transformation of habits. In the context of recent military intervention by Western powers in other countries, such as Iraq and Afghanistan, often with an explicit goal of "regime change" or "building democracy," Mead's universal project, although legitimate in the eyes of some Western politicians, raises justifiable questions about the legitimacy of Western "democracies" imposing their system and institutions on other societies.[77]

Conclusion

In his critical review of Mead's work, Hans Joas points out that during Mead's lifetime his influence was almost limited to a few colleagues and students at the University of Chicago.[78] After his death, the school of "symbolic interactionism" appropriated Mead's social psychology. To this end, the American sociologist Herbert Blumer, a former student of Mead, was instrumental in refashioning Mead's social psychology to sociology. Thus, Mead came to be seen as the school's "progenitor," even though, until the 1980s, his ideas remained somewhat "marginal,"[79] referenced, along with Cooley and Durkheim, as important for the understanding of the internalization of cultural norms and mores. Outside the United States, some European scholars (e.g. Lev Vygotsky, Mikhail Bakhtin, Jürgen Habermas) were openly receptive to Mead's work. For example, Habermas identified Mead as the principal inspirer of his *Theory of Communicative Action* (1981).[80]

Since the 1980s, sociologists have attached greater importance to Mead's ideas. Although the dominant focus has been on Mead's theoretical grasp of the unity of the individual or microsocial interactions and socializations, a "reconstruction" and reinterpretation of Mead's social psychology has focused on the societal or macrosociological and reformist components of Mead's ideas, which, it is argued, were erased, together with his radical ideas on social reform, by Herbert Blumer.[81] That Blumer's interpretation of Mead has become dominant within North American sociology, Jean-Francois Côté argues, can still be seen in contemporary social theory that rarely employs his social psychology beyond a "cursory understanding" of the "self" in its interactions with "others." Moreover, the dominant interpretations of Mead do not take into account his concept of society.[82] George Ritzer, for example, confidently asserts that Mead's work "largely lacks a macro sense of society."[83] As Côté rightly points out, a reinterpretation of Mead's dialectic views of the self and society go well beyond the focus on Blumerian symbolic interactionism to theories of societal self-transformation. In sum, Mead's theory of self and society defines his place in the classical social canon.

FURTHER THINKING:

How does Mead's theory of the self explicitly link to his concept of society? Thinking about Mead's ideas on communications, what is the role of rhetoric in contemporary political discourse and social change?

FURTHER READING:

The following are useful secondary sources on G.H. Mead: J.D. Baldwin, *George Herbert Mead: A Unifying Theory of Sociology* (London: Sage, 1986); G.A. Cook, *George Herbert Mead: The Making of a Social Pragmatist* (Urbana: University of Illinois Press, 1993); Jean-Francois Côté, *George Herbert Mead's Concept of Society: A Critical Reconstruction* (Boulder, CO: Paradigm, 2015); Hans Joas, "The Emergence of the New: Mead's Theory and Its Contemporary Potential," in *Handbook of Social Theory*, ed. George Ritzer and Barry Smart (London: Sage, 2001), 89–99; and L. Athens, "Domination: The Blind Spot in Mead's Analysis of the Social Act," *Journal of Classical Sociology* 2, no. 1 (2002): 25–42. Also see further readings at the end of the book.

Notes

1   Hans Joas, *G.H. Mead: A Contemporary Re-Examination of His Thought* (Cambridge, MA: MIT Press, 1985), 7, and cited by Alex Law, *Social Theory for Today* (London: Sage, 2015), 244.

2   Jean-Francois Côté, *George Herbert Mead's Concept of Society: A Critical Reconstruction* (Boulder, CO: Paradigm, 2015), 2.

3   Hans Joas, "The Emergence of the New: Mead's Theory and Its Contemporary Potential," in *Handbook of Social Theory*, ed. George Ritzer and Barry Smart (London: Sage, 2001), 89–99.

4 Joas, "The Emergence of the New," 95.

5 Côté, *George Herbert Mead's Concept of Society*, vii.

6 George Ritzer, *Classical Sociological Theory*, 5th ed. (New York: McGraw-Hill, 2008), 433.

7 Côté, *George Herbert Mead's Concept of Society*, viii.

8 Joas, "The Emergence of the New," 89.

9 Côté, *George Herbert Mead's Concept of Society*, 103.

10 Côté, *George Herbert Mead's Concept of Society*, 111.

11 Faris, reviewing *Mind, Self and Society* in 1936, pointed out that the title of the book followed the "reverse order" to that which the organization of Mead's ideas would seem appropriate: "Not mind and then society: but society first and then minds within that society." Ellsworth Faris, "Review of *Mind, Self and Society* by George H. Mead," *American Journal of Sociology* 41 (1936): 810, and cited by Côté, *George Herbert Mead's Concept of Society*, 112. It is outside the scope of this chapter to explore the controversy surrounding the passage from *George Herbert Mead's Social Psychology* (Chicago: University of Chicago Press, 1964) to sociology, but interested readers should consult chapter 4 of Côté's book, which we quote at length in this chapter.

12 Morris provides a bibliography of Mead's writings, chronologically arranged, comprising 68 papers. Côté also notes that most of Mead's articles published in his lifetime are available through the Mead Project website at Brock University (www.brocku.ca/MeadProject). Côté, *George Herbert Mead's Concept of Society*, xvi.

13 Joas, "The Emergence of the New," 90.

14 J. Valsiner and R. Veer, "On the Social Nature of Human Cognition: An Analysis of the Shared Intellectual Roots of George Herbert Mead and Lev Vygotsky," *Journal for the Theory of Social Behaviour* 18, no. 1 (1988), 117–36, p. 127.

15 John Dewey, "The Reflex Arc Concept in Psychology," *Psychological Review* 3, no. 4 (1896): 357.

16 Cited in George Herbert Mead, *Mind, Self and Society*, ed. Charles W. Morris (1934; Chicago: University of Chicago Press, 1974), 3.

17 Mead, *Mind, Self and Society*, 105.

18 Côté, *George Herbert Mead's Concept of Society*, 51

19 As quoted in William James, *Pragmatism* (1907; Cambridge, MA: Harvard University Press, 1975), xxiv.

20 Cited by Alex Law, *Social Theory for Today* (London: Sage, 2015), 241.

21 Wilhelm Dilthey, *Introduction to the Human Sciences, Selected Works*, vol. 1, ed. Rudolph A. Makkreel and Rodi Frithjof (Princeton, NJ: Princeton University Press, 1989), 208, 211, 213, and cited by Côté, *George Herbert Mead's Concept of Society*, 128.

22 Ritzer, *Classical Sociological Theory*, 416.

23 Georg Simmel, *The Philosophy of Money*, ed. David Frisby (London: Routledge, 2004), 296.

24 Charles Horton Cooley, "Looking-Glass Self" (1902), in *The Production of Reality: Essays and Readings on Social Interaction*, ed. Jodi O'Brien (Thousand Oaks, CA: Pine Forge Press, 2011), 6.

25 Ritzer, *Classical Sociological Theory*, 432.

26 Côté, *George Herbert Mead's Concept of Society*, 10.

27 Côté, *George Herbert Mead's Concept of Society*, 11.

28 Côté, *George Herbert Mead's Concept of Society*, 103.

29   G. Jacobs, "Influence and Canonical Supremacy: An Analysis of How G.H. Mead Demoted C.H. Cooley in the Sociological Canon," *Journal of the History of Behavioral Sciences* 45, no. 2 (2009): 117–44, and cited by Côté, *George Herbert Mead's Concept of Society*, 129.

30   George Herbert Mead, "What Social Objects Must Psychology Presuppose?", *Journal of Philosophy, Psychology and Scientific Methods* 7 (1910): 177, and cited by Côté, *George Herbert Mead's Concept of Society*, 11–12.

31   Mead, *Mind, Self and Society*, 6.

32   Mead, *Mind, Self and Society*, 7.

33   Mead, *Mind, Self and Society*, 140.

34   Mead, *Mind, Self and Society*, 133.

35   Mead, *Mind, Self and Society*, 140.

36   Joas, "The Emergence of the New," 91.

37   Mead, *Mind, Self and Society*, 6.

38   Mead, *Mind, Self and Society*, 14.

39   Mead, *Mind, Self and Society*, 133–34.

40   Côté, *George Herbert Mead's Concept of Society*, 53.

41   Mead, *Mind, Self and Society*, 151.

42   Mead, *Mind, Self and Society*, 151.

43   Mead, *Mind, Self and Society*, 155.

44   Joas, "The Emergence of the New," 92.

45   Côté, *George Herbert Mead's Concept of Society*, 46.

46   Joas, "The Emergence of the New," 92.

47   Joas, "The Emergence of the New," 92.

48   Mead, *Mind, Self and Society*, 47.

49   Mead, *Mind, Self and Society*, 175.

50   Mead, *Mind, Self and Society*, 199.

51   Mead, *Mind, Self and Society*, 259.

52   We quote Côté's argument at length in this section.

53   Mead, *Mind, Self and Society*, 261–62.

54   Mead, *Mind, Self and Society*, 262.

55   Mead, *Mind, Self and Society*, 261.

56   Côté, *George Herbert Mead's Concept of Society*, 59.

57   Côté, *George Herbert Mead's Concept of Society*, 151.

58   Mead, *Mind, Self and Society*, 262.

59   Mead, *Mind, Self and Society*, 252.

60   Mead, *Mind, Self and Society*, 221.

61   Law, *Social Theory for Today* (London: Sage, 2015), 244.

62   Mead, *Mind, Self and Society*, 256–57.

63   Côté, *George Herbert Mead's Concept of Society*, 73.

64   George Herbert Mead, "Natural Rights and the Theory of Political Institution," *Journal of Philosophy, Psychology and Scientific Methods* 12 (1915): 152–53, and cited by Côté, *George Herbert Mead's Concept of Society*, 74.

65   Mead, *Mind, Self and Society*, 309.

66 Mead, *Mind, Self and Society*, 263.

67 Côté, *George Herbert Mead's Concept of Society*, 77.

68 Mead, *Mind, Self and Society*, 281, 310.

69 Côté, *George Herbert Mead's Concept of Society*, 89.

70 Côté, *George Herbert Mead's Concept of Society*, 70–71.

71 Mead, *Mind, Self and Society*, 318.

72 Mead, *Mind, Self and Society*, 318.

73 Côté, *George Herbert Mead's Concept of Society*, 179.

74 See, for example, Deborah Tannen, *You Just Don't Understand: Women and Men in Conversation* (New York: Ballantine Books, 1990), and Deborah Tannen, *I Only Say This Because I Love You* (New York: Ballantine Books, 2001).

75 B. Hart and T.R. Risley, *Meaningful Differences in Everyday Experience of Young American Children* (Baltimore: Brookes Publishing, 1995).

76 See an early study: B. Bernstein, "A Public Language: Some Sociological Implications of a Linguistic Form," *British Journal of Sociology* 10, no. 4 (1959): 311–26.

77 Côté, *George Herbert Mead's Concept of Society*, 181.

78 Joas, "The Emergence of the New," 95.

79 Joas, "The Emergence of the New," 96.

80 Joas, "The Emergence of the New," 97.

81 Côté, *George Herbert Mead's Concept of Society*, xi.

82 Côté, *George Herbert Mead's Concept of Society*, xi.

83 Ritzer, *Classical Sociological Theory*, 433.

PART IV
CLASSICAL SOCIAL THEORY TODAY

16. Concluding Thoughts on the Classical Canon

If we educate our graduates in the inevitability of tooth-and-claw-capitalism, it is hardly surprising that we end up with justification for massive salary payments to people who take huge risks with other people's money. If we teach that there is nothing else below the bottom line, then ideas about sustainability, diversity, stakeholders, responsibility and so on become mere decoration.

—Martin Parker, 2018[1]

Since 2017 the scale of the financial crisis has placed that relationship between democratic politics and the demands of capitalist governance under immense strain. Above all, this strain has manifested itself ... in a crisis in the political parties that have historically mediated the two.

—Adam Tooze, 2018[2]

AS GEORGE MONBIOT SAYS IN THE EPIGRAPH TO THIS BOOK, ideas matter. Without the dominant infrastructure of capitalist ideology, and the justifying narratives it disseminates, the current grotesque levels of social inequalities and ecological destruction would be considered intolerable. Monbiot is writing about how ideas determine whether human ingenuity and capacity serve society and the planet or work against it. The purpose of this chapter is to draw some general conclusions about the continuing relevance of classical social theory, even in the age of Apple, Amazon, Google, and Facebook. As dramatized in director Robert Zemeckis's 1985 film *Back to the Future*, the present and the future depend on the route taken in the past. Where sociology is going in the future depends upon its past and how sociologists have intellectually traveled from the past to the present. The preceding chapters have attempted to show that the ideas of classical social thinkers have shaped the present world and our understanding of it. Marx, Durkheim, and Weber; Wollstonecraft, Martineau, Luxemburg, and Perkins Gilman; Du Bois and Mead—all were, without doubt, social thinkers. But they were also storytellers. As Noah Richler observes, stories provoke public discourse and play a role in societal conflicts. Stories reflect the world back to us, constituting the frames—mental structures that shape the way we see the world—around which we build our system of morality, values, and truths.[3] What these social thinkers have given us in their eminent works, ranging from *A Vindication of the Rights of Woman, Capital,* and *The Division of Labor in Society* to Weber's *The Protestant Ethic and the Spirit of Capitalism* is a series of grand narratives on modernity, each as distinctive and insightful as any to be found in the celebrated novels of their age.

The lasting classical legacy may be summarized by a series of concepts—*materiality, morality, rationality, gender, race,* and *culture*—that can be used to examine modern society.[4] We believe these ideas will continue to shape social theory and research, just as they continue to exert profound influence on intellectual inquiry, public consciousness, and human agency in the context of global capitalism. In this post-Trump and post-Brexit era, therefore, the ideas of the classical theorists should become part of the mental fixtures of every educated citizen because these concepts continue to exert so profound an influence on intellectual inquiry, public consciousness, and human agency.

A major theme running through this book has been a stress on the continuities as well as the discontinuities across time. In post-Brexit Britain and in the United States, according to Trump, immigration makes societies more fragmented. However, the emergence of mass social movements and societal conflict was undoubtedly part of the context for the development of post-nineteenth-century social theory. From working-class struggles for democracy to the suffragettes, to the American Civil War and anti-slavery struggles, European and American history is one of contestation. As Malik (2018) observes, the fractures of nineteenth-century Britain and the United States expose "the myth that, until disrupted by immigration, nations existed as organic political and cultural communities defined by a 'collective consciousness.'"[5] The sojourn into social history underscores that societies have always ruptured along class, religious, and ideological divides. These dynamic pre-1914 social developments provided the context of the classical works of Marx, Durkheim, Weber, Du Bois, Mead, and the early feminist thinkers.

The development of social theory has built upon the ideas of earlier philosophers and public intellectuals and these have to be contextualized adequately if we are to appreciate their relevance. Thus, we can only really appreciate Marx's critique of consciousness if we know what debates on religion took place in his lifetime. The Enlightenment movement was not a unified body of thinking but was internally fractured and riddled with contradictions. The inconsistencies of Enlightenment views on slavery and women's rights provide examples of these contradictions. Nevertheless, the very public debates between the typically rationalist and secular Enlightenment ideology and the conservative philosophical reaction to it have left a legacy in the form of classical propositions about the nature of society. These ideas about society profoundly influenced and shaped the classical canon we study today.

The Classical Triumvirate

In part II of *Capitalism and Classical Social Theory*, we examined the original classical triumvirate of scholars: Marx, Durkheim, and Weber. We began our journey into the canon with Karl Marx. At the center of Marx's social theorizing is the primacy of capitalist production and the way this shaped the political and social life of the society. For Marx, society is created by purposive praxis, and it is material conditions that determine human consciousness. Durkheim, in contrast to Marx, believes society is self-creating, exists over and above the individual, and wields an immense power. Also in contrast to Marx, Weber believes that society is the fragile outcome of human interaction, so change in the realm of ideas is at least as important as change in the processes of economic production. Marx's multifaceted conception of alienation in its political, religious, philosophical, and economic forms has had a lasting effect on the work of later sociologists and social philosophers. As we have noted, Marx's critique of consciousness is worthy of our attention for more than historical reasons. In contemporary debates on religion, multiculturalism, and the public discourse on Christianity and Islam, Marx's philosophical concepts continue to be insightful and suggestive, and they remain a fertile source for social theorizing. Turning to Marx's methodology, we argued for the continued significance of Marx's dialectic. The dialectic, which helps us to understand connections between disparate processes and events, allows us to think creatively about the apparent contradictions that lie at the heart of globalization in a post-Trump world. The dialectic can, for example, help us to conceptualize both the intensified conflict over the earth's shrinking reserves of natural resources and the rise of a more effective opposition to the economic sources of global climate change.

Marx's conception of history provides a series of interrelated structural concepts through which to interpret the development of the past and to expose contradictory social phenomena in the present. These ideas encourage us to see the present society in historical-materialist terms. They underlie C. Wright Mills' notion of the sociological imagination, which requires us to relate personal troubles to the history of the social transformations that typically lie behind them.[6] For example, researchers have confirmed that mental illness, obesity, and reduced life expectancy are far greater in the least well-off in society.

Our sociological imagination should also help us make the connection between "capital behavior" and global warming. Throughout the twentieth century, sociology tended to neglect how the engine of modernity was so dependent on the natural world. This despite the fact that Marx's brilliantly original nineteenth-century analysis of industrial capitalism highlighted its *modus operandi* to sap both "the soil and the laborer." Capital is implicated within the processes and practices that generate increases in global temperatures, which have risen by at least 0.74°C over the past century.[7] As we write in the summer of 2018, extreme weather has brought record temperatures in the mid-40°C; lethal fires to North America, Europe, North Africa, Australia, and Japan; and deadly monsoon floods in the southern Indian state of Kerala. As we noted, Marx was well aware of the effects of resource-fueled capitalism and how the efforts of capital focused on the subjugation and exploitation of the living planet. He observes, "Capitalist production, by collecting the population in great centers ... disturbs the circulation of matter between man and soil, ... it therefore violates the conditions necessary to lasting fertility of the soil."[8] Despite the potential for high-carbon societies to self-destruct, our institutions and the efforts of Western governments seem to be "concentrated not on defending the living Earth from destruction, but on defending the machine that is destroying it."[9]

Cliché has it that we live in a post-ideological age in which grand narratives have been discredited and discarded, much like the US and UK steel industry of the twentieth century.[10] Ideology, however, continues to run deep through Western governments' foreign and economic policies and, importantly, through the academic scaffolding and curricula of university business schools. As Martin Parker's compelling critique argues, both the explicit and the hidden curriculums taught generally in business schools aim ultimately to produce a frictionless planet for the benefit of capital. Within business schools, which form part of what Thomas Picketty in *Capital in the Twenty-First Century* calls an "apparatus of justification," neoliberalism and capitalism are "assumed to be the end of history, an economic model which has trumped all others, and is now taught as a science, rather than ideology."[11] Significantly, we suggested that Marx's ideas on ideology are highly relevant in modern political economy and sociology as a means to analyze the

nexus between the realm of ideas and those of neoliberalism and economic nationalism pursued by the political far right. This relevance is
illustrated in the work of Canadian writer Naomi Klein in *The Shock
Doctrine*, which documents the ascendancy of the ideology of US global
laissez-faire capitalism:

> Since the fall of Communism, free markets and free people have
> been packaged as a single ideology that claims to be humanity's
> best and only defence against repeating a history filled with mass
> graves, killing fields and torture chambers. Yet in the Southern
> Cone [South America], the first place where the contemporary
> religion of unfettered free markets ... was applied in the real
> world, it did not bring democracy; it was predicated on the over-
> throw of democracy in country after country. And it did not
> bring peace but required the systematic murder of tens of thou-
> sands and the torture of between 100,000 and 150,000 people.[12]

In *The Division of Labor in Society* Durkheim presents a theory of
social evolution that contains the interplay between structural or material
factors such as population size and cultural ideas. His analysis centers
on the importance of culture and morality because the division of labor
presupposes a prior morality and the development of a culture of anomie
results from rapid social change that prevents new habits and moral
values from becoming embedded in organic society. A concern with moral
regulation is the central theme of Durkheim's major studies on suicide,
religion, and education. Durkheim identified anomic and egoistic suicides
as the main currents of suicide in organic societies due to a lack of regulation and integration. In his major studies he refers to the implications of
his analysis by pointing to the need for the development of a new morality
that matches new social arrangements.

In each of his major studies, Durkheim makes brief references to
human nature and the individual's need for social regulation. In his discussion of education, his portrayal of children as egoistical and asocial[13]
reflects his general view of the human being as a bundle of desires
that need to be channeled for the sake of social order.[14] Durkheim is
sometimes interpreted as being influenced by a conservative reaction to
social change,[15] but this is to neglect his more radical views on property
ownership, his anti-clericalism, and his commitment to state-provided
secular education. Turner argues Durkheim's sociology of morality is not
a conservative theory; rather, it is a "socialist response to the negative
impact of an anarchic economy on moral life."[16] If Durkheim thought
that the free market of his day was anarchic and prone to anomie,

then his theory has been given a new relevance by the neoliberal advocacy of minimal interference in markets, free trade between countries, and individualism: anomie has become globalized.

Durkheim's analysis of anomie due to a lack of regulation has the potential to be applied to economic activity within markets. Individual passions could only be limited to avoid social and personal harm, in Durkheim's analysis, if society provided moral regulation and placed restrictions on the desires of individuals. The neoliberal aspiration to allow individuals to pursue unfettered financial goals in unregulated markets opens up the possibility that they may develop an intense desire for wealth or power—or, in another word, *greed*. The leaking of millions of files from two major law firms that handle secret offshore investments for corporations, politicians, celebrities, and other super-rich individuals shows the extent to which tax evasion underestimates actual capital income[17] and the reluctance of the mega-rich to part with their money. Most of the banking in offshore tax havens is perfectly legal, but it raises serious ethical problems about the role of tax havens and the greed shown by rich individuals and corporations in their unwillingness to meet their tax obligations as a source of global inequality.[18]

In 1991, Stjepan G. Mestrovic[19] and John E.T. Eldridge[20] discussed the unleashing of greed and consequent financial disasters and business scandals as symptomatic of contemporary anomie. Their Durkheimian analysis was certainly out of step with the dominant assumptions of the leaders of finance and politics in the 1990s and up to the 2008 GFC (global financial crisis or crash). In 2005, prior to the GFC, Alan Greenspan, the US Federal Reserve chairman, complacently believed that the deregulated financial system with its complex financial products was "a far more flexible, efficient, and hence resilient financial system than the one that existed just a quarter-century ago."[21] During his period as British prime minister, Gordon Brown also advocated deregulation, famously calling for "light touch regulation" of the banking and financial sector.[22] The near collapse of the banking sector can be interpreted as a product of anomie. Although Paul Mason's account of the financial collapse of 2008 is not written from a Durkheimian perspective, his concluding analysis supports anomie theory. As he writes, "In the first week of October 2008, a deregulated banking system brought the entire economy of the world to the brink of collapse. It was the product of giant hubris and the untrammelled power of a financial elite."[23] With the failure of Lehman Brothers, it became obvious that global markets did not govern themselves. Indeed, their dysfunction threatened to implode the entire global economy.[24]

Max Weber's work on methodology in social science research still informs epistemological considerations today. We explained that Weber emphasized that, in both the natural and social sciences, facts never speak for themselves—they require interpretation—and research methods are always shaped by the researcher's cultural values and politics. In short, research methods cannot be separated from ideology. Weber's value-freedom/value-relevance dichotomy, as well as his use of singular causal analysis, his theory of social action, the application of *Verstehen* as a distinct mode of understanding, and the nature and purpose of ideal-type constructs are commonly referred to today. Central to Weber's discussion of social action is the notion of *Verstehen* or "interpretative understanding." According to Weber, social phenomena are identified not by their external characteristics but by social inquiry, which captures humans' inner states through interpretative understanding. Weber's essays—which chart the boundary between values, judgments, and epistemological neutrality—have been given canonical status in most introductory texts on social research methods. What emerges from Weber's work on social inquiry is that historical understanding is always interpretative, and, therefore, there is no one way of understanding capitalist modernity. Instead, multiple histories are relevant to the writer's values and interests. Thus, his contribution to social research methods foreshadows postmodernist thinking, in particular, its challenge to the project of creating a universal human history or other meta-narratives. Finally, we emphasized that Weber's rich and complex approach to human inquiry remains relevant to sociology today. As qualitative researchers Norman K. Denzin and Yvonna S. Lincoln observe, "The interpretive *bricoleur* understands that research is an interactive process shaped by his or her personal history, biography, gender, social class, race, and ethnicity, and by those of the people in the setting. The political *bricoleur* knows that science is power, for all research findings have political implications. There is no value-free science."[25]

We have examined Weber's well-known thesis on ascetic Protestantism and capitalism as well as some of the substantive areas of his sociology: social class, power, and bureaucracy. We discussed how difficult it is to impose a single overarching theme onto Weber's writings but suggested, as others have, that his conception of rationalization is a unifying theme. We examined his classic work on ascetic Protestantism and explained that, in contrast to Marx's theories, Weber's narrative of societal development avers that the growth of Western capitalism cannot be explained through wholly material and structural forces. Moreover, Western capitalism is embedded in the interconnected process of rationalization. We explained that Weber's thesis on rationalization informs his theories of social class, politics, and bureaucracies. Although Weber differed profoundly with some aspects of Marx's analysis of capitalism and class, Weber's theory of class reflects Marx's thinking: the ownership or the absence of property constitutes basic class divisions, and unambiguous economic interest is a factor producing class. As we explained, Weber departs from Marx in emphasizing that the level of skill embodied in labor power may be a form of property that produces class differentiation, and, thus, a social class situation is ultimately a market situation. For Weber, access to resources such as training and education affect an individual's position in the labor market and, in turn, strongly influence his or her overall *life chances*. To illustrate the continued relevance of Weber's work, we pointed out that Erik Olin Wright has combined the approaches of both Weber and Marx to formulate an influential theory of class.[26]

We also explained that theories of power, domination, and the state are pivotal to Weber's political sociology and that Weber's account of the political process is "resolutely elitist."[27] The modern state is necessarily based on domination and coercion, and bureaucracies are the purest form of legal-rational authority, according to Weber. We discussed Weber's pessimistic view of individual liberty within modern society and stressed that his iron cage metaphor is one of the most influential analogies in general critiques of modernity. In 2018, when President Donald Trump was accused of "autocratic envy" of his Russian counterpart, President Vladimir Putin,[28] Weber's observation is prescient: "It is as if in politics ... we were deliberately to become men who need 'order' and nothing but order, who become nervous and cowardly if for one moment this order wavers, and helpless if they are torn away from their total incorporation in it."[29] We next extended the discussion on Weber's theories of rationalization and bureaucracy. Here we explained that Weber understood bureaucracy to be the most efficient means of administration and realized that it produced unintended consequences for the overall functioning of rational institutions. His theory that rational systems could produce irrationalities, such as the dehumanization of those within them, as well as threaten creativity and leadership placed Weber in an ambiguous relationship with modernity. We also suggested that George Ritzer's discussion of McDonaldization provides an excellent example of the applicability of Weber's rationalization theory and of his ideas on the irrationality of rationality.

Another important strength of Weber's sociology is its continuing relevance in debates on capitalism and global warming. Like Marx, Weber recognized the finitude of the planet's fossil resources and the "heedless consumption of resources, for which there are no substitutes."[30] Contemporary sociologists draw on Weber's ideas to make the argument that ecological problems cannot be understood without making the ideological connections between Christianity, Western rationalism, and society's domination and exploitation of natural resources.

The work of social theorists Ulrich Beck, Anthony Giddens, Michael Mann, and W.G. Runciman represent a renaissance of Weberian historical sociology. This intellectual genre recognizably draws upon the tradition founded by Weber and eschews historical materialism, arguing that global capitalism and contemporary change and processes are caused by the interaction of several irreducibly distinct forms of power and domination. German sociologist Ulrich Beck argues that the contemporary wave of global capitalism produces a "detraditionalized" social life: "Those who live in this post-national, global society are constantly engaged in discarding old classifications and formulating new ones. The hybrid identities and cultures that ensue are precisely the individuality which then determines social integration. In this way, identity emerges through intersection and combination, and thus through conflict and other identities."[31] Weber's intellectual legacy is evident. Beck's analysis of contemporary global capitalism is inexorably paradoxical: society and social action are constituted out of conflictual arenas that are simultaneously closed, national, individualized and transnationally open, and defined in opposition to one another.

Expanding the Canon

Capitalism and Classical Social Theory has extended the traditional canon to include a selection of early feminist writings. These early social thinkers used their gender as a standpoint from which to expose what they saw as the androcentrism of "Enlightenment thinking" and early social theory. Marx and Engels, for example, presented gender relations in class societies as dominated by and secondary to property relations, and they viewed patriarchy as secondary to and derived from society's mode of production rather than an autonomous form of social inequality. The classical feminist ideas examined have played an important role in shaping and reshaping contemporary interpretations of gender, and, importantly, the ideas and theories that early feminist thinkers and activists have produced have influenced many of the educational, legal, and political reforms that have improved opportunities for women and their quality of life. Mary Wollstonecraft's *A Vindication of the Rights of Woman*, published over 225 years ago, was the first celebrated feminist manifesto.[32] It enunciated the principles of emancipation: an equal education for girls and boys, an end to sexual discrimination, and a right for women to be defined by their profession, not their partner. These principles have resonance in contemporary society. Mary Wollstonecraft and Harriet Martineau used the language of slavery to define women's status. As heirs of the European Enlightenment, these pioneers considered the oppression of white women as connected to the oppression of black female slaves and of slaves in general in eighteenth-century America.

Mary Wollstonecraft lived in a society challenged by the ideas of the French Revolution, prior to the establishment of university-based sociology. She brought to her task a formidable background in Unitarian rationalism and the ideas of radical reformers. Wollstonecraft did not argue for women's essential equality with men. She felt that, in fair competition, men would still be ahead. But she argued strenuously that women should be allowed to participate, as fully as they were able, in the making of society. Such participation would enhance both male and female virtues and contribute to the progress of society. Her writings were provocative calls to extend the Enlightenment ideals of liberty and equality of opportunity to everyone. Harriet Martineau attained an exceptional education for a woman of her time, and she was also strongly affected by Unitarian rationalism. She was contemporary with Auguste Comte and translated his major work into English. She was, nonetheless, a very different kind of social theorist. Martineau's books on sociological methods of observation and grounded theory building, as well as her critical theorizing about the anomalies of slavery and the political invisibility of women, set a standard that remains very high.

Rosa Luxemburg, by contrast, was a leading Marxist theorist and socialist who championed the cause of imprisoned prostitutes and supported the suffragette movement. In *The Accumulation of Capital*, she critiques Marx's theory of capitalist reproduction, and in so doing she produced the first modern theory of under-consumption. The Achilles heel of under-consumption theory is: What if capitalism does find a way of overcoming the low spending power of the majority? Luxemburg was compelled to search for an objective rationale for the breakdown of capitalism. The essence of her thesis was that mature capitalism can, at least in the short term, offset under-consumption by constantly expanding across the globe for "untrammelled accumulation," and this impulse is the economic motivation for the colonial wars between the superpowers. For Luxemburg, the outcome is the dialectical phenomenon that mature capitalist countries provide ever-larger markets for, and become increasingly dependent upon, one another, yet they compete ruthlessly for trade relations with non-capitalist countries. The invasion of Iraq by the United States and its ally Britain, as well as how Trump's economic nationalism, most spectacularly manifested in his "America first" trade policies, impact China and the European Union illustrate that Luxemburg's work remains "richly relevant" in the era of neoliberal capitalism.

As the historian Adam Tooze observes, economics and geopolitics are intertwined and the idea that the global economy is a realm beyond politics or the play of global power is a self-serving illusion.[33] The British economist Paul Mason[34] also argues that Luxemburg remains relevant because she identified a critical factor for the debate on "post-capitalism" today: the importance of an "outside world" for systems that successfully adapt.

Charlotte Perkins Gilman represents another thread of feminist thought. Perkins Gilman's use of evolutionary theory as an argument for the superiority of women and for the implicit inferiority of non-whites and immigrants from non-Western countries cannot be justified by scientific research. However, her work, grounded in her own experiences as a woman and as an observer of women in her society, contains arguments about the family, education, occupational opportunity, and also the social origins of crime and retarded development, all of which remain significant in sociological theory. Women's challenge to the traditional sociological canon has been carried out, from the beginning, in an activist as well as intellectual way. This intellectual activism of women was grounded in the social experiences that they so eloquently attempted to change.

We extended the canon further by examining the distinctive contribution of W.E.B. Du Bois to the development of social theory. Contemporary theories about the social construction of identity, race, and racial inequality can be traced back to the pioneering work of Du Bois. The work of Du Bois, which has contributed to questions of racial colonialism, racial enslavement, and the role of race in the dehumanization of the African American, serves as a model.[35] As we explained, his intellectual legacy is unquestionably related in complex ways to the sociocultural context in which it was shaped. The transformation of the United States, from an agrarian society to an economic and political superpower, provided the empirical backcloth to Du Boisian social thought in much the same way that the Industrial Revolution in Western Europe provided the context for Marx, Weber, and Durkheim. Du Bois's early studies appeared at the same time as Jack London's *The People of the Abyss* (1903), which described white working-class poverty in London's East End, and Upton Sinclair's *The Jungle* (1906), which exposed the appalling labor conditions in the American food industry. Du Bois was witness to and had personal experiences of structured racism, American apartheid, and Jim Crow laws.

Finally, in this new edition we draw on the work of Canadian sociologist Jean-Francois Côté to examine the legacy of George Herbert Mead.[36] Although Mead's analysis of the social self and society was almost limited to a few colleagues and students during his lifetime, the University of Chicago's school of "symbolic interactionism" posthumously appropriated his social psychology. To this end, the American sociologist Herbert Blumer was instrumental in refashioning Mead's social psychology to sociology, but minus his radical ideas on social reform and society. Until the 1980s, Mead's ideas remained "marginal," even though some eminent scholars in Europe were openly receptive to Mead's work. Over the last four decades, sociologists have attached greater importance to Mead's theoretical grasp of the unity of the individual or "microinteractions" and socializations. We have highlighted a "reconstruction" of Mead's work that focuses on the societal or "macrosociological" components of Mead's ideas. As such, we have emphasized Mead's dialectic views of the self and society that go well beyond the focus on Blumerian symbolic interactionism to theories of societal self-transformation. Thus, we argue Mead's theory is relevant today and defines his place in the classical social canon.

In this period, the academic field of sociology emerged around a few white men—most notably, in France, around Émile Durkheim; in Germany, around Max Weber; and, in the United States, around William Graham Sumner (1840–1910), Lester F. Ward (1841–1913), Edward A. Ross (1866–1951), and Charles Cooley (1863–1929). At the same time, the inner cities in both America and Europe were abysmally overcrowded and rife with poverty and crime. Cities were also sites for periodic widespread social unrest. Writing about England in the decade before World War I, when new social, political, and economic forces—including the suffragette movement—were challenging European liberalism, Paul Johnson wrote, "England, on the eve of war, was in a state approaching revolution—only our submersion in a general European catastrophe averted a crisis of our national fortunes. Our parliamentary democracy itself was, perhaps, saved in the mud of Flanders."[37] Thus, the development of American sociology, like its European counterpart, was motivated by the sense that there was a crisis in the affairs of bourgeois society, by a Zeitgeist that something needed to be done to prevent society's disintegration or transformation into a different, less desirable societal form.[38] The idea that humanity was divided by "race" penetrated the dominant ideology of the period almost as deeply as the notion of "progress" itself. Swedish author Sven Lindqvist in *Exterminate All the Brutes* (2007) shows how nineteenth-century intellectual thought served the European imperial project. In 1799, Charles White argued that Europeans were inherently superior to "darker races." And, in Germany in 1893, Alexander Tille, drawing on British writers, made the remarkable proposition that "it is the right of the stronger race to annihilate the lower."[39]

This is the intellectual lineage that was part of Du Bois's university education. In *The Philadelphia Negro, The Souls of Black Folk,* and

Darkwater, Du Bois transcended disciplinary boundaries and genre to examine the interplay of class and race, the intersection of racial segregation and social inequality and injustice, and the incompatibility of an inclusive sociology with official liberal bourgeois social theory. Richly populated with a myriad of racial vignettes exposing brutal fragments of social injustice, *The Souls* has as its *leitmotif* the unveiling of American racism and of its effects on metropolitan identity. Du Bois's sociology shares with Georg Simmel and George Herbert Mead a focus on the microsociological issues of social interaction and differentiation; neither is similar to the "meta-narratives" promulgated by Marx, Durkheim, and Weber. The veil and the double self concepts are Du Bois's best-known contributions to social theory. The veil filters and organizes information that is transmitted across the divide, obscuring the process in which whites and blacks act to exchange perceptions and ultimately shape their own identities. This transmission process, of course, extends to popular culture, with those on each side of the divide nurturing and supporting their own music, songs, and artists.[40]

Charles Lemert plausibly argues that excluding *The Souls* from the sociological canon caused a kind of blindness among white sociologists because they did not see clearly beyond the veil. Also, Du Bois was himself excluded from the sociological canon because, Lemert argues, "He, and others in his position, having been veiled, were not clearly visible."[41] This observation, then, resonates with our comments on the neglected voices of Wollstonecraft, Harriet Martineau, and other early feminist writers. Judith Blau and Eric Brown[42] argue that there are significant convergences between the ideas of George Herbert Mead, Georg Simmel, and Du Bois, especially in regards to their characterization of the development of social identity as a complex, highly malleable process shaped by sociocultural and economic power. Moreover, Du Bois's analysis of the intersection of race, class, double-consciousness, and power is situated in the distinctive experience of African American history. Even more important, his discussion of identity speaks to the present. At a time of mass global migration and allegations in 2018 that Donald Trump used racial epithets, including the taboo "N-word" about White House staff,[43] language that would not surprise Du Bois in 1918, *The Souls* is particularly relevant for sociology in this historical moment. Blau and Brown, for example, argue that the mature Du Bois's conception of race anticipated contemporary debates about the self in terms of cosmopolitanism and hybridism. *The Souls* is also germane for how sociologists pose questions about social justice. Racism takes many discrete forms and actions, and it is from this concrete perspective that sociologists ought to address questions of social justice.

Class, Gender, and Race in the Age of Austerity

Class, gender, and race are important principal social statuses affecting many aspects of everyday life, including social inequalities. In this section, in what has been called the "age of austerity," we review some of the enduring debates about class, gender, and race. This discourse attests to an analytic dissatisfaction with the interpretations of society that privilege one, such as class, over equally important dimensions like gender and race, among others.[44] On one side of the debate, some argue that class is more determinative of African American life chances in the United States than race.[45] Since the 1970s, as the number of middle-class blacks increased, a marginalized underclass was left behind in increasingly impoverished inner-city ghettos. In the Canadian and US context, theories of class-based inequalities tend to find less traction among students and the wider population than they do in, say, the UK and Europe. However, in the age of neoliberalism and a decade after the 2008 banking implosion and "austerity economics," class has come to play a greater, not lesser, role in determining rewards and wealth, quality education, health and life expectancy, and social justice.[46] As Mike Savage points out, people who are positioned at the bottom of the social hierarchy—the "precariat class"—tend to be less "visible" in research in contemporary class relationships.[47]

Despite popular support for liberal attitudes across a range of social issues, there appears to be "a hardening of stigmatization" of those in the precariat class. According to Richard Wilkinson and Kate Pickett, while most people claim to deplore class divisions, many continue to dismiss progressive demands to reduce income differences as just "the politics of envy."[48] The growth in income inequality and the precariat is producing new instabilities in society, and, in terms of post-Trump, post-Brexit, and post-factual politics, it is argued that the precariat class are "increasingly frustrated and angry, but also dangerous because they have no voice, and hence they are vulnerable to the siren calls of extreme political parties."[49]

Gender issues also have a significant effect on life chances, and play a fundamental role in the way women have been perceived and treated in the workplace and society. The allegations against Harvey Weinstein in 2017, for example, are just one illustration of the dynamics between powerful men on the one hand and vulnerable women on the other. However, sexual harassment and misogyny are products of wider society, and most women outside of Hollywood will have either experienced sexual harassment or discrimination in the workplace, or domestic violence at home, or know someone who has. There are many jobs that are overwhelmingly occupied by women as a result of patriarchy and gender-based assumptions. However, domestic employment, as shown in

Du Bois's *The Philadelphia Negro*, has been disproportionately occupied by black women not only because of traditional gender- and race-based associations but also because of the propensity of upper-class white women to contract out domestic labor. So race is obviously a factor in this situation, and black women experience dual forms of subordination. They experience "black machismo" and sexism—which are affected by the traditional dichotomies between socially constructed "masculinities" and "femininities"—as well as racial biases and discrimination.[50] The stratified permutations of class, gender, and race distinctions are evident when, for example, a white middle-class woman exploits or expresses anger at a black working-class domestic worker over whom she feels relatively powerful; yet she may be relatively powerless in relation to her male partner.[51] As these examples suggest, class-, gender-, and race-based exploitation and discrimination are intimately interrelated, and, at the same time, each should not be reduced to a mere function of the other.[52]

As we enter the third decade of the twenty-first century, class, gender, and race continue to profoundly shape the life experiences of all people in North America and Britain. This fact has been well-documented in extant research and, to some extent, is commonly understood.[53] In Wilkinson and Pickett's *The Inner Level*, the authors plot the long-term trends in income inequality among a group of rich countries including Canada, the United States, and Britain. The trend from around 1980, when Canadian Prime Minister Brian Mulroney, US President Ronald Reagan, and UK Prime Minister Margaret Thatcher were elected, started an upward trajectory after a long decline, and by the early twenty-first century had returned to levels of income inequality not seen since the 1920s.[54] Accompanying the upward trend has been social acceptance for the income gap between the rich and the poor to widen. Minimum-wage rates close to subsistence level, as well as extremely high salaries at the top of the income pyramid, are also endured. Data from the Canadian government's census show that income inequality in Canada has risen during the decade 2005–15. Income rose by 12.7 percent for the working class, compared to 16.4 percent for the top 10 percent.[55] Similarly, in the US, top executives received an average pay raise of 17.6 percent in 2017–18 while their employees' wages increased by just 0.3 percent over the year. The CEOs of America's top 350 companies earned 312 times more than their employees on average in 2017.[56] In the UK chief executives of FTSE 100 companies are paid a median average of £3.45 million a year, which is 120 times the £28,758 average pay of UK workers.[57]

Although the matter of global inequality is extraordinary complex, the statistics are truly breathtaking. There are 1,542 dollar billionaires in the world, of which the top 500 own $5.3 trillion. Booming stock markets enabled them to increase their wealth by 23 percent in 2017. Thirty-six million people are dollar millionaires. They make up 0.7 percent of the world's adult population and own 46 percent of global wealth. Seventy percent of the world's population has assets of less than $10,000 and owns 2.7 percent of global wealth.[58] Meanwhile, at the other end of the spectrum, about 3 billion people, or almost 50 percent of the world's population, live on less than $2.50 a day.[59] Wilkinson and Pickett show that, in more unequal societies, health, violence, teenage birth rates, drug abuse, child well-being, and poor education performance of school students "develop steeper social gradients and so bigger differences in outcomes between rich and poor."[60] The processes responsible for income inequality are, in part, explained by Marx's theory of exploitation. It is not primarily the result of the behavior of greedy or unethical employers; neither is it the result, as President George W. Bush said in 2002 after the collapse of WorldCom and Enron, the nefarious behavior of a few "bad apples." Rather, it is an innate feature of the capital-labor relationship itself—the buying and selling of labor power. The capitalist who refuses to engage in the exploitation of workers will most likely lose out to competitors who close their eyes to such issues. The system preserves those who accept the primacy of the profit motive, and it makes losers of those who do not. The only way to step out of the system is to change it.

As we explained, Karl Marx's *Capital* has made an immense contribution to the sociological analysis of technological change and management. Marx's pioneering work on the effects of machinery has morphed into what is known as labor process theory, which seeks to expose the social and class interests behind technological change. Marx's analysis has relevance to contemporary debates on "jobless growth." Automation and AI systems, the so-called third wave of digital technology, are making labor superfluous to capitalist production. On this, Mike Davis reminds us of Marx's warning found in *Capital*: "It is capitalistic accumulation itself that constantly produces ... a relatively redundant population of laborers ... and therefore a surplus-population."[61] And critical sociological studies of management conceptualize management as a control mechanism that advances and protects the economic and political interests of the ruling dominant class. Marx's analysis centers attention on the dominant imperative that management must realize a satisfactory degree of control over antagonistic capital-labor relations. In other words, these relations must be controlled as much as is necessary to secure the efficient extraction of profit in the form of surplus value.

Another major achievement of Marx's economics was the correct prediction of the growth of multinational companies and global markets. For Marx, the logical tendency of capitalism is to work toward the concentration and centralization of capital, and the predictable effect of this tendency is corporate control over markets; with this control, larger corporations had the capability of destroying smaller competitors. We cited Apple, Amazon, and the US retailer Wal-Mart as examples of this tendency. Contemporary wisdom predicts that multinational corporations will operate in accordance with universal principles that will result in a convergence of markets and business practices. Thus, globalized capitalism will drive wages down and erode employment standards and lead to the transfer of production from relatively expensive labor markets (e.g., North America) to less expensive ones (e.g., China and India). We can also predict, in a post-SUV economy, the transfer of production to societies with weak carbon emission controls, as well as the transfer of pollution from environmentally regulated societies (e.g., the European Union) to less regulated ones (e.g., China and India).

The social theories of Marx, Durkheim, and Weber can be readily applied to contemporary trends in the labor market as well. For example, it has become expected in some occupational fields such as the media, fashion, journalism, the arts, advertising, law, and charities that prior "work experience" through internships is a requirement to gain entry to permanent work. As parents often pay the interns' living costs and, in growing numbers, a fee for the privilege of an internship, the system amounts to a massive subsidy to employers. Some internees may regard the exchange of free labor for work experience, employment contacts, and professional references as a fair exchange, especially because it gives them an advantage over those whose parents cannot pay so their children can make contacts with employers or gain work experience. Agencies have sprung up to sell internships with companies in the United Kingdom, the United States, China, and Australia, and internships are also auctioned online.[62] From a Durkheimian perspective, there is an unjust dimension to such practices, as access to employment following work as an intern gives an advantage to young people who have parents who can support them for several months, thus skewing the allocation of work from a "spontaneous" one based upon natural inequalities. The practice also resonates with Weber's theory of social class and status. One could argue that internships enable upper- and middle-class parents to use their wealth and economic networks to effectively buy professional training for their dependents, thus reinforcing their dominant position in the social hierarchy. With regard to contemporary debates on global capitalism, we have tried to show that Marx, Durkheim, and Weber have provided a legacy of insightful social theory that still resonates in the global capitalism era.

The legacy of early feminist social theorists is also relevant today. Although from the 1970s, more varieties of feminist perspectives have appeared on the intellectual landscape, including liberal to radical and black feminist thought, our introduction to classical feminist ideas and scholarship sought to demonstrate their importance in shaping and reshaping the contemporary feminist discourse. In the dark "age of austerity," gender differentiates across a variety of outcomes, such as employment and health. According to a Cranfield University report, the percentage of women in leadership positions on FTSE 100 boards has flatlined for a fourth successive year at 9.7 percent, and the percentage of women on FTSE boards has increased slightly to 23.7 percent.[63] Although women are good at flying planes, 99 percent of pilots are men. Women with equal qualifications have to work six hours to receive what a man will earn in five; nevertheless, women run a much greater risk of losing their jobs.[64] A 2018 survey at the BBC found that on average men there were paid 9.3 percent more than women, which is better than the UK national average pay gap of 18.1 percent. However, it was discovered that nearly 500 BBC employees were being paid less than colleagues in a similar role due to their gender.[65] Research has continued to explore how gender and class affect other social outcomes, such as access to health care. For example, Merzel's study found that working-class women receive less consistent primary health care.[66] A survey of 3,200 new mothers in the UK found that around one in nine had been dismissed, made compulsorily redundant, or treated so poorly they had to leave their job. Scaled up to the general population, this means around 54,000 mothers in the UK lose their jobs every year.[67]

Contemporary feminist perspectives incorporate class, race, and gender into their analyses, as illustrated by Judith Rollins's American sociological study *Between Women: Domestics and Their Employers*.[68] Rollins studied black working-class women who worked as domestics for white middle- and upper-class women, and this situation allowed her to explore both the commonalities among women and the differences between them based on class and race positions.[69] One commonality was that gender reinforced the historical pattern that women, much more than men, have been assigned domestic work. The study also emphasized the Weberian notion of "status"; for white middle-class women, the ability to hire other women to do socially devalued household work was status-enhancing. According to Rollins, another distinction between the women was that domestic workers had to endure a "ritual of subordination," such as the paternalistic attitude and behaviors of their employers and acts of "linguistic deference," for example, being called "girl." As Chancer and Watkins argue, new perspectives on gender "have made it virtually impossible to ignore the relationship between gender and other forms of discrimination such as ones based on class and race."[70]

Du Bois's contribution to social theory is highly relevant to contemporary theories on race, multiculturalism, race-based discrimination, and inequality. The litany of racial inequality and injustice in the UK, the United States, and Canada is a long and shameful one. In this "age of austerity," 10 percent of black people in the UK were unemployed in 2016 compared to 4 percent of white people.[71] Black people are eight times more likely to be stopped and searched by police

The employment of black working-class women as domestics for white upper-class women reveals both commonalities among women and differences between them based on class and race positions. For white middle-class women, the ability to hire other women to do socially devalued household work is status-enhancing. Analyses of the connections between class, gender, and race show the limits of reductionist perspectives on the social world.

than white people.[72] And in the United States, young African American men were nine times more likely than white Americans to be killed by police officers in 2015.[73] Black people all too often experience the reality of police racism. When 21-year-old black Mauro Demetrio was arrested during the 2011 summer riots in London, the police officer who arrested him said, "The problem with you is that you will always be a nigger ... you will always have black skin ... don't hide behind your skin."[74] Even though Demetrio had secretly recorded the comments, the judge acquitted the police officer of criminal racist abuse after two consecutive juries failed to reach a verdict. One hundred and twenty years after *The Philadelphia Negro* was published, minority communities on both sides of the Atlantic continue to call for society to be free of racial discrimination and for legislation and institutions to address the "race problem." Race plays a central role in United States politics, a point demonstrated by Barack Obama's election victories. As was the case in 2008, race was crucial in the 2012 election, with 93 percent of African Americans, 73 percent of Asians, and 71 percent of Latino people voting for Obama.[75] The 2016 presidential election again showed a major social division around race, with 89 percent of African Americans, 66 percent of Hispanics, and 65 percent of Asians voting for Hillary Clinton.[76]

Class, Gender, and Race in the Age of Post-Trump

The election of Donald Trump in November 2016 and the UK referendum decision in June 2016 to leave the European Union ("Brexit") sent shock waves through the political systems of both countries and the wider world. Trump was a reality TV star with no political experience and a maverick outsider. Trump matters because the United States affects the entire global capitalist system.[77] The overall vote to leave the EU produced a margin of 52 percent to 48 percent (Scotland and Northern Ireland voted to remain); the result shocked Europe and went against the policies of the main UK parties. As previously discussed, both outcomes have been seen as protest votes of mainly white working-class voters against unemployment, growing inequality, and immigration.

Analysis of exit polls following Trump's election show patterns of voting that indicate deep social divisions and point to the continuing relevance of the classical sociological tradition around class, gender, and race. CNN's Edison national election poll of 24,537 voters at 350 polling stations shows that though "disaffected, economically insecure white blue-collar voters" helped Trump win in "rustbelt states such as Michigan, they cannot explain the new Republican president's performance nationwide."[78] Trump's supporters came mainly from white voters both male and female, most ages and education levels, and from middle and higher income groups. White voters, who constitute 69 percent of the total, voted 58 percent for Trump and 37 percent for Clinton. Non-white voters, who made up 31 percent of the electorate, voted 74 percent for Clinton and 21 percent for Trump. White men opted 63 percent for Trump and 31 percent for Clinton. Non-college-educated whites were mainly Trump supporters—72 percent of men and 62 percent of women. Of male college graduates, 54 percent of males and 45 percent of women opted for Trump. Trump was also more popular than Clinton among white voters aged 18–29 (Trump 48 percent and Clinton 43 percent). Clinton won 88 percent of the black vote and 65 percent of the Latino vote, which in each case was a few percent below Obama's popularity with these groups.[79] Clinton was more successful in attracting the votes of poorer Americans with incomes of less than $50,000 per year.

Millions of working-class Americans have been left behind and have endured a long trend of wage stagnation. Average wages for blue-collar workers have increased by only 0.3 percent between 2017 and 2018. The widening income gap between the top 5 percent and the rest can be attributed partly to a decline in trade union membership and loss of bargaining power because of anti-union labor policies and globalization.[80] The decline in the economic position of average families and consumers is indicated by the reduction in the portion of national income going to workers: 56.8 percent in 2017 compared with 64.5 percent in 1973. Income growth has been skewed toward the richest 20 percent of workers, who enjoyed a 27 percent increase in the period 1979–2016 compared with those in the bottom fifth whose real wages declined slightly.

This decline is due to a lower presence of unions in the workplace as membership fell from 28 percent of all workers in 1956 to 10 percent in 2016. In the private sector only 5 percent of workers belonged to a union.[81] President Trump promised to champion America's working class, and in 2017 unemployment fell. But at the same time, workers' rights have been attacked, making workers less secure and less safe as regulations that neoliberals believe are burdens on business are rolled back. There are more than 90 pieces of legislation planned to weaken protection for workers. It is proposed to expand the use of 16- and 17-year-olds in the logging industry, though under adult supervision, and there is a proposal to roll back a 2015 ban on under-18s from working with toxic pesticides.[82] President Trump's appeal to workers does not seem to be based on improving the balance of power between capital and labor.

Donald Trump is well known as a denier of global warming and climate change, and he is also opposed to regulations on business designed to halt global warming or maintain clean air and water, which he claims "kill jobs."[83] Trump's decision to withdraw the US from the Paris climate deal gained much publicity, and his administration has been quietly rolling back environmental policies and regulations designed to protect air and water quality. During the leadership of Trump appointee Scott Pruitt, and with the help of Republicans in Congress, the Environmental Protection Agency initiated many pro-polluter policies that contradicted its public health and environmental protection mission. By early July 2018, the Trump administration had targeted 76 rules designed to protect the environment, with 46 rules overturned and 30 rollbacks in progress. These regulations have been removed or weakened in favor of easing energy extraction policies, "often as a direct response to petitions from oil, gas and coal companies. Mr. Trump has argued that supporting the fossil fuel industry strengthens the economy"[84] and that deregulating business creates jobs. Harvard University researchers calculate that scrapping environmental regulations could lead to at least 80,000 extra deaths per decade and cause respiratory problems for more than 1 million people.[85] Thus, social inequalities are exacerbated as those on low pay, who are more likely to work and live in polluted environments, suffer a disproportionate amount of harm.

Gender issues have become a source of conflict and resistance since the election of Donald Trump. Key issues for the feminist movement are the gender pay gap, women's reproductive rights around the availability of abortion and contraception, and resistance to sexual harassment. A survey of more than 300 US occupations reveals a gender pay gap across almost all occupations. In 2016 the median earnings for women was $40,675 and for men was $50,741. Women were most likely to be employed in lower-paying jobs.[86] President Trump is associated with restrictive policies on abortion and contraception. He was the first sitting president to address the March for Life, an annual anti-abortion gathering, and he instituted a policy that restricts the US government's funding of international family planning organizations that offer "abortion-related services." Since the inauguration of Trump, women have marched and opposed what they perceive as threats to women's control of their bodies. The #MeToo movement has grown around sexual misconduct, bringing down well-known men in entertainment, media, and politics and transforming the position of women in workplaces.[87]

Race has also been at the center of Donald Trump's presidency. His presidential campaign included promises to ban immigration from Muslim countries and to eliminate immigration from Mexico by building a wall between Mexico and the US. The frequently used promise to put "America first" is a code or "dog whistle" with a history that goes back over a century in its association with American populism, slavery, and white nationalism[88] and would be recognized by the black writer W.E.B. Du Bois. In August 2017 armed white nationalists, neo-Nazis, and Ku Klux Klan members demonstrated and chanted racist slogans in protest at plans to remove a statue of Confederate general Robert E. Lee from a park in Charlottesville, Virginia. A civil rights protester was killed when a young man drove a car into a crowd.[89] Initially, Trump blamed "both sides" for the violence in Charlottesville and claimed there were "very fine people on both sides." Under widespread international pressure Trump was obliged to condemn racism and the far right groups involved in the rally.[90] Donald Trump's description of African nations and Haiti and El Salvador as "shithole countries" in a public meeting led to condemnation from the UN and leaders of many states for his racist remarks.[91]

In the context of a growing politicization of race, the Pew Research Center notes that there has been a doubling of the share of Americans who see racism as a "big problem" in society—up from 28 percent in 2011 to 58 percent in 2017.[92] The Trump administration is set to roll back Obama-era policies known as "affirmative action," which were designed to increase diversity in educational environments by encouraging admissions policies that considered racial and environmental factors in the admissions process.[93]

Class, Gender, and Race in the Age of Post-Brexit

Brexit has not happened (at the time of writing), but it is possible to refer to the impact of the decision to leave in the post-referendum period and look at some of the speculation regarding change in a post-Brexit United

Kingdom. The UK has a notably high level of income inequality compared
to other European countries. After direct taxes and benefits, the bottom
10 percent had an average disposable income of £9,644 in 2015–16 while
the top 10 percent had nine times that (£83,875). Those in the ninth
richest decile only had around 60 percent of the income of the top 10
percent. The richest 10 percent have incomes on average 24 times larger
than the poorest. The richest 1 percent enjoyed much higher incomes
than the average for the top 10 percent: the top 1 percent had an average
income of £253,927 in 2012 and the top 0.1 percent had an average
income of £919,882. The poorest fifth of society have only 8 percent
of total income compared with the richest fifth that receive 40 percent.
Wealth distribution in the UK is even more unequally distributed, with
the richest 10 percent of households owning 45 percent of all wealth and
the poorest 50 percent a mere 8.7 percent.[94]

The British educational system has a poor record at enabling
working-class children to achieve high academic levels. Children receiving free school meals and the pupil premium[95] are 27 percent less likely
to achieve good school grades compared to children from rich families.
In her research on British education, Diane Reay (a leading British education researcher) is quoted in a London School of Economics paper as
saying that different standards and resources are provided to children
from different class and ethnic backgrounds.[96] In this context, the OECD
stated that social mobility in Britain has stalled and that a "child of a
parent with low educational attainment has only a 21 percent chance of
gaining a degree-level qualification compared with 71 percent of those
with parents who have a college degree."[97]

It is impossible to avoid speculation about the effects of Brexit on
women at work, levels of services, and family budgets.[98] Economists predict
a reduction in GDP for the UK ranging from 1.5 percent to 9.5 percent
depending on how closely the UK adheres to existing arrangements with
the EU. "No deal" scenarios are believed to be the most damaging. If
the UK leaves the EU, new trade deals may be less favorable than those
enjoyed currently by the UK as a member of the EU. Exit from the EU
may negatively affect women as workers if the economy contracts. Much
of the legislation protecting workplace rights originated in Europe, so
there is concern about future legal protection. There is also uncertainty
about the impact of Brexit on women as consumers, as EU consumer law
provides the framework for consumer rights in the UK. Trade deals with
non-EU countries may involve acquiescing to practices not accepted by
the EU because the UK will be in a weaker position; for example, the
US wants to export chlorinated chicken and beef containing hormones.
A break with the EU on world trade rules is estimated to cost the average

UK household £580 per year in future, which would have the highest impact on the poorest households.

The campaign to leave the EU produced slogans such as "Vote leave, take control" and "We want our country back," but, as Prime Minister Theresa May is discovering, the UK's efforts to "take back control" does not mean that the EU, the United States, and China fall into line. The UK lacks the economic "heft."[99] Living standards have declined due to austerity, but "to distract us from these national failings, we have been encouraged to blame immigration and the EU."[100] There was a spike in hate crimes in the weeks following the referendum, indicating a legitimation of racism, but as Jon Burnett states, it was given legitimacy by the forms of racism implicit in national policies and debates over reducing immigrant numbers and combating Muslim terrorism. "In this context, it is indicative that certain messages previously belonging to [the] far right are now found in dominant policy decisions."[101]

The deep embeddedness of racist policies was illustrated when it emerged that hundreds of immigrants (often referred to as the "Windrush" generation) who had come to Britain to contribute to the UK's post-war reconstruction were denied their legal status and suffered by losing their citizenship, work, and benefits under a general government policy of providing a "hostile environment" that emerged from Conservative pledges to drastically reduce immigration.[102] A likely focus of the sociology of race relations in the post-Brexit UK will be the study of immigration policies and forms of institutional racism designed to make the UK an unattractive destination for immigration.

At the time of writing it is unclear under what terms the UK will leave the EU, if at all. For Will Hutton and Andrew Adonis, "the Brexit referendum was above all a clarion call from left-behind Britain that it will no longer tolerate being ignored and neglected."[103] They go on to argue that Brexiters want a neoliberal, "Thatcherism in one country" typified by unregulated markets, a small state, and extreme inequality, They counterpose this bleak vision by advocating remaining in Europe, embracing a European vision, and creating a stakeholder capitalism with socially responsible employers, fairer taxation, greater representation for the regions, and a widening of social mobility.

These contemporary studies and reports show how far class, gender, and race differentiate across a wide range of outcomes, such as income, education, health, social mobility, sociocultural exclusion and participation, and sociopolitical attitudes and power. For example, there is an intersection of poverty and violence against women, with reports of women being entrapped into selling their bodies in exchange for rent money.[104] Studies also indicate that the classical social legacy continues to be highly relevant and connected to a variety of national contexts in this age of late modernity.

Our journey through the works of the classical social theorists is now drawing to a close. The entire scaffolding of this text rests on one series of questions: What is the nature of postmodern society, are its features inevitable, or can it be transformed? Who can lead a transformation of society? And what is the cause of and solution to the corporate takeover of nature and the environmental crisis? These are the questions that we posed at the beginning of this book. A search for answers will bring each new generation of critical social scientists to the classical social theorists.

Notes

1 Martin Parker, *Shut Down the Business School* (London: Pluto, 2018), 20.

2 Adam Tooze, *Crashed: How a Decade of Financial Crises Changed the World* (London: Allen Lane, 2018), 614.

3 Noah Richler, "Novel Thinking Needed on Both Sides," *The Globe and Mail*, October 10, 2006, 11; also see George Lakoff, *Don't Think of an Elephant* (White River Junction, VT: Chelsea Green, 2014).

4 See Larry Ray, *Theorizing Classical Sociology* (Buckingham, UK: Open University Press, 1999), 8.

5 Kenan Malik, "Myths about Shared Culture Have No Place in the Citizenship Debate," *The Observer*, November 4, 2018, 22.

6 C. Wright Mills, *The Sociological Imagination*, 40th anniversary ed. (New York: Oxford University Press, 2000), 3–4.

7 For an introduction to the sociology of climate change, see John Urry's *Climate Change and Society* (London: Polity Press, 2011); for a polemical account of the link between society and climate change, see also George Monbiot's *How Did We Get into This Mess?* (London: Verso, 2017).

8 Robert Tucker, ed., *The Marx-Engels Reader* (New York: Norton, 1972), 416.

9 Monbiot, *How Did We Get into This Mess?*, 99.

10 Dominic Sandbrook, "The Death of Ideas," *New Statesman*, August 6, 2009, http://www.newstatesman.com/uk-politics/2009/08/ideas-ideological-politics-age.

11 Parker, *Shut Down the Business School*, 35.

12 Naomi Klein, *The Shock Doctrine* (Toronto: Alfred Knopf, 2007), 121.

13 Émile Durkheim, *Moral Education* (New York: Dover Publications, 2002), 26.

14 Steven Lukes, "Alienation and Anomie," in *Philosophy, Politics and Society*, 3rd series, ed. Peter Laslett and W. G. Runciman (Oxford: Blackwell, 1967), 134–56.

15 Robert A. Nisbet, *The Sociological Tradition* (London: Heinemann, 1967), 16–19.

16 Bryan S. Turner, *Classical Sociology* (London: Sage Publications, 1999), 108.

17 See Thomas Piketty, *Capital in the Twenty-First Century*, trans. Arthur Goldhammer (Cambridge, MA: Harvard University Press, 2014), 281.

18   Juliette Garside, Holly Watt, and David Pegg, "The Panama Papers: How the World's Rich and Famous Hide Their Money Offshore," *The Guardian*, April 3, 2016, https://www.theguardian.com/news/2016/apr/03/the-panama-papers-how-the-worlds-rich-and-famous-hide-their-money-offshore. See also Nick Hopkins and Helena Bengtsson, "What Are the Paradise Papers and What Do They Tell Us?", *The Guardian*, November 5, 2017, https://www.theguardian.com/news/2017/nov/05/what-are-the-paradise-papers-and-what-do-they-tell-us.

19   Stjepan G. Mestrovic, *The Coming Fin De Siecle: An Application of Durkheim's Sociology to Modernity and Postmodernism* (London: Routledge, 1991).

20   John E. T. Eldridge, Peter Cressey, and John MacInnes, *Industrial Sociology and Economic Crisis* (Hemel Hempstead, UK: Harvester Wheatsheaf, 1991).

21   Paul Krugman, *End This Depression Now* (New York: W.W. Norton, 2012), 51.

22   Hannah Furness, "Regulating the Banks: What Politicians Used to Say about the City," *The Telegraph*, July 4, 2012, http://telegraph.co.uk/news/politics/9376534/Regulating-the-banks-what-politicians-used-to-say-about-the-City.html.

23   Paul Mason, *Meltdown: The End of the Age of Greed* (London: Verso, 2009), 173.

24   Tooze, *Crashed*.

25   Norman K. Denzin and Yvonna S. Lincoln, *Handbook of Qualitative Research* (Thousand Oaks, CA: Sage, 2000), 6.

26   See Erik Olin Wright, *Classes* (London: Verso, 1985); Erik Olin Wright, *Class Counts: Comparative Studies in Class Analysis* (Cambridge: Cambridge University Press, 1997).

27   Alex Callinicos, *Social Theory: A Historical Introduction* (Cambridge: Polity Press, 2007), 175.

28   Veronica Stracqualursi, "Ex-CIA Director: Trump Has 'Autocratic Envy' Toward Putin," *CNN News*, March 3, 2018, https://edition.cnn.com/2018/03/02/politics/michael-hayden-donald-trump-vladimir-putin-cnntv/index.html.

29   Quoted by Reinhard Bendix in *Max Weber: An Intellectual Portrait* (New York: Doubleday Anchor Books, 1962), 464.

30   Max Weber, *The Protestant Ethic and the Spirit of Capitalism* (London: Unwin, 1939), 181, and cited by Urry, *Climate Change and Society*, 40.

31   Ulrich Beck, "Living Your Own Life in a Runaway World: Individualism, Globalization and Politics," in *On the Edge: Living with Global Capitalism*, ed. Will Hutton and Anthony Giddens (London: Jonathan Cape, 2000), 164–74. See also W. G. Runciman, *A Treatise on Social Theory* (Cambridge: Cambridge University Press, 1997); W.G. Runciman, "The Selectionist Paradigm and Its Implications for Sociology," *Sociology* 32, no. 1 (1998): 163–88; Michael Mann, *The Sources of Social Power* (Cambridge: Cambridge University Press, 1993); Anthony Giddens, *The Consequences of Modernity* (Cambridge: Polity Press, 1990).

32   Charlotte Gray, "Feminism's First Manifesto," *The Globe and Mail*, November 15, 2008, D14.

33   Tooze, *Crashed*.

34   Paul Mason, *Postcapitalism: A Guide to Our Future* (London: Penguin Books, 2015).

35   Tukufu Zuberi, "W.E.B. Du Bois's Sociology: The Philadelphia Negro and Social Science," *Annals of the American Academy of Political and Social Science* 598 (September 2004): 146–56, see page 147.

36   Jean-Francois Côté, *George Herbert Mead's Concept of Society: A Critical Reconstruction* (Boulder, CO: Paradigm, 2015).

37 Paul Johnson, "Preface," in *The Strange Death of Liberal England*, by George Dangerfield (London: Paladin, 1970), 10.

38 Eric Hobsbawm, *The Age of Empire, 1875–1914* (London: Abacus, 1994).

39 Quoted by George Monbiot, "Colonised and Coloniser, Empire's Poison Infects Us All," *The Guardian*, October 8, 2012, 30, http://www.guardian.co.uk /commentisfree/2012/oct/08/empire-torture-kenya-catastrophe-europe.

40 See, for example, Todd Boyd, ed., *African Americans and Popular Culture* (Westport, CT: Praeger, 2008).

41 Charles Lemert, "A Classic from the Other Side of the Veil: Du Bois' *Souls of Black Folk*," *The Sociological Quarterly* 35, no. 3 (1994): 383–96, see page 388.

42 Judith R. Blau and Eric S. Brown, "Du Bois and Diasporic Identity: The Veil and the Unveiling Project," *Sociological Theory* 19, no. 2 (2001): 219–33.

43 Omarosa M. Newman, *Unhinged: An Insider's Account of the Trump White House* (New York: Gallery Books, 2018).

44 See Lynn S. Chancer and Beverly Xavier Watkins, *Gender, Race, and Class: An Overview* (Malden, MA: Blackwell Publishing, 2006), and Pierre W. Orelus, *Rethinking Race, Class, Language, and Gender: A Dialogue with Noam Chomsky and Other Leading Scholars* (Lanham, MD: Rowman & Littlefield, 2011).

45 Derrick Bell, *Faces at the Bottom of the Well: The Permanence of Racism* (New York: Basic Books, 1992); Michael Hughes and Melvin E. Thomas, "The Continuing Significance of Race Revisited: A Study of Race, Class, and Quality of Life in America, 1972 to 1996," *American Sociological Review* 63 (1998): 785–95; Douglas S. Massey and Nancy A. Denton, *American Apartheid: Segregation and the Making of the Underclass* (Cambridge, MA: Harvard University Press, 1993); William Julius Wilson, *The Truly Disadvantaged: The Inner City, the Underclass, and Public Policy* (Chicago: University of Chicago Press, 1987).

46 See, for example, Linda McQuaig and Neil Brooks, *The Trouble with Billionaires* (Toronto: Penguin, 2010); Janny Scott and David Leonhardt, "Shadowy Lines That Still Divide," in *Class Matters*, by *The New York Times* (New York: Macmillan, 2005).

47 Mike Savage, *Social Class in the 21st Century* (London: Pelican Books, 2015).

48 Richard Wilkinson and Kate Pickett, *The Inner Level* (London: Allen Lane, 2018), 231.

49 Savage, *Social Class in the 21st Century*, 351. See also James Bridle, *New Dark Age: Technology and the End of the Future* (London: Verso, 2018).

50 R.W. Connell, *Masculinities: Knowledge, Power, and Social Change* (Berkeley: University of California Press, 1995); Michele Wallace, *Black Macho and the Myth of the Superwoman* (London: John Calder, 1979).

51 Judith Rollins, *Between Women: Domestics and Their Employers* (Philadelphia: Temple University Press, 1985).

52 Chancer and Watkins, *Gender, Race, and Class*.

53 Margaret L. Andersen and Patricia Hill Collins, *Race, Class, and Gender: An Anthology*, 3rd ed. (Belmont, CA: Wadsworth Publishing Co., 1998).

54 Wilkinson and Pickett, *The Inner Level*, 238. Note that, according to the authors, this overall pattern reflects the strengthening, and then the weakening, of the labor movement, and the ascendency of the political ideology of neoliberalism espoused by Thatcher et al.

55 Andrew Jackson, "Census Data Shows Income Inequality Remains a Major Challenge," *The Globe and Mail*, October 8, 2017.

56 Dominic Rushe, "US Chief Executives Enjoy 17% Pay Rise as Workers' Wages Stall," *The Guardian*, August 17, 2018, 29.

57 Rupert Neate, "An Honest Year's Work? Excessive Pay in Focus on 'Fat Cat Thursday,'" *The Guardian,* January 4, 2018.

58 Rupert Neate, "World's Megarich Now Worth a Combined $6tn," *The Guardian,* October 27, 2017.

59 Luisa Kroll, "The 2013 Billionaires List," *Forbes,* March 25, 2013, http://www .forbes.com/sites/luisakroll/2013/03/04/inside-the-2013-billionaires-list-facts-and -figures/; Arundhati Roy, *Public Power in the Age of Empire* (New York: Seven Stories Press, 2004), 23; Anup Shah, "Poverty Facts and Stats," *Global Issues,* http://www.globalissues.org/article/26/poverty-facts-and-stats.

60 Wilkinson and Pickett, *The Inner Level,* 233.

61 Tucker, *Marx-Engels Reader,* 422. See also Mike Davis, *Old Gods, New Enigmas* (London: Verso, 2018), Chap. 1; and Bridle, *New Dark Age.*

62 Rachel Williams, "Career-Boosting Internships for Sale," *The Guardian,* May 24, 2011, http://www.guardian.co.uk/education/2011/may/24/internships-sold-work -experience-students.

63 Julia Kollewe, "Fewer Women in Top Jobs at FTSE 250 Firms," *The Guardian,* July 18, 2018.

64 See Paul Seabright, *The War of the Sexes: How Conflict and Cooperation Have Shaped Men and Women from Prehistory to the Present* (Princeton, NJ: Princeton University Press, 2012).

65 Graham Ruddick and Jamie Grierson, "BBC Gender Pay Gap: Male Staff Earn 9% More than Female Colleagues," *The Guardian,* October 4, 2017.

66 Cheryl Merzel, "Gender Differences in Health Care Access Indicators in an Urban, Low-Income Community," *American Journal of Public Health* 90, no. 6 (2000): 909–16.

67 Alexandra Topping, "Maternity Leave Discrimination Means 54,000 Women Lose Their Jobs Every Year," *The Guardian,* July 24, 2015.

68 Rollins, *Between Women,* and cited by Chancer and Watkins, *Gender, Race, and Class,* 46.

69 We draw here on Chancer and Watkins, *Gender, Race, and Class,* 46–48.

70 Chancer and Watkins, *Gender, Race, and Class,* 48.

71 Gov.UK, Ethnicity Facts and Figures, https://www.ethnicity-facts-figures.service. gov.uk/work-pay-and-benefits/unemployment-and-economic-inactivity /unemployment/latest.

72 Vikram Dodd, "Stop and Search Eight Times More Likely to Target Black People," *The Guardian,* October 25, 2017.

73 Jon Swaine, Oliver Laughland, Jamiles Lartey, and Ciara McCarthy, "Young Black Men Killed by US Police at Highest Rate in Year of 1,134 Deaths," *The Guardian,* December 31, 2015, https://www.theguardian.com/us-news/2015 /dec/31/the-counted-police-killings-2015-young-black-men.

74 Benjamin Zephaniah, "The Police Don't Work for Us," *The Guardian,* October 26, 2012, http://www.guardian.co.uk/commentisfree/2012/oct/26/police -dont-work-for-us.

75 Ed Pilkington, "The Fresh Coalition that Led to Second Election Win," *The Guardian,* November 8, 2012, 6–7.

76 Roper Center for Public Opinion Research, "How Groups Voted 2016," https:// ropercenter.cornell.edu/how-groups-voted-2016.

77 Tooze, *Crashed.*

78 Jon Henley, "White and Wealthy Voters Gave Victory to Donald Trump, Exit Polls Show," *The Guardian,* November 9, 2016.

79   John Henley, "White and Wealthy Voters Gave Victory to Donald Trump, Exit
     Polls Show." The discrepancy of 1 percent between the survey cited above and
     the one by the Roper Center quoted earlier is probably due to differences in the
     interview samples or even the "rounding up" process. Their consistency serves to
     emphasize the importance of race in US politics.

80   Pedro Nicolaci Da Costa, "Here's Why Millions of Americans Feel Left Behind
     by the Economic Recovery," Business Insider UK, http://uk.businessinsider.com
     /inequality-near-historic-highs-wages-stagnant?r=US7IR=T.

81   Da Costa, "Here's Why Millions of Americans Feel Left Behind."

82   Dominic Rushe, "Employee Rights: Has Trump Made America Great for Its
     Working Class?" The Guardian, January 26, 2018.

83   Oliver Milman, "Trump's Alarming Environmental Rollback: What's Been
     Scrapped So Far," The Guardian, July 4, 2017.

84   Nadja Popovich, Livia Albeck-Ripka, and Kendra Pierre-Louis, "Environmental
     Rules on the Way Out Under Trump," The New York Times, July 6, 2018,
     https://www.nytimes.com/interactive/2017/10/05climate/trump-environment
     -rules-reversed.html.

85   Popovich, Albeck-Ripka, and Pierre-Louis, "Environmental Rules on the
     Way Out."

86   Amy Newcomb, "Women's Earnings Lower in Most Occupations,"
     US Census Bureau, https://census.gov/library/stories/2018/05/gender-pay-gap
     -in finance-sales.html.

87   Sabrina Siddiqui, "How Has Donald Trump's First Year Affected Women?",
     The Guardian, January 18, 2018.

88   Sarah Churchwell, "Death of a Dream," The Guardian Review, April 21, 2018.

89   David Smith, Oliver Laughland, Pat Owen, and Mark Oliver, "Trump Finally
     Condemns Charlottesville Racism, Days After Violence," The Guardian, August
     14, 2017.

90   Smith, Laughland, Owen, and Oliver, "Trump Finally Condemns
     Charlottesville Racism."

91   Patrick Wintour, Jason Burke, and Anna Livsey, "'There's no other word but
     racist': Trump's Global Rebuke for 'Shithole' Remark", The Guardian,
     January 13, 2018.

92   Samantha Neal, "Views of Racism as a Major Problem Increase Sharply,
     Especially Among Democrats," Pew Research Center, August 29, 2017,
     http://www.pewresearch.org/fact-tank/2017/08/29/views-of-racism-as-major
     -problem-increase-sharply-especially-among-democrats/. See also "Most
     Americans Say Trump's Election Has Led to Worse Race Relations in the U.S.",
     Pew Research Center, December 19, 2017, http://www.pewresearch.org.

93   BBC, "Affirmative Action: Trump 'to Scrap' College Racial Bias Policy,"
     July 3, 2018, https://www.bbc.co.uk/news/world-us-canada-44703874.

94   The Equality Trust, "The Scale of Economic Inequality in the UK,"
     https://www.equalitytrust.org.uk/scale-economic-inequality-uk.

95   The pupil premium is an additional payment given to publicly funded schools in
     England in order to reduce social disadvantage. Schools can claim extra funding
     for children who receive free school meals, are in local authority care, or have
     been adopted from local authority care.

96   London School of Economics, "England Is Still Educating Different Classes for
     Different Functions in Society," http://blogs.ise.ac.uk/politicsandpolicy/uk
     -educating-different-classes-for-different-functions/.

97   Phillip Inman, "OECD Says Inequality Has Risen in Richest Nations Since 1990s
     as Social Mobility Declines," The Guardian, June 16, 2018.

98   "Exploring the Economic Impact of Brexit on Women," Women's Budget Group and Fawcett Society, March 2018.

99   Tooze, *Crashed*.

100   Danny Dorling, "Brexit: The Decision of a Divided Country," *British Medical Journal* 354 (2016): 3697.

101   Jon Burnett, "Racial Violence and the Brexit State," in *Race & Class*, Institute of Race Relations 58, no. 4 (2017): 85–97.

102   Anne Perkins and Amelia Gentleman, "Government Knew for Years that Windrush Generation Hurt by 'Hostile Environment,'" *The Guardian*, April 23, 2018.

103   Will Hutton and Andrew Adonis, *Saving Britain: How We Must Change to Prosper in Europe* (London: Abacus, 2018).

104   Andrew Whitaker, "Campaigners Demand State Inquiry into Scotland's Sex for Rent Scandal," *The Herald*, June 3, 2018, http://www.heraldscotland.com/news/16266066 .Campaigners_demand_state_inquiry_into_Scotland_s_sex_for_rent_scandal/.

Further Reading
and Sources

The Classical Triumvirate: Marx, Durkheim, and Weber

KARL MARX

Selected primary sources

Engels, Friedrich. *The Condition of the Working Class in England*. Moscow: Progress Publishers, 1973.

Marx, Karl. *Economic and Philosophical Manuscripts of 1844*. London: Lawrence & Wishart, 1974. Also available in *The Marx-Engels Reader*, 2nd ed., edited by Robert C. Tucker, 66–125. New York: Norton & Company, 1978.

———. "Thesis on Feuerbach." In *The Marx-Engels Reader*, 2nd ed., edited by Robert C. Tucker, 143–45. New York: Norton & Company, 1978. Written in the spring of 1845.

———. *The Poverty of Philosophy*. New York: International Publishers, 1982. First published in Paris and Brussels in 1847.

———. "Wage Labour and Capital." In *The Marx-Engels Reader*, 2nd ed., edited by Robert C. Tucker, 203–17. New York: Norton & Company, 1978. First published in 1849.

———. "The Eighteenth Brumaire of Louis Bonaparte." In *The Marx-Engels Reader*, 2nd ed., edited by Robert C. Tucker, 594–617. New York: Norton & Company, 1978. First published in 1852.

———. *Grundrisse*. London: Penguin Books, 1973. Written in 1857–58.

———. Preface to *A Contribution to the Critique of Political Economy*. Moscow: Progress Publishers, 1977. First published in 1859.

———. *Capital*. Vol. 1. London: Lawrence & Wishart, 1970. First published in German in 1867.

———. *Capital*. Vol. 2. London: Lawrence & Wishart, 1974. Written in 1863–78 and edited for publication by Engels in 1885.

———. *Capital*. Vol. 3. London: Lawrence & Wishart, 1971. Written in 1863–83 and edited and completed by Engels after Marx's death; first published in 1894.

Marx, Karl, and Friedrich Engels. *The German Ideology*. New York: Prometheus Books, 1998.

————. *The Communist Manifesto*. London: Penguin Books, 2002. Written in 1847 and published in 1848.

Selected collections

Bottomore, Thomas Burton, and Maximillian Rubel. *Karl Marx: Selected Writings in Sociology and Social Philosophy*. London: Pelican, 1963.

McLellan, David. *Karl Marx: Selected Writings*. Oxford: Oxford University Press, 2000.

Tucker, Robert, ed. *The Marx-Engels Reader*. 2nd ed. New York: Norton & Company, 1978.

Selected secondary sources

Acton, Harry Burrows. *What Marx Really Said*. London: MacDonald, 1967.

Arthur, Chris. "Hegel's Master-Slave Dialectic and a Myth of Marxology." In *Marx, Myths and Legends*. http://marxmyths.org/chris-arthur/article.htm. Originally published in the *New Left Review* (November–December 1983): 67–75, and revised by the author.

Barbalet, J.M. *Marx's Construction of Social Theory*. London: Routledge, 1983.

Carver, Terrell, ed. *The Cambridge Companion to Marx*. New York: Cambridge University Press, 1991.

Clarke, Simon. *Marx's Theory of Crisis*. London: Macmillan Press, 1994.

Cohen, Gerald A. *Karl Marx's Theory of History*. Princeton, NJ: Princeton University Press, 2000.

Cornforth, Maurice. *Historical Materialism*. London: Lawrence & Wishart, 1962.

Davis, Mike. *Old Gods, New Enigmas*. London: Verso, 2018.

Elster, Jon. *Making Sense of Marx*. Cambridge: Cambridge University Press, 1985.

Fine, Ben. *Marx's Capital*. London: Macmillan, 1975.

Freedman, Robert. *Marx on Economics*. London: Pelican, 1962.

Jones, Gareth Stedman. *Karl Marx*. London: Penguin, 2017.

Larrain, Jorge. *Marxism and Ideology*. London: Macmillan Press, 1983.

McLellan, David. *Marx Before Marxism*. London: Harper Torchbooks, 1970.

McLennan, David. *Marx*. London: Fontana Press, 1975.

————. *Karl Marx: The Legacy*. London: BBC Publications, 1983.

Morrison, Ken. *Marx, Durkheim, Weber*. 2nd ed. London: Sage, 2006.

Rigby, S.H. *Marxism and History*. Manchester: Manchester University Press, 1998.

Swingewood, Alan. *Marx and Modern Social Theory*. London: Macmillan, 1975.

Wheen, Francis. *Karl Marx*. London: Fourth Estate, 2000.

Wood, Allen W. *Karl Marx*. London: Routledge, 2004.

Worsley, Peter. *Marx and Marxism*. London: Routledge, 2002.

Wolff, Jonathan. *Why Read Marx Today?* Oxford: Oxford University Press, 2002.

ÉMILE DURKHEIM

Selected primary sources

Durkheim, Émile. *The Division of Labour in Society*. New York: The Free Press, 1997. Originally published in 1893.

———. *The Rules of Sociological Method*. New York: The Free Press, 1938. Originally published in 1895.

———. *On Suicide*. London: Penguin Books Ltd., 2006. Originally published in 1897.

———. *The Elementary Forms of Religious Life*. Oxford: Oxford University Press, 2001. Originally published in 1912.

———. *Education and Sociology*. New York: The Free Press, 1956. First published in 1922.

———. *Moral Education*. New York: Dover Publications, 2002. First published in 1925.

———. *The Evolution of Educational Thought*. London: Routledge & Kegan Paul, 1977. First published in 1938.

Selected secondary sources

Bellah, Robert, ed. *Emile Durkheim on Morality and Society*. Chicago: University of Chicago Press, 1973.

Fenton, Steve. *Durkheim and Modern Sociology*. Cambridge: Cambridge University Press, 1984.

Giddens, Anthony, ed. *Durkheim: Selected Writing*. Cambridge: Cambridge University Press, 1972.

———. *Durkheim*. London: HarperCollins, 1997.

Lukes, Steven. *Émile Durkheim: His Life and Work: A Historical and Critical Study*. Harmondsworth, UK: Penguin Books, 1973.

Parkin, Frank. *Durkheim*. Oxford: Oxford University Press, 1992.

Pearce, Frank. *The Radical Durkheim*. 2nd ed. Toronto: Canadian Scholars' Press, 2001.

Pickering, William S.F., ed. *Durkheim Today*. Oxford: Berghahn Books, 2002.

Stedman Jones, Susan. *Durkheim Reconsidered*. Cambridge: Polity Press, 2001.

Thompson, Kenneth. *Émile Durkheim*. Revised ed. London: Routledge, 2002.

MAX WEBER

Selected primary sources

Weber, Max, *The Protestant Ethic and the Spirit of Capitalism*. London: Penguin, 2002. First published in 1904–1905.

———. *Economy and Society*. Edited by Guenther Roth and Claus Wittich. 2 vols. Berkeley: University of California Press, 1968. First published in 1921.

———. *The Sociology of Religion*. Boston: Beacon Press, 1964. First published in 1921.

———. *General Economic History*. Translated by Frank H. Knight. New York: Dover Publications, 2003. First English translation by F.H. Knight in 1927. Original publication compiled by S. Hellmann and M. Palyi from Weber's students' notes on his 1919–20 lectures.

———. *The Methodology of the Social Sciences*. Translated by Edward Shils and Henry A. Finch. Glencoe, IL: The Free Press, 1949.

Selected secondary sources

Albrow, Martin. *Max Weber's Construction of Social Theory*. London: Macmillan Press, 1990.

Bendix, Reinhard. *Max Weber: An Intellectual Portrait*. New York: Anchor Books, 1962.

Dawe, Alan. "The Relevance of Values in Weber's Sociology." In *Max Weber and Modern Sociology*, edited by Arun Sahay, 37–66. London: Routledge, 1971.

Eliaeson, Sven. *Max Weber's Methodologies*. Cambridge: Polity Press, 2002.

Freund, Julien. *The Sociology of Max Weber*. London: Penguin Press, 1966.

Gerth, H.H., and C. Wright Mills, eds. *From Max Weber: Essays in Sociology*. London: Routledge, 1970.

Hamilton, Peter, ed. *Max Weber: Critical Perspectives*. London: Routledge, 1991.

Hennis, Wilhelm. *Max Weber's Central Question*. Translated by Keith Tribe. Newbury: Threshold Press, 2000.

Ray, Larry J., and Michael Reed, eds. *Organizing Modernity: New Weberian Perspectives on Work, Organization and Society*. London: Routledge, 1994.

Ringer, Fritz. *Max Weber's Methodology*. Cambridge, MA: Harvard University Press, 1997.

Runciman, W.G. *A Critique of Max Weber's Philosophy of Social Science*. Cambridge: Cambridge University Press, 1972.

Sayer, Derek. *Capitalism & Modernity: An Excursus on Marx and Weber*. London: Routledge, 1991.

Tribe, Keith, ed. *Reading Weber*. London: Routledge, 1989.

Turner, Bryan S. *Max Weber: From History to Modernity*. London: Routledge, 1992.

———. *For Weber*. London: Sage, 1996.

Turner, Stephen P., ed. *The Cambridge Companion to Weber*. Cambridge: Cambridge University Press, 2000.

Turner, Stephen P., and Regis A. Factor. *Max Weber and the Dispute over Reason and Value*. London: Routledge, 1984.

Expanding the Canon: Wollstonecraft, Martineau, Luxemburg, Perkins Gilman, Du Bois, and Mead

MARY WOLLSTONECRAFT

Selected primary sources

Wollstonecraft, Mary. *Thoughts on the Education of Daughters with Reflections on Female Conduct in the More Important Duties of Life*. Clifton, NJ: Augustus M. Kelley Publishers, 1972. First published in 1787.

———. *A Vindication of the Rights of Woman*. Edited by Miriam Brody. London: Penguin Classics Books, 2004. First published in 1792.

———. *A Vindication of the Rights of Men; A Vindication of the Rights of Woman; An Historical and Moral View of the French Revolution*. Oxford: Oxford University Press, 1994. First published between 1790 and 1795.

Selected secondary sources

———. *Ahead of Her Time: A Sampler of the Life and Thought of Mary Wollstonecraft*. Selected and arranged by Ella Mazel. London: Routledge, 1995.

———. *The Collected Letters of Mary Wollstonecraft*. Edited by Janet Todd. New York: Columbia University Press, 2003.

Wollstonecraft, Mary, and William Goodwin. *A Short Residence in Sweden and Memoirs of the Author of "The Rights of Woman."* Edited by Richard Holmes. London: Penguin, 1987.

Selected online sources

Project Gutenberg has available various Wollstonecraft writings, including *Maria; Or the Wrongs of Woman.* See www.gutenberg.org/browse/authors/w#a84.

The Online Library of Liberty has available *A Vindication of the Rights of Men, A Vindication of the Rights of Woman,* and *An Historical and Moral View of the Origin and Progress of the French Revolution.* See https://oll.libertyfund.org /people/mary-wollstonecraft.

HARRIET MARTINEAU

Selected primary sources

Martineau, Harriet. *Autobiography.* Edited by Linda H. Peterson. Peterborough, ON: Broadview Press, 2007.

———. *Harriet Martineau's Autobiography.* Edited by Maria Weston Chapman. Boston: James Osgood, 1877.

Selected secondary source

Logan, Deborah Anna. *The Hour and the Woman: Harriet Martineau's "Somewhat Remarkable" Life.* Dekalb: Northern Illinois University Press, 2002.

Selected online sources

Harriet Martineau's Autobiography (2 volumes) and *Memorials of Harriet Martineau.* Edited by Maria Weston Chapman. Boston: James Osgood, 1877. Available from the Online Library of Liberty. See https://oll.libertyfund.org/people/harriet -martineau.

Quotidiana has available various essays by Harriet Martineau, including "Experience and Progress," "Household Education," and "On Marriage." See http://essays .quotidiana.org/martineau.

The Online Books Page has available several Harriet Martineau writings. See http:// onlinebooks.library.upenn.edu/webbin/book/browse?type=lcsubc&key=Martineau %2c%20Harriet%2c%201802%2d1876.

ROSA LUXEMBURG

Selected primary sources

Luxemburg, Rosa. *The Accumulation of Capital.* London: Routledge, 2003. First published in 1913.

———. *The Crisis in the German Social-Democracy.* New York: Howard Fertig, 1969.

———. *The Industrial Development of Poland.* Translated by Tessa De Carlo. New York: Campaigner Publications, 1977.

Selected secondary sources

Ali, Tariq. *The Dilemmas of Lenin.* London: Verso, 2017.

Evans, Kate. *Red Rosa: A Graphic Biography.* London: Verso, 2015.

Rowbotham, Sheila. "The Revolutionary Rosa N." *The Guardian*, March 5, 2011. https://www.theguardian.com/books/2011/mar/05/rosa-luxemburg-writer-activist-letters.

Scott, Helen. *Rosa Luxemburg: Reform or Revolution*, Chicago: Haymarket Books, 2008.

Waters, Mary-Alice. *Rosa Luxemburg Speaks*. New York: Pathfinder Press, 1970.

Selected online sources

Rosaluxemburgblog. https://Rosaluxemburgblog.wordpress.com.

Rose Luxemburg Internet Archive. www.marxists.org/archive/luxemburg/index.htm.

CHARLOTTE PERKINS GILMAN

Selected primary sources

Perkins Gilman, Charlotte. *The Yellow Wall-Paper*. New York: Feminist Press, 1973. First published in 1892.

———. *Women and Economics: A Study of the Economic Relation between Men and Women as a Factor in Social Evolution*. New York: Harper & Row, 1966. First published in 1898.

———. *Concerning Children*. Boston: Small & Maynard, 1900.

———. *The Home: Its Work and Influences*. New York: Macmillan, 1903.

———. *Human Work*. New York: McClure & Phillips, 1904.

———. *Social Ethics: Sociology and the Future of Society*. Edited by Michael R. Hill and Mary Jo Deegan. Westport, CT: Praeger, 2004. Originally published in serialized form in 1914.

———. *The Charlotte Perkins Gilman Reader*. Edited by Ann J. Lane. New York: Pantheon, 1980.

———. *Charlotte Perkins Gilman: A Nonfiction Reader*. Edited by Larry Ceplair. New York: Columbia University Press, 1991.

———. *The Abridged Diaries of Charlotte Perkins Gilman*. Edited by Denise Knight. Charlottesville: University Press of Virginia, 1994.

Selected secondary sources

Deegan, Mary Jo. *Jane Addams and the Men of the Chicago School, 1892–1918*. New Brunswick, NJ: Transaction Books, 1990.

Deegan, Mary Jo, ed. *Women in Sociology: A Bio-Bibliographical Sourcebook*. New York: Greenwood Press, 1991.

Kelly, Gary. *Revolutionary Feminism: The Mind and Career of Mary Wollstonecraft*. London: Macmillan Press, 1996.

Lengermann, Patricia M., and Gillian Niebrugge-Brantley. *The Women Founders: Sociology and Social Theory 1830–1930*. Boston: McGraw-Hill, 1998.

Selected online source

Radcliffe Institute for Advanced Study, Harvard University. "From Woman to Human: The Life and Work of Charlotte Perkins Gilman." https://www.radcliffe.harvard.edu/schlesinger-library/exhibition/woman-human-life-and-work-charlotte-perkins-gilman.

WILLIAM EDWARD BURGHARDT DU BOIS

Selected primary sources

Du Bois, W.E.B. *The Philadelphia Negro*. Philadelphia: University of Pennsylvania Press, 1996. First published in 1899.

———. *The Souls of Black Folk*. New York: Dover Publications, 1994. First published in 1903.

———. *Darkwater: Voices from Within the Veil*. New York: Dover Publication, 1920.

———. *Black Reconstruction in America, 1860–1880*. New York: Harcourt Brace, 1935.

———. *The Autobiography of W.E.B. Du Bois: A Soliloquy on Viewing My Life from the Last Decade of Its First Century*. New York: International Publishers, 1968. Published posthumously.

Selected secondary sources

Blau, Judith R., and Eric S. Brown. "Du Bois and Diasporic Identity: The Veil and the Unveiling Project." *Sociological Theory* 19, no. 2 (2001): 219–33. https://doi.org/10.1111/0735-2751.00137.

Lemert, Charles. "W.E.B. Du Bois." In *The Blackwell Companion to Major Classical Social Theorists*, edited by George Ritzer, 333–54. Malden, MA: Blackwell Publishing, 2003.

Levering, David Lewis, ed. *W.E.B. Du Bois: A Reader*. New York: Henry Holt, 1995. See especially pages 610–18.

Marable, Manning. "Black Intellectuals and the World They Made." In *The New Black History*, edited by Manning Marable and Elizabeth K. Hinton, 1–16. New York: Palgrave Macmillan, 2011.

Robinson, Cedric J. *Black Marxism: The Making of the Black Radical Tradition*. Chapel Hill: North Carolina Press, 2000. First published in 1983.

Sundquist, Eric J., ed. *The Oxford W.E.B. Du Bois Reader*. New York: Oxford University, 1996.

Selected online sources

Various writings of W.E.B. Du Bois are available at http://www.webdubois.org/wdb-sources.html.

GEORGE HERBERT MEAD

Selected primary sources

Mead, G.H. "Review of le Bon, *Psychology of Socialism*." *American Journal of Sociology* 5, no. 3 (1899): 404–12. https://doi.org/10.1086/210901.

———. "Suggestions Toward a Theory of the Philosophical Disciplines." *Philosophical Review* 9, no. 1 (1900): 1–17. https://doi.org/10.2307/2176354.

———. "The Relations of Psychology and Philology." *Psychological Bulletin* 1, no. 11 (1904): 375–91. https://doi.org/10.1037/h0073848.

———. "Review of Jane Addams, *The Newer Ideal of Peace*." *American Journal of Sociology* 13 (1907): 121–28.

———. "The Philosophical Basis of Ethics." *University of Chicago Record* 12 (1908): 108–10.

———. "Social Consciousness and the Consciousness of Meaning." *Psychological Bulletin* 7, no. 12 (1910): 397–405. https://doi.org/10.1037/h0074293.

———. "What Social Objects Must Psychology Presuppose?" *Journal of Philosophy, Psychology and Scientific Methods* 7, no. 7 (1910): 177.

———. "Natural Rights and the Theory of the Political Institution." *Journal of Philosophy* 12, no. 6 (1915): 141–55. https://doi.org/10.2307/2013371.

———. "Cooley's Contribution to American Social Thought." *American Journal of Sociology* 35, no. 5 (1929–30): 693–706. https://doi.org/10.1086/215189.

———. "The Philosophies of Royce, James, and Dewey, in Their American Setting." *International Journal of Ethics* 40, no. 2 (1930): 211–31. https://doi.org/10.1086 /intejethi.40.2.2377976.

———. *Mind, Self and Society*. Chicago: University of Chicago Press, 1974. First published in 1934.

Selected secondary sources

Athens, L. "Domination: The Blind Spot in Mead's Analysis of the Social Act." *Journal of Classical Sociology* 2, no. 1 (2002): 25–42. https://doi.org/10.1177/14687 95X02002001672

Baldwin, J.D. *George Herbert Mead: A Unifying Theory of Sociology*. London: Sage, 1986.

Cook, G.A. *George Herbert Mead: The Making of a Social Pragmatist*. Urbana: University of Illinois Press, 1993.

Côté, Jean-Francois. *George Herbert Mead's Concept of Society: A Critical Reconstruction*. Boulder, CO: Paradigm, 2015.

Joas, H. "The Emergence of the New: Mead's Theory and Its Contemporary Potential." In *Handbook of Social Theory*, edited by George Ritzer and Barry Smart, 89–99. London: Sage, 2001. https://doi.org/10.4135/9781848608351.n8.

Selected online source

Brock University, Mead Project. See http://www.brocku.ca/MeadProject.

Credits

Figures

10.1   Fritz Ringer, *Max Weber's Methodology: The Unification of the Cultural and Social Sciences*, Cambridge, MA: Harvard University Press, Copyright © 1997 by the President and Fellows of Harvard College.

15.3   Adapted from Yrjö Engeström, *Learning by Expanding: An Activity-Theoretical Approach to Developmental Research*, Helsinki: Orienta-Konsultit, 1987.

Illustrations

5.1   Nick Hedges, "Girl Pulling Lever on a Drilling Machine, Lee Howl Pump Factory Tipton, 1978." Copyright © Nick Hedges, reproduced by permission.

5.2   Copyright © Steve Allen/Shutterstock.com.

5.3   Copyright © smereka/Shutterstock.com.

6.1   Copyright © Mike Dotta/Shutterstock.com.

7.2   Copyright © Sergej Cash/Shutterstock.com.

9.1   Courtesy of The Schøyen Collection MS 4629, Oslo and London.

9.3   Copyright © Associated Press.

10.2   Copyright © dominika zarzycka/Shutterstock.com.

13.4   Courtesy of the Rosa Luxemburg Foundation and Karl Dietz Verlag Berlin GmbH.

14.1   C.M. Battey, "W.E.B. Du Bois," c. May 31, 1919. Courtesy of the Library of Congress.

15.1   Copyright © The History Collection/Alamy Stock Photo.

15.2   Don Coltman, "CWAC Baseball Team," 1943. Courtesy of the City of Vancouver Archives.

16.1   Copyright © Pictorial Press Ltd/Alamy Stock Photo.

Text

Index